IRVING HOWE

GERALD SORIN

IRVING HOWE

A Life of Passionate Dissent

New York University Press • *New York and London*

NEW YORK UNIVERSITY PRESS
New York and London

© 2002 by New York University

Library of Congress Cataloging-in-Publication Data
Sorin, Gerald, 1940–
Irving Howe : a life of passionate dissent / Gerald Sorin.
p. cm.
Includes bibliographical references and index.
ISBN 0-8147-9821-7 (cloth : alk. paper)
1. Howe, Irving. 2. Jews—New York (State)—New York—Biography.
3. Critics—New York (State)—New York—Biography.
4. Jewish radicals—New York (State)—New York—Biography.
5. Jews—New York (State)—New York—Intellectual life.
6. New York (N.Y.)—Biography. 7. New York (N.Y.)—Intellectual life. I. Title.
F128.9.J5 S665 2002
974.7'100492'0092—dc21 2002008168

For Myra

Contents

All illustrations appear as an insert following page 162

Preface

IRVING HOWE rose from Jewish immigrant poverty in the depression-ridden East Bronx of the 1930s to become one of the most important public thinkers in America, preeminent in three major fields of general interest: radical politics, literature, and Jewish culture. Howe was the personification of the New York Intellectual. But he was also something more. A man of great passions, he was deeply committed to social reform, ardently devoted to fiction and poetry, in love with baseball, music, and ballet, and with life itself.

By the time he died in 1993 at the age of seventy-three, Howe was known most widely for his award-winning book *World of Our Fathers* (1976), a richly textured portrayal of the East European Jewish experience in New York. This book represented a culmination of Howe's own "reconquest of Jewishness"—his personal journey from alienation to repossession. But Howe had also won extraordinary attention and admiration over the course of a half-century for his prodigious output of illuminating essays on American culture that appeared in a host of periodicals, including *Partisan Review, Commentary*, the *New Republic*, and *Harper's*. These essays proved him to be not only a brilliant critic but one, like his contemporary Alfred Kazin, dedicated to the "common reader." And to the end Howe remained a fierce opponent of the postmodernists whose literary studies became increasingly inaccessible to anyone but academic specialists.

In a somewhat smaller circle he was also known for his indefatigable promotion of democratic socialism. Largely through *Dissent*, the quarterly journal he edited for nearly forty years, Howe (unlike most of the other New York intellectuals of his generation, including Nathan Glazer, Seymour Martin Lipset, and Irving Kristol), remained passionately committed to the socialism that had attracted him in his youth. And although his socialism changed from a revolutionary commitment to a personal ethos, Howe never retired from the battle for a more just, more humane, more cooperative society.

One of his colleagues has called Irving Howe a "triathlon man"—
an intellectual athlete whose development and achievements proceeded along three tracks—political, literary, and Jewish.[1] These tracks
usually ran smoothly parallel to one another, sometimes meeting tangentially, or even merging, as in Howe's *Politics and the Novel* (1957),
Voices from the Yiddish (1972), and *The American Newness: Culture and Politics in the Age of Emerson* (1986). Occasionally the tracks could collide.
Intensified political activism, in his work with the Democratic Socialists
of America (DSA), for example, or with SANE, or giving attention to the
never-ending phone calls, fund-raising, and editorial drudgery for *Dissent*, could drain energy from the literary and creative track. On the
other hand, the unrelenting "steady work" of politics could sporadically push Irving Howe back into the respite and pleasure of a "world
more attractive," of "doing something absolutely pure," like his collaboration with Eliezer Greenberg in translating and editing Yiddish literary works.[2]

While Howe continued to see politics as "a central human activity,"
he toiled at times to reconcile his desire to live the introspective, reflective life of a writer with his need to contribute actively to progressive
social change, or what he called "remembered fantasies about public action." He struggled mightily with the tangled attractions and frustrations of literary critic, socialist editor, and political activist. Some of this
dilemma is reflected in Howe's delicate and stirring essay on Lawrence
of Arabia, a dramatic and tragic figure who was representative of the
modern hero torn between action and withdrawal—action that could
stamp "intelligence and value upon a segment of history," and withdrawal that could allow reflection upon the meaning of human existence.[3]

Howe did manage to combine the contemplative and the active
partly through his instructive presence as a spokesman for culture at
the crossroads of literature and politics, as in his many seminal and
provocative essays, including "This Age of Conformity" (1954), "The
New York Intellectuals" (1968), and "Writing and the Holocaust"
(1986). And sometimes he simply emphasized the inward or the out-
ward on different days of the week: working at *Dissent* or with the DSA
on Tuesdays and Wednesdays, for example, and writing essays on Wallace Stevens and Robert Frost on Thursdays and Fridays. Whether he
had successfully synthesized his literary and political aspirations, however, was less important a question for Howe than whether his political

conscience led him to support good causes, and whether his critical consciousness led him to write pieces up to the standard of the essayists he most admired, George Orwell and Edmund Wilson.

But as is clear in Howe's life and writing, and in the disputes he entered—disputes about Ezra Pound and T. S. Eliot, Ralph Ellison and Hannah Arendt, race and multiculturalism, Marxism and postmodernism—critical consciousness and political conscience continued to inform one another. This process of mutual reinforcement moved Howe to enlarge his dedication to literary modernism with a broader, more humane conception of creative writing, and helped him produce work—political, literary, and Jewish—which was analytically sharp, lucid, accessible, and ethically meaningful.

In 1934, less than a year after he became a bar mitzvah in a store-front shul in the East Bronx, Irving (Horenstein) Howe, at the age of fourteen became a "socialist"—a member of the Young People's Socialist League, an admirer of Socialist party leader Norman Thomas. Of "Jewish consciousness," Howe later admitted, he had had little at this time. In retrospect, however, he came to see how important Jewishness—secular Jewishness—was to his life. "It meant, on the one hand," he said, "a home atmosphere of warm and binding love" and a communal atmosphere of mutual responsibility; "and it meant, on the other hand, an atmosphere of striving, of struggle to appropriate those goods of American life which to others come almost automatically."[4]

Irving Howe would remain on the left for the rest of his life, even as he appropriated some of those goods, including the English language and American literature, on his way to becoming an outstanding writer of literary and social criticism. He continued, in fact, to call himself a socialist to the end. And as a young man just out of the army he would begin his "reconquest of Jewishness" as he came to recognize more fully how much he and his socialism had been formed by Jewish tradition and community—a tradition and a community he would celebrate in *World of Our Fathers*.

Celebration is only part of the picture, however. For it is also possible to trace Howe's intellectual development along the three tracks—socialism, literature, and Jewishness—as a story of lost causes and "marginal hopes."[5] In America, the flame of socialism flared more than once in the first third of the twentieth century and again, momentarily, in the 1960s; but in America's open, pluralistic society so marked by heterogeneity, individualism, and a national psychology of mobility and progress, socialism has long since been extinguished. Moreover, the socialist idea had been poisoned, perhaps irreparably, because of the way it had been implemented and applied, especially in the totalitarian Communist regimes of the Soviet Union, its puppet states, and China. The idea was so badly damaged, in fact, by its confused association with Stalin and Mao and their murderous means, that Irving Howe, who was devoted to democracy above all, contemplated, along with some of his associates at *Dissent*, dropping the socialist label altogether.

But even after the socialist idea took another brutal beating in the late 1960s when one deluded faction of the Students for a Democratic Society turned to Maoism and another, the Weathermen, to terrorism, Howe retained the socialist label. It had become, however, less an ideology or political formula or program of institutional and economic arrangements, and more the name of Howe's "desire," his vision of a less competitive, more fraternal society. And he continued to promote that fraternity, even as he remembered that a "fanatic idealism can be put to ghastly service." He continued to promote egalitarianism, without overblown or naive expectations, exemplifying Antonio Gramsci's "pessimism of the intellect, optimism of the will."[6]

In the realm of the study of literature, Howe was also disappointed, but again not completely defeated. He had believed that good analysis and good criticism, in addition to an adequate supply of pencils, required a sharp, incisive intelligence, vast knowledge of history and the humanities, a sensitivity to questions about conduct and consequences, concern about the struggle for meaning and authenticity, and reflectiveness about aging and death (quite a requirement, actually). In short, unlike the deconstructionists and the novelist-philosopher William Gass, whom Howe took to task in his posthumously published *A Critic's Notebook* (1994), Howe continued to believe that *life* is indeed the subject of fiction, and that literature is the subject of literary criticism. Unsurprisingly then, he had no patience for the postmodernists and their convoluted theorizing and their impenetrable jargon. Nor did he have anything but contempt for Marxist academics, who, having failed to make their revolution in the streets, took over English departments in the universities and proceeded to reduce literature to a predictable and insipid sociology of gender, race, and class. Howe continued, however, even in the face of seemingly insuperable odds, to make the good fight for intelligible and humane literary study.

In *World of Our Fathers*, Howe honored a Jewishness infused with secular messianism. Even while warning against its excesses, Howe acclaimed the thirst for, and the deeply felt expectation of producing a better world on this earth through collective action. He thought this Jewishness, and even its more modest political expression in democratic socialism, was at death's door, overcome by social mobility and assimilation. Indeed, *World* had often been described by reviewers, and even by Howe himself, as an elegy. But here, too, as with both democratic socialism and the intrinsic value of literature, Howe retained an admittedly slim, but nonetheless palpable "margin of hope"—his hope for Jewish continuity, a continuity partly based on those dimensions of the Jewish experience that "prompted some of us to a certain kind of politics," the politics of left-liberalism.[7]

Irving Howe kept no diary or journal. He did not make or retain copies of letters he sent, nor did he save those he received. His family has been cooperative, permitting me to quote generously from Howe's published works and to use several photographs in their possession. But they were reluctant to support an "authorized" biography and would not share personal information or stories about Irving. With the help of his many writings (over six hundred items), however, and his many letters scattered in the archival collections of others, dozens of interviews with his associates and students, friends, and critics, and a number of important secondary works on the New York intellectuals, I have been able to explore here Howe's three rich and intersecting journeys from sectarian polemicist to broadly humane and erudite literary critic, from Trotskyist revolutionary to democratic socialist, and from "lost young intellectual: marginal man twice alienated,"[8] to what he himself called "partial Jew."

Irving Howe changed not only ideologically, but temperamentally as well. It is rare that Howe is discussed without some mention of the apparent rudeness or abrasiveness that surfaced in his years as a public figure. Even his co-editor and friend, Michael Walzer, said that Howe's "abrasiveness came naturally, as naturally as his intelligence." And *Dissent* board member and contributing editor Todd Gitlin admitted that "Irving . . . could be maladroit [and] fierce."[9] On the other hand, Howe worked hard at "diplomacy." He never did fully transcend his sharp, polemical style—a residue of the New York streets as well as of his early Marxist training—but the many available obituaries and the dozens of personal interviews I conducted indicate that he had an abiding kindness for people, even for most of the people with whom he argued.

Perhaps most important in this regard, Irving Howe, over time, grew less harsh on his adversaries for the most part, and more open and self-questioning in his political positions and in his literary criticism. Daniel Bell, with whom Howe took issue on many social and political questions, said, in remembering Howe, that the ideas people held were less important than the way in which they held them. Howe would no doubt have disagreed with this idea, too. But for Bell, Howe in his post-Trotskyist phase—that is, in the bulk of his adult life—was "just a mensch. A sweet mensch."[10]

Not a bad thing to be. But Howe was, in addition, a hero of sorts. When he wrote that Ignazio Silone, the Italian novelist and former Communist, exhibited a "heroism" that was "a condition of readiness, a talent for waiting, a gift of stubbornness . . . [a] heroism of tiredness," Howe was describing himself as much as he was writing literary criticism.[11] Howe's "gift of stubbornness" was neither a sentimental attachment to outworn traditions, cultural or literary, nor a blind devotion to a depleted and degraded political dogma. It was a principled commitment to the ideal of democratic radicalism, to a true egalitarianism, and to the never-ending struggle for decency and basic fairness in the face of social injustice and the frustrations of everyday life.

In the twentieth century, the century of Auschwitz, the gulag, and global interethnic mass murder, it has been hard to sustain political certainties and difficult to take pride in one's humanity. To have lived a life of conviction and engagement in this era is a rare achievement. Irving Howe lived such a life.

The Trauma of Sharply Fallen Circumstances

World of Our Fathers

IN ONE OF those odd coincidences of "Jewish geography," David Horenstein and Nettie Goldman, Irving Howe's parents, had lived as teenagers in the *shtetlekh* of Bukovina (between Russia and Romania), and had arrived in the United States in 1912 on the same boat. But they did not get to know each other until they met in the Bronx, where they spent the next thirty-five years together.[1]

When Irving was born on June 11, 1920, and throughout the 1930s and '40s, the Bronx neighborhoods in which the Horensteins lived were predominantly Jewish, and Yiddish was the language of the home, streets, and shops. At the newsstands, popular Yiddish dailies, including the *Forverts* and *Der Tog*, sold as well as or better than English-language papers. The Yiddish language, a significant carryover from the Old World, provided parents who spoke the foreign tongue an element of familiarity in an alien land. Their young children, therefore, often started school knowing Yiddish better than English. This was true for Alfred Kazin and Daniel Bell and many other children of Jewish immigrants who later would be counted among the New York intellectuals.[2] And it was certainly true for Irving Howe, who could both read Yiddish and speak it.

The public school proved to be an arena in which immigrant children began to differentiate themselves from their parents. Howe recalled an instance of this process of distancing from his very first day: "I attended my first day of Kindergarten as if it were a visit to a new country. The teacher asked the children to identify various common objects. When my turn came she held up a fork and without hesitation . . . already trying to distinguish myself . . . I called it by its Yiddish name:

'a goopel.' The whole class burst out laughing at me with that special cruelty of children." That experience, Howe said, "is one of the most vivid memories of my life. I felt terribly humiliated." And "that afternoon I told my parents that I had made up my mind never to speak Yiddish to them again, though I would not give any reasons. It was a shock for them, the first in a series of conflicts between immigrant and America."[3]

Despite his theatrical announcement at the tender age of five forsaking the so called *mamaloshn*, Howe, while growing up, read the Yiddish papers—mostly "on the sly." They were "very amusing," Howe said, "and . . . after I began to get a little more intellectual I found to my astonishment that I could get more out of *Der Tog*"—which had the best Yiddish writers—"than out of American papers."[4]

What looked like complete rejection, then, was really an exercise in ambivalence for Howe, whose denials later turned into extraordinary affirmations. Howe's translating and editing work with Yiddish poets and writers, beginning in the 1950s, was for him part of a "reconquest of Jewishness," a repossession and reformulation of ethnic identity. So, too, was Howe's work on *World of Our Fathers* (1976), a monumental, and implicitly autobiographical book that reflected his search for authentic, coherent, and enduring Jewish meaning in the collective experience of ordinary Jewish men and women.

This is not to suggest that the family conflict in the immigrant ghettos was unreal or always "resolved" over time. The generational struggles, resentments, and disappointments were intense, and pervasive. Daniel Bell, who witnessed these tensions in the lives of so many of his contemporaries, thought that the "bulk of Jewish immigrants" experienced anxiety over adjusting to the New World—an anxiety they "translated into the struggle between fathers and sons." And Lionel Trilling, a leading member of the predominantly Jewish New York intellectuals, wrote that in his time "we *all* were trying to find a release from our fathers."[5] In this, Irving Howe was no exception.

At eight or nine, Irving used to play ball in an abandoned lot not far from his parents' grocery store in the West Bronx. If Irving was late coming home for dinner, his father would come out, still wearing his white apron, shouting from a distance—"Oivee!" This Yiddish twist, or "mutilation" as Howe described it later, always produced amusement among the onlookers, and in him a sense of shame; and though he would come in to eat—"supper was supper!"—he would often skip on ahead of his father as if to indicate there was little, if any, connection between them. Nearly forty years later Howe admitted still feeling shame, not so much from having been publicly embarrassed, as from having been mortified—for no good reason—by his father's behavior.[6]

Time and distance offered a chance for perspective on this typical, perhaps inevitable, kind of interaction between immigrant fathers and native-born sons. But for the children it was already a sign of difference, an early hint of the alienation that would grow between foreign-born parents and their Americanizing children. And it did begin early, as we saw with Howe's kindergarten experience. Differentiation and alienation were especially pronounced for those children who became intellectually inclined like Trilling and Kazin, or Ruth Gay, Vivian Gornick and Kate Simon, or Daniel Bell and Irving Howe. Their whole experience and their search for truth led them to an increasing relativism, to the necessity of choosing values and not merely internalizing those with which they were raised.[7]

But as Howe put it later, "it seems unlikely that anyone can . . . simply decide to discard the [tradition] in which he has grown up. Life is not that programmatic; it is rare that the human will can be that imperious; and a tradition signifies precisely those enveloping forces that shape us before we can even think of choices."[8] In 1961, at the age of forty, Howe also said, "Only now do I see the extent to which our life . . . was shaped first by the fact that many of us came from immigrant Jewish families." Even a family like Irving's, which was no longer strictly observant in faith or behavior but whose entire life was informed and shaped by Jewishness, provided a moral context and an "essential goodness of soul," that Howe said was unmatched by anything he ever found outside the Jewish immigrant community. "We did not realize then how sheltering it was to grow up in this world." And there is the proverbial rub. Only much later, after having left home, too late for the parents, did Irving and some of the other very bright boys and girls from the working class see the extent to which their lives had been formed, and formed positively, by their immigrant families and by their nearly all-Jewish environment. In the New York of their youth, they came to realize that "the Jews still formed a genuine community reaching half-unseen into a dozen neighborhoods and a multitude of institutions." Within the family and within the shadow of these institutions— *landmanshaftn,* mutual-aid societies, philanthropic associations, labor unions, and even the store-front *shuln*—Irving Howe and his cohort, without seeking it, had found "protection of a kind."[9]

In one of those *shuln*, "ramshackle and bleak with its scattering of aged Jews" and "run by a poor rabbi trying to eke out a living," Irving, in 1933, became a bar mitzvah. His mother baked a *lekach*, a honey cake, and if the bar mitzvah wasn't any benefit to him, as Howe later claimed, "it was a benefit to ten old men [who] . . . had something to eat that day."[10] In preparation for the traditional ritual, Irving had attended *heder*—reluctantly, by his own admission, and sporadically, because the family had not always been able to put aside enough for tuition. At those times, Irving's father, though not well educated in Jewish sources, would himself "make a pass at teaching [him] a little Hebrew."[11]

Heder was not the only thing for which there were inadequate funds. The Horensteins, although rarely if ever hungry, were always poor and had become even poorer after the crash of 1929. In 1930, less than a year into the Great Depression, Irving's parents lost their grocery business, and the family was plunged into severe poverty. Forced to move from a relatively middle-class area in the West Bronx (a relatively narrow strip lying between Jerome Avenue and the Harlem River) to Jennings Street, one of the "worst streets" in a working-class neighborhood of the East Bronx, ten-year old Irving experienced a transition that he said "was very difficult . . . perplexing and painful."[12] Later he compared this drop in social status to that suffered by Nathaniel Hawthorne and Herman Melville: "I, too," Howe said, "had experienced 'the trauma of sharply fallen circumstances.'"[13]

It was the ambition of most families in the East Bronx to reach a point in life where they could afford to become residents of the West Bronx. But the Horensteins had been forced to make the reverse journey. It was not as bad as returning to the Lower East Side, many remembered, but it was bad enough.[14] Even if one had not been located on the tree-lined Grand Concourse with its proliferation of food stores, ice-cream parlors, and specialty shops, to live in the West Bronx meant to enjoy the best the city had to offer, including relatively modern buildings, many with elevators. The East Bronx, in contrast, was grim. Dilapidated frame houses and muddy brown or gray walk-up tenements predominated, and trees outside of Crotona Park were extremely rare.[15]

The move to the East Bronx for David, Nettie, and Irving, as for many other families, was not only a drop in social status, but also a decline in living standards. The Horensteins had to move in with Irving's grandmother, who lived in a badly aged five-story tenement building. The halls on the ground floor were poorly lighted, and the stairwells were dark and "spooky" and retained the smells of too many people living together. From the courtyard, especially in summer, one could hear the noises emanating from two dozen other kitchens and the screeches of as many clotheslines.

Worst of all, the cramped apartment the Horensteins were forced to share already sheltered Depression-idled uncles and aunts saving on rent. Unemployment in the East Bronx, as elsewhere, "was bad, very bad," Howe remembered. In fact, disproportionate numbers in the East Bronx were on relief or were employed short term with the Works Progress Administration, and nearly everyone needed to squirrel resources.[16] For almost three years Irving slept on a folding cot in a room he occupied along with his grandmother and aunt. "No doubt," Howe said, half seriously, this suffocating "arrangement accounts for some of my subsequent psychic malformations."[17]

When things got even worse in 1931 and 1932, Howe's father would say with characteristic grim humor, "At least we're not on Fox Street." But the Horensteins were only three short blocks north of Fox Street and clearly fearful of further descent, social and physical. "We were very close to destitution," Howe recalled. And "the pain of this," he said, was "overwhelming."

Irving suffered some pain on the streets as well. He had difficulty adjusting to the "toughies," as he called them, and he longed for the more carefree days of the West Bronx, where he had had no hesitation in leaving his apartment to play stoop-ball or, better yet, baseball—a game he continued to love throughout his life.[18] Living in the East Bronx educated Howe in the "hardness of existence." Here, during the Great Depression, he grew to adolescence and political consciousness. The streets, with their narrow tenements and sharply rising stoops, their alleyways and vacant lots and hiding places, toughened and roughened the children of immigrants by schooling them in the actualities of American urban life. Here, beyond the immediate reach of teachers and parents, Irving came to be pretty fast on his feet and developed a rather sharp tongue, and learned other strategies of survival as well. These streets could induce a "bruising gutter-worldliness," a "hard and abrasive skepticism" that echoed well into adulthood.[19] But the streets were also a place where Irving and the friends he eventually made could roam—away from the adult-dominated territories of home, school, and shop—tasting the delights of freedom, the mysteries of sex, and the excitement of the unpredictable.[20]

Still, Howe, even in the last year of his life, remembered his social descent "from the lower middle class to the proletarian—the most painful of all social descents," as "the great event of [his] childhood." He said that the sudden and confusing change in circumstances, in a childhood he characterized as not especially happy up to that point, was "like having everything fall out from under you."[21] At the same time, however, the "great event" which forced his parents into the physically oppressive and enervating wage labor of the garment industry also helped shape and develop Howe's lifelong commitment to the labor movement and his most powerful and enduring political values.

Howe remembered his mother coming home exhausted every evening, after ten hours of work and a 45-minute subway ride. She ended her week with a $12 paycheck. "My father, who stood all day over a steaming press-iron [came] home during the summer months with blisters all over his body. When the great strike of the garment workers was called by the ILGWU in 1933 my folks, who had had no experience with unions before, responded immediately."[22] Even Howe's mother, Nettie, who had never been on a picket line before, went out. To Jewish workers like Irving's parents, the idea of scabbing was inconceivable; as inconceivable, Howe said, "as conversion to Buddhism." So, like tens of thousands of others, David and Nettie Horenstein picketed, borrowed money for food, and stood fast. When the strike was over, Nettie brought home her first new paycheck of $27 for the week. "It seemed like heaven," Howe remembered; "we felt freer, better, stronger," and prouder, too, that they had helped accomplish this for themselves.[23]

The Horensteins moved to new, less crowded quarters. They were still living in a poor neighborhood near Crotona Park in the East Bronx, but they had meat on the table at least once a week "and many other small things" that, according to Irving, "made life much more agreeable." Irving's mother could even buy him some "grown-up shirts" for his birthday, and since that time, Howe said, "I've always had a thing about shirts."[24] And now the family could also afford an occasional outing to the movies or to Yankee Stadium. But the "best times were at home in the comfort of our innerness," Howe remembered fondly, as when "my father and I sat in the kitchen dipping bits of apple into glasses of hot tea," or as "on those Sunday evenings when there was enough money to indulge in delicatessen."[25]

Although Howe's parents did not stay particularly active in the union that helped bring them these moments and these things, "they paid their dues faithfully, and if a strike was called, they were the first to go out."[26] In the East Bronx, as in many other parts of urban America, the Jewish labor movement—especially its socialist element with its tradition of fervent protest—exerted an enormous moral power in the Jewish community. It not only helped produce and organize a collective consciousness, it reinforced the "inner discipline" Jews already felt to look after one another. This was the ethic with which Irving Howe grew up, the ethic of solidarity. Almost half a century later, he said, "I still believe in it."[27]

The experience of downward mobility, the "great event" that had helped shape Howe's political convictions, also turned Irving to the world of books and ideas, and pulled him "out of the unreflective routine of ordinary childhood." At eleven and a half or twelve he began "to read voraciously" in school and out. There existed in the public school classrooms of the East Bronx, Howe said, a moral and intellectual energy, with "kids [who] were very much engaged" and a faculty with "no notion of working for the lowest common denominator." Some of his teachers, Howe insisted, even in junior high school as well as at the all-boys DeWitt Clinton High School, "were at least as good as the people you now have in colleges and perhaps a shade better."[28]

Teachers reinforced the drive for perfection that Jewish immigrant school boys—the overwhelming majority of the students—had learned at home. Jewish parents may have feared the educational system because of the inexorable way it put distance between themselves and their children, but they were in awe of that system as well. Irving's parents may not have known, as he put it, "what the hell it was all about," but they had "a blind, sweet trustfulness of the public schools."[29] And they, along with other Jewish parents, typically praised academic achievement, especially in their boys, not only as a route to material comfort, but as an early assurance that Jewish children would not "go bad."[30] "Anything less than absolute perfection in school," Alfred Kazin wrote of his youth in Brownsville, "always suggested to my mind that I might fall out of the daily race, be kept back in the working class forever, or—dared I think of it?—fall into the criminal class itself."[31]

This drive for "absolute perfection," Irving Howe believed, was internalized by many Jewish boys and led to "precocity, . . . moral quest and self judgment, a neurotic need for perfection" not only in school, but for success, and even eminence, afterward.[32] Although high school teaching was about as far as Howe's parents' aspiration for him extended, this was in fact relatively far in depression-conscious America, and Irving, particularly as an only child, felt the burdens and advantages of parental high hopes. He admitted that "Jewish immigrant boys" like himself "felt enormously driven as everyone says—and some were lucky like me, in having good mothers, not all Jewish mothers being like [Philip] Roth's Mrs. Portnoy."[33]

Nettie Horenstein certainly instilled the idea of success in Irving. She held the family together, however, "not by a mere idea," but, as Howe put it, "through energies out of her depths." As if she were fulfilling the most positive aspects of the stereotype of the Jewish mother, Nettie apparently bloomed through sustaining others. Even while troubled herself and exhausted from working in the garment industry, she helped Irving adjust a little to the roughness of his new neighborhood, she helped her husband transcend the shame of having lost his business, she helped relatives in even more desperate straits than herself, and she helped Irving's grandmother keep house. She also tried to maintain whatever Jewishness the Horensteins had not yet abandoned. On Friday night especially, that Jewishness flickered to life "with a touch of Sabbath ceremony a few moments before dinner," and "it came radiantly to life during Passover," when through the rituals of the *Seder* "traditional dignities shone."[34]

Even in the worst of times, between 1930 and 1934, Howe's parents, like many other immigrant Jews, nurtured a "margin of hope," a hope fixed passionately upon the United States and upon their child. "Whatever their faith or opinions," Howe wrote, "they felt here in America the Jews had at least a chance, and as it turned out they were right." Irving's parents, despite their sense of his growing separation from them, did not impede his acculturation. His mother took him out of the neighborhood to see the movie *All Quiet on the Western Front*, and Irving "watched the tears stream down her face as the butterfly moved across the final frames"; another time he went with his father to Yankee Stadium and sat only a few dozen yards from Babe Ruth, the most popular man in the Bronx.

By the 1930s, as Eastern European Jews drew sustenance from the new world as well as the old, trips to the movies and to Yankee Stadium had become part of the immigrant milieu. They did not necessarily signify, as Howe would have it later, that his parents were ready for him to start his journey out of their "little world" into "the great one outside." The Horensteins, like many other Jewish immigrant parents, were ambivalent. And they undoubtedly still harbored fears about "losing" their son even as they encouraged a degree of Americanization and tried to help him find a way out of the physical labor to which they were chained.[35]

Academic achievement was seen as a way out, and school books were thought of as tools for mobility. This added a new dimension to the fact that books were already considered intrinsically good by most Jewish parents, a point illuminated by a story Howe liked to tell. When at age thirteen Irving was confined to bed with scarlet fever and unable, for nearly six weeks, to go to the library himself, he sent his father to fetch a bunch of books—the collected poems of Keats, Milton, and Wordsworth. The librarian, Howe guesses, probably looked at David Horenstein "with considerable disbelief." But only for a moment. For she must have had "some idea of these crazy Jewish kids." And of their parents, too. Like many Jewish immigrants, Howe's mother and father had "something like a semi-religious faith that books were good," even when they owned no books themselves.[36]

Books also helped to refine Irving's politics. Reading moved him to reinterpret the "great event" of his own downward social descent; he now saw that what had happened to him and his family, and to many of his Bronx neighbors, was not merely that "things had changed unpleasantly" in a complex and confusing way after 1929, but that "things had gone profoundly wrong."[37] Only after he had read a number of the books recommended by his high school teachers—"some of them slightly to the left"—and digested Sherwood Anderson's reports in the mid-1930s about North Carolina textile workers, did Irving more fully understand the implications of his change in circumstance: that poverty and inequality were not merely economic conditions, but political ones, the result of unjust social arrangements. Thinking about it in 1961, Howe wrote:

> I am struck by how little I saw as a boy in the thirties of hunger and suffering, though surely there was no lack of either in New York and I was quite prepared to notice both. I knew, of course, the shacks of Hooverville on Riverside Drive, the lines of people waiting before store-fronts rented by the welfare agencies, the piles of furniture on top of which sat the children of evicted tenants, the panhandlers

slouching on Fourteenth Street, the idle men standing day after day near the rowboats of Crotona Park. But while the East Bronx was a place of poverty, it kept an inner discipline: Jews felt obligated to look after each other.[38]

But after he learned about the troubles of people he did not know, Irving Howe's sense of his own deprivation grew keener, and his understanding of its sources grew clearer.[39] This combination of personal and family trouble, on the one hand, and intellectual stirring, on the other, made for the beginnings of political consciousness in him and in many other boys and girls in his generation. It certainly served to prepare Irving for "the movement."

And the movement—a collection of left-wing, anti-Stalinist groups —flourished in the East Bronx. Politics, especially left-liberal politics, was, to use Howe's expression, "meat and drink" in the immigrant Jewish section. Republicans were rumored to be in the vicinity, but none were ever sighted. On the other hand, the Communists, in the mid- to late 1930s, were beginning to transcend a narrow sectarian period and to grow.

Although fragile, the Socialist Party also had a visible following in the neighborhood. More important, *socialism*, for many immigrant Jews in the Bronx and elsewhere, was "not merely politics or an idea, it was," as Irving Howe said, "an encompassing culture, a style of perceiving and judging through which to structure our lives."[40] Alfred Kazin, too, remembered that "'socialism' was a way of life" among the immigrant Jews and their children. His mother and father voted for the Socialist Party, as did the parents of Nathan Glazer and Daniel Bell, and all, including the parents of Irving Kristol and Irving Howe, belonged to the left-leaning ILGWU or the Amalgamated Clothing Workers Union. Everyone he knew in New York, Kazin said "was a socialist, more or less."[41]

A pervasive Jewish culture with an emphasis on political radicalism gave the East Bronx a distinct character in the Depression era and prompted some of the most vigorous neighborhood protests. In his own neighborhood, Irving Howe often heard the socialist leader Jacob Panken's indignant soapbox denunciations of capitalism, along with his practical calls for incremental reform of the system. This combination attracted large Yiddish-speaking audiences. The socialist Workmen's Circle *shules* in the East Bronx were also well attended, and Abe

Cahan's socialist *Forverts* had a very wide circulation. There were, too, some eight or nine "circles" of the Young People's Socialist League (YPSL) scattered about the Bronx. And the Yiddish school on Wilkins Avenue, where one of the circles held its weekly meeting on Sunday night, was only blocks from Irving's home.

Given this "encompassing culture" of socialism, and Irving's sense that the world was falling apart in the 1930s, "it was a very normal thing," as Howe said, "for a kid [like him] with some sort of introspection and intellectuality to turn to politics."[42] Perhaps what needed to be explained, according to Howe, was "not why some of us became radicals in the thirties, but why others did not." Certainly Howe's "heritage of Jewish sensibility," the historical consciousness he absorbed "literally at the kitchen table," and his having breathed in Yiddishkayt and socialism from a milieu saturated in both, made it likely that the politics he turned to would be leftist politics. And so at YPSL, Irving, at age fourteen, found a "home of sorts."[43] Here he engaged in lengthy discussions and debates, and occasional street meetings. Most of these took place in Jewish neighborhoods. But sometimes, recalling their mission to reach out to the American working class, the YPSL group ventured into gentile sections. In Irish areas, especially near Fordham Road in the northwest Bronx, their meetings were often broken up by young street toughs, and Irving and his friends learned to stay away. In Harlem, however, this "handful of white kids," speaking against racial discrimination, could set up a platform on 125th Street and Lenox Avenue and experience no sense of risk from the black audience, which was at least mildly interested—or bemused by the spectacle.[44]

The movement produced a milieu within which a young person could feel a sense of enlargement and discovery, the excitement of entertaining and refining ideas about a better social order, or even about revolution. But by his own admission, Howe had "wandered into the ranks of Socialist youth, as much from loneliness as conviction."[45] Having moved some distance from, but not all the way out of, the world of his parents, Irving, like many other young Jewish men and women, sought roots in a new one. The socialist movement provided rich soil, and a very special community. "There was a sense of chaos, of disintegration" in the world, Howe explained, and "the socialist view seemed to suggest a conceptual frame by which one could structure and give meaning to these very difficult experiences." The movement provided a context within which, for Irving and others, "everything seemed to fall into place: ordered meaning, a world grasped through theory, a life shaped by purpose." In the movement, one gained a coherent perspective upon all events, local and global, a sense of "knowing," and a feeling that one was sophisticated. Even a youngster in high school could enjoy "a privileged relationship to History," and a sense that one's ideas could help change the world.

Without at all dismissing the substance of the radical ideas involved, or the sincerity with which they were held, it is possible to recognize, along with Howe himself, that what many described as socialism's attraction has some parallels with religious conversion. Within the socialist movement, young Jewish radicals thirsted for a future of international brotherhood in which they fully believed; but they could settle, in the meantime, for being bound to a group life that demanded time and loyalty, and which at least embodied the long-term redemptive goal.[46]

The movement had another advantage for the young people in transition from the immigrant community to the larger world, young people in the process of secularization but still informed by the values of *tikn olam* (the injunction to repair or improve the world) and *tsedakah* (action to promote social justice). Radicalism did not force them to make a total break with their parents; indeed it provided a bridge, a degree of continuity with their own recent Jewish past and traditions. A significant minority of the Jewish immigrant parents were socialists and militant labor activists. As importantly, the general Jewish electorate, particularly in New York (but also Philadelphia and Boston), from the turn of the twentieth century had repeatedly demonstrated its left-liberal proclivities and a remarkably broad interpretation of its group interest. Jews in the northeastern cities persistently crossed ethnic and party lines to vote for candidates they felt represented the social justice values they cherished.[47]

Many believed these values were embedded in Jewish religious culture. Indeed, Jewish radicals in the first decades of the twentieth century argued that socialism was a secular version of the Judaic prophetic tradition. The more pious Jews in the community were unlikely to be influenced by such arguments and were not inclined to support socialism or other liberal tenets. But the more numerous secularizing Jews were enveloped in an urban ethnic culture in which either socialism or liberalism or simply "humanistic" values were appealing and linked in some way with their continuous identity as Jews.[48] Howe told us in

World of Our Fathers that some of "the ideological styles of Jewish immigrant socialism became, paradoxically, a way of breaking out of the confinements of immigrant Jewish life." But this also implied that one could conquer a new world without abandoning the old one entirely. When the children of immigrants, then, joined left-liberal movements like socialism and Communism in disproportionate numbers in the 1920s and 1930s, it was not so much out of generational rebellion as a product of socialization.[49]

The autobiographies of radicals and former radicals indicate that private conflicts between parents and children over student activism were unusual and generally not very heated.[50] This was certainly true for the Horensteins. Irving's entry into "the little world of socialism" probably struck his less radical parents as part of the inevitable process of acculturation and maturation as their child reached out for the greater society. They disapproved of Irving's politics, but without much conviction. Once, when bakers went on strike in the East Bronx, about fifteen blocks from the Horenstein apartment, Irving and his YPSL circle, anxious to aid the proletariat, rushed to the scene. Some days later Irving's father asked him what he had had against that baker. "'A poor man who tries to make a living, and you tell people not to buy his bread.'" Though he fancied himself at least a passable street orator, Irving, perhaps recognizing the justice of his father's question, now "found not a word to say." Nor was there much more objection from his father. The Horensteins worried some about the behavior of their only son, but they objected more, Irving remembered, to his "lateness, a result of wandering the streets with cronies" after socialist activities, than to the activities themselves.[51]

Moreover, socialism was familiar and less frightening to the Horensteins and many other Jewish families than Communism. The parents of Julius Rosenberg and of Ethel Greenglass (Rosenberg), for example, though themselves steeped in the milieu of Jewish socialism, were desperately worried about their children, whose whole lives were caught up in the Young Communist League and who were later convicted and executed for espionage. Socialism resembled more closely the moods and dynamics of the lives actually lived by the immigrant Jews. Unlike Communism, which seemed so sure of itself and whose adherents, to borrow novelist Sherwood Anderson's language, "really meant it," socialism, like the transitional culture constructed by East European Jews in America was marked by a deeply rooted skepticism, a sense of irony and compassion, and even humor.[52] In any case, as early as the mid-1920s Jewish interest in Communism, though pronounced, was dissipating. Jewish cultural and religious institutions had been destroyed in the Soviet Union and thousands of Jewish leaders had been imprisoned or killed.

And the attempt by the American Communist Party to co-opt the Jewish unions tarnished the movement at home. Moreover, a commitment to the Communists involved a higher ratio of risk, potential ostracism at school, submission to the discipline of a more stringent organization, and certainly, by 1934, a blindness to Stalinist betrayals and perversions of socialist ideals. Irving, to the relief of his parents, was never tempted. He stayed in the YPSL throughout high school, associating mainly with the activist sons of old-time officials in the leftist garment unions, and he remained a fervent anti-Stalinist socialist at the City College of New York, which he entered in 1936.

2

Illusions of Power and Coherence at CCNY

World of College Politics in the 1930s

"IT WAS UNDERSTOOD that a Jewish boy like me would go to college," Howe said. "How could it be otherwise," he asked, "when the central credo of the immigrant world was, 'my son should not work in a shop?'" Most shopworkers, however, did not send their sons to college; a future in small business was the much more likely option. But Irving's parents had not been able to save enough to set him up in business, and his strongly developed socialist politics would have spoken against this choice in any case. In 1936 there was also nothing much else to do, except perhaps unskilled work in the garment center. The thought of Irving working in this industry horrified his parents, who had had too full a taste of those wretched jobs themselves. So not very strong physically, and terrifically bright, Irving was sent to college.[1]

The Horensteins, like most immigrant families during the Depression, could not even begin to think about the $600 a year it would take to send Irving to Columbia University, the city's preeminent college, or even the lesser amount it would cost at New York University. Moreover, unofficial quotas were in place in both institutions in the 1930s. The combination of the Depression and restricted Jewish admissions, especially at Columbia, the training ground for the Protestant elite, made the tuition-free City College of New York (CCNY) a logical choice for Irving Howe and other Jewish boys.

The actual cost of City College, aside from the sacrifice of the very modest potential income of the employable sons, was about 30 cents a day: 10 cents for the round-trip subway ride and about 20 cents for food. Irving could sometimes get away with as little as a quarter![2] With unemployment high, entrance into the school became increasingly

15

competitive, and in the 1930s and 1940s CCNY continued to attract an impressive collection of Jewish talent, including Alfred Kazin ('35), Daniel Bell ('39), Irving Howe ('40), Irving Kristol ('40), Earl Raab ('40), and Nathan Glazer ('44), among others who would go on to become social scientists, professors, and journalists.

Howe and many of the others struggling to escape the immigrant world took it for granted that college was an arena for political and intellectual development as well as for the construction of new identities. They sometimes pursued these activities in class, but more often, especially in Howe's case, outside of class. Bright, inquisitive students found the faculty unstimulating. Irving Kristol, for example, thought CCNY "a pretty dull educational place," and Howe ranked his teachers as mediocre, quite poor or simply hopeless. The college, with its low pay and fifteen-hour-a-week teaching load, could not attract a very distinguished faculty, and some of the best students avoided the classroom. "Unless there was an exceptionally good teacher, I didn't go to class very much," Howe told an interviewer in 1982. "After all, I had important business to attend to, political business."[3]

Occasionally, there were politics of a sort in the classroom itself. In one of his English courses, for example, Howe admitted that, as a fervent anti-Stalinist Marxist, he had written a formularized "'class analysis' of Edmund Spenser's poetry." The instructor, whose political ideas, Howe remembered, were probably not very far from his own, kindly suggested that there was much more to the world than Howe could yet recognize. The teacher gave him a B- and wrote on the paper, "The trouble is you confuse a sunset with the decline of civilization," which Howe later thought "wasn't a bad comment." But even at the time he knew his paper was "no good." Trotsky had taught him "not to treat literature in crude political terms," Howe said, but "I had written the paper in that vein. . . . It was a lapse."[4] And "the Stalinist teachers," Howe recalled with some glee, "we tormented." Irving, in his sophomore year, had written a composition about the persecution of writers in the Soviet Union, and he slyly volunteered to read it aloud in a class taught by one of the Stalinist instructors. "I kept reading until the guy was going out of his mind," he said. "But, all [the teacher] did," Howe continued, with a hint of triumph, "was correct the punctuation."[5]

The most lively and intense political discussions, however, took place outside of class in the alcoves of the college lunchroom. Although you could, in the late 1930s, buy on campus for as little as 15 cents "a memorably generous and highly seasoned chopped liver sandwich," most boys brought their lunch from home. They usually ate it standing up, leaning against the large oak tables on the window side of the grim cafeteria, a gloomy, pungent room with a wide staircase at one end that led down to open toilets. "Even we who came from the slums," Irving Kristol remembered, judged the cafeteria "an especially slummy place."[6] That image, however, for most of the CCNY graduates who became New York intellectuals and have provided accounts of their college careers, faded in the face of the indelible memories of the political intensity of the cafeteria alcoves and the vivacity and tenaciousness with which they all, before, during, and after lunch, confronted the problems and dismal prospects of the thirties.[7]

The alcoves, Daniel Bell remembered, "became a kind of—not Hyde Park, per se, but essentially a *kheyder* [Jewish school room] . . . where you were constantly disputing." There were dozens of alcoves representing religious, cultural, ethnic, and political groups as well as athletic teams. But the most important alcoves for the sons of Jewish immigrants were Alcove 1 and Alcove 2, representing a wide array of left and left-leaning political opinion. One student remembered that in Alcove 1, "the radicals ranged from right-wing Socialists . . . to splinters from the Trotskyist left wing. In between was a bewildering variety—Austro-Marxists, . . . Socialist centrists and Socialist Left-Wingers, Kautskyites, followers of the Independent Labor Party in England, the Lovestoneites, Brandlerites, and many another group, faction, or splinter. . . . We also had in our midst philosophical anarchists, supporters of the IWW, and all kinds of sympathizers, fellow-travellers, and indeterminists."[8] What held this strange conglomeration together was the powerful presence, only a few feet away, in Alcove 2, of members of the pro-Stalinist Young Communist League (YCL), led by none other than Julius Rosenberg.

Political life on campus, even in the 1930s, when America witnessed its "first mass student movement," was confined to a minority of students—as it always is.[9] A great number of CCNY students (80 percent of whom were Jewish) were driven by personal ambition and family pressure and were neither interested in politics, in any activist sense, nor in intellectual pursuits. Many were at the school as refugees from the Depression, as much for "lack of anything better to do than with any particular goal in mind." Others thought vaguely about civil service jobs or high school teaching.[10] But in several of the alcoves, particularly numbers 1 and 2, politics was all. Alcove 2, with more than one hundred YCL regulars and several sympathetic and supportive professors including Morris Schappes, was the most populous of the political alcoves. But even in this era of the Popular or People's Front (c. 1935–39), when the Communist Party, touting the idea that Communism was "Twentieth Century Americanism," celebrated Jefferson and Lincoln, and assumed an identity as an organization bent on compromise, coalition, and reform, Alcove 2 could rarely mobilize more than five hundred students for a demonstration, out of a CCNY population of some 20,000.

Alcove 1, where Irving Howe, Daniel Bell, and Irving Kristol spent much of their time, had fewer than thirty regulars and no professors, and they were fortunate if they could attract audiences of fifty or more. Anyone who was on the anti-Stalinist left was therefore considered an ally and a potential recruit for Alcove 1. Seymour Melman, for example, the future radical economist and professor of industrial engineering, was the leader of a left-wing Zionist group (Avukah) which tried to make a synthesis of Zionism and socialism. Nathan Glazer, who overlapped one semester at CCNY with Howe, was also a member of this group, as was Harold Orlans who went on much later to become an editor of *Dissent*. Because Zionism was perceived by the Trotskyists as a variety of bourgeois nationalism, Howe and others in his immediate circle "didn't go along" with what Avukah was trying to do. But, he said, "we formed a bloc [with them] so to speak . . . because they were anti-Stalinist." And despite "disagreements about Zionism we could work together on concrete political issues. We [became] good friends because Avukah was moving toward us politically, and anyhow they were nice kids." Howe admitted that he had had "a deep, blind hostility to the Zionist movement." But he found, even at seventeen, as he would throughout his career, "that life was richer than ideology," and he would not allow political differences (with the exception of Stalinism and fascism) to preclude alliances or, for that matter, camaraderie or relationships based on shared tastes in literature, music, or sports.[11]

In Alcove 1, from about 10 in the morning to about 5 P.M., the aspiring intellectuals had what Israel Kugler, the future union activist and professor of social science, called "the counterpart of a floating crap game—only our dice," he said, "were political arguments on all issues affecting the world."[12] Irving Howe had studied opinions on every one of those issues and expressed himself very sharply, quickly earning his college nickname "Fangs." He was, according to Irving Kristol, an "intense ... pillar of ideological rectitude" who "incessantly and nervously twist[ed] a cowlick" as he enunciated his authoritative points on whatever the current question was.[13] Often in the library or in Alcove 1, and rarely in class, Irving learned more on his own and with his socialist friends by "boning up intellectually." He prepared diligently for debate within his own circles but also, and especially, with the students in the YCL.

Out of sympathy with the ideals of the Soviet Union, many well-intentioned YCL youngsters were forced to try to justify, among other things, the Moscow Trials of the mid-1930s, the bloody purges of the old Bolsheviks, the Communists' murder of anarchists and socialists in the Spanish Civil War, and the self-glorification of Stalin as a model of Communist virtue and wisdom. The young Stalinists typically tried to counter the arguments of the Trotskyists by heckling and bullying. But occasionally the groups came to blows, and Irving was physically assaulted more than once. Although tall, having already reached his full height of six feet, Irving was thin, gangly, and not terribly athletic, and he is unlikely to have given back as good as he got. But of course "the main contribution of the Trotskyist youth groups and socialists," Howe insisted later, was not in fisticuffs. It was "in the fight against [Stalinism's] totalitarian perversion of Socialism. . . . And," he said, "I think we were right."[14]

It is possible that Irving and the other anti-Stalinists were not only right, but also effective in making their case against the Communists. In 1937 the YCL issued an edict prohibiting their members from speaking to, or even arguing with, the coalition of socialists in Alcove 1. "No more debates," they were told. "You don't talk to class enemies and fascists." Irving and his friends, however, would occasionally taunt the members of the YCL, sometimes rousing them into discussion. Of course, as alumnus and later law professor Philip Selznick recalled, at CCNY in those days "having a discussion meant arguing about something and doing it at the top of your lungs."[15] There was one of our fellows "with a foghorn voice," Irving remembered with some amusement, "named Sammy Portnoy, and he would stand in Alcove 1 and hold up a socialist paper, a left-wing paper, and yell, 'Read about Stalin the Butcher.'" This and similar declamations provoked debate. And while many student Communists, under the watchful eyes of Julius Rosenberg, obeyed the gag order, over the next several years an increasing number moved away from the YCL and the Communist Party.[16] Irving Howe's moral intensity, logic, and command of the historical materials may have had an impact on the consciousness of some in the YCL, but he too could be challenged, troubled, and moved. Most troubling, "yet somehow fascinating," Howe wrote much later, "was the handful of independent leftists who took anti-Stalinism for granted but kept chopping away at our Marxist and Bolshevik assumptions. I found them hard to cope with, for while I did not know this, they formed a kind of presentiment of where some of us were going to end politically"—as democratic socialists with the emphasis firmest and fullest on democratic.[17]

Before reaching that last stage of political development, however, Irving Howe's socialism would go through a number of revisions, beginning with his move to Trotskyism. In 1936, Irving's freshman year, the Socialist Party was in a state of precipitous decline. The New Deal had stolen some of the Socialists' thunder, and Norman Thomas's 900,000 presidential votes in 1932 had dropped to 187,000. Much of the trade-unionist old guard had been driven out of the party by so-called militants who, impatient with compromise and incremental material gains, called for a more combative, even revolutionary socialism. And the Socialist Party confused itself and many of its followers in its wavering between maintaining ideological "purity," and supporting, however critically, some of the more progressive reforms, and reform proposals, of the Roosevelt administration.

A last push toward annihilation of the Socialist Party came from the brilliantly polemical and monolithic Trotskyists who entered the party in 1936, aiming either to create a new left-wing anti-Stalinist coalition or, as a temporary tactic, to recruit and convert socialists to Trotskyism. The Trotskyists were not very different politically from socialists on the Left, but according to Irving Howe, they brought with them "an aura of certainty" about why the Russian Revolution had succeeded initially, why it had been betrayed, and how it might yet recur. They also carried with them the aura of their great and exiled leader, and held fast, unlike the conflicted socialists, to a claim for revolutionary purity. Irving was impressed. When they were expelled from the Socialist Party in August 1937, Howe and "a tiny group" of other "enchanted captives" followed the Trotskyists and headed "straight into the hermetic box of a left-wing sect," the Socialist Workers Party (SWP), which the Trotskyists formed in January 1938.[18]

It may have been only a small number from Howe's group that went along with the Trotskyists, but at the national level they took two or three times as many people out of the Socialist Party as they had come in with, and their leader, James P. Cannon, said later: "The Socialist Party was put on the sidelines. This was a great achievement, because [the SP] was an obstacle in the path of building a revolutionary party." In 1982, a more mature Howe, in criticism of the tragically wasteful internecine warfare of the Left, said, "Of such achievements, the history of American radicalism has had no lack, though Cannon never quite managed also to put bourgeois society or Stalinism on the 'sidelines.'"[19]

By 1940, the year of his graduation from CCNY, Howe would have a falling out, though not a complete break, with the Trotskyists, disagreeing with "the Old Man" over the nature of the Soviet Union, which Irving thought was neither democratic nor a worker's state. Howe would continue to believe that democracy was an absolute prerequisite for any society, and he never wavered in the conviction that socialism without democracy would not be socialism at all. He left the SWP and joined the Worker's Party (WP), but even as he moved farther and farther away from Trotsky's ideas, Howe would continue to see the former Lev Bronstein as a figure of heroic and tragic dimension, "an embodiment of past grandeur, a voice of corrosive honesty attacking the terror and corruption of Stalin, a thinker in the great Marxist tradition, a revolutionist of exemplary fearlessness." But he also saw him as a deeply flawed man, unable to transcend the epiphanies he experienced in making the Revolution, or to see far enough past his early investment in, and commitment to Bolshevism, to apply the same "corrosive honesty" to Bolshevism's pre-Stalinist history.[20]

From late 1937 to 1940, however, Irving (now using the party name of Hugh Ivan) led the Trotskyists at CCNY. He was the "theoretician" of the group, Daniel Bell recalled, and "commissar of the revolution." Bell, a social-democrat,[21] would often taunt the Trotskyists about the Kronstadt rebellion in 1920, when Trotsky ordered the shooting of dissident sailors who had earlier helped initiate the Russian Revolution. Unlike many of the others, Irving knew all about Kronstadt, but according to Bell, he defended Trotsky's action as "historical necessity."[22]

Howe told an interviewer, only months before he died in 1993, that Bell's story was essentially correct. "We thought we were discussing revolutionary or Marxist strategy. But as I see it now, we were often engaged in more fundamental ethical questions" about violence, and especially about ends and means. For example, Howe said, Daniel Bell "kept raising the question of . . . Kronstadt . . . and he would argue that Trotsky had evaded the painful aspects of this. . . . We tried to rebut him, but not too successfully." Bell, Howe said, "left a permanent mark upon my consciousness which not too many years later, led me to move in his direction."[23] Howe's remarks not only confirm Bell's story but exhibit the habits of the true intellectual: a readiness to question one's own political positions and ideas—which have been acquired at some cost; a readiness to undertake yet another revolution of the mind—a readiness Irving Howe would demonstrate more than once over the years.

Throughout these many changes there was a singular consistency that showed itself clearly in Howe's growing attachment to democracy, even if not yet to what he called the "bourgeois democracies." In part, this increasing commitment can be explained by the constant Communist "shout-downs" to which Irving and his friends in the Trotskyist movement had been subjected. Victimized by harassment, they came to recognize more directly and fully the value of freedom of thought and speech.[24] Howe's democratic proclivities became even clearer to him following a debate between Trotsky and the democratic pragmatist John Dewey in 1937. After hearing Dewey's remarks, Irving confided to a friend that, although he remained something of a Trotskyist, in this instance he supported Dewey, mainly for his democratic position. He shared the philosopher-educator's conviction that the idealist ends of socialism could not be achieved by terrorism and dictatorial means without those ends becoming hopelessly perverted.

Trotsky had argued that the bourgeoisie was "by its imperialist methods of appropriation . . . destroying human culture generally." But the bourgeoisie is tenacious, he said, it does not want to abandon power, and it "thereby threatens to drag after it into the abyss the whole of society. We are forced to tear off this class and chop it away. The Red Terror is [justified as] a weapon used against a class that, despite being doomed to destruction, does not wish to perish."[25] Thus, Trotsky made history into a sacred force to which everything must be sacrificed, and he displayed the implacable arrogance of the revolutionary who believes that a more just and decent society will emerge out of a dialectical process, despite the criminally inhumane quality of the means employed. While Irving continued to hate capitalism and the bourgeois democratic states that sustained it, he rejected Trotsky's "morally arrogant" defense of the idea that capitalist exploitation justified any and all means to achieve social justice.[26]

Even in the People's Front period when Stalinism was at its most popular among radicals and liberals in the United States, Howe, and several members of his small band of CCNY Trotskyists, held out against the antidemocratic totalitarianism that Stalinism or any association with it represented. Many left-leaning and liberal Americans who never so much as entertained the idea of joining the Communist Party, even in its new nonrevolutionary Popular Front phase, mistakenly saw the Soviet Union after 1935 as in the throes of a kind of supercharged New Deal, as the last best hope against Hitler, and as the most reliable bulwark against the fascism that had overtaken much of Europe. But Irving, along with other members of the YPSL, remained a ferocious critic of the Popular Front, objecting to Socialist alliances with bourgeois institutions and states that continued to support imperialism, as well as to alliances with Communists, whom he saw as merely masking their antidemocratic intentions with Popular Front rhetoric.[27]

Irving Howe and other leaders of YPSL during this period of the Popular Front saw themselves as more truthful, and more genuinely radical, than the Communists. Indeed, one of the major campaigns of YPSL was directed against the Communist students who aligned themselves with Western "liberalism" and who were thereby deemed insufficiently anticapitalist, antiwar, and anti-imperialist. The YPSL warned in its national newspaper, *Challenge of Youth* (which Irving helped edit), and in a 1937 leaflet most likely written by Howe, that the "main enemy," American capitalism, was at home, and that FDR was diverting attention to this fact by "trying to line up the working class for the next imperialist war." Later in the year, the group argued that the only correct program against the coming war was "the struggle for the revolutionary overthrow of the government." Only a workers' government, they insisted, "can really ensure peace." Many of "the ideas that we had at the time," Irving told an interviewer much later,

> ideas of social revolution—seem now half-baked or irrelevant to American conditions. But then you must remember that the situation in the thirties was so utterly different from what it is today, there really was a feeling of apocalypse. . . . There was the feeling that we were living at the end of the world.[28]

In 1938, Howe and other YPSL-Trotskyists, in a move they saw as contributing in a small way to delaying the "apocalypse," organized a "Strike against Imperialist War," a demonstration featuring speeches by James Burnham, James T. Farrell, and Sidney Hook. A little later, Irving himself edited the "CCNY Red Book," a mimeographed pamphlet that protested cuts in funding for education, called for sit-down strikes, and denounced CCNY as "a striking example of the intellectual bankruptcy of the capitalist class."[29]

While Howe and other Trotskyist youth organizers indefatigably attacked both the Stalinist totalitarianism of the Communists and their Popular Front alliances with capitalist elements, they were attacked, in turn, by the YCL as agents of fascism, especially for their refusal to support coalitions of left-liberal groups that included Communists. The hostility of the Communist-Trotskyist conflict poisoned the political atmosphere to such a degree as to preclude any genuine dialogue about the Popular Front. Irving Howe and the Trotskyists remained caught up in anti–Popular Front mania, condemning any joint activities with nonsocialists as regressive. The Communists, even though they would cooperate with the U.S. government's successful attempts in 1941 to convict Trotskyists as subversive revolutionaries under the Smith Act (1940), continued to attack Trotskyists and other left-wing dissidents and independent radicals as treacherous counterrevolutionaries.

The Communists' critique of the Trotskyists was especially severe whenever the Trotskyists dared to criticize the excessive, sometimes murderous, repressions of non-Stalinist dissidents by the republican government of Spain. That government had come to power legitimately as a Popular Front coalition of Communists, socialists, and even anarchists in 1936 but was forced to fight an unsuccessful civil war against Franco's fascist minions until 1939. Irving Howe and other Trotskyists were implacable enemies of Franco and fascism; but in 1937, after the Popular Front coalition in Spain fell apart, they were also severe critics of the newly reorganized, Communist-dominated republican government and some of the antifascist forces loyal to it.

They pointed out, for example, that La Pasionara, the courageous defender of Madrid against Franco's forces, was also a Stalinist who ruthlessly persecuted political opponents on the non-Stalinist left. They explained to listeners that the Communists, who controlled much of the republican military effort, took the lead in fighting against other left groups, including the anarchists and the anti-Stalinist Marxists, Partido

Obrero Unificada Marxista (POUM). And they reminded their audiences that the Loyalist government of Spain allowed the Russian secret police (NKVD) to kidnap and murder Andres Nin, the leader of POUM. By making these points, Irving and his friends were complicating the Spanish question in ways that could seem insufferable to many.

Their attacks were dazzlingly intelligent and factually correct, but they placed Howe and his comrades in the awkward position of saying there was something wrong with their own antifascist side. This especially troubled "true believers" at a time when fascism threatened to take over most of Europe, and socialist movements were in retreat. Most students dismissed Irving Howe's arguments out of hand. As one socialist student activist put it: "I am not a split personality, one of those who can both support and oppose," those working "to defeat fascism in Spain. . . . Therefore my support [of the Loyalists] is full," and one might add, purposefully blind.[30]

It was somewhat easier after the Nazi-Soviet Non-Aggression Pact of August 1939 to paint Stalin with the brush of fascism, and to move students and others away from blind support of Communist activities in Spain and elsewhere.[31] Irving Howe and his Trotskyist friends walked around feeling that in one sense they "had been 'confirmed' since Trotsky had predicted a Hitler-Stalin pact." But, Howe said, "we also felt that we were at a terrible historical point, the two main totalitarian dictators, the two monsters, had come together [and we felt] that a war was certain to follow very soon. We all expected that."[32]

There were also some battles to be fought at home. Earlier, in February 1939, the German-American Bund staged a pro-Hitler rally in New York City which attracted enough members of various far-right groups to fill Madison Square Garden. Irving and his friends mobilized and distributed anti-Nazi, pro-socialist leaflets calling for a counter-demonstration in the streets. Thirty or forty thousand people showed up, and Irving felt that the Trotskyists had now entered into "a significant relationship with the masses." Later, of course, he realized "it was nothing of the sort." But at that particular moment, he said, "we were able to touch the sentiments of large numbers of New Yorkers, probably mostly Jewish New Yorkers."[33]

At the time, Irving Howe and his friends made little of this Jewish connection. They claimed to be in possession of a "worldview" and above "national identity." They believed that being "born Jewish was an accident" and not something significant. But as Howe realized later, "the sheer thickness" of Jewish life and Jewish radical politics in New York were "crucial" in making him who he was, and indeed in sheltering him and his comrades as they railed against capitalism and "bourgeois democracy" (which also sheltered them) and nationalism. Their Jewishness at this point in the late 1930s and through the mid-1940s was suppressed, at best tacit, and, for Irving at least, marked by a powerful sense of tension between Jewish home life "with its sweet poignancy and embittered conflicts," and the political life he had chosen "with its secret fellowship and sectarian vocabulary."[34]

The thought of bringing his college friends home, then, was for Irving "inconceivable." The conflict he felt between his family, so stamped by Jewishness, and school, the arena in which he aspired to be an internationalist Marxist with a totally secular, nearly absolutist ideology, was too strong—or Irving was too weak or uncourageous to defend one against the other. But there was a paradoxical kind of synthesis of these warring elements reflected in Howe's later recognition that "the whole idea of escaping from Jewishness is itself a crucial part of the Jewish experience." And even at the time there was an uncanny dimension of similarity between home and school that obviated a complete breaking away from one or the other. For CCNY, like Irving's junior high school and like DeWitt Clinton High School, was overwhelmingly Jewish. Indeed, at times, especially in Alcoves 1 and 2, where rough disputation was the order of the day, college seemed like a continuation of life in the Jewish neighborhoods of New York.

Sometimes this was true in class as well. One of the few classes Irving Howe attended with any regularity was Morris Cohen's course in philosophy, the atmosphere of which was described by another student, Sidney Hook, as "not unlike that of a Yeshiva," or at least the give-and-take world of the immigrant neighborhoods.[35] Cohen was a brilliant and remorseless practitioner of the Socratic method, but as he himself admitted, he had more of a "Jewish argumentative" style and less of Socrates' courtesy. Being in Cohen's class, Irving said, was often "terrifying," and only certain kinds of students could have withstood it. Still, many remember Cohen as challenging and engaged, a good teacher, especially for "Jewish boys . . . indifferent to the prescriptions of gentility, intent on a vision of lucidity."[36]

In this way, the Jewish community enclosed one, at school as well as at home or on the street. Even when "you found a job," Howe wrote later, "it was likely to be in a 'Jewish industry,' and if you went to college it was still an essentially Jewish milieu." So, "what you believed, or said you believed, did not matter as much as what you were, and what you were was not nearly so much a matter of choice as you might care to suppose."[37] In the late 1930s, ordinary New York Jews, like Irving's parents, David and Nettie Horenstein, knew that Jewishness was not something one *chose*, and in this respect, Howe said self-critically, their "instincts were sounder, both morally and practically, than that of the radicals" like himself who chose "party names," like Hugh Ivan, for example, that did not sound Jewish. Irving, however, who was to graduate from CCNY as Horenstein, dropped the Hugh Ivan identification and began immediately thereafter, in the summer of 1940, to use the name Howe (which he adopted legally in 1946) in his writings and public appearances. Although he would say later that pseudonyms expressed "a decided rejection of Jewishness," we need to wonder in his case whether keeping the name "Irving" (an American name widely used by Jews) did not reflect confusion or ambivalence about Jewishness rather than outright rejection.[38]

Still, after movement meetings, it was not immediately to his Jewish home that Irving returned, with or without his radical friends. Instead, there was a good deal of walking the streets together, away from the pressures of family, but also of politics. The movement was often exciting, inducing in Irving a pride in belonging to the "vanguard," intensifying in him a fascination for the idea of history, and opening him further to the pleasures of the intellect and the thrust and parry of argument. But there were also frustrations: isolation, a sense of smallness and futility, factional fights over the "correct line" filled with the vanity of overblown rhetoric, heavy-handed sarcasm, and a seemingly unbreakable attachment to intellectual agility rather than reflection, to dialectic rather than investigation and analysis.

As much as Irving and his friends enjoyed political activity and argument, escape was often necessary. There were movies to see—usually sophisticated and challenging European art films in which "class" was not the only thing that mattered. And there were free concerts at the Metropolitan Museum of Art, where such un-Marxist feelings as aestheticism and romanticism could find a "sanctioned outlet in Beethoven and Schubert." Howe and his friends had intense cultural and intellectual interests that did sometimes test their politics; but they never imagined the idea of a genuine conflict between engagement and taste. "We wanted the socialist revolution *and* avant garde modernism," Howe rightly remembered, "Trotsky and Joyce, Marx and Stravinsky, everything that seemed bold and truthful."[39]

One of the people, in the late 1930s, who helped Howe construct a temporarily viable synthesis between activism and aesthetics was his friend and fellow Trotskyist, Noah Greenberg. Together, during the week, they distributed socialist literature. But on Saturday nights Howe and many other young people in the movement would pile into Greenberg's little apartment on East 14th Street to submit themselves to his recordings of baroque and medieval pieces and to his enthusiastic and ultimately enchanting musical teaching. Greenberg, who remained politically active even as he went on to a distinguished career in music, was Howe's "first music teacher" and, as Irving put it, "a damned good one." Music remained one of Howe's abiding passions right up to the moment of his death.[40]

There was also more reading one could do, beyond Marx's *The Eighteenth Brumaire of Louis Bonaparte* or *Das Kapital* or Trotsky's *The Revolution Betrayed*. Edmund Wilson's classic book of literary criticism, *Axel's Castle*, for example, though not fully comprehended by Irving Howe, made a powerful impression on the sixteen-year-old and may even have lit a small fire of ambition in the future literary critic. There were the great modernists James Joyce and Marcel Proust and Thomas Mann to master; and here Irving and the other young Trotskyists did not have to find "excuses" for their deviance from the socialist line. For Trotsky himself was a skillful literary critic. The concluding chapters of his *Literature and Revolution*, which Howe devoured, fulminated against the idea of a strictly "proletarian culture," promoted the works of Shakespeare, Pushkin, and Dostoevsky, and predicted lyrically that "socialist man" would scale great cultural heights, going beyond even Goethe and Beethoven.[41]

Moreover, Irving and several other students of Alcove 1 read *Partisan Review*. A Communist magazine from 1934–35, *Partisan Review* was revived in 1937 in the hope of bringing a "cleansed" Marxism, an anti-Stalinist Marxism, together with literary modernism in the struggle against bourgeois society. The young students did not necessarily understand the articles even after two or three readings. Nor did they yet see fully the ultimate tension, if not contradiction, between modernism and Marxism. The political implications of modernism were often potentially reactionary, as with T. S. Eliot, Ezra Pound, and D. H. Lawrence. Modernism was also mainly subjective and fragmentary, occasionally mystical, and often engaged with nihilism, as with Samuel Beckett, Louis-Ferdinand Celine, and Ernest Hemingway. None of this sat very neatly with Marxism's faith in rationality, politics, and future historical victory.

But Irving, who read *Partisan Review*, "with passion" from the "very first issue," felt, along with the other young idealists, that the "journal was a major accession to [their] side" and appreciated the magazine's commitment to everything that seemed brave and beautiful. And Marxism and modernism did, after all, share important concerns. Both were attentive to the moral squalor of industrial society, and both were alienated from the prevailing values of middle-class society. Therefore, despite the tensions between Marxism and modernism, Irving and his friends wanted the synthesis to work, and they thought it could in *Partisan Review's* equal and simultaneous attention to political conscience through Marx and Trotsky, and to critical consciousness through Kafka, Dostoevsky, and Eliot. And "with T. S. Eliot," Howe joyously recalled, "I fell crazily in love." Howe defended this attraction later by saying that Eliot's reactionary politics were muted some by his "many profound insights into the decadence of society." The young Irving knew Eliot was "a reactionary . . . but didn't really care." He was "in love more with the rhythms and music of [Eliot's] verse than its meaning." Once again, life, for Irving Howe, showed itself to be richer than ideology.[42]

When Irving was not listening to music, or playing the violin (at which he was "pretty good"), or watching films, or reading the modernist masters, he occasionally attended the "socials" given by different branches of the movement.[43] He remembered these, perhaps incorrectly, he said, as "drab and awkward." But here, as in many movement activities, unlike at DeWitt Clinton, an all-boys high school, or at CCNY, an all-male college, there were bright, interesting, strong, and "sexually attractive" young women. These students, some as young as fifteen and still in high school, were very much ahead of their moment. And despite the fact that they often came up against subtle and not-so-subtle sexual condescension and insensitivity from many young men, they were determined to behave as if an announced sexual equality was a reality.

Apparently charmed by Irving's mix of social awkwardness and political intensity, several women, including an articulate and stunningly attractive brunette, Rickie (Rochelle) Kimmel, moved into Howe's orbit. At socialist gatherings, Rickie said, Irving was "always sitting there twisting a lock of his hair in his fingers." When he acquired a new "girl friend . . . he'd come to meetings and sit there and twist *her* hair." And there may have been as many as a half-dozen new girl friends in a three- or four-year period. It is rumored that some men attached themselves to the movement primarily for the "sexual action" available among "liberated" women. But Irving was clearly a committed socialist, and while sexually assertive he was no libertine.[44]

Indeed, "from [his] little peak of rectitude," Howe "looked down upon" some women at the farthest edges of the movement who constituted a "bohemian minority." He admitted that he "was afraid of the rumored dissoluteness" of those "who moved in and out of one another's apartments—that wasn't how we had been taught to live in the Bronx. To have been raised in a working-class family, especially a Jewish one, means forever to bear a streak of puritanism which, if not strong enough to keep you from sexual assertion, is strong enough to keep you from very much pleasure."

This may be part of the explanation for the fact that Irving Howe married and divorced three times, before he settled in, for the last seventeen years of his life, with his fourth wife. In any case, Howe said (perhaps reflecting the general culture of dating in New York), physical experience was one thing, but "we were programmatically untrained to engage with personal experience at all. The fate of the world hung heavily on our shoulders, yet we asked few questions about the lives, feelings, inner thoughts of those who were supposed to be our partners in making a new society."[45]

In the meantime, as Irving was nearing graduation in June 1940, he thought the old society was "breaking down," indeed "collapsing." At commencement exercises, sitting next to Irving Kristol and Earl Raab, Howe listened to speeches about "careers lying ahead of you." Having no expectations of ever finding jobs, Irving and the others "burst out laughing." And they continued to laugh, Howe said, when another "dummy . . . reassured us we would not have to face a war."[46] The commencement speeches were wrong on all counts. The war did come for the United States, and until that time, there were relatively few jobs.

3

The Second World War and the Myopia of Socialist Sectarianism

THE WAR THAT Howe had been assured he would not have to face became a palpable presence in his life little more than a year after his graduation. He would serve four years in the army and spent even more time thinking about the nature of the global conflict and its potential consequences for the advance of socialism. Still very much a sectarian ideologue in this period, he deluded himself about the meaning of World War II, insisting it was little more than a battle among equally abhorrent imperialist powers. And he sustained a virtually unwarranted hope that the disruptions of the war would create the context for a workers' revolution, not only in Europe but even in America.

In the meantime, between the end of school in 1940 and the beginning of his army experience in 1942, Howe needed work. During summers as a teenager, he had had a small number of very short-lived odd jobs. He was fired after only a day or two by a supermarket manager who accused him, justly, of dumping into a sewer circulars he was supposed to be distributing. And he was fired, within days as well, by a shopkeeper who worriedly watched while "this stringbean of a boy with glasses" struggled to carry rolls of linoleum. Given his "work history" and the state of the economy, it did not seem to Howe, fresh out of college, that his employment opportunities were exactly glowing.

But he did find work in the summer of 1940 that paid sixteen dollars a week, a relatively attractive wage for a young man who lived at home and paid no rent or board. This job, in a Long Island City factory that manufactured pinball machines, actually lasted several weeks, but again Irving, along with two of his colleagues, was fired summarily—this time for "talking union" to the other men in the shop. "We left," Howe wrote, "ashamed of our ineptitude but delighted to be free of the shop." Although he would from time to time do union organizing work and recruiting for the Workers Party (WP), Howe was never fully comfortable with either activity. He could have gone West immediately after graduating to help build a working-class base for the socialist movement. But he did not "join this trek to the proletariat; some inner resistance," he said, "some hard grain of sense, kept me in New York."[1]

While Howe may have been able to work in a shop only temporarily, he could not assume the state of mind of women and men who had no choice but to be there regularly. Perhaps even more important, although Howe in 1940 thought of himself as a political person with unusually wide cultural interests rather than as an intellectual, he had a powerful desire to write—to continue the kind of socially critical journalism he had begun in college. And this writing would eventually help ease, but never entirely erase, the tension he felt between his cultural interests and his political activism.

Howe's journalistic talents were quickly recognized by Max Shachtman, the principal editor of the Trotskyist monthly *New International*, to which Howe had contributed articles in 1941. Leaders of the Workers Party who founded *Labor Action* in 1940 also admired his work and political passion. They appointed him editor of the weekly (which also remained under Shachtman's general direction) in late 1941. This job, managing a periodical with a circulation of close to 50,000, not only satisfied, for a time, Howe's need to combine his writing and his activism, it allowed him to move out of his parents' home into a Greenwich Village apartment, and it reinforced his commitment to New York and to Shachtman.[2]

Irving Howe had followed Shachtman, whom he admired greatly, out of the Socialist Workers Party (SWP) in 1940. They had split with the more orthodox Trotskyists, who continued to see the Soviet Union, even under Stalin, as a socialist entity, and defended Russia's actions in public even when they disagreed privately, as with Russia's invasion of Finland in 1940. Howe had first heard Shachtman speak when he came to CCNY in 1937 to debate the validity and morality of the Moscow Trials with Morris Schappes, a Stalinist professor of English who in 1936 had temporarily lost his post at the college. Howe and his friends, despite their anti-Stalinism, had defended Schappes's academic freedom at the time and even joined in a sit-down demonstration demanding his reinstatement. In 1937, however, in Doremus Hall, the large (and, on this day, filled to capacity) chemistry lecture room, it was Schappes's Stalinist political position that was on trial, and it was demolished.

Howe remembered being "stunned" by Shachtman's brilliant polemics and staccato attack on Schappes's case. Later, Schappes claimed that he merely appeared at the event in order to assert that he would not debate with an enemy of the working class. But several students, including Howe, recalled the afternoon quite differently. Schappes had made a brief presentation insisting that the Moscow defendants were guilty (because they had confessed), and then he denounced Shachtman at length. But Shachtman savagely, contemptuously, tore the trial "evidence" to shreds and refuted, incontrovertibly, the claims in the "confessions." According to one student in the audience, even the members of the Young Communist League (YCL) looked shattered as they left the hall.[3]

Howe was deeply impressed with Shachtman's passionate, "high-wire virtuosity" and Marxist principles. He would remain a devotee of Shachtman for some time. Even after they diverged ideologically—Max crossing Howe's path to the left in the late forties, and then again to the right in the late sixties—Howe continued to admire him. Howe contributed occasional pieces to Shachtman's *New International* throughout the 1940s and into the early 1950s. And in addition to editing Shachtman's *Labor Action,* Howe often wrote half the articles for that four-page paper himself. He worked hard at this four or five days a week, taking only twenty minutes out for lunch at a café on West Fourth Street, a short distance from his apartment.

Even after he was drafted into the army in June 1942, Howe, under the by-line R. Fahan (*rote Fahan?*—Rosa Luxembourg's "Red Flag"?), R. Fangston, or simply R. F., continued to contribute articles to both periodicals while stationed on Long Island, later in western Pennsylvania, and finally, until 1946, in Alaska. More than thirty years later, in preparation for writing his intellectual autobiography, *A Margin of Hope,* Howe reread these radical papers and he "blush[ed]" at "the ready-made assurance with which [he] wrote" when he was in his twenties. It is not difficult to see why. His political ideas and style in the early 1940s are almost always marked by stridency, and occasionally by a naive utopianism, especially about the near-future possibilities of redemptive socialist revolutions in Europe and the United States. His essays are also too often marred by arrogance and reductionist ideology, much of it having to do with the "bankruptcy" of social democrats and liberals, but especially with the "imperialist nature" of all sides in World War II.

In 1941 before assuming the editorship of *Labor Action*, Howe, in the *New International*, in only his second published article, acerbically attacked the journalist Louis Fischer, a former Stalinist, as a "king of philistines and prince of liars" who had established "a record of filth and hypocrisy." Howe might have ignored Fischer or even forgiven him, Fischer having, after all, abandoned Stalinism to become a vociferous critic. But by Howe's standards, Fischer was continuing to sin, this time in his "hysterical support" of World War II, or what Howe liked to call "the second imperialist world war."[4] In the same issue, referring to the English and French and to those in the United States advocating American entry into the war against Hitler, Howe wrote that the "bourgeois democrats try to lull themselves (and others) with the illusion that the roots of this war are an ideological repugnance for Fascism, rather than imperialist rivalry."[5]

Two months later and within days of the first appearance of Howe's name as managing editor on the masthead of *Labor Action*, the United States was suddenly thrust into the "imperialist rivalry" by the Japanese attack on Pearl Harbor. The lead article in the first post–Pearl Harbor issue was a front-page manifesto declaring that the "noble hatred of tyranny has been cunningly exploited by the imperialist statesmen of the so-called democracies for the purpose of whipping up pro-war sentiment among the masses of the people." The article does attack the Nazi state for its crimes against the peoples of Europe and for "its cruel destruction of the labor movement in Germany," but it took the position, espoused for years to come, that the war was "between two great imperialist camps" struggling over "which shall dominate the world."[6]

In 1982 Howe wrote that he and others in his sectarian circle, in the early 1940s, still "upholding the banner of Lenin and Trotsky" and "trapped between an inherited ideology and a perceived reality," had moved to a position of implicit "critical support" for the war. And he admitted the "deep error" of not making the support explicit.[7] But, Howe, undeniably, overstated his case. He did, in 1942, allow himself to be drafted, as did many other Trotskyists, including Emanuel Geltman, Irving Panken, and Julius Jacobson. And he did say in a letter from the army in 1945 (perhaps only because of the prying eyes of the military censor) that it was "undoubtedly . . . necessary for this country to enter into a military alliance with Russia in order to defeat Hitler."[8] But

Howe's voluminous writings during the 1940s indicate nothing like support for the war, critical or otherwise. In a *Labor Action* article on December 29, 1941, for example, Howe berated liberals, the vast majority of whom were for the war against Hitler, for having been "sucked into the fold of Rooseveltian capitalism." No one who supported the war escaped his wrath: not the trade unions which supported FDR; not the left-liberal magazines, the *New Republic* and the *Nation* which editorialized for national unity; not even Norman Thomas, whose Socialist Party, according to Howe, did not take an explicitly oppositional stance on the war.[9]

There was no question that Irving Howe and other Shachtmanite Trotskyists hated Hitler. A representative pamphlet issued by the Workers Party in 1940 joined the cry to "Stop Hitler." If he is not stopped, the WP argued, "trade unions and workers' organizations everywhere will be destroyed. The workers will be reduced to starvation wages and slave conditions of labor, Jews will be driven once more into ghettos and will have to scrub streets under the whips of storm troopers. Negroes will be pushed still further into the slums and swamps of oppression and misery where they have lived so long. Hitler must be stopped, for Fascism spares none."[10]

Yet the pamphlet was entitled "This Is Not Our War." For Howe and the others it was the capitalists' war. The WP Trotskyists believed, as Howe wrote in 1942, that the war presents a "picture of the capitalist world gone mad—profits, profits above all. Everything else is just so much hogwash designed to trick the unwary into surrendering their lives for these profits." In the same year, Howe also attacked the divided editorial board of *Partisan Review* (PR) for taking no position on the war, the "one issue," he said, "on which nobody can be [silent]." In the same article, Howe chastised the PR editors for publishing "letters from England which are uniformly pro-imperialist." He focused particularly on George Orwell's letter which asserted that "'to be anti-war in England today is to be pro-Hitler.'" Howe wanted to know how it is that "this preposterous statement—fit for the garbage pails of the *New Republic* or the *Nation*—goes unchallenged by the editors!"[11]

Many years later, no longer a brash twenty-two-year-old blinded by sectarianism, Howe favorably quoted remarks made by Orwell in 1942: "When one thinks of the cruelty, squalor, and futility of war . . . there is always the temptation to say: 'One side is as bad as the other. I am neutral.' In practice, however, one cannot be neutral, and there is hardly such a thing as a war in which it makes no difference who wins. Nearly always one side stands more or less for progress, the other side for reaction." Howe also specifically admitted that Orwell's position supporting the war against the Nazis had made perfect sense. For a brief interval, Orwell, like Howe, had enunciated a semi-Trotskyist line critical of the bourgeois West. But when the war came, Howe wrote, Orwell "had the good sense—not all his co-thinkers did—to see that his earlier views on combating fascism had been abstract, unreal. . . . He supported the war yet remained a radical, steadily criticizing social privilege and snobbism."[12]

Howe clearly regretted not having taken this position himself. But he did not seem to want to remember just how consistently and for how long he had kept up his attack on the bourgeois democracies and on American participation in the war against Hitler. Throughout the 1940s, Howe continued to hammer home the theme of struggle between two imperialisms, neither worthy of support. In May 1942 he wrote that the war is an indication that "we are living [through] the literal last convulsions of capitalist society in decay." Both sides, he said, "fight for the retention of the reactionary status quo." In January 1943, Howe, now in the army and writing under his R. Fahan by-line, said, "Roosevelt has discovered the obvious: an imperialist war can be conducted only by imperialist means [and] the New Deal has been completely shunted aside." The war, Howe concluded, is "conducted as a conservative war of big business. Big business is firmly entrenched in the Washington saddle." In 1944 he again attacked liberals who can "see no moral discrimination between their overflowing love of humanity and their support of British, American and Stalinist imperialism in the war." And as late as 1947 Howe in several pieces continued to describe World War II as a war between allied and axis imperialism.[13]

It is difficult, if not impossible, to explain satisfactorily the blindness of Irving Howe and other intellectuals who failed to make the kind of lesser-evil distinctions George Orwell made in the early 1940s, especially in the case of the war against Nazism, which Michael Walzer, Howe's student in the 1950s and co-editor of *Dissent*, has appropriately called a model of the "just war."

The intellectuals themselves, including Irving Howe, subscribed to the following kind of rationale: socialism and capitalism are not only mutually exclusive, they completely exhaust the possible alternative forms of society. Fascism, Howe said again and again, is, after all, a form of capitalism—capitalism in its last desperate paroxysmal stage. Therefore, whether the bourgeois democracies triumph or fascism triumphs, capitalism will be the winner and the working classes the losers. Although Stalinism, fascism, and capitalism look like different social systems, and although capitalism temporarily maintains "comparatively attractive" political and economic conditions, they are, Howe argued, all "reactionary social systems and a choice [among them] would be necessary only if one abandoned the socialist perspective."[14]

The way out of the dilemma, then, was not by aiding the countries occupied by the Gestapo or in opening a second front to help England. Instead, the hope, "in this world of chaos and destruction," Howe wrote rather rhapsodically in 1942, lay with "the star of socialism [which] shines with constancy and promise. Not the ceaseless war, the chaotic postwar disintegration, the dictatorial brutality which capitalism promises, but the peace, the freedom, the human brotherhood which socialism alone can bring. That is our road." Echoing sentiments Howe had announced as early as his CCNY days, the editorial position of *Labor Action* was that the only road out of war, and the only "way to sever ties between the Hitler regime and German soldiers" was "to fight for worker's governments in the Allied countries."[15]

It is not surprising that some readers of *Labor Action* were taken aback by the paper's stance. The *California Eagle*, a black newspaper, the *St. Louis-Star Times*, and the *Christian Science Monitor* all accused *Labor Action* of "play[ing] Hitler's game," and insisted that the paper's neutralism favored a victory for fascism, Hitlerism, and Japanese imperialism. Howe was kept busy from March through May 1942 trying to counter these kinds of attacks. Typically, he wrote, "We *are* in favor of a defeat of fascism. We believe, however, that an indispensable prerequisite . . . is the establishment of workers' and farmers' governments in the Allied countries."[16]

This meant, of course, that the working classes in England and the United States, and perhaps even in France and Eastern Europe, were expected to prepare for civil war, or at least to sabotage war efforts by strikes and by passive resistance against their governments, including the democratic governments fighting Hitler. Class victory by workers in America and England would presumably operate as a focal point and move the German people to overthrow their own fascist government. Only a kind of systematic delusion—to which isolated sectarians are particularly vulnerable—could have sustained these hopes about an

America whose working classes had for the most part supported the New Deal, or for a Europe in which Germany had destroyed socialist trade union movements at home, as well as in every country the Nazis occupied.

Irving Howe, perhaps desperate to believe that socialist movements were still operating underground in Europe, had grossly overestimated their strength. He and his fellow Trotskyists had also underestimated the "ferocious urge to total domination" that characterized Nazism; and in their insistence that the Nazi version of fascism was merely German capitalism in its death throes, they failed, as Howe later admitted, to recognize that the society created by the Hitler regime was "something qualitatively new in its monstrousness."[17]

This discounting of Nazism except as a form of fascism meant, too, that Irving Howe, and the many other radical Jews on the staffs of *Labor Action* and the *New International*, would not pay great attention to the unique and tragic fate of European Jewry. In 1983, Howe, haunted still by the ghastly reality of the Holocaust and by his less than fervent response to it in the 1940s, came close to admitting this. In answer to historian Lucy Dawidowicz's charge in *Commentary* magazine that hardly any Marxist group during World War II ever gave a passing thought to the Jews of Europe, Howe wrote: "The Socialist Left, like (I would say) every other group on the political spectrum, should have done and said more than it did about the European Jews. . . . A large portion of what the Socialist Left did say was rigid, sectarian, doctrinaire, and quite indefensible. Some of it now seems to me stupid."[18]

But Howe did go on to cite a number of examples of significant concern by the Socialist Left, including the Jewish Bund (which Dawidowicz inexplicably rejected as not socialist), Norman Thomas, and Trotsky himself, who, as early as 1932, warned that if a new world war broke out, the Jews of Europe would suffer physical annihilation. Howe also asked Albert Glotzer, who had been the editor (as Al Gates) of *Labor Action* while Howe was in the army from 1942 to 1946, and keeper of the archives, to supply him with citations from the paper to refute Dawidowicz. Glotzer quickly sent Howe eleven titles relating to the plight of European Jewry.[19]

In fact, by my count, there were at least twenty-three pieces on the victimization of European Jewry and nearly another dozen pieces on anti-Semitism in the United States and Europe, that appeared in *Labor*

Action between June 1940 and December 1947. These included such things as a lengthy article on the Warsaw Ghetto (May 25, 1942), attacks on the British government's indifference to Jewish refugees (September 13 and October 5, 1943), and a report on the reappearance of anti-Semitism in Poland (September 9, 1946). Other important articles included "Jews in France Doomed to Certain Death" (June 24, 1940); "UN Policy Dooms European Jews" (September 6, 1943); "American Jewish Conference Reveals Terrible Plight of World Jewry" (September 27, 1943); "No Let Up in Nazi Torture of Jews" (February 7, 1944); and Howe's own essay, "The Jews of Europe" (August 26, 1946), in which he described the conditions of the displaced-persons camps, dealt with postwar anti-Semitism, and asked:

> Will the last pathetic remnant of European Jewry expire in the DP camps? Are the doors of the world to be closed to them in their last agony? No one who still functions on the level of humanity, no one who still responds as a human being rather than a robot can fail to urge, with the Workers' Party, that the doors of the United States, Palestine, and whichever other country they wish to go to, be opened to the Jews of Europe.

From the army, just prior to his departure for Alaska in November 1944, Howe had also written a letter to Glotzer expressing horror about "a grisly article" he had read in the *American Mercury* about the Warsaw Ghetto. "It made me sick for two days," Howe wrote. "God, what incredible butchery—and how nobly and heroically did the Jews fight, for once! It is a terrible shame that the American press has neglected this so much; most readers don't know anything about it; don't you think it would still be worthwhile if someone wrote about it?"[20]

Clearly, Irving Howe was not unconcerned about the Jews of Europe during the war or afterwards, but his deepest convictions probably lay elsewhere. This was true not only for Howe, but also for many of the New York Jewish intellectuals. Although the full extent of the Nazi-perpetrated horrors remained hidden until after the war, there was evidence by December 1942, which mounted afterward, that a genocide of unprecedented proportion was being committed against the Jews. Other New York Jewish intellectuals, not on the left, such as Marie Syrkin, Ben Halpern, and Ludwig Lewisohn, were very much concerned with anti-Semitism abroad; and they were obsessed with the

Holocaust and with the apparent lack of concern over the Nazi genocide among American Jews generally.[21]

It is remarkable, therefore, how little exploration of the "Jewish question" there was among the radical intellectuals both before and during the war. Many of them, Daniel Bell recalled, wanted to be seen, and to see themselves, as "liberated universalists," and despite their radicalism, they had "a great fear of open discussion" about Jewish issues. To talk of explicitly Jewish questions would have marked the radicals as provincial, something to be avoided at all cost. It would have meant being stuck, intellectually if not physically, in the ghetto, left behind in what Saul Bellow would later describe as "the old system."[22] About the silence surrounding prewar anti-Semitism and Hitler's blatant discrimination against the Jews in the mid-1930s, Alfred Kazin later admitted, "If [the Jewish] intellectuals had gone on a great deal . . . about the Jews . . . the way, for example, the Yiddish press did, they would have seemed a good deal less 'American,' less assimilated."[23] Unfortunately, the reluctance to focus on the Jews carried over into the war years. But Kazin did produce in 1944 a notable exception to the general lack of explicit attention to the destruction of European Jewry. In a short piece in the *New Republic*, he was the first to argue for an extended sense of responsibility, indeed guilt, for the crimes committed by the Nazis. "Something has been done—and not by the Nazis—which can never be undone," Kazin wrote. "Something has been set forth in Europe that is subtle, and suspended, and destructive. . . . That something is all our silent complicity in the massacre of the Jews."[24]

Howe himself wondered out loud later, and asked others too, why his and their response to the Holocaust was so belated. William Phillips, the longtime editor of *Partisan Review*, said Howe "was haunted by the question of why our intellectual community, particularly in the pages of *Partisan Review*, had paid so little attention to the holocaust in the early forties." Howe phoned Phillips before he wrote his 1982 memoir, *A Margin of Hope*, and asked him to lunch. Howe wanted to know "why we had failed to respond more strongly to the gravity of events. . . . Neither of us knew the proper answer," Phillips said, "but we tended to believe that our residue of Marxist thinking and our preoccupation with the [imperialist] nature of World War Two—distracted us from the mind-shattering slaughter of European Jewry."[25]

"One's first response" to the Holocaust, Howe wrote in *Margin*, "— not the sole response, but the first—had to be a cry of Jewish grief. For me, alas, that would only come a little later," when, as he put it, he "had become less ideological and more responsive morally."[26] For the meantime, at least through the 1940s, the fear of the heresy of "Jewish nationalism," the continued attachment to Marxist categories which blocked any understanding of the real nature of Nazism, and perhaps the incomprehensible enormity of the event itself kept the Holocaust from a central place in Irving Howe's consciousness.

In dozens of letters from his army post to Al Glotzer between July 1944 and September 1945, Howe mentioned the Jews only once, in connection with the Warsaw Ghetto uprising. He talked mainly about his loneliness, his life in the military—"monotonous and terrifyingly boring," his voracious reading (more than 150 books in fourteen months), the dangers of Stalinism and Soviet imperialism, and his organizing work for the Workers Party, which Howe continued to do while on occasional leave.[27] And the political articles he wrote for the *New International* and *Labor Action* between 1942 and 1945 as R. Fahan, or R. Fangston, also had little to do with the Jews of Europe. They were mostly about the evils of capitalism, racism in the United States, and the desperate need for socialist revolution everywhere. Although Howe supported racial integration even within the framework of capitalism, he insisted that only socialism would bring real justice to American blacks—just as he insisted that only socialism would end anti-Semitism. Class and class exploitation and not race or religion were the critical factors for Howe.[28]

As late as December 1946, Howe, now back home, wrote a piece for *Labor Action* called "Genocide or Socialism" in which he contended that "the conception of genocide is not merely applicable to those peoples that fell victim to Nazism. Increasingly, it becomes descriptive of capitalist civilization as a whole." And in 1947 in the *New International*, Howe reviewed a book about the concentration camps without ever mentioning the Jews. He insisted that David Rousett's *The Other Kingdom* was the very best work on the subject because it "places the concentration camps within the framework of capitalist society."[29]

Not the Jews but the "absolute rottenness of the capitalist system" and the need for socialist revolution remained Howe's central concerns during the war and even after the war. And this concern persisted even as he saw other intellectuals in the postwar "period of reaction" take "flight from Marxism." In 1946 Howe attacked Dwight Macdonald in the pages of *Politics*, Macdonald's own magazine, which had taken

Howe on as a part-time assistant. "Macdonald and his friends," Howe wrote pointedly, were among the many "backsliders" who refused to recognize the revolutionary potential of the proletariat. Howe believed, despite much evidence to the contrary, that the major social forces that could drive the working classes to revolt persisted. "The working classes of all countries *do* revolt," Howe argued, adding rather desperately, "sporadically, in disorganized fashion, it is true, but they still revolt."[30] Throughout 1947, Irving Howe continued to bemoan what he saw as the selfish and cowardly retreat of the intellectuals from Marxism, and in October he added that they were not only fleeing radical politics, but politics altogether.[31]

This was a tragic retrogression, Howe thought, because, as he continued to insist, there is true justice only in a socialist society, and the only way to establish socialism—an authentic workers' government—in the United States was "revolutionary militancy" by the masses and their socialist leaders.[32] Yet the war hardly produced the socialist revolutionary movement Howe had anticipated. Instead, in these so-called flabby capitalist democracies, the war produced an extraordinary popular will to resist fascism and a deeply felt conviction that the Nazis had to be demolished even if at high cost. And in the war's aftermath, the economies of Western Europe, resisting Marxist predictions, underwent an extraordinary revival.

Even in the face of the resilience of capitalist society, then, what remained paramount in Howe's consciousness was the need to redeem the Western democracies through socialism. But there were other things on his mind as well. In addition to his copious overseas correspondence with Al Glotzer, Irving was also busy answering letters from Thalia Phillies. A small, dark-haired, strikingly good-looking Trotskyist working on her doctorate in classical studies at Columbia University, Thalia began writing to Howe at the request of her brother-in-law, Nicholas Syracopoulos, a Workers Party activist in Ohio. Howe had written to Syracopoulos about his loneliness in the army, and asked for mail. Too busy with party work and his own law practice, Nicholas asked Thalia to write instead.[33]

The letters Irving and Thalia exchanged do not survive, but their correspondence blossomed into a romance and then a marriage in 1947. This was actually, for Howe, a second marriage. Mentioned nowhere in his autobiography or in his several published memoir-essays is Anna Bader, another young Trotskyist and the daughter of Orthodox Jews, whom Howe somehow found time to pursue and marry in 1941, despite his rigorous editing schedule. His work, however, did keep him and his new wife apart most of the time. Anna Bader, described by several associates as pretty, brazen, and physically demonstrative, had to undergo treatment for psychological problems, which, according to friends of the couple, were probably exacerbated but not caused by her relationship with an intense, often preoccupied Irving. In any case, they were separated in less than a year and divorced in 1946, when Howe was demobilized.[34]

In between writing to Thalia Phillies and Al Glotzer, Howe also kept himself busy reading books from a fairly substantial army-base library, and he had occasional outings with women. "Despite all my bitching, moaning . . . groaning, [and] whining," he said in 1945, "I'm still alert, reading like a fish, even having one or two dates (on one of which, I proudly relate to your skeptical ears, I nearly got drunk)." Howe also gained "a little relief" from his tedious job of "processing" personnel records, all alone, in an abandoned mess hall, by listening to music and developing new tastes. He told Glotzer that he was "turning increasingly to the romantics. The attitude . . . which we had of snobbishly turning up our noses at Tchaikovsky, Brahms, Berlioz, Franck, etc.," Howe said, "seems very childish to me now."[35]

In the barracks, because he read "deep" books, Howe came to be known as "the prof," a label laden with respect as well as a touch of hostility. Occasionally, Irving also found himself arguing, softly, about racial and religious matters with an unworldly Southern Baptist boy he had befriended. And he had to rebuke another Southern soldier, who often made disparaging remarks about Jews. Wanting to be Howe's "buddy" and even promising to risk his life for him if they ever saw action, the soldier was surprised and hurt by Irving's anger, and the relationship ended in sullen silence. But in general, in the closeness of barracks life, Howe felt among the soldiers, mostly workers and farmers, an "unasserted sympathy" that was part of the common human effort of "making do."[36]

Every few days Howe also had long, rambling phone conversations with "Ira," a newly made friend who also had a monotonous job at another location on the army post; and nearly every Sunday, Alaska weather permitting, Irving and Ira walked two or three miles to Anchorage for a meal together. Their talks, occasionally lasting hours, might concern anything not too immediately personal, ranging from

books read to "lascivious recollections of pastrami sandwiches" con-
sumed. With Ira, Howe "was able to retrieve a few fragments of New
York culture." Together, Howe said, "we could remind ourselves who
we were, New Yorkers, Jews, and I at least a radical . . . we helped each
other survive" army life.[37]

There was not much else, however, in the way of intellectual give
and take. Howe "kept reading regularly and hard." But he felt "a little
irritated and sterile" without the interchange of opinion, [and the] conflict of ideas."[38] Enforced isolation and steady reading, however, did
bring about a gradual intellectual change. Howe remained "passionately caught up with politics," but he broadened his learning and had
time for introspection, and so began to escape the singleness of mind
that had inspired the ideological commitments of his youth.

In early writings, prior to his entering the army, Howe had exposed
the kind of arrogant certainty and political narrowness exhibited by
young radicals not yet experienced in doubt and ambiguity. In his first
book review in 1941, for example, he discussed *The Defenders*, a novel by
Franz Hoellering about the suppression of the Austrian proletariat in
1934. "Hoellering has neither the intensity of [Andre] Malraux nor the
depth of [Ignazio] Silone," Howe wrote, and his book has many "technical imperfections." Indeed, the novel "winds itself into a serious contradiction which destroys it." This failure, the twenty-one-year-old
Howe had the nerve to say, is "not unusual for a young writer." Yet
Howe was favorably disposed to *The Defenders* for political reasons. The
book is "an extraordinarily moving account of one of the most heroic of
all proletarian struggles; and as such," Howe concluded, "it deserves to
be read by all to whom the working class revolution is more than a mere
reminiscence of past youthfulness."[39]

This last remark, in addition to promoting political over literary
value, was an indirect criticism of those intellectuals who had abandoned their radicalism in the late 1930s and early 1940s. Howe continued his critique in February 1942, this time against the editors of *Partisan Review*. His article in the *New International*, "The Dilemma of Partisan Review," attacked the magazine for its attitude of "haughty
independence" from the struggles of the militant working classes.
Howe acknowledged that he had admired *Partisan Review* in the late
thirties, when it "was the only magazine in the country which attempted to relate Marxism to the cultural life of our time." He also
agreed with the more recent position of *PR* that writers and artists re-

quired "complete artistic and intellectual freedom," especially from party discipline. Nonetheless, he insisted along with Trotsky that "the writer or artist must necessarily take his stand with the revolutionary proletariat," something, in Howe's estimation, *PR* did not do. Indeed, in Howe's view, *PR*'s "independence" and consequent failure to move forward to "a consistent clear socialist doctrine" caused the editors inevitably to "retrogress . . . into toleration of the status quo."[40]

In the same issue of the *New International*, Howe, in a style typical of him for this period, made severely caustic remarks directed at John Dos Passos. Like Van Wyck Brooks and Archibald MacLeish, Dos Passos was one of several writers and critics whose disillusionment with communism and fear of fascism in the late 1930s had turned him back to American tradition and the democratic inheritance. Reviewing Dos Passos's *The Ground We Stand On*, Howe ridiculed the author's newfound admiration for Jeffersonian democracy by calling the book "Crumbling Ground" and by accusing Dos Passos of moving "from a vague belief in a vague Marxism to an even vaguer confusion." Dos Passos, Howe complained, talked only about the "people in general," not classes, and he never mentioned "economic arrangements." *The Ground We Stand On* "then is a complete failure." Its "sole virtue," Howe maintained, resided in the fact that it represented "the failure of the conscientious groping of a man whose mind at present can only be described as in a seriously preoccupied muddle."[41]

Just prior to being drafted in July 1942, Howe published a similarly vituperative piece on John Steinbeck's *The Moon is Down*. He mercilessly described the novel as "a colossal literary fraud," filled with politically unsophisticated "airy abstractions," a book which gives not even a hint "of the motivations which might impel resistance to Nazi conquerors."[42] This kind of overly politicized, polemical writing contained little hint of Howe's later humane judiciousness and sensibilities. But, slowly, through the late forties and beyond, Howe's critical work evolved into a more temperate and broadly sophisticated literary commentary.

As early as October 1942, after only one month of post–basic training army life and the opportunity it provided for reading and introspection, Howe, in reviewing Ignazio Silone's *The Seed Beneath the Snow*, took a step away from "the totality of the political" in his literary criticism. He asked that Silone's novel "be judged by the pleasure and stimulation afforded the reader" rather than be "analyzed as a political document." Otherwise, Howe feared that this latest work of Silone's was "likely to be cavalierly dismissed by radicals as merely another instance of intellectual backsliding reflecting Silone's retrogression from Marxism to a strange variety of primitive, revolutionary Christianity." Such an attitude, Howe warned, "despite its political good intentions, would result in a failure to appreciate a literary masterpiece of our times."

While Silone's "ideological creed does not appear very attractive to the radical reader," the Italian novelist, Howe argued, continues to be "a man of great sincerity and honesty, a man who in a period of intellectual surrender remains an uncompromising rebel and a man (most important of all) who is one of few genuinely great writers of our time." Let it be remembered, Howe wrote, echoing his early love for T. S. Eliot and pressing his newly developing perspective, "that two of the world's literary masterpieces, Dostoevsky's *Crime and Punishment* and Tolstoy's *War and Peace*, are expositions of reactionary ideologies. That does not prevent any sensible person from reading them again and again."[43]

Several months later, in a review of Alfred Kazin's classic work of criticism, *On Native Grounds*, Howe also indicated a growing willingness to express appreciation of the literary value of good writing with which he disagreed politically. He still believed, and would continue to believe (as in the later case of the poet Ezra Pound) that the seriously flawed politics of a writer results, almost inevitably, in a deterioration in literary merit of that writer's work. But Irving Howe could praise Kazin for his "brilliant . . . youthful freshness and vivacity" even as he disagreed with his "New Dealish . . . liberalistic nationalism." He also took issue with Kazin for his "savage attack" against the conservative New Critics (Allen Tate, John Crowe Ransom, Richard Blackmur, et al.). Howe, like Kazin, thought that the group placed an inordinate, if not absolute, premium on form; but, whatever the political implications of their work, Howe argued, they were talented critics who had "done much to reawaken respect for economy, discipline, and technical competence."[44]

In the army, Howe continued to grow intellectually as he gave himself the kind of multidisciplinary education he had missed at City College. Reading novels and nonfiction, taking notes on important books and passages, and studying, among other things, history, economics, German, and anthropology, Howe came to recognize that "there was far more in the world—more thought, more knowledge and even uncertainty" than his earlier convictions had led him to suppose. He developed a taste for complication which was, as he put it later, "necessarily a threat to the political mind."[45]

Indeed. It was a threat as well to relations with fellow socialists. From October 1946 to the fall of 1947, Howe, back home from the army, became embroiled in a fierce and complicated debate with his colleagues in the Workers Party over the work of Arthur Koestler. The *New International*, the journal of the WP, published in the summer of 1945 a critical review by Peter Loumos of four of Koestler's books. More than a year later, another WP member, poet Neil Weiss, wrote to the *New International* protesting that Loumos, blinded by his Marxist political bias, had failed to provide an objective evaluation of Koestler's work. He went so far as to indict the *New International*'s reviewers in general for their persistent "theological tub thumping" attacks on political antagonists.

In a generally sympathetic response to Weiss's criticism, Irving Howe warned against "the gross error of judging a novel merely by political standards." Koestler's literary impressionism, Howe admitted, was no substitute for analytically rigorous discussion of politics. But what was "so exciting" about Koestler, what made him well worth reading, "even when we disagree with his every word," Howe wrote, is his nearly inimitable ability to "touch the heart of the modern problem," to illuminate the growing complexity of world politics. Reflecting the wide learning he had achieved in the military (like Melville's Ishmael who called whaling his "Harvard," Howe called the army his "graduate school"), Howe emphatically urged readers to recognize that "there is more than one universe of discourse in human existence; politics is not the totality of life."[46]

Loyalists in the WP were not about to let Howe have the last word. Albert Gates (Glotzer), the editor of the *New International* and Max Shachtman's closest collaborator, tried to justify the original critique of Koestler, whom Glotzer demoted from novelist to "writer of fictionalized current events." Glotzer, who had had a warm and copious correspondence with Howe when he was in the army, was now "shocked" that Howe had come to Koestler's defense. Why Irving Howe's letter took Glotzer by surprise in 1946 is a bit of mystery, given that Howe had written some similarly "politically incorrect" things about Silone and Kazin in 1942 and 1943. Moreover, as everyone knew, Howe, though often severely critical of *Partisan Review*'s politics, diligently read the periodical for its unflagging championship of modernist literature and the autonomy of art.

In any case, Glotzer accused Howe of overreacting to Stalinist excesses, particularly the vulgar political coding of literary texts that had discredited the Communist literary movement in the 1930s. There may be some truth in this. But Glotzer was badly mistaken in thinking that Howe's demand of readers to evaluate novels on more than political grounds meant a call for a total separation of literature and politics. Howe understood, as he made clear both in his response to Glotzer and in his developing career (especially in his classic statement, *Politics and the Novel*, 1957), that no author writes in a vacuum, in a value-free or belief-free zone, and that no human life, relationship, or institution is untouched by the political and social structure of the community in which it resides.

Glotzer had made a very crude attack on Howe, dismissing him as a bourgeois critic who eschewed "method," by which he meant, of course, Marxist method. Howe, in turn, characterized Glotzer as a man determined to judge literature narrowly, not by party line as did the Stalinists, but as if fiction were merely a convenient vehicle for political content. Howe went on to say that intelligence, knowledge, and experience were more important in literary criticism than Marxism, and that Marxism, because it is only "a theory of historical analysis and social action . . . contributes little to an *evaluation* of a work of art." Elsewhere and earlier, Howe had been even more explicit in devaluing the Marxist approach to creative writing. Marxism, Howe said, often "clarifies things about literature or art," especially their connection to the social milieu, but it "seldom illuminates their specific manifestations," and almost always ends as reductionism.[47]

Irving Howe came to realize during the exchanges over Koestler that a dogmatic approach to literature was not a monopoly of the Stalinists. Even Trotskyists could insist on treating novels as political programs, despite the fact that Trotsky himself had said, "Art must make its own way and by its own means. Marxian methods are not the same as the artistic."[48] Howe concluded that "being a revolutionary socialist does not necessarily prevent one from being a cultural philistine" and took yet another step away from narrow-minded sectarianism.[49] Much later in another context, Howe, referring to some former American Communists, said "most changes of thought occur hesitantly, and language always lags behind impulse and feeling." He could easily have been speaking about himself. It would take another five years before he formally broke with the WP (renamed the Independent Socialist League in 1949) in 1952, but the seeds of disaffection had been firmly planted in the Koestler dispute.[50]

Toward the end of that dispute, in the summer of 1947, Howe decided "to drop the whole matter" and to keep his "private opinions on . . . literary matters out of the *New International*."[51] He submitted an essay on James Farrell to *Partisan Review* rather than the WP periodical, convinced that what he had to say about Farrell and literary criticism would only keep the imbroglio going. In this he was surely right. For although Irving Howe, like his Trotskyist cohort, admired Farrell's anti-Stalinist Marxism, unlike them he could charge the novelist-critic with reducing "literature to an anterior political or sociological concept." In practice, Howe wrote, Farrell "cannot reconcile himself to the view that literature is a human activity requiring no . . . social sanction." He concluded, however, by asserting his continued belief in "social criticism," a considerably complex social criticism, that can employ "Marxism with subtlety and [with] regard for its limitations." Although Howe, much later, thought his attack on Farrell, a political ally, shamefully gratuitous, it did represent a growing complexity in Howe's literary consciousness.[52]

Howe's disaffection from the literary opinions of the *New International* and to a lesser extent from the WP itself was nurtured and reinforced by his growing ambition to be a writer. By the end of 1947 he had had three pieces published in *Partisan Review* and two in *Commentary*. Established in 1945 by the American Jewish Committee, *Commentary* was clearly a *Jewish* magazine. But it opposed Jewish "nationalism" and tried to provide an "unparochial" alternative to *Jewish Frontier* and *Reconstructionist*, one that would attract Jewish writers like Howe who saw themselves as universalists. Edited by former Stalinist Elliot Cohen, *Commentary* succeeded in drawing many of its contributors from the same community of intellectuals as the resurrected *Partisan Review* of a decade earlier. Howe told an interviewer in 1981 that in the 1940s he did not dream of being a writer or a literary critic; his ideal was to be the "editor of a great socialist daily in the United States." But in the army, Howe said, "almost against my wishes, I was able to educate myself with true breadth and learn enough to avoid the narrowness of ideology. I left Alaska and, in a way that even now I am not clear about, I knew I wanted to be a writer."[53]

Within the political activist, apparently, there had been beating, for some time, the secret heart of a literary intellectual.[54] As early as 1944, Howe was contemplating writing a book about the novelist Sherwood Anderson, and just prior to being shipped to Alaska he spent his last weekend pass visiting Clyde, Ohio, Anderson's hometown and the model for his *Winesburg, Ohio*. Perhaps the desire to distinguish himself as a writer went back to his days at CCNY when he had read Edmund Wilson's *Axel's Castle*, and where he had taken a course in literary criticism. "The professor, a man named Stare," Howe remembered, "spent half the semester reading almost line by line through Aristotle's *Poetics*. And I loved that," Howe said. "I loved the close attention and analysis that he gave to the text. And I guess this . . . must have prefigured my later decision to become a literary critic."[55]

Whatever the origin of Howe's desire, in Alaska he had been inflicted with the virus of heresy, and with the slow but steady erosion of his strict adherence to Marxist theory, there began to emerge from him the kind of sophisticated, erudite work for which he would later come to be known and respected. And as with many other New York intellectuals, Howe's gradual disengagement from the bonds of Marxist universalism, a process powerfully advanced by the Holocaust, allowed him, as we shall see, to discover his Jewish self in his work.

4

The Postwar World and the Reconquest of Jewishness

THE WAR OVER, and knowing now he would not be killed, Irving Howe was "wild to live." From Alaska in late November 1945 he joked in a letter to Al Glotzer, "I've just about finished with the local library, and therefore consider it time to go home."[1]

Back in the Bronx in January 1946, Howe immediately visited his parents. His father seemed much older, bent from too many years of work with the press iron; his mother, clearly ill, was yellow with jaundice and the cancer that would kill her about ten months later. Irving would not stay for the "few days" his parents requested. Just before moving into his own apartment on East 107th Street with two friends, he revisited his parents, and, apparently needing a physical symbol of connection, a "last battered token" of the immigrant years, he took from their place an old, beat-up folding chair—a chair he kept for years.[2]

G.I. unemployment insurance of twenty dollars a week enabled Howe to work for *Labor Action* for many months without pay. He quickly returned to the typewriter, banging out articles for the socialist weekly as well as for the *New International*, and a little later for Dwight Macdonald's independent radical magazine, *Politics*. The goal of the Left, Howe continued to insist, remained the same as it had been before the war, to "destroy . . . the illusion that Stalinism or Social Democracy can bring Socialism" and to "build . . . a revolutionary party which can."[3] It seemed as if Howe had recaptured his past. "But it does not work," he wrote later. "One must learn that the past is not subject to the reach of the will." And soon, only about six months after demobilization, Irving Howe had hesitations about continuing with sectarian radical journalism.

By November, in a review of Karl Kautsky's book on Social Democracy, Howe admitted "wryly" that "almost every revolutionary theoretician yearns [for] a life of secluded scholarship." Howe neither achieved nor really fully desired such a life. Politics would always remain critically important to him. But his words indicated his need for "nourishment in the common air," and his need to be more deeply involved with the study and independent evaluation of literature.[4]

In the meantime, "half in the movement and half out," and especially as his unemployment insurance ran out, Irving Howe had to earn a living. In the summer of 1946 he wrote to Dwight Macdonald telling him that he had done "some reviews and writing" for *Commentary* that had been warmly received. "I think I could sell," Howe said, but in the meantime he asked if Macdonald could help him with "some little side line that is regular?"[5] Howe found more work than money as an editorial assistant at *Politics*, where he reworked articles, and wrote, under the pen name Theodore Dryden, a monthly feature evaluating (mostly attacking) articles in other periodicals. Howe was paid fifteen dollars a week—most weeks: too often he had to remind Macdonald to send him a check.

That Howe was working for *Politics*, a kind of halfway house for independent leftists who were bored with sectarian Marxism but thoroughly opposed to postwar conservatism, made some in the movement uncomfortable. But his friends in the Workers Party finally agreed that Irving could operate as a technical aide at *Politics* as long as he desisted from "editorial collaboration" with this magazine full of "deviations" from Trotskyism. Macdonald was kind enough not to tease Irving about this, probably because, as Howe wrote later, "he saw that I was heading down the slopes of apostasy and there was no need to push."[6]

At the time, however, and for two or three years longer, Howe, publicly and perhaps out of his own ideological ambivalence, continued to declare himself a loyal member of the WP, which was still, at least nominally, a Trotskyist organization. And when Macdonald in the summer of 1946 published "The Root Is Man," his antirevolutionary manifesto deemphasizing ideology in the face of the more important need to promote nonviolence and to transcend the "inherent evil" in human nature, Howe was infuriated. He attacked what he saw, correctly, as Macdonald's pacifism and ridiculed his abandonment of political involvement in the name of some higher standard of morality. Morality "was determined by class situation and class conflicts," Howe argued, not human nature, as Macdonald seemed to suggest. Although he would change his mind in the not-too-distant future, Howe in 1946 continued to reject the idea that there was anything fixed in human nature. He believed, as he had written in 1943, that "the human being is a *completely adaptable organism*, molded by the society in which he finds himself and capable, under certain conditions, of changing that society."[7]

While Macdonald was trying to decide whether or not to publish Howe's diatribe against him, he received a letter from Irving explaining that "our political lines have diverged so widely that all we can really do is note the differences and let it go at that. I should of course be pleased if you'd print [my response], because it is the only contribution sent you by a practicing Marxist, that is one who functions in a group." Later, Howe wrote again, saying, "I am certain that you will find my piece an unsatisfactory presentation—which makes it even."[8] Macdonald finally decided to print Howe's essay "The Thirteenth Disciple," perhaps because, as Macdonald's biographer said, "Howe had struck a nerve."[9] But out of his legendary stinginess or out of personal pique, Macdonald determined to run it not as an article, but as a "communication"—for which he would not have to pay. Howe gave his permission, saying, "I didn't write it to get rich," and "certainly the *New International* wouldn't pay a penny more for it than you. I want it in *Politics*," Howe admitted, "because it'll reach people who wouldn't otherwise see it and because it may help me personally."[10]

Despite the feud, Howe continued to write for *Politics*, but in the several weeks of late summer 1946 he made no new submissions. Irving had "suffered the shock of . . . discovering the imminent death of [his] mother from cancer, which" as he told Macdonald, "made it impossible for me to work for a while, but I guess there's no alternative but to get into the swing again. So drop me a line."[11] Macdonald did just that, eliciting more writing from Howe, and they remained friends, although they did not try to hide their disagreements. The disagreements were overstated, in any case. After all, Howe himself, whether consciously or not, had begun to withdraw gradually from the Trotskyist movement that Macdonald had earlier left behind. In fact, only months after his exchange with Macdonald over ideology and morality, Howe resigned from the editorial board of *Labor Action*.

Howe needed more room to breathe. He also needed a wider audience and more money, especially after marrying Thalia Phillies (his army correspondent) in 1947, and after *Politics* disappeared late in that same year—along with his fifteen dollars a week. He took a job as part-time assistant to Hannah Arendt, who was editor of Schocken Books at the time. For $150 a month, Irving wrote copy for book jackets, fine-tuned translations, and did other literary chores. He also worked at doing synopses of novels for Paramount Studios, which was looking for film script material. Phyllis Jacobson, one of Howe's associates in the movement, had the same job at Warner Brothers, and they helped each other by trading synopses. This lasted about a year, and then in 1948 Howe accepted a part-time job as a book reviewer for *Time*, the news magazine which he had only recently criticized as having a "capsuliz-ing, English-twisting, high-speed, omniscient-reporter approach."[12]

Irving Howe and everyone he knew held *Time* in contempt, but only one 800-word review for that magazine would produce seventy-five dollars each week, and Howe's financial troubles would be over. Still, as a socialist and an uncompromising highbrow, Howe hesitated and expressed his reservations to Philip Rahv, the co-editor of *Partisan Review*. Rahv laughed and told Howe it was better to do "dirty work" for one who paid well than for a dozen "bosses" who paid badly. Even though Irving's wife Thalia had recently secured a position teaching Latin and Greek for $1,900 a year in a private day school in Princeton, New Jersey, to which they moved, Howe felt that they needed the extra money from *Time*. Moreover, he wanted to be less dependent upon free-lance writing, which he continued to find "a wretched business." As important, and perhaps a signal that on Howe's list of socialist priorities women's equality was not very high, he thought it even "more wretched to be supported by a wife."

Finally, "lured by Satan's finger of gold," he took the job, comforting himself partly by the fact that he was not being asked to write reviews of political books, and partly by the presence on *Time*'s staff of other literary figures. Howe became friendly with Nigel Dennis, who grew to be a first-rate satirist; with James Agee, who had achieved a small degree of fame for his book *Let Us Now Praise Famous Men* (1941), and with Robert Fitzgerald, a gifted poet. Howe continued writing for *Time* until 1953. This enabled him to keep his head above water finan-cially, and even to purchase an automobile. "We have invested in that great American institution, a Chevrolet," he wrote Trilling in 1950, which "makes me feel more substantial socially but very precarious physically."[13]

Even more important for Howe's sense of propriety was that during those years with *Time*, a place he described with some embarrassment as "the devil's den," he did do his "own work" at home as he had promised himself. He coauthored a book on the United Auto Workers (UAW), wrote critical and enduring studies of the life and work of Sherwood Anderson and William Faulkner, began work on "a big book" on American Communism, and produced several essays that would constitute the core of *Politics and the Novel*.[14] All of this was major work, a stunning accomplishment reflecting Howe's extraordinary breadth of interests, his complex critical imagination, and his increasingly sophisticated politics.

Howe's writings on the UAW (1949), in an era of increasing racial friction, included significant attention to the question of race relations. He was very sympathetic to the UAW and the CIO (Congress of Industrial Organizations), unions which had pledged themselves to nondiscrimination policies and had "acted vigorously to defend the Negro workers." He especially praised the work of the UAW's fair employment practices department and its persistent push among working men and women for racial equality. Although still much more focused on class than race as a critical force in society, Howe by the late 1940s understood that racism was not merely a "symptom" of capitalism. He knew, too, that the injustice and wastefulness of discrimination could be ameliorated within the presocialist framework of "bourgeois democracy." He was not only supportive of the integrationist efforts of the industrial labor unions, but also of the Urban League, the NAACP, and A. Philip Randolph, president of the Brotherhood of Sleeping Car Porters, who had been indispensable to the success of what Howe saw as campaigns for elemental justice—the desegregation of the defense industry in 1941 and of the armed forces in 1948.[15]

Throughout his work on the UAW, in which Howe emphasized economic justice, he made the case for racial justice and fraternity. These two themes were also important for Howe in his work in the early fifties on Faulkner, whose attitudes on race, as on gender and class, were often violently contradictory. The great southern writer's early portraits of blacks were little more than stereotyped products of a racist culture. *Sartoris* (1929), for example, perpetuates rather than explores Southern racial caricatures. But, as Howe demonstrated, Faulkner, though never completely shedding his racist inheritance, did grapple with it, and

after 1930 in novel after novel he subjected conventional southern attitudes about race to corrosive examination.

Faulkner remained befuddled and conflicted on the question of
race, but he did experience a steady enlargement of sympathies, and his
black protagonists grew from predictable stock figures to complex characters like Joe Christmas in *Light in August* (1932) and Lucas
Beauchamp in *Absalom, Absalom* (1936). Faulkner never endorsed the
equality of the races, and his fear of miscegenation remained explicitly
evident in *Absalom, Absalom* and *Go Down, Moses* (1942). But evident,
too, was Faulkner's awareness of the tortured injustice of race relations
in the South, and in his work the search for a "lost fraternity" of black
and white was always at the center. Howe, for whom "a fraternity of
companions" was "morally finer" even than a formal equality, responded very positively to this image. It spoke not only to an ideal in
relations between the races but to Howe's notion of the good society
generally.[16]

At the same time that Howe was producing some of his most enduring and most socially conscious work, he was trying hard to adjust
to the far from fraternal quality of Princeton, a picture-book Ivy League
place he never really learned to like. Not until after he left in 1953 did
he realize just how much he had been repelled by the "chilled graces"
of both the town and the university. During his nearly five-year stay,
Howe regularly fled the "Anglophile snobbery" of Princeton and
rushed off to New York at least once a week, sometimes for the entire
weekend.[17] New York could be "demoralizing," even "paralyzing," he
told Lionel Trilling in 1948, but Irving needed the noise, the challenge,
and even the "tension" of the city. Princeton, Howe felt, had only one
good thing going for it—"the advantage of being close to New York,
without being in it."[18]

But Princeton had other advantages, too, especially its lively literary life, which centered mostly around Richard Blackmur and his small
coterie of associates in the university's English Department. Between
Blackmur, a New Critic, suspicious of streetwise New Yorkers and wary
of leftist politics, and Howe, once described as a radical "Jew-boy in a
hurry," there was some cultural and temperamental distance. But like
Howe, Blackmur was an autodidact, a man with no Ph.D. (indeed, no
B.A.), who had mastered English literature through private reading.
And apparently wanting friendships "that might break past the insu-

lating circle of his fame," Blackmur was receptive to Howe, and Howe to him.

Howe, who had no official connection to Princeton University, got even closer to several of Blackmur's teaching assistants. John Berryman, for example, who eventually won widespread recognition and acclaim as a boldly original and innovative poet, was Irving's neighbor in the university-owned Prospect Street Apartments, and he and Howe had frequent conversations. Somewhat bewildered by Berryman's intense and frenetic style, Howe nonetheless told Trilling, "I can think of nothing more stimulating, even if exhausting, than talking to John Berryman. He's one of the few people I know in whose goodness and sense I have complete trust."[19] The relationship, however, came to a rather abrupt halt when Howe told Berryman he was not particularly enchanted with Rimbaud, the nineteenth-century French poet. Rimbaud's embrace of "chaos," which Berryman replicated, troubled Howe. He preferred to be comforted by Marx and history and, unlike Rimbaud and Berryman, he did not define himself primarily as a victim, a fellow sufferer acutely oppressed by modern malaise. This meant that Irving Howe, in Berryman's eyes, was something of a philistine and no longer worth talking to.

With Delmore Schwartz, another of Blackmur's teaching assistants, Howe had a similar discussion but with different results. "Do you sometimes get up in the morning," Schwartz asked, "and feel that you can't even bring yourself to tie your shoelaces?" Although Howe said that he had had his bouts of depression, he also admitted that they had never quite led to immobilization. Schwartz, unlike Berryman, was not particularly disappointed in this "failure" of Howe's. Though a deeply troubled man, Schwartz mostly resisted the notion fashionable among postwar intellectuals that depression and neurosis were somehow beneficial. He also respected Howe's attachment to politics and rationality. There was also a deep mutual interest in baseball, "the most lucid product," according to Schwartz, "of American life." And Schwartz, in whose writings and voice Howe had always heard "a note almost familial," stayed friendly until his untimely death.[20]

Much later, in conversation with Marshall Berman about Schwartz and Berryman, Howe said he "lacked their inner conflicts" and wondered if that meant there was "something wrong" with him.[21] But he did have inner conflicts, even if not so powerful as those haunting his

Princeton neighbors, and he would go through additional, quite serious bouts of depression in the late 1950s and early 1960s. Unlike Berryman and Schwartz, however, Howe was neither tormented by psychic illness nor addicted to the nonrational, and he avoided the tragic, self-destructive course followed by the two poets. Schwartz, depleted by inner demons and the drugs and alcohol he used to repel them, died broken and alone outside his dismal hotel room in New York in 1966, and Berryman committed suicide by leaping off a bridge in Minneapolis in 1972.[22]

Irving Howe, though still very much a modernist in the late 1940s and early 1950s, was always deeply committed to coherence and to life, values no doubt internalized by him as a young man growing up in the Jewish immigrant milieu of the Bronx. Moreover, only recently out of the military, Howe still felt "wild to live." In fact, he was so devoted to life that he was ready to bring more of it into the world. In the fall of 1948 he wrote to Lionel Trilling, "So many of our friends alternate between telling us how wonderful babies are (as we can see for ourselves!) and then what a nuisance they are, that we breathe hot and cold. But we'll have one, I hope in the not too distant future."[23]

Irving Howe's fervent attachment to life was consistent and showed up again, explicitly, shortly after Berryman plunged to his death. In 1973, in an essay on the literature of suicide, Howe discussed Isaac Babel's story "In the Basement" in which a Jewish grandfather thwarts his thirteen-year-old grandson's attempt to drown himself. After pulling him out of a water barrel, the grandfather said to his unconscious grandson, "I am going to take a dose of castor oil, so as to have something to lay on your grave." This speech may seem coarse, even barbaric, Howe wrote, but the story ends with the boy coming to, and the grandfather stalking about the room whistling. "That whistle," Howe insisted, "signifies a melody of gratification," and the grandfather's seemingly vulgar behavior was "a way of enforcing the urgency of the commandment to life." Howe went on to say, "There is a rich tradition here, expressed tragically by another Russian-Jewish writer, Osip Mandelstam, who said when his wife proposed that they commit suicide before Stalin's police could come to arrest them, 'Life is a gift that nobody should renounce.'"[24]

In Saul Bellow, who was also at Princeton in the late 1940s, Howe found a comrade in life affirmation. Bellow had already won something of a reputation among a small group of mostly Jewish intellectuals with his first two novels. He was, like Berryman and Schwartz, a teaching assistant for Blackmur, and he, too, became an associate of Howe's. "Bellow, Berryman, and Schwartz," Howe told an interviewer in 1988, "were hangers-on in Princeton, with part-time jobs in creative writing, while hankering for full-time positions in the English department. And I was a hanger-on of hangers on."[25] Bellow was "sturdier" than Berryman and Schwartz, "very strong-willed and shrewd in the arts of self-conservation," Howe remembered, and "he understood that while endurance may not guarantee distinguished work, it sometimes enables it."[26] In many if not all of the novels he went on to write, including *Humboldt's Gift* (1975), a fictionalized life of Delmore Schwartz, Bellow demonstrated an irrepressible faith in a moral ethic, perhaps even in God, but certainly in the idea—one shared by Howe—that life is a great gift not to be renounced.[27]

Howe found yet another sturdy, strong-willed friend in the Princeton sociologist Dennis Wrong. The long walk along Nassau Street from Irving's small split-level home on Grover Avenue (purchased with the help of a GI loan in 1949) to Firestone, the main Princeton University library, took him past Wrong's house; and he frequently stopped in. The two men also often dined together at Lahiere's on Witherspoon or at The Annex on Nassau Street. "Irving hardly needed me to talk about literature," Dennis Wrong said, what with Blackmur, Berryman, Schwartz, and Bellow around, but "politics and social criticism were another matter." In the early 1950s Dennis Wrong was in the process of moving away from socialism toward a more generalized left-liberalism, but Howe respected his opinions and intelligence and his general take on important new books. They read and discussed together David Riesman's *The Lonely Crowd*, C. Wright Mills's *White Collar*, Czeslaw Milosz's *The Captive Mind*, and Hannah Arendt's *The Origins of Totalitarianism*. And Howe, deeply impressed by Ralph Ellison's *The Invisible Man*, which "tells us how distant even the best of whites are from the black men that pass them on the street," lent Wrong his review copy from *Time*, insisting that he read the new novel at once.[28]

Despite these seemingly abundant social and intellectual connections, Howe, partly out of resentment at being a mere "hanger-on of hangers-on," expressed serious dissatisfaction with life in Princeton. "Everyone grubs along," Howe wrote to Trilling in the summer of 1948, "turning out too much stuff, especially those trying to win tenure in a university. . . . People are too busy, in Princeton, for instance to live.

Swallow a few more books instead of taking a walk on a lovely night.
. . . I know because I am tempted by the same thing, and even see myself in an odd sort of competitive relationship to the people in the universities. In fact, rather unhappily, I've concluded that I shall one of
these days have to try to get into a university, though not to make it my
main emphasis."[29]

Prior to the late forties, no significant number of Jews had been welcome in the English or history departments of the prestigious universities. But things were beginning to change. Trilling, who in 1932 had become the first Jew in the English Department at Columbia University,
was appointed professor in 1948. Oscar Handlin had been at Harvard
since 1939, and Delmore Schwartz had also been teaching there for several years before he arrived in Princeton in the early 1950s. Irving Howe
could think seriously, therefore, about an academic position in 1948.
And in October he told Trilling, "For a long time I've had a strong urge
to teach, and I secretly suspect that one of the reasons I attack the academy is that, since I only have a bachelor's degree, it won't let me in. I
think I'd be a good teacher too."

Irving Howe had a chance to test himself as a teacher, when in the
fall of 1948 he taught a group of adults in New Jersey. Mostly Jews who
had escaped the garment industry in New York to become chicken farmers in the Lakewood district, they were, Howe said, "an extremely interesting group." The kind of people Irving Howe would celebrate later
in *World of Our Fathers*, these "semi-intellectuals" had had a discussion
group going for years and then asked Howe to teach them about the
modern novel. They chose the books themselves: *The Red and the Black,
Brothers Karamazov, Huckleberry Finn, Portrait of the Artist, The Trial*—a remarkable selection of masterful writers representing five different na-
tionalities whose work was "political" in the richest sense of that word.
And Howe was delighted. It was all "rather fantastic and wonderful,"
Howe thought. "The whole experience exhilarated and buoyed me immensely," he told Trilling, and "I mean to try to do more [teaching]. But
then my trouble is that I want to do everything at once."[30]

Indeed. Howe continued in these same years, 1948–1952, to publish
occasional items in *Labor Action* and *New International*, even as he was
distancing himself from the Trotskyist movement. But his most important pieces, more than two dozen, went to *Commentary* and *Partisan Review*, magazines he had published with before, beginning in 1946. From
1946 on, Howe's pieces indicate and help illuminate some mildly

reawakened stirrings of Jewishness, as well as a corresponding gradual disengagement from Marxist orthodoxy. Howe's very first essay in *Commentary* (August 1946) was a review of Isaac Rosenfeld's *Passage from Home*. The novel, which had initially attracted Howe because Rosenfeld had once been a Trotskyist, involved the eternal and universal pattern of conflict between father and son, here made graphic in an immigrant Jewish family. It made an "overwhelming impression" on Howe, "no doubt," he said later, "because it touched elements of my own experience that I had willed to suppress." Almost immediately after finishing the book, Howe, "with hardly a thought of publication," poured out his "unused feelings" in two thousand "overwrought words."[31]

Apparently still proud of this first effort for *Commentary*, Howe, nearly thirty-six years later, reprinted a section of the review in *A Margin of Hope*:

> I recall with emotion, for it impinges upon my own life—as so many other Jewish readers will feel the book does—a scene at the end of the novel where, after Bernard's return [from a flight from home], his father faces him in judgment and confession. . . . "He got up from the bed and walked about the room, stopping before the bookcase and looking at my books. He always seemed to regard them as strange and remote objects, symbols of myself, and thus related to him—it was with his money that I had bought them—and yet as alien and hostile as I myself had become. My father ran his hand along a row of books. . . . "
>
> Nobody who has been brought up in an immigrant Jewish family and experienced the helpless conflict between the father, who sees in his son the fulfillment of his own uninformed intellectuality, and the son for whom that very fulfillment becomes the brand of alienation . . . can read this passage without feeling that here is true and acute perception.[32]

After the review appeared, Isaac Rosenfeld himself, in his inimitable style, sent a note of praise to Howe, scribbled on brown wrapping paper. He liked the fact that Irving was able to use the "Marxist method" undogmatically in literary criticism. And *Commentary* editor Clement Greenberg, apparently surprised that a Marxist like Howe could write an essay that was not particularly class centered, commended him for his flexibility and encouraged him to submit more.

Irving Howe followed up in October with his thinly disguised autobiographical essay, "The Lost Young Intellectual: A Marginal Man Twice Alienated."

An editor's note at the start of the piece described Howe and his politics and listed his credentials (including, on the G.I. bill, one semester of graduate work in literature at Brooklyn College). The note went on, rather coyly, to say "any implied resemblance between [Howe] and the young intellectuals described in this article is, we are assured, quite unwarranted." Any doubt, however, about the autobiographical nature of Howe's essay is dispelled by the examples he drew upon from his own life and from the lives of friends and associates, and by Howe's sudden switch to the first-person midway through the narrative.

"The Lost Young Intellectual" portrays a young secular Jew alienated from his immigrant past, and yet uncomfortable in the modern American present. The piece is a nearly perfect example of Howe's ambivalence about his immigrant origins and reveals his continuing struggle with the question of Jewish identity. It is almost equally divided between tender reminiscences of Yiddishkayt and the Jewish family on the one side, and sharply drawn incidents of alienation, conflict, and humiliation on the other. Howe insisted, however, on the meaninglessness of these recollections, positive or negative, for, he claimed, they harm the young Jewish writer for whom "Jewishness is really no longer a vital part of . . . life." This, Howe wrote, "*is nothing about which to moralize or judge*; it is in the circumstances unavoidable."[33]

Yet Irving Howe, his protestations to the contrary notwithstanding, appears even in this early *Commentary* piece to be searching for his own Jewish roots. At the very least, in this essay he recognizes the indelible quality of his Jewishness and struggles to come to terms with it. The lost young intellectual, Howe wrote, continues to experience "in his flesh the brand of his people." Using the image of a "brand" as a metaphor for Jewish identity was highly evocative in the post-Holocaust context and suggests that Howe's rhetoric had been influenced, consciously or otherwise, by his knowledge of the death camps. More explicitly, Howe wrote, feelings of connection and "a sense of communal martyrdom" are stirred in the Jewish intellectual by the murder of Jews in a Polish pogrom, "because in a very real and bitter sense it is he, too, against whom the pogrom has been committed: it is his blood that stains the streets of Kielce."

And if, as he described it in the essay, Howe, still fresh from conversations with his intellectual, universalist friends on "Kafka or Existentialism or Chagall's technique," sat somewhat uncomfortably at a Passover Seder, he was, after all, at that Seder, with his family, saturated in ceremonies which he wants to reject, but which "stir in him feelings of continuity." Howe was not alone in this. Many intellectuals, even as they wrote about their "alienation," continued to resonate to Passover. Isaac Rosenfeld's *Passage from Home*, for example, opens with an affectionate description of a Seder night: "Passover has always been my favorite holiday," says the novel's narrator.[34]

But the Jewish intellectual, with his emphasis on rationality and universalism, Howe argued in the essay, cannot, even if he wished to, return either to traditional Judaism or Zionism, and he cannot commit himself to the reconstruction of a specifically Jewish culture. It is difficult to be a Jew in the modern era, Howe said, and, in Christian America "just as difficult not to be one." Howe concluded—in a paragraph with little relation to the rest of the piece—that this problem of rootlessness might someday be resolved, if in the United States a "society appears in which both the Jewish intellectual and his people, along with everyone else, can find integrity, security and acceptance."[35]

Perhaps this vaguely "socialist solution" was the farthest he thought he could go in a liberal bourgeois magazine like *Commentary*, but Howe need not have hidden anything since he had been clearly identified by the editors as active in radical politics. It is more likely that Howe no longer firmly believed, as he had in the past, that anti-Semitism "becomes dangerous only when it is deliberately fostered by capitalism" or that Jew hatred dies only when "humanity as a whole gains socialist liberation." In any case, neither a class analysis nor a revolutionary point of view was explicit in "Lost Young Intellectual." Instead, there was a personally detailed, intriguing wrestling match with the knotty difficulties of Jewish identity. Irving saw himself as "the rootless son of a rootless people." But he could find consolation and dignity "in the consciousness of his vision, in the awareness of his complexity, and in rejection of self-pity."[36]

Once more, then, what could look on the surface like disaffection from Jewishness contained the seeds of reengagement. This was made even clearer in the late fall of 1946 when Howe, given the dizzying task of selecting *any* book to review from the highly piled stacks of review copies in the office of *Partisan Review*, chose *The Old Country*, a collection of short stories by the great Yiddish writer Sholom Aleichem. This could hardly have been an accident. When Philip Rahv, the venerable and voluble editor of *Partisan Review*, saw what Howe had chosen, he only smiled. "Even among big talkers," Howe later reminisced, "some things don't have to be spelled out."[37]

In his essay for *Partisan Review*, Howe, like Sholom Aleichem himself, did pay some attention to class. He showed, for example, that the Yiddish writer was a severe judge who was ready to point out the internal stratification and deprivations of the shtetl world. But Howe also demonstrated that Sholom Aleichem "wrote with love and warmth of the communal tradition [and] defended its ethos" of mutual responsibility. Howe was careful to warn intellectuals against glorifying this "spiritual integration of Sholom Aleichem's world" as a substitute for politics. That world, Howe argued, could not endure in the face of modern civilization and was in "its last tremor of self-consciousness before dissolution." But throughout the piece, and in his later work with the great Yiddishist Eliezer Greenberg, beginning in the 1950s and running through the 1980s, Howe manifested a deep appreciation and affection for Yiddish literature.[38]

When he began publishing his "little pieces" in *Partisan Review*, Irving said, "I swelled with a secret pride, feeling I had made my way into the best literary magazine in America. It seemed to me that I was stepping into 'another world,' a community bright with freedom, bravura, and intimate exchange. I also feared this world, suspecting it might weaken my already weakened political commitment." Howe was afraid, too, that he might not be ready for *Partisan Review*, arguably the country's most prestigious and influential voice of highbrow culture. He wondered if in the same arena as Philip Rahv, Sidney Hook, and Harold Rosenberg, he "could hold to [his] bit of space."[39]

But neither fear of political backsliding nor of "intellectual sharpshooters" held Irving back. By the late 1940s, and after more than a dozen discursive essays, Howe's identification with *Partisan Review* was such that wherever he delivered an invited lecture, he was most often introduced as a writer for that magazine. "That didn't totally define me," Howe told an interviewer in 1975, "but it was almost sufficient." Yet Irving Howe never felt that he was "really part of the inner group" at *Partisan Review*.[40] "I don't feel at home . . . in any place," Howe wrote to Lionel Trilling in 1949, "not among my radical friends who view me with suspicion, nor among literary people who hold the same view for diametrically opposite reasons, nor among the *Time* people who think of me as an 'intellectual,' nor even among the PR [Partisan Review] people."[41] Perhaps out of a not unwarranted worry that he was drifting farther from his colleagues at *Labor Action* and from his comrades in socialist sectarianism generally, Irving liked to see himself "to the left" of the *Partisan Review* crowd politically.[42]

Whatever the accuracy of Howe's perception in this regard, he, like so many others associated with *Partisan Review*, was molded intellectually by the temporary, fertile, but tense union between the cultural modernism and independent radicalism that defined the magazine, and he continued to write fairly regularly for *Partisan Review* through the late 1960s. But Howe's association with the editors, writers, and readers of *Partisan Review*—essentially "the New York intellectuals," as he labeled them in 1968—was not exactly harmonious or mutually supportive. This was "a gang of intellectual freebooters," Howe wrote later, "whose relations with one another more closely resembled the jungle of Hobbes than a commune of Kropotkin."[43] One "does not feel oneself to be working in any sort of community," he told Trilling. "Is it romanticizing," he asked, "to think that during the thirties the atmosphere was different in this regard?"[44]

The New York intellectuals were not a community. They did not, for example, despite their preoccupation with one another, read one another's works in progress, nor did they refrain from attacking one another in reviews.[45] There were, however, several shared concerns that kept the group, including Irving Howe, tenuously attached. Almost all the members of the founding generation of the New York intellectuals, including Philip Rahv, William Phillips, Edmund Wilson, Lionel Trilling, and Meyer Schapiro, had been socialists, and several of them Communists. All tended to view things, including literature and art, in their social and historical contexts while simultaneously holding to the belief in the independence of artists and the irreducible quality of artistic works. This issue—the autonomy of art—brought the original *Partisan Review*, founded in 1934 as a Communist Party youth group organ, to an early end in 1935. Editors Rahv and Phillips refused to accept the party's Stalinist dictate that mediocre proletarian novelists like Tom Kromer and Jack Conroy were to be touted as "great," while modernist, experimental poets with politically reactionary inclinations like T. S. Eliot and William Butler Yeats were to be condemned as decadent.

An anti-Stalinist *Partisan Review*, revived in 1937, attracted a second generation of New York intellectuals, including Mary McCarthy, Delmore Schwartz, William Barrett, Saul Bellow, Nathan Glazer, Isaac Rosenfeld, Irving Kristol, Alfred Kazin, and Irving Howe. Many but not all of them were especially interested in literature, and many were "modernists"; but all were intellectuals on the left, men and women interested in radical politics and the play of ideas. Trotsky was a linchpin here, and most of the younger radicals, including Irving Howe, fastened onto his example of pursuing both intellectual and political goals. "Trotsky made history, and kept an eye on history," Howe wrote later. "He was a man of heroic mold, entirely committed to the life of action, but he was also an intellectual who believed in the power and purity of the word."[46]

Many of the left intellectuals, including Howe, in the late 1930s and 1940s put too much value in Trotsky, idolizing his skills, exaggerating his contributions, and failing to see his odious darker side. But, recognizing in Trotsky their own hopes for themselves, they resonated to this model of revolutionary will and energy who was also a brilliant and iconoclastic man of letters. It is also likely—certainly possible—that the connection between the *Partisan Review* intellectuals and Trotsky was reinforced by their shared Jewish origins.[47]

Several members at the very core of the group, Dwight Macdonald, Mary McCarthy, William Barrett, F. W. Dupee, James Baldwin, and Elizabeth Hardwick, for example, were not Jewish. And several at the periphery of the group (Howe calls them "cousins")—Robert Lowell, James Agee, John Berryman, and Ralph Ellison—were also Gentiles. You didn't have to be Jewish, then, to be a New York intellectual, but it helped. The Kentucky-born writer Elizabeth Hardwick claims that she came to New York in order to *be* a "Jewish intellectual," and William Barrett describes an atmosphere so "pervasively Jewish" around *Partisan Review* and its associated circles that he often forgot that he was "not a Jew after all."[48] The "Jewishness" Barrett and Hardwick and others experienced vicariously, and the Jewishness that the New York intellectuals lived, often unwittingly, consisted of shared experiences growing up in an urban, Yiddish-speaking immigrant community, the style and rhythm of language that were products of that milieu, a hunger for dialectic, a sharp method of argumentation laced with skepticism and irony, and an emphasis on rationalism, but also a set of moral priorities having to do with social justice.

Irving Howe in 1968 in an influential, definitive essay implied that, for the first generation of New York Jewish intellectuals—Lionel Trilling, Philip Rahv, Meyer Schapiro, Paul Goodman, and others—Jewishness as sentiment and cultural source played only a modest role in their conscious experience. As late as 1944, Trilling, for example, could still say: "As the Jewish community now exists, it can give no sustenance to the American artist or intellectual who is born a Jew. And so far as I am aware, it has not done so in the past. . . . I know of no writer in English who has added a micromillimeter to his stature by "'realizing his Jewishness.'" Trilling in the late 1940s, hearing that Howe was working on Sholom Aleichem and Peretz, told him rather bluntly: "I suspect Yiddish literature." Irving, who treated the Yiddish writers with the same passionate intensity he directed toward Turgenev, James, and Faulkner, later confessed to a colleague that this remark hurt and angered him deeply. Though they became friends, he never forgave Trilling, "since he didn't know a damned thing" about Yiddish. Trilling's own conscious Jewishness, he himself said, "consisted in feeling that I would not, even if I could, deny or escape being Jewish. Surely it is at once clear how minimal such a position is." And he suggested that it was "the position of most American writers of Jewish birth."[49]

Trilling and many of the other first-generation New York Jewish intellectuals, including Sidney Hook, Harold Rosenberg, Clement Greenberg, and Lionel Abel, only a few years removed from immigrant neighborhoods in the Bronx and Brooklyn, proclaimed themselves, in the late 1930s and into the early 1940s, "radical internationalists, spokesmen for cultural modernism, men of letters transcending 'mere' ethnic loyalties." But, despite these proclamations there was, as Howe said, "something decidedly Jewish" about them, those intellectuals who, prior to the Second World War, began to cohere as a recognizable group around *Partisan Review*.[50] Many of these universalist "founding fathers" of the New York intellectuals resisted assertions or identifications of Jewishness, but a common Jewish heritage, at least at the level of personal understanding and intellectual sympathies, helped draw many of them together into a tighter circle. That was certainly true of Howe and others of the second generation, especially in the years after World War II and the Holocaust.

The Jewish immigrant milieu in which the second-generation New York intellectuals had been raised marked them as separate but also incited in them, as it had in the first generation, "fantasies of universalism." Many, including Irving Howe, even as they gravitated toward things Jewish, continued publicly to reject and even ridicule any and all versions of "Jewish nationalism." For example, although he had had two pieces published in *Commentary* in 1946, Howe complained elsewhere that while that magazine had many virtues, it was "given to the unwarranted attempt to discover a 'Jewish angle' in everything."[51]

In June 1948 in yet another *Commentary* essay Howe called himself "completely irreligious," and, from a distance that kept him blissfully ignorant, he deplored what he saw as the shallow suburbanism of institutionalized American Judaism. And when a number of New York intellectuals, including Harold Rosenberg, Leslie Fiedler, and Irving Kristol, tried to make Jewishness a vital part of their lives by returning to Judaism, Howe characterized the attempt as "a sickeningly sentimental business. . . . A sheer phony, self-induced, uncritical nostalgia for something that never was."[52] As for himself, he said, "I have no belief in and feel no need for supernatural sanction or support. More than most intellectuals I remain loyal, not to one or another doctrine, but to the underlying values of the 1930's."[53]

But there was a residue of Jewishness in Irving Howe and other Jewish intellectuals, even as they maintained the rhetoric of internationalism. Howe remembered that among the *Partisan Review* crowd surprising assertions about Jews and Jewishness often "broke through" that rhetoric. He recalled, for example, reading, in the late 1940s, Clement Greenberg's attack on Arthur Koestler for going along with the negative "majority gentile view" of the East European Jews. "It is possible," wrote Greenberg, "to adopt standards of evaluation other than those of Western Europe. It is possible that by 'world-historical' standards the European Jews represent a higher type of human being than any yet achieved in history. I do not say that this is so, but I say it is possible and that there is much to argue for its possibility." Howe recalled experiencing a "rather . . . pleasant shock" when he first encountered this passage. Other *Partisan* writers "may have felt a twinge of embarrassment before these words," Howe said, but he suspected that Greenberg had also expressed some of their deeper feelings.[54] And he believed that if one were "to go through the first twenty years of *Partisan Review*" one would see just "how frequently Jewish references, motifs, and inside jokes break past the surface of cosmopolitanism."[55]

Howe, though he did not admit it to himself at the time, had been pulled initially toward *Partisan Review* by something that broke past his own "surface of cosmopolitanism." From the very first issue in 1937 in which Delmore Schwartz's story "In Dreams Begin Responsibilities" appeared, there was in *Partisan Review*, Howe said, a distinctly urban tone and a string of Jewish cultural allusions that made young Jewish intellectuals hear "a voice that seemed our own, though it had never really existed until Schwartz invented it."[56]

Other intellectuals who heard that voice included Leslie Fiedler as well as Saul Bellow and Isaac Rosenfeld (known in high school as Zinoviev and Kamenev, the dissident Bolsheviks).[57] This cluster of young men, all studying in the Midwest, all products of Yiddish-speaking households who proclaimed and took joy in their Jewishness, gravitated in the late 1930s to *Partisan Review* and the New York group. Fiedler said that in dealing with *Partisan Review* he had the sense of beginning his own "autobiography," that is, "my life as an urban American Jew, who came of age intellectually during the Depression; who discovered Europe for the imagination before America; who was influenced by Marxist ideas . . . ; who wanted desperately to feel that the struggle for a revolutionary politics and the highest literary standards was a single struggle; whose political certainty unraveled during the second World War."[58]

Irving Howe could easily have said the same. What is important here, in the striking similarity, is Jewishness. Even though this meant different things to different members of the group, Howe said that

when up against the impenetrable walls of gentile politeness we would aggressively proclaim our 'difference,' as if to raise Jewishness to a higher cosmopolitan power. This was probably the first time in American cultural history that a self-confident group of intellectuals did not acknowledge the authority of Christian tradition.

A whole range of non-Christian references was now reaching at least some American literary people, terms like Hasidism, place names like Chelm, proper names like Sholom Aleichem. *Partisan Review* printed some, if not enough criticism of Yiddish writers—Isaac Rosenfeld on Peretz and me on Sholom Aleichem; the magazine was just starting to confront its anomalous position as the voice of emancipated Jews who nevertheless *refused to deny their Jewishness*.[59]

This refusal took on additional intensity with revelations about the Holocaust. In the late forties, as Howe admitted, "the murder of the Jews had not yet become a major theme of discussion among the New York writers," and it would take several more years before their "low-charged guilt" became more than a "quiet remorse." But, unable to talk about the Holocaust itself, Howe and many of the others began in the postwar years to talk about themselves as Jews. "At least some of us," Howe wrote later with bracing honesty, "could not help feeling that in our earlier claims to have shaken off all ethnic distinctiveness there had been something false, something shaming. Our Jewishness might have no clear religious or national content, it might be helpless before the criticism of believers; but Jews we were, like it or not, and liked or not."[60] And what Howe wrote about Isaac Rosenfeld in 1962 he could have easily written about himself: "While Jewish to his bones, he sought a way of leaping beyond those constraints which in our time are signified by Jewishness—and all that stood in his way was his body, his country, the times, history."[61]

Even before the war, when Howe and the others "did not think well or deeply on the matter of Jewishness" and "felt no particular responsibility for its survival or renewal . . . the fact of Jewishness," Howe confessed, "figured much more strikingly than we acknowledged in public."[62] And after the war, although Howe still did not identify with a Jewish tradition, he grew increasingly concerned with Jewish themes. Even at what looked like his most estranged state, as we saw in his 1946 essay, "Lost Young Intellectual," Howe was not unaware of the fact that only an accident of geography and the vagaries of immigration separated him and his intellectual Jewish friends from those who died at Auschwitz.

Still, Howe continued to want to avoid overly "narrow habits of response and to embrace universalist values." He was not alone. As Daniel Bell once put it: "Most of us—intellectual Jews who have grown up in Galut [exile] and live our lives as cosmopolitan beings—accept in varying degrees the unresolved and perhaps irreconcilable tension between parochial identities, with all [their] emotional tugs, and universal aspirations."[63] Howe and other Jewish writers had "universal aspirations." They avoided a pronounced Jewish identification, and even as many remained alienated from the bourgeois republic of American democracy, they eagerly sought membership in the cosmopolitan republic of American letters.

This ambition prevented Irving Howe and many other New York intellectuals, for a time, from facing up to and speaking out loud about "Jewish questions," including the anti-Semitic sentiments of some of their favorite modernist writers. This was especially the case with T. S. Eliot. Howe was not particularly disturbed by the patrician anti-Semitism of Henry Adams, whom he dismissed as "nutty on the subject of Jews," or the plebeian anti-Semitism of Theodore Dreiser, who "when not writing novels, was the sort of ignoramus you could run into at any bar." But passages about Jews in the work of Eliot and other great modernists like Ezra Pound caused Howe significant pain. That literary modernism could sometimes align itself with reactionary movements like anti-Semitism, Howe said, "was intensely embarrassing and required either torturous explanations or complex dissociations."[64]

Eliot was not above lines replete with representations of Jews as loathsome, subhuman creatures whom the world would be well rid of:

> The rats are underneath the piles
> The jew is underneath the lot.
> (from "Burbank with a Baedeker: Bleistein with a Cigar")

> Rachel nee Rabinovitch
> Tears at the grapes with murderous paws.
> (from "Sweeney among the Nightingales")

> My house is a decayed house,
> And the jew squats on the window sill, the owner
> Spawned in some estaminet of Antwerp,
> Blistered in Brussels, patched and peeled in London.
> (from "Gerontion")[65]

It is hard to dismiss these examples, and many others, in Eliot's poetry as mere aberrations, mere slippages into old-fashioned, conventional Jew-hatred.[66] It is more accurate to say that although anti-Semitism does not define Eliot or his poetry, there *is* an active Jew-hatred at work. This conclusion is reinforced when we also take into consideration Eliot's own public pronouncements. For example, in a series of lectures at the University of Virginia in 1933, only a few weeks after Hitler and the Nazis came to power in Germany, Eliot said:

The population should be homogeneous; where two or more cultures exist in the same place they are likely either to be fiercely self-conscious or both to become adulterate. What is still more important is unity of religious background; and reasons of race and religion combine to make any large number of free-thinking Jews undesireable. There must be a proper balance between urban and rural, industrial and agricultural development. And a spirit of excessive tolerance is to be deprecated.[67]

But Howe was attuned to the "inner vibrations" of Eliot's poetry and to its "profound awareness of the moral turmoil . . . that afflicted serious persons." Turning to Eliot not so much for answers as for questions, Howe "had little desire to be critical, especially of what might be passed over as a few incidental lines of bigotry."[68] Others, too, including the distinguished Jewish poet Karl Shapiro, saw Eliot as virtually "untouchable," indeed, as "Modern Literature incarnate." The "handful of insults in the poetry," said Cynthia Ozick in 1993, "I swallowed down without protest . . . [Eliot] was poetry incarnate, and poetry is what one lived for." And Leslie Fiedler went so far as to say that "[t]he Jewish intellectual of my generation cannot disown [Eliot] without disowning an integral part of himself."[69]

Part of what Leslie Fiedler called "a special affinity" between Eliot, the expatriate anti-Semite, and "certain free-thinking Jews" is explained by the fact that the great poet had made the journey from provincial St. Louis to cosmopolitan London. The New York intellectuals, Irving Howe wrote later, were not likely to match Eliot's "hauteur," but "perhaps they could negotiate a somewhat similar journey from Brooklyn or the Bronx to Manhattan." Moreover, Irving had felt, even in his orthodox Marxist phase in the late 1930s, that "the central literary expression of the time was a . . . poem by a St. Louis writer called 'The Waste Land,'" full of thrilling modernist images of alienation, moral dislocation, and historical breakdown.[70] This perceived "outsider" quality of the poet—even after his having announced himself a devout Christian—prompted Howe and others, despite enormous differences in belief, to feel a kinship with Eliot. In any case, to Eliot's anti-Semitism, Irving Howe had only a muted response, a sign, he admitted later, of a troubling discomfort over the divisions between the aesthetic and the ethical, and the struggle between Jewish identity and an ambition to be part of the larger intellectual scene.[71]

Some years after the Second World War, "when the shock of the Holocaust" had finally registered, Howe saw that none of the usual categories of thought of the New York intellectuals—neither Marxism nor modernism—was sufficient to grasp the meaning of the historic enormity. Only then did he and others begin to look back upon modernism and the idea of rootlessness and the style of alienation with a certain questioning. It was "not exactly rejection" of modernism, Howe said, "but [a]questioning" of complete alienation from the community, general and Jewish.[72] And it was the Ezra Pound affair, redolent with Holocaust associations and representative of modern anti-Semitism, that delineated more sharply, for Howe, the points of conflict between his ethical/political values and literary modernism.

In 1949 a group of very distinguished writers, including W. H. Auden, Robert Lowell, and Allen Tate, voted to give the prestigious Library of Congress Bollingen Award to the poet Ezra Pound, the unrepentant fascist and a man of questionable sanity, who during the war years had broadcast via Rome radio vicious anti-Semitic propaganda in English. With the exception of Dwight Macdonald, who for his own idiosyncratic reasons found the decision "the brightest political act in a dark period," the New York writers were distinctly unhappy with the award.

Those who defended giving the prize to Pound argued that he was a great poet, and his political opinions, even if reprehensible, should be kept separate from judgments about the poetry. This was something that Irving Howe was eager to respect. Pound was indisputably a brilliant, radically innovative artist, and a man who selflessly championed the work of others, including James Joyce and T. S. Eliot, two of Howe's favorite writers. But there remained the deeply troubling question of the anti-Semitic passages in Pound's verse:

> *Petain defended Verdun while Blum*
> *Was defending a bidet.*

> *the yidd is a stimulant and the goyim are the cattle in gt/proportion*
> *and go to saleable slaughter with the maximum of docility.*
> *(from the "Pisan Cantos")*

These detestable, "irresponsible opinions" and many others just like them were not isolated instances or peripheral to the verse. They were, even according to Allen Tate, one of the awarding judges, contaminations "right in the middle of the poetry."[73] Howe was angry enough to consider the Pound award a conscious provocation, and he made his views widely known. Dwight Macdonald, in a letter to Howe in May 1949, said he was "really floored by the attitude taken by many of my friends, including yourself, on the Pound award. . . . I am not convinced by the arguments of your side, which seem to me illiberal and specious."[74] This demurral from an old friend did not stop Irving Howe; on the contrary, he continued to be critical of Pound and the problem of anti-Semitism in literature generally.

In August 1949, Howe, in *Commentary*, attacked American novelists who perpetuated classic stereotypes of the Jew, negatively as alien exploiter or "positively" as prophetic progressive or angelic victim. Few writers escaped Howe's wrath. F. Scott Fitzgerald, Ernest Hemingway, and John Dos Passos were spared because they created Jewish characters who, while not always admirable, were complex and fully human. But Jewish writers like Mike Gold, Budd Schulberg, Jerome Weidman, and Sholem Asch were special targets for Howe because of their gratuitously negative portrayals of stick-figure Jews, or because the "positive" caricatures they constructed were "all the more malicious in that their creators intend[ed] no malice." Two months later, in a *Commentary* magazine symposium on Jewishness and the English-language literary tradition, Howe went after non-Jewish authors primarily, insisting that "it is not only necessary, but right that we say exactly what we feel about the anti-Semitic remarks or passages of even the greatest modern writers." Passing references to "clever" or "grubbing" Jews by modern writers—and here Howe probably had in mind Thomas Wolfe, Henry James, Edith Wharton, and others—were even more distressing, Howe argued, than the common anti-Jewish attitudes expressed in Chaucer, Marlowe, or Shakespeare. For from the time of Chaucer, "to our own there has been some progress at least in what the intellectual minority considers the desired norm of civilized conduct." Moreover, while Shakespeare was not exempt from the nearly universal anti-Semitism of Elizabethan England, "he has given his Merchant of Venice," Howe said, "a dramatic tension impossible in the kind of anti-Semitic diatribe that can be found in Pound's Cantos."[75]

While there was "nothing we should 'do' or wish to 'do,'" Howe continued, about Dickens's Fagin or Chaucer's Prioress's Tale or Eliot's landlord spawned in Antwerp, except live with the pain, we should not, he said "let any notions about the inviolability of literature or the sacredness of art sway us from expressing our spontaneous passionate feelings about those contemporary writers who succumb, willingly or not, to anti-Semitism. We must beware of what Clement Greenberg has rightly called the culture-sickness of this age, the sickness which permits people to excuse or justify the most dreadful behavior and the most vicious ideas in the name of culture." Indignation against anti-Semitic writing "is often insufficient, but sometimes," Howe concluded, "it is the only condition of dignity."[76]

Howe clearly opposed the Pound award, but he and others were still tying themselves into aesthetic knots in their attempts both to resist giving Pound the prize, and to reaffirm the idea of artistic autonomy. Clement Greenberg and William Barrett, on the other hand, insisted that the aesthetic is not the primary category for human life; life includes art, they said, but it is finally more important than art. Howe was not quite as direct, and as he later admitted, he should simply have said, at the time, that Pound's vicious anti-Semitism ultimately corrodes his poetry and substantially lowers its value as literature.[77] Karl Shapiro, the only Bollingen judge to vote against the award, had said just that, and unlike Howe had stood up to be counted as a Jew, refusing to honor lines of poetry encrusted with Jew-hatred. Shapiro's strong position cost him friends and the favor of influential critics, and in the aftermath of the Pound affair the career of this highly esteemed poet and 1944 Pulitzer Prize winner limped toward near anonymity.[78]

Later Howe recognized Shapiro's superior moral courage and he concluded, with Greenberg and Barrett, that "if aesthetic perceptions and ethical judgments . . . clash . . . the ethical should . . . be given priority." Howe remained a "free-thinker," but he finally recognized "enough of a Jew" within himself to admit that, in addition to opposing the award, he should have said more explicitly "great poet or not, Pound shared the responsibility for the Holocaust and no decent person ought to honor anyone of whom that could truthfully be said. We should simply have seconded Karl Shapiro's explanation of why he . . . had been unable to go along with the award: 'I am a Jew and I cannot honor anti-Semites.'"[79]

Simultaneous with the Pound debate, another important Jewish controversy was unfolding, this one surrounding Jean Paul Sartre's *Anti-Semite and Jew* (1948). Howe thought the French existentialist's book had "reduced both Jew and anti-Semite to bloodless timeless essences." Indeed, Sartre, writing from a point far removed from Jewish experience and with only the thinnest knowledge of Jewish tradition, claimed that the Jews "have no history" and were bound together only by anti-Semitism. According to Sartre's reductionist notions, Jew-hatred alone created Jewish consciousness, and anti-Semitism was nothing more than a consequence of the social wrongs of capitalist society. The answer to the "Jewish question," then, was relatively simple: socialism and/or assimilation of Jews into the larger society. Not many years earlier, in his quest for universalism and in his adherence to Marxist categories that reduced anti-Semitism to a mere disorder of transitory capitalism, Irving Howe had said strikingly similar things. But now in 1948, his response to Sartre's writing was much more complex and proved to be a crucial step in his slow, halting, but ultimately affirming reconquest of Jewishness.

Howe appreciated Sartre's sharply detailed descriptions of the psychology of the anti-Semite, and his recognition that the damage done the Jews by an endless series of dispossessions was enormous. He was also grateful that the philosopher wrote with good will and an analytical fire that elevated the discussion of the "Jewish question" to a significant theoretical level. But Howe also recognized that "the book suffered from an extreme ahistoricity," which denied Jews autonomy, a self-affirmed tradition, and even the right to survival, "whether in the actual world of capitalism, or the dreamed-of world of socialism."[80] Howe published nothing of his own at the time on Sartre, but he liked Harold Rosenberg's 1949 *Commentary* essay "Does the Jew Exist? Sartre's Morality Play about Anti-Semitism."[81] If Sartre's book provoked one to think hard about Jewish matters, Howe said, "Rosenberg's polemic prompted a distancing from Sartre's categorical excesses." To Sartre's remark that "the Christians . . . created the Jew," Rosenberg responded that "the opposite is, of course, the case: the Jews created Christianity." He went on to argue, against Sartre's portrayal of Jews as a people without community or history, that the Jews, thought to be on the verge of dying for thousands of years, "have shown that without being a race, a nation, or a religion, it is possible . . . to remain together in a net of memory and expectation."[82] Howe, a man whose Jewishness had "no fixed religious or national content," felt that Rosenberg spoke for him, and he saw the essay as a turning point in his life. Although Rosenberg's essay was marked by religious sensibility, Howe believed that it was written "from neither a religious nor theological premise." Rosenberg wrote as a spokesman for "the partial Jew," which is the way Howe saw himself: a Jew "acknowledging links with the past, yet also forming himself through a multiplicity of identities."[83]

Acknowledging links with the Jewish past, however, led Howe neither to a transcendence of, nor a forthright confrontation with his "troubled sense of Jewishness," and he continued to see himself and other New York intellectuals as "inauthentic" Jews, who gave no really "serious thought" or "unblocked emotion" to the Jewish "situation." The question of Israel was a case in point. From 1947 to 1949, *Partisan Review* published no articles on the emerging Jewish state, even while lesser-known figures, whom historian Carole Kessner calls "the 'other' New York Jewish intellectuals," writers like Marie Syrkin, Ben Halpern, and Ludwig Lewisohn, paid full attention to and wrote affirmatively in *Jewish Frontier* and the *Menorah Journal* about the beleaguered Jews of Europe and Palestine.[84]

In an interview in 1982, Howe said: "I would be lying if I said I was tremendously excited by the formation of Israel in 1948. It didn't at first touch me very much per se—it got to me only later, when it was in danger. I was for the state; I thought it was okay. But I wasn't so deeply stirred emotionally as I would be" in the years following the Six-Day War in 1967. Howe had felt "an underglow of satisfaction" when Israel declared its independent existence but admitted that his "worn opinions," his universalist antinationalist biases, and his recognition of the reality of the "Arab Question" kept him from open joy. Only later did Irving see that "being happy about the establishment of Israel, perhaps the most remarkable assertion . . . a martyred people ever made—didn't necessarily signify a conversion to Zionist ideology."[85]

That realization took some time, nearly twenty years actually. In the meantime, in the late 1940s and early 1950s, Irving Howe's main intellectual journey, fraught with its own peculiar difficulties, consisted of a break from his earlier orthodox, anti-Stalinist Marxism.

5

Toward a "World More Attractive"

IN THE LATE 1940s, in the aftermath of the war and the Holocaust, Irving Howe "could no longer think of [himself] as any sort of orthodox Marxist." He "remained a socialist," he said, "but what I meant by that changed a good deal."[1] Howe had begun a "reconquest" of his Jewishness; he had become more open-minded about literature; more committed to democracy as the sine qua non of socialism, and less optimistic about the near-term future of worker-based revolution. These changes led, as we began to see in the debate over Arthur Koestler in 1946, to disagreements with the Workers Party (WP) and eventuated in a complete break by 1952. Less than a year later, Howe would begin his long career in university teaching with an eight-year stint at Brandeis.

The beginning of the end of Howe's connection to the WP came in September 1946 when he published a review of a translation of Trotsky's *The New Course* in which he raised questions about Trotsky's strategy in the struggle against Stalin. During the consolidation of the revolution, Howe wrote, "Trotsky made the error of seeing the economic issues as predominant. . . . But . . . they were entirely secondary to the one burning problem of democracy." Proper economic planning, Howe argued, "may have been impossible without workers' democracy, but a successful struggle for workers' democracy was the best way to make possible proper economic planning." Howe knew he might raise some hackles among the more orthodox Trotskyists with these comments, and he therefore concluded, in his own defense, that "if we criticize *The New Course* in order to learn certain lessons for the future, in order to once more reassert *the forever necessary statement of the indissolubility of socialism and democracy*, then we are engaging in a useful activity."[2] Howe's attempt to preempt criticism, however, seems to have had the opposite effect. His colleagues in the WP not only accused Irving of "anti-Marxism," but attacked him later for being too "hot-headed and impatient" in his responses to their accusation.[3]

Howe's political differences with the leaders of the WP continued to intensify and erupted openly in 1948 after Stalin's takeover of Czechoslovakia. In a full-page article in *Labor Action* in early March, Howe announced his "feeling of discouragement" about the future of socialism, his disgust with the workers who apparently gave active support to the Stalinist coup, and his rather startling conclusion that "the world today is in a far worse state than ten years ago when Hitler overran Europe." Howe did go on to say that it is still "possible for men to act" or at least to "keep alive . . . that flickering, but still beautiful dream" of socialism. But the article emphasized that "only the most sober realism, only, if you will, the most honest pessimism can possibly serve as a basis for discussion."[4]

Howe's coworkers in the movement were troubled. They especially took issue with Howe's depiction of the Czech workers as having cooperated with the Stalinists. The men and women in the factories, mills, and mines, they insisted, had "defiance in their hearts" and would "never yield . . . to oppression and exploitation" by the Stalinist system of "bureaucratic collectivization." And they accused Howe himself of standing paralyzed with fear before Stalinism, a crime hardly better, they said, than succumbing to it.[5]

In April, Irving Howe was not only expressing doubts about workers, he came close to defending "bourgeois liberalism," which he insisted had indeed had a proud history of defiance. A vital liberalism had "stood at the head of the great revolutions of the 18th and 19th centuries, sweeping aside the crowns of kings," Howe said. And we socialists, he argued, must keep alive liberalism's relevant beliefs, "its emphasis on democratic rights, on human individuality, and human diversity. What they talked about we must make real."[6]

By the summer of 1948 Howe was telling Dwight Macdonald: "I haven't considered myself a Trotskyist in any strict sense of the word for some time now. I've been undergoing a rather painful soul-searching and will probably arrive at a terminus soon. My ideas are changing."[7] A critical point in his intellectual development came when, after rereading *The Federalist Papers* in 1948 (at the suggestion of Hannah Arendt and at about the same time of his admission to Macdonald), Howe "began to see that certain elements of traditional political theory could not be reduced to categories of class analysis" and that the countervailing powers James Madison talked about were necessary for the maintenance of democracy in any society, including socialist society.[8]

But even as he was championing the indispensability of democracy as the foundation of a viable, moral socialism, and even as he was expressing disagreement with his colleagues in the Trotskyist movement, Howe maintained a militant socialist rhetoric. He even defended the Workers Party as the last best hope for socialism in the United States. Late in 1948 he attacked the Socialist Party as backwardly sectarian and bureaucratic, singling out its leader, Norman Thomas (a man he formerly admired, and would again), as one of the "most astonishing muddleheads this country has ever seen."[9] He attacked intellectuals, accusing them of pursuing "fascinating career choices" in academia, publishing, and government, and becoming "defanged" and spiritually enervated in the process. And early in 1949 he attacked his former college classmate Daniel Bell for suggesting that socialists should work inside the Democratic Party as "intellectual catalysts." Howe insisted that such a policy would turn socialists into "intellectual stooges" and would only serve the interests of the capitalist exploiters, the real power behind both major American parties. Howe vigorously condemned the Democratic Party and effusively praised the WP as "the only alive, democratic center of socialist rebellion in the U.S." He urged intellectuals to continue to struggle for "independent class action and the rebuilding of an independent socialist movement."[10]

As late as the fall of 1949, in the *Anvil*, a periodical published by the New York Student Federation Against War, Howe urged young people to "at least be willing to take chances with their lives and to commit themselves in their hopes and dreams" rather than "accept a living intellectual and moral death as the price of creature comfort." He went on to criticize those ex-radicals, some of whom still claimed to be socialists "in a sort of way," who are "today comfortable labor bureaucrats." Their number, Howe said, "is appalling, the mark of the suicide of a generation of Americans."[11]

Perhaps the bitter diatribe against Bell and Howe's attacks on the increasing complacency of some socialists and former revolutionaries were manifestations of his own inner conflicts over radical activism. He admitted much later that as early as 1946 he was "inwardly starting to waver in his opinions," and that he wrote some especially radical polemics "as if to suppress these doubts."[12] Howe may even have been aware of this problem at the time. "I do not rise as a defender of the true faith" of Marxism, Howe said in 1951. "Whoever cares about such matters knows that I consider Marxism in a state of intellectual crisis and that I am myself subject to this crisis."[13] And he had indeed been subject to it for quite some time, as we have seen. By the late 1940s, in fact, Howe found it difficult even to attend meetings of the WP, although it too was changing.

In the face of the historical realities and the growing sense that it was not only Stalin, but Lenin and Trotsky and even Bolshevism itself that were inherently and inexorably repressive, the bulk of the WP membership had moved some distance, even if not as far as Irving Howe, since the late thirties. "We wanted at first," Howe remembered, "to show that we remained good Marxists, but every time we thought about a problem, we moved farther from Leninism and closer to social democracy."[14] By 1949 Max Shachtman, the virtual "guru" of the WP, and most of his followers no longer expected to see a violent worker overthrow of capitalism in the United States. They gave up on Bolshevik revolution, renamed themselves the Independent Socialist League (ISL), and took on a new role as a "socialist conscience" within the broader left movements of the early fifties. In practice, however, the ISL was still caught up in sectarian squabbles and factional struggles and remained as marginal and as small as the five-hundred-member WP had ever been.[15] Irving Howe, on the other hand, was now very much a part of a larger intellectual community—in Princeton, and at *Partisan Review* and *Commentary*. He was increasingly dissatisfied with the hermetic quality of the sectarian movement.

Early in 1949, two of Irving's closest associates in the movement, Stanley Plastrik and Emanuel "Manny" Geltman (party names "Henry Judd" and "Emanuel Garrett") also expressed frustration with the WP, especially with its opposition to the Marshall Plan, the vast American program for the economic recovery of war-torn Europe. Plastrik and Geltman, and Howe too, had come to see that the West's struggle against Stalinist expansionism was not merely an imperialist adventure, but was, like their own anti-Stalinism, a battle for democracy. They were clearly losing faith in a "third camp" solution, the emergence of a viable socialism that would eliminate the need to choose between Stalinism and capitalism. It was important, then, to stop the spread of Stalinism, and so they argued, but to no avail, for endorsing the policy of

American economic aid to Europe and for supporting democratic anti-Communist governments on the continent.[16]

By 1951 in the context of the Korean War, even Max Shachtman began making statements implying that his faith in a "third camp" solution was weakening. Not wanting to do anything that would facilitate a Communist victory in East Asia, Shachtman went so far as to urge that the ISL stop opposing the U.S. war in Korea. Irving Howe welcomed this proposal, but he wanted to go farther. He pushed, again without success, for an ISL announcement of "critical support" for the U.S. effort in Korea and for the West generally in its battle against totalitarian Communism.[17]

In the same year, Howe and Plastrik, Irving's primary ally in inner-party battles, urged the ISL to make *Labor Action* over into a more "weighty and serious" paper, one that did "not merely replay . . . the old records," one which would speak to more than sectarian concerns, without the tone of "sectarian agitation." This failing, they proposed starting a quarterly journal, something along the lines of Dwight Macdonald's now-defunct *Politics*, under the auspices of the ISL but open to a variety of viewpoints on the anti-Stalinist Left. Again, however, Shachtman was not interested. Still, not until October 1952, several months after this rebuff, did Howe and Plastrik resign from the ISL.[18]

They submitted a lengthy explanation that affirmed their intention to remain democratic socialists. "Our motive in leaving the ISL is a conviction that it has ceased to be useful for advancing the cause of democratic socialism or for providing a lively center in which its problems can be discussed." The ISL was no longer viable, Howe said, because it was torn between its "healthy fumblings towards a new view of American socialism" and its immobilizing Trotskyist roots.

The main thrust of the Howe-Plastrik statement was its fervent anti-Stalinism. Since the historical energies were not available currently to bring about a "third camp," they said, it was time, certainly, to give up this concept and cooperate with the Western world against Stalin. "We are opposed to war," they continued. "We believe in the need to cooperate with whatever forces resist this tendency while also resisting the advances of Stalinism. But as democratic socialists our place is in the . . . democratic world, no matter how sharp our criticisms of its bourgeois leadership." Howe and Plastrik insisted that the struggle between Stalinism and the West is not merely a struggle for the imperialist division of the world, but also, in terms of consequences, more fundamentally a struggle between two ways of living: between democracy, however marred, and the most bestial totalitarianism ever known.

Consequently, they went on—here radically distancing themselves from a position Howe had taken during the Second World War—"we do not believe socialists can retire to some isle of rectitude more or less equidistant from both sides." Instead, they said, they must propound the idea that "the defeat of Stalinism can best be achieved through political means," while recognizing simultaneously that *the survival of democracy as we know it, is indispensable for socialism, for the working class, for humanity.*"

Howe and Plastrik were opting for what some took to calling a "second and a half camp" position, insisting that they retained "every right to criticize the bourgeois leadership for its policy vis-à-vis Stalinism," but they did so from the "frank recognition" that they were "aligned with the West in its struggle against the Stalinist World." Indeed, they intended to act as the "socialist wing of the West." And they asked others to join them in the battle, declaring that "the whole heritage of civilization is at stake." In the meantime, they would engage in "the major task of socialists today . . . sustained intellectual activity, mainly with the aim of reorienting and reeducating ourselves."[19]

Max Shachtman responded by branding Howe a traitor, despite the fact that Irving had been seen by many as Shachtman's protégé. Shachtman may have "stood for democracy" and may have used "the rhetoric of openness and pluralism," as several of his followers claimed, but as these same followers confessed, Shachtman had been "brought up as a Stalinist" and remained one in terms of style and methodology. Shachtman characterized Howe as suffering from long-term personal and psychological problems and said that his resignation from the ISL was simply the most recent expression of his "political instability." He proceeded to read Howe out of the movement. The major responsibility of the moment for revolutionaries, Shachtman claimed, was to maintain a socialist organization in order "to keep alive the great socialist traditions of the past and present for the coming generations." Anyone, Shachtman said, who abandons this duty "with a slick slogan like 'We Support the West' identifies himself with one of the imperialist powers or camps and ceases to be, in the real sense of the word, a socialist."[20]

In addition to their important differences over "supporting the West," personal elements were also involved in the tensions between

Howe and Shachtman. Howe's increasing literary productivity, including his innumerable articles for important periodicals and the recent publication of his books on Sherwood Anderson (1951) and William Faulkner (1952), probably elicited some resentment in Shachtman, who had unfulfilled literary aspirations of his own. According to Julius and Phyllis Jacobson, members of the ISL who stayed on board, Shachtman recognized and envied Irving's talent, knew it would be appreciated outside of the movement, and believed that Irving would be "seduced" by bourgeois magazines and opportunities for intellectual prestige. But instead of encouraging Howe to be a writer who could bring a revolutionary perspective or vision to the "outside," Shachtman was distinctly unsupportive. "When [Irving Howe] began to write 'outside,'" Manny Geltman said, "he got a lot of flack." And not only from Shachtman, but even from the novelist James Farrell, who asked Irving, "Why do you have to appear in the non-party press when the party press is available to you?"[21]

Invited to an ISL membership meeting in New York to "explain" his resignation further, Irving Howe was reported to have complained there that the organization, among other things, seriously impeded his literary activity.[22] Howe wanted a much larger audience with wider, deeper, and more complex interests; and he had in any case come to the conclusion that the party press was moribund and irrelevant. This did not mean, however, as Shachtman would have it, that Howe was no longer a socialist. It did mean that he would suffer "inner divisions" for many years, torn between the refinement of literary life and the "relaxed will" that Lionel Trilling spoke about, on the one side, and the struggle of political life with its demands of necessity and conscience, on the other. Looking back on the internal conflicts he experienced in the early fifties and afterward, Howe asked: "Had not after all, so entirely political a man as Trotsky once remarked that for him the world of letters was always "a world more attractive?" It was more attractive, Howe admitted; but it was not, all the same, a world to which he could "totally yield."[23]

Though Irving Howe was clearly driven by "that taste for complication which is necessarily a threat to the political mind," he never yielded totally to the world of letters. He withdrew into it more fully from time to time, especially when beleaguered by the frustrations of politics, but that simply meant that he would occasionally take an extra day or two a week away from action in the public arena or from writing about politics. And even this could trouble him. When Howe was working on Sherwood Anderson and William Faulkner in the late 1940s and early 1950s, he worried aloud to Manny Geltman, who had followed Irving out of the ISL, about his writing about literature "when I should be writing about politics." But when he wrote on politics, Geltman remembered, Howe "chided himself" for not writing about literature.[24]

Even while Howe worked on the "literary" topics of Anderson and Faulkner, he was in fact beginning to put together materials for a book on the American Communist Party. And in addition to occasional political pieces for the "party press," which were dwindling in number, he did "political" essays for *Partisan Review, Commentary,* and the *New Republic* on race, labor unions, populism, socialism, and the respective politics of C. Wright Mills, Henry Adams, and F. O. Matthiessen.[25] Howe eviscerated Matthiessen's *From the Heart of Europe,* a book which revealed the influential Harvard scholar's positive attitude toward Stalinism on the continent and toward the Communist-dominated Henry Wallace movement in the United States. Howe hated Wallace and all he stood for, calling him dangerously irresponsible and "the most boring humorless egomaniac on the American political scene since William Jennings Bryan." He attacked Matthiessen mercilessly for acquiescing "in the absurd distinction between political freedom and economic freedom" and for accepting the most "brutal and corrupt" political behavior in the name of "socialism." He ended his essay by repeating the charge that Matthiessen had been seduced by the "pseudosocialist rhetoric" of those who "jailed, exiled, and murdered" genuine radicals abroad, a conclusion indicative of Howe's unwavering anti-Stalinism and his unrelenting commitment to the politics of democratic socialism.[26]

One could argue, too, that the literary works on Anderson and Faulkner themselves were not without their political dimensions. Just prior to the publication of his major Anderson study in 1951, Howe had had an essay in *Commentary* on Sherwood Anderson and the "power urge" in which he identified a significant element of authoritarianism in the writer's work. In some contexts, Howe wrote, an image of Anderson as "a deeply plebeian and democratic writer" was justified, but in too many others, such as *Marching Men* (1917), Howe found only "a defense of political mindlessness," a "lust for power," and "an authoritarian potential which is buried deep within . . . a certain kind of plebeian revolt."[27]

In the full book on Anderson, Howe expressed admiration for the writer's "never-diminished feeling for the Southern workers" (something that had strongly impressed Howe as an adolescent), but he paid less attention to Anderson's explicit politics, especially his belated conversion to Communism, dismissing it all as intellectually lazy and irresponsible. Howe did, however, pay attention to the "implicit politics" of Anderson's best work, *Winesburg, Ohio*.[28]

Howe thought Anderson's writing, especially *Winesburg*, was important in American culture "as the expression of a sensitive witness to the national experience," the experience of transition from an agrarian, provincial society to an industrial, modern society. "No novelist, no historian," Howe said, has depicted this segment of the American past "with an intimacy and poignancy superior to Anderson's." Anderson's characters had become divorced by the "national experience" from their natural environments, from their communities, and from their unfulfilling and generally oppressive work. Instead of being bound together in fraternity, an image evoked tirelessly by Howe, Winesburg's residents, Anderson's "grotesques," are alienated from any authentic sources of emotional sustenance.[29]

The stories of Winesburg, Howe said, present an image of a fundamental illness in American social relations, hidden by superficial health but expressing itself in a fearful and sour loneliness. But the final effectiveness of Anderson's prose, Howe contended, resided in its invocation to community, "in its prevalent tone of tender inclusiveness." The ultimate unity of the book, Howe said, "is a unity of feeling, a sureness of warmth, and readiness to accept Winesburg's lost grotesques with the embrace of humility."[30]

Perhaps in reaction to Lionel Trilling's critique of Anderson in the *Liberal Imagination* and Alfred Kazin's basically negative evaluation in *On Native Grounds*, Howe attempted to rescue Anderson's reputation.[31] He did not judge him a great writer, but he argued that Anderson's work, especially *Winesburg, Ohio*, deserved a lasting place, if only a minor one, in the national literature. "There were a few moments when [Anderson] spoke," Howe said, as almost no one else among American writers had, "with the voice of love." Indeed, Howe insisted that Anderson had "created a small body of fiction unique in American writing for the lyrical purity of its feeling."[32] Howe's praise also implied that in the early Cold War atmosphere of "defeated radicalism," Anderson's concern with ordinary and relatively inarticulate people could be of some political use: making American intellectuals face up to their retreat from the idea of fraternal community.

Sherwood Anderson, like Howe, had an abiding interest in organic community, with its vibrant tradition of plebeian fraternity, whether real or imagined. This helps explain Howe's initial attraction to Anderson, and perhaps to William Faulkner as well. Faulkner, with his emphasis on communal agrarianism, Howe thought, dramatized as few other American novelists could the "clash between traditional mores no longer valued or relevant and a time of moral uncertainty and opportunism."[33]

Howe's study, one of the earliest book-length explorations of Faulkner's fiction, exemplifies his continued interest in literary modernism and is yet another example of his ability to admire a great writer despite that writer's conservative tendencies. In writing about the South, Howe said, Faulkner was writing about every place. Like Hemingway's *The Sun Also Rises* and Fitzgerald's *The Great Gatsby*, Faulkner's work was driven "not merely by the sense of regional disintegration" but by the sense of "universal human crisis." Howe was most impressed with what he called Faulkner's "greatest theme," the "welling love for . . . 'the lowly and invincible of the earth'" who suffer the consequences of social change but who "'endure, and endure and then endure.'"[34] Howe, of course, did not see Faulkner's agrarian social vision as a viable solution for the United States, the most industrialized country in the world. But he insisted that Faulkner's "implicit politics" deserved consideration as an invocation to fraternity, something Howe valued even more than equality and as a sign of "a fundamental quarrel with modern life, an often brilliant criticism of urban anonymity."[35] His admiration for the ideology of Faulkner and other Southern agrarians as "image" or "myth" rather than political prescription seems to foreshadow Irving Howe's later description of his own socialism as "moral impulse" rather than as a blueprint for the radical reconstruction of society. It also reflects the idea that for Howe, socialism was as much a way of conserving the best of the past (the perceived or mythic past perhaps, but the past nonetheless), as it was a desire for, or a sensibility toward, an improved future.

Irving Howe would never fully solve the problem of how to bring together, in harmony, literary reflectiveness with an eagerness to engage the world in behalf of left-liberal ideas. But in his attention to what he called "the literature of loss," and especially in his work with

Anderson and Faulkner, he seems to have come to tentative terms with the idea that between the life of the mind and the life of politics, there is not only disharmony, but some vital connection too.

Another case in point was Howe's reaction to Lionel Trilling's *The Liberal Imagination*, a collection of essays critical of, but not opposed to liberalism, which aimed at "putting under some degree of pressure the liberal ideas and assumptions of the present time."[36] Howe was attracted to Trilling's intention to deepen liberalism philosophically and to save it from its smug glibness and simple-minded rationalism. And he appreciated the difficult questions Trilling raised about liberalism's ability "to cope with the disorder, the violence, the sheer inexplicable evil that the twentieth century had thrown up in such abundance."[37] But Howe was irritated with Trilling's too easy inclination to criticize politics from the point of view of art; and he bridled at Trilling's insistence, even as he acknowledged its partial truth, that "the literary life was inherently more noble than the life of politics." To accept this idea fully, Howe said, "could have been disabling at a time when politics was essential."[38]

Politics remained essential for Irving Howe. Although he admired and befriended Trilling, indeed, was in correspondence with him throughout the late forties and early fifties, and was being aided by him in his work on Sherwood Anderson, Howe quarreled with many of Trilling's points. He berated him for the political consequences, perhaps unintended, of his basic position on liberalism. Trilling, Howe argued, identified liberalism mainly with Communists and "fellow-travelers," thus mistaking liberalism's shabby, degenerated forms as fundamental to it. Liberalism, Howe insisted, is better associated with a code of intellectual tolerance and freedom, with the life of reason, with secularism and a confidence in the power of people to help direct their own fate.

In these senses, Howe said, we all presumably wish to be or should be liberal. And while liberalism has sometimes been "a political doctrine that . . . has meant the support of capitalism" (where, Howe said, "at least a few of us get off the train"), in post–New Deal America liberalism has also meant a militant political activism in support of progressive social change and in behalf of at least a measure of egalitarianism. Although Lionel Trilling considered himself a liberal, adhered to the values of reason and tolerance, and was a strong defender of civic freedoms, the effect of his essays, his critique of the "liberal imagination," Howe argued, was to discourage people from this post–New

Deal variety of liberalism and to supply an increasing number of intellectuals with an excuse for their new mood of accommodation to the status quo.[39]

Accommodation was something Howe himself consciously resisted in the early fifties, as he had all along. He refused to turn away from the evidence of distress in American society and in the American character, evidence hidden under the emergence of an unprecedented affluence and the shield of increasing national power. Even as he favorably compared an incomplete, imperfect American democracy to Stalinist totalitarianism, Howe refused to join in the consensus of opinion that was complacently positive toward the American ship of state and toward those institutions and values that former radical intellectuals had only a few years earlier dismissed as "bourgeois democracy."

In the mid-to-late 1940s, in the aftermath of depression and war, the emphasis in the serious journals had not been on recovery, national self-esteem, and a brighter future, but on alienation, anxiety, disorientation, and guilt. Articles about Kafka or Dostoevsky or French existentialism and on the "crisis of reason" or "the failure of nerve" filled the pages of *Partisan Review*, *Commentary*, and the *Nation*. Even the titles of well-known books had announced a mood of depression, distress, and despair: Saul Bellow's *The Dangling Man* (1944) and *The Victim* (1947), Robert Lowell's *Lord Weary's Castle* (1946), Randall Jarrell's *Losses* (1948), Arthur Miller's *Death of a Salesman* (1949), David Riesman's *The Lonely Crowd* (1950), William Styron's *Lie Down in Darkness* (1951), Carson McCullers's *Ballad of a Sad Café*. All were portraits in the alienation of "modern man." And for the eight or nine years following the Second World War this alienation was also the focus of sociology and psychiatry.

With the intensification of the Cold War, however, the American model began to look increasingly attractive compared to the Soviet Union, and there was a growing tolerance, if not downright appreciation, for liberal democracy, even on Irving Howe's part. Moreover, with the dramatic economic recovery still underway in the 1950s at home and abroad, intellectuals could actually begin to think about steady jobs, reasonable standards of living, even prosperity. All of this, especially "the leisure of the theory class," as Daniel Bell put it, humorously twisting Thorstein Veblen, made it easier for writers and critics to give up their radicalism and their sense of alienation, even though their "post-Marxist deconversions" were gradual and sometimes tortured.[40] "Abandoning Marxism came to resemble mass rituals of contrition,"

Howe said later, "sometimes liberating, since you shook off the phantasms of ideology, but often rather sad," since some intellectuals forfeited serious criticism, hope, and commitment.[41]

Among the many former radicals who by the early fifties no longer considered themselves socialists of any variety (some of whom moved considerably to the right) were Martin Diamond, political scientist; Leslie Fiedler, literary critic; Gertrude Himmelfarb, historian; Seymour Martin Lipset, sociologist; and Irving Kristol, journalist. Irving Howe was an outstanding exception. He too was no longer a Trotskyist, or even an orthodox Marxist, but his steadfastness as a radical critic of American society and his endurance as a socialist continued unabated. This was clear in Howe's behavior and writings throughout the fifties, beginning with the symposium in print organized in 1952 by *Partisan Review* called "Our Country and Its Culture."

Partisan editors William Phillips and Philip Rahv solicited responses from a large number and very wide spectrum of New York intellectuals (but no women) that included Jacques Barzun, Richard Chase, Sidney Hook, Irving Howe, Norman Mailer, C. Wright Mills, Arthur Schlesinger, Jr., Delmore Schwartz, and Lionel Trilling. They posed several questions, including the following: "To what extent have American intellectuals actually changed their attitude toward America and its institutions? . . . Where in American life can artists and intellectuals find the basis of strength, renewal, and recognition now that they can no longer depend fully on Europe as a cultural example and a source of vitality? . . . If a reaffirmation and rediscovery of America is under way can the tradition of critical non-conformism (going back to Thoreau and Melville and embracing some of the major expressions of American intellectual history) be maintained as strongly as ever?"[42]

The very pronouns of the title "Our Country and Our Culture" and the way the questions were framed suggested that affirmations of America were in order. And affirmations were certainly encouraged by the editorial statement that "[t]he American artist and intellectual no longer feels 'disinherited' . . . [M]ost writers no longer accept alienation as the artist's fate in America; on the contrary, they want very much to be part of American life." The responses about the American present and future, were, predictably, mostly positive. But even among the so-called affirmers like Reinhold Niehbur and Philip Rahv himself, there were significant demurrals. "No intellectual life worthy of the name,"

Niehbur wrote, "can be at ease with the massive spiritual, moral and cultural crudities, which seek to make themselves normative in a civilization."[43] Rahv said: "The illusion that our society is in its very nature immune to tragic social conflicts and collisions has been revived, and once more it is assumed that the more acute problems of the modern epoch are unreal as far as we are concerned. And in their recoil from radicalism certain intellectuals have now made that easy assumption their own."[44] Several of the others, including Chase, Trilling, Hook, and Schlesinger, talked about sustaining a necessary dissidence from within American culture and about the need for a critical nonconformism to go along with the reaffirmation and rediscovery of America.

A very small handful of others, however, directly denounced the assumptions of the symposium itself. Norman Mailer, for example, asked: "Is there nothing to remind us that the writer does not need to be integrated into his society, and often works best in opposition to it? . . . [I]ntegration, acceptance, non-alienation, etc., etc. has been more conducive to propaganda than art."[45] Irving Howe, perhaps the most intense and vociferous nonaffirmer, criticized the editors for their loaded questions and their untestable declamation that writers now "want very much to be part of American life." Howe said, "I cannot react with enthusiasm, or distaste" to such a statement "until I am told which part of American life." It seemed more sensible to Irving Howe to take America piece by piece. "Then one can admire our easy-going manners and be disturbed by the drive against civil liberties; enjoy baseball but distrust mass culture . . . ; respect the democratic tradition, [but] feel disturbed by the trend toward conformism; and more."

Howe was unquestionably sincere in his criticism of America, and he continued for a few years into the 1950s to be very attached to the idea of his own alienation. But with Delmore Schwartz, Isaac Rosenfeld, Alfred Kazin, and several other dissenting New York Jewish intellectuals, Howe was also very much an American. He, like the others, reflected the nervous energy, quick intelligence, and tumultuous spirit of the big American city. And again like the others, Irving Howe, despite an apparent preference for the sophistication and political subversiveness of the great European literary masters like Joyce and Kafka, early came to see the value of the American writers. Alfred Kazin was especially appreciative of literature produced on "native ground"; Schwartz and Rosenfeld admired Hawthorne and the New England Transcendentalists; and Howe was very much drawn to Faulkner and Anderson and Frost, eventually even growing in his appreciation of Emerson. He also, like Schwartz and Rosenfeld, loved baseball.

Although Howe in his piece for the symposium reiterated yet again that America, "a once vigorous society," was reaching its end because "capitalism as a world system is exhausted, economically and spiritually," and although he said once more that Marxism seemed to him "the best available method for understanding and making history," he made it abundantly clear that he preferred America and the "inadequate democracy of the capitalist world" to any system that denied political freedom. "Totalitarianism is a social evil distinct from any we have known," Howe said. And between the limited freedom of the capitalist world and the total repression of the Stalinist world, Howe insisted "there is the difference between life, however afflicted, and death." The socialist intellectual, then, "must try to defend democracy with some realism *while maintaining his independence from and opposition to the status quo.*"[46]

In Irving Howe's mind, maintaining independence meant, in part, remaining institutionally unattached. Howe saw his part-time employment at *Time* magazine not as a sell-out but as a compromise required by the basic costs of living. And although his anti-institutional strictures included the academy, Howe, as we saw in his correspondence with Lionel Trilling, did flirt with the idea of university teaching. Whatever reluctance he may have had in regard to an academic attachment was reduced somewhat by the needs of his growing family. In November 1951, while still living in their small split-level house on Grover Avenue in Princeton, Thalia Howe gave birth to Nina. Irving was delighted to be a father. "Nina," he wrote to a friend only days after his daughter's arrival, "is a dream." Four months later he was still enthralled. "There is simply no experience like fatherhood," he said. "My little girl . . . is a great source of joy."[47]

But Thalia's job at Miss Fine's Day School for Girls and Irving's freelance writing barely covered expenses. While Thalia was pregnant, Irving, in June 1951, took a job as a visiting instructor at the University of Vermont. "I am playing professor for 2 weeks," he told Richard Chase. Howe enjoyed the new experience but not entirely. Almost immediately he found that his preference for a method-free criticism and a personally insightful reading of texts was resisted. "All these earnest graduate students here," he complained, "hounding me about SYM-BOLS; there isn't a noun in a novel they don't find a symbol in." Looking for sympathy from Chase, Howe wrote: "Criticism gets to be such a dreary business doesn't it?"[48]

The following summer, Howe was in Seattle teaching at the University of Washington. Again he had a number of complaints, but overall a positive encounter. His students knew intimately the disputes among literary critics, Howe said, "quite as Yeshiva students had once known the inner exchanges of Talmud commentators." But whether they had read Tolstoy or Stendahl, or any literature, as distinct from literary criticism, was by no means clear to Irving. The students apparently regarded Howe as an amateur because his approach to criticism, unlike the New Critics they favored, was historically grounded and often spontaneous and pragmatic. And they found amusing their teacher's admiration of Edmund Wilson, whom they dismissed as a mere journalist. But they liked Irving Howe, finding him "fresh" in both senses of the word.[49] And he liked them; and he liked his colleagues, too.

In the English department, Howe, perhaps to his own surprise, was less comfortable with the leftist disciples of Vernon Parrington and more at home with Arnold Stein, Robert Heilman, and other New Critics, all of whom were adherents of Richard Blackmur, Allen Tate, John Crowe Ransom, and other "reactionary" Southern agrarians. The New Critics rejected socialism and quarreled with American liberalism. And there were doctrinal differences between them and Howe, especially their radical commitment to form, rhetoric and tone, and their general inattention to historical background and biography. Despite all of this, Howe found the New Critics appealing. He liked their penchant for close reading of poetry and their insistence that a literary work had a value of its own beyond what it "said" about something else, and beyond the emotions it aroused in a reader. More important, he found among them "a kind of largeness of spirit," a "kindness" he said he had difficulty finding among intellectuals in later years.[50]

He also saw in their agrarian vision, as he had with Faulkner, a "myth" that could serve not so much as a map to the future, as a useful tool for criticizing the present, "an idyll reflecting their desire." It may have been this stay at the University of Washington and his study of the Southern writers that helped Howe apply this same idea to his socialism, which only two years later he characterized as "the name of our desire." He would continue to use that phrase, as well as the words "myth" and "image" to describe his socialism, which he came to see eventually less as a political than a personal persuasion, less as a plan for the future than a moral influence, a way of measuring American culture against a utopian ideal.[51]

In any case, Irving Howe enjoyed his summer as an instructor on the Northwest coast, and despite the fact that he once again, this time in a letter to Granville Hicks, described his teaching as "playing" a role, he began to take the idea of a university career more seriously. In August he was telling Richard Chase: "Teaching as such tempts me greatly; it seems, also, a way to earn a living without doing the often unpleasant hack work I do now," especially for *Time* magazine. But at the same time, Howe said, "I have an instinctive, probably irrational suspicion of the academic environment." Moreover, with Wisconsin senator Joseph McCarthy's antiradical crusade in full swing in the early fifties, Howe anticipated "increasing pressure on political dissidence" in the universities. Worst of all, he said, "I doubt if I have the patience to go through the degree wringer. All I have is a bachelors."[52]

But Howe did have two important literary studies, especially the Faulkner book, which was a pioneering work and is still in print after four editions. These easily could have served as substitutes for doctoral dissertations. In the 1950s, with the universities virtually flooded with war veterans studying under the G.I. Bill, even mavericks like Howe could be admitted to faculties, though not without hazing, some of it not very good natured, from the more traditional scholars. Also, Howe had had by now a number of important teaching experiences. He had taught adults in New Jersey in 1948, and graduate students in Vermont in 1951 and in Seattle in 1952. Irving had another very valuable teaching opportunity when he was invited to present the Christian Gauss Lectures at Princeton University in the spring of 1953. Richard Blackmur directed the seminars, and he had invited Paul Tillich, Edmund Wilson, and Leon Edel as the senior lecturers, and Howe as the junior. Dwight Macdonald and Hannah Arendt had also been lecturers in the early fifties, as had Delmore Schwartz in 1949. Irving Howe was thrilled and a bit awed to be in such lustrous company, and he attended all the sessions with Wilson and Tillich, dutifully doing his homework in preparation. His own lectures were on politics and the novel, the nucleus of a book he published by the same name in 1957. The book benefited from the lively informed exchanges with a small audience, usually fewer than twenty invited guests, who sat around a table in a Firestone Library seminar room. The experience further enhanced Howe's interest in teaching.[53]

His familiarity with a variety of classroom settings made him more attractive to the academy. In 1952 an invitation to apply for a position at Sarah Lawrence was followed by a series of interviews at the Bronxville school, fifteen miles north of New York City. Howe wondered why some faculty members asked questions while others did little more than smile politely. After being rejected, Howe learned that the quiet ones were Stalinist fellow-travelers unwilling even to consider a candidate with Howe's Trotskyist sympathies, especially one with no graduate degree.[54]

None of this, however, was a problem for Brandeis University, it-self an upstart institution. Located in Waltham, Massachusetts, a sub-urb of Boston, Brandeis was founded by American Jews in 1948, and the administration of the young school was determined to build a first-rate faculty to rival Harvard across the Charles River. Lewis Coser, an anti-Nazi émigré, who was teaching sociology at Brandeis, had be-come acquainted with Irving Howe in the early forties at *Labor Action*, where Coser (party name, Louis Clair) wrote a weekly column on Eu-ropean events under the pseudonym Europacus. Although at that time they maintained only a business relationship, in the early fifties Coser urged Howe to apply for a position in the English department. In 1953, the year his second child, Nicholas, was born, Howe sent in an appli-cation.[55]

He was interviewed by a faculty committee which included Simon Rawidowicz, a historian of Jewish thought; Ludwig Lewisohn, for-merly a Freudian critic and in the 1950s a student and proponent of Jew-ish nationalism; and Joseph Cheskis, who taught French and had a thick Yiddish accent. The early spring afternoon was apparently not going very well for Howe until he mentioned in passing that he was working with the Yiddish poet Eliezer Greenberg on an anthology of Yiddish sto-ries in English translation. Smiles broke out, as did Yiddish, which everyone spoke for the rest of the session. "Is there another professor of English in the country," Howe asked later, "who can say that his first job interview was conducted in Yiddish?"[56]

Irving Howe, only a little surprised after that exercise in Yid-dishkayt, was hired. The committee filed a positive report to Abram Sachar, the president of Brandeis, who was willing to overlook the absence of the doctorate and, as important, the unconventional polit-ical pasts of exciting candidates who had proven their merit outside the academy. Still, Irving Howe's suspicion of the university did not completely disappear. "I'm becoming, alas, a professor (at Brandeis)," he told the poet Theodore Roethke, "and I don't like it too much, but there it is." Howe, whose most important models for literary criticism, George Orwell and Edmund Wilson, had always worked outside the academy, worried about the potential loss of independence and a gradual, even unconscious retreat from radicalism, or worse: the abandonment of the critical stance, the very raison d'être of the intellectual.[57]

Howe also worried about whether the university would "protect" him should he come up against the McCarthyites. Many professors in the early fifties had been called before investigating committees, and approximately 150 had lost their positions. The pressures were worst in New York and California, but few major universities escaped at least token firings. He told Coser in the spring of 1953, before he actually signed his contract with Brandeis, that he feared the congressional investigations. "Right now they're on the ex-CPers," Howe said, "but their capacity for making distinctions, or their desire, is limited. What would it matter to them that someone like me has always been anti-Stalinist?" Ultimately, Howe's question to Coser was: "What would the likely reaction of the Brandeis people be to any such trouble? Are they badly frightened?" He was most worried about Sachar: "My guess is that he'd cave in."[58]

Coser could not vouch for Sachar's standing firm if there were a direct major assault by McCarthy, but he thought he could be depended on if there were only minor harassments. Not entirely satisfied, Howe came aboard anyway in the fall of 1953. And by the end of his first semester he seemed to relax a bit. He told Richard Chase that Brandeis "is pretty loose in structure, the bureaucracy not having hardened yet, so that one has much freedom." Faculty life was not perfect, Howe said, "but when I remember having to churn out a review for *Time* for 5-1/2 years, once a week . . . ."[59]

At Brandeis in the fifties, a remarkable institution "mixing college, political forum, and kibbutz," Irving Howe found a place, he said, where "the life of the mind was engaged with [a] passion" unequaled elsewhere. What counted most, Howe said, were the students—several hundred offbeat, "prematurely New Leftist" young people, most of whom had a quarrelsome love of politics and literature. Teaching at Brandeis could be "exhilarating and terrifying," and often Howe would come out of class needing to change his shirt. Howe's students included Martin Peretz, the future owner-editor of the *New Republic*; Michael

Walzer, later to be one of the nation's leading political philosophers; Judith Bordovko (Walzer), who went on to become Dean of Humanities at the New School for Social Research; and Jeremy Larner, award-winning novelist and screenwriter. They could think discursively and write elegantly, and Howe sometimes thought he had little to teach them. They say otherwise.[60]

Judith Walzer, at the invitation of several of her friends who thought Irving Howe was "very special," visited one of his classes. "I was very impressed," she said, "and although a history major I went on to take several courses with him. Ultimately, he was responsible for my doing graduate work in literature." Howe had an informal, open classroom style, which was very different from the European and European-educated faculty who were teaching at Brandeis in the 1950s. They were more attuned to "the authority principle," but Irving, Walzer said, was "interested in us. He helped us discover that the things *we* thought were interesting. It made the classroom experience memorable."[61]

Some students were more interested in what *Irving Howe* thought. In a class on Henry James and Mark Twain, Howe, assuming the stance of skepticism, took apart various interpretations of James's story "The Liar." At the end of the hour, never having voiced his own opinion, Howe started walking out. A group of students led by Jeremy Larner, apparently wanting "the truth," surrounded their teacher shouting to no avail: "You can't do this to us!" At other times Howe did deliver "the truth," especially when students seemed deaf to the fact that in life and literature there were irresolvable dilemmas, problems that simply would not yield to reason. At such times Howe might ask: "'Suppose you were reading a novel that showed Nazis as *characteristically* kind to Jews, how would you respond?" Instead of attacking the question by saying, for example, that no sane person could write such a book or even imagine such a situation, the students, Howe said, would mumble, with some discomfort, about the need to allow the writer's imagination to run free. At this Howe would explode, he confessed, saying that if he were reading such a book he would throw it out the window.

More often, Howe delivered the "truth" indirectly. Jeremy Larner remembered a class in which he gave an assigned talk on Huck Finn, charging Twain with "writing a lousy ending." Larner insisted that Twain neither understood what he had created in Huck's defiance of fire and brimstone by helping the slave Jim escape, nor came to terms with the irony of their having escaped into the deeper South. Instead,

Larner argued, Twain "copped out" in the conclusion, satirizing a medieval romance and reintroducing Tom Sawyer. Howe took an opposing position, citing Lionel Trilling's authoritative argument that the ending was symbolically and morally coherent. He got the rest of the class to agree with him, Larner said, before he turned around "and then showed why he thought I was right after all!" Howe did a similar thing when Marie Boaz, the daughter of the noted anthropologist Franz Boaz, analyzed the fall of Socrates. When she finished, Larner recalled, Howe asked the class to put themselves in the position of the Athenians and vote. They all voted against Socrates. A dismayed but unruffled Irving Howe said: "'Now you know how these things happen; and I am ashamed of you.'" Many students admitted later that this kind of experience in Howe's classes made them reexamine values, and even life-choices.[62]

The very first course Michael Walzer took with Irving Howe was for him a life-defining experience. He went home for winter break and told his parents: "I don't want to be a lawyer; I want to be an intellectual," and a left-wing intellectual at that. With some sense of amusement and gratitude as well as with what I took to be a smidgen of regret, Walzer also said that Howe had elicited "so much respect from me that I probably never, even at *Dissent*, got completely away from the teacher-student relationship in my interactions with Irving."

Howe did some "teaching" outside the classroom, too. "A group of us who thought of ourselves as the Brandeis left," Walzer recalled, "determined that we were no longer going to wear ties in the campus dining room." Howe, who continued, since Princeton, to dress quite fashionably in the style of the Ivy League, asked him: "Michael, is this important?" Not waiting for an answer, Howe said: "This is *not* important; you can wear a tie. Save your energy and whatever credit you have in the world for more fundamental things. There really are more important political issues." Six years later, in 1960, Walzer, on "assignment" for Howe at *Dissent*, was not only writing about the civil rights sit-ins at the lunch counters of Woolworth stores in the South, he was helping organize those demonstrations. And he got involved in the Northern Support movement which picketed forty Woolworth establishments in the Boston area. Irving Howe was mainly interested in the reportage and analysis for *Dissent*, Walzer said, but this time he heartily approved of the activism.[63]

In Howe's classes there was no stinting on work. "We read a book a week," Judith Walzer recalled, "and wrote papers as often." Howe taught respect for the word, many students remembered, and several said "he actually taught us *how* to read." And he certainly expected students to read. On a day when they were to discuss James's "The Awkward Age," there were no responses to Irving's questions. After confirming that no one had read the book, he "very calmly, with no anger, gathered up his books and papers, and said as he left: 'We have nothing to talk about.'" Everyone was embarrassed, Judy Walzer said. "No one wanted that to happen again. And it never did."[64]

Not all assessments of Howe's teaching were positive. Some indicted Irving for treating students, women particularly, with very little patience. "He was unpleasant and dismissive to me," one student complained, "acting as if a woman, especially a pregnant woman, could not possibly be serious." And Howe, according to others, could be "prickly and intolerant" of women, particularly the "Miami Beach types" or "those who would sit and knit in the back of the class." Even a female student who admitted that "Irving was dramatic and exciting; a star, a great teacher," also said, "Years later I noticed that in his course on the English novel he included no women writers—not even Virginia Woolf."[65] On the other hand, Judith Walzer said that Irving's apparent belief that "the intellectual life belonged to men" did not show up in class. "'Smart' was what counted," she said, "not gender." And Rachel Sugarman (Price), a literature major who took four courses with Howe, said she saw no differences in Howe's treatment of male and female students. "He simply did not brook stupidity well," she said, "whatever the source or gender."[66]

Most students, women and men, thought Irving Howe was a marvelous teacher, but many thought he could be intimidating. Martin Peretz, who took a course with Irving on the English novel, said: "Irving was an extraordinary lecturer; but he taught a little bit by terror. Some people were not given easily to asking questions. And Irving was not above publicly identifying a question as stupid." Larner, too, remembered that Irving "had little time for fools and delighted in drawing some piece of cant from a too-assured pupil."[67] Howe himself confessed that his Brandeis teaching experience was not entirely rosy. "Wasn't there a quantity of aggression," he asked, "some of it needless, in my classroom style?" Irving Howe worried later in *Margin of Hope* that some students, especially those undistinguished though "perfectly harmless" young men and women, had suffered as victims of his intellectual pride. "For the effect of my teaching," he said with brutal honesty, "could be to make them aware of their deficiencies without providing a way to overcome them."[68]

With the Brandeis faculty, too, Irving Howe had a mixed but generally positive experience. He had a close and abiding relationship with sociologist Lewis Coser, a fellow democratic socialist and cofounder of *Dissent* magazine (which was virtually born on the Brandeis campus). The same held true for Philip Rahv, who came aboard in 1957 as a professor of literature; but the friendship eroded as Rahv, partly out of a fearful overreaction to McCarthyism, had become, temporarily, less and less "political." Howe and Herbert Marcuse, a professor of philosophy and a Stalinist sympathizer, clashed several times, once rather dramatically in public debate over the 1956 Hungarian revolution. For the poet and Yiddishist Marie Syrkin, who became the first female professor of an academic subject on the faculty of Brandeis, and whom Howe later came to admire and befriend, he had, at the start, little respect. He did not as yet think one could be a committed Zionist like Syrkin and also be an intellectual. And it is rumored that Howe initially opposed granting Syrkin tenure at the university.[69]

Howe's most important collegial association at Brandeis was with the poet and classicist J. V. Cunningham. Despite an enormous gap in their political inclinations, Cunningham became the one faculty member Howe regarded as his teacher. Perhaps the fact that both men were "contentious, rudely charming" and determinedly plebeian, and that both despised the false gentility of many academics, allowed them to work together well. Whatever the case, Howe admired Cunningham enormously and from him "learned that scholars need not be the musty, irrelevant sort of drones some of us had foolishly supposed them to be." From Cunningham, Howe said, "I learned that scholarship can be as serious [and] exalted a calling as the intellectual life and that often enough the two could unite."[70]

Howe also had a mixed relationship with Abram Sachar, the president of Brandeis. Sachar considered Howe's appointment to the university in 1953 "a major coup," but he and Irving often sharply disagreed. For example, when Sachar told Irving in 1955 or 1956 that his course could not be titled Yiddish literature, they quarreled, the president demanding that the course be called Jewish literature or Hebrew literature. But Howe insisted on the Yiddish label and he went to the Brandeis board, which, in an unprecedented move, overrode Sachar. And by 1957 Howe was on the Faculty Organization Committee which sought more power in relation to the president.[71]

Despite the friction between them, there were positive moments. When the first issue of *Dissent* was published in January 1954 with its clarion call for a new socialism, Howe and Lew Coser were not sure how Sachar, characterized by some faculty as incorrigibly middle class, would react. They decided to submit the new magazine just as they would any other faculty publication and sent the president a copy. Back came a letter from Sachar saying that the leftward thrust of the magazine is "not at all my opinion, but more power to you boys." And he never gave them any trouble. Howe also admired Sachar's ability to raise funds for Brandeis from wealthy Jews of East European origin who, with little education, were in awe of learning. The faculty saw Sachar as a philistine, Howe said later, but the faculty could not appreciate that in Sachar's hands "philistinism was being raised to the level of genius."[72]

Irving Howe never came to be completely comfortable with university life, neither at Brandeis, nor at Stanford (where he taught from 1961 to 1963), nor even at the City University Graduate Center where, beginning in 1963, he spent the bulk of his teaching career. He could not escape, nor did he want to escape the sense of being a "semi-outsider." Howe never published in the academic journals; he was "more a 'man of letters,'" he said, "or a literary intellectual" than a scholar.[73] But he did come to see that scholarship could have a value and dignity of its own. Even if there were professors who were small-minded and arid, Howe said, "others really cared about ideas and possessed a quiet learning that made [my] own absorption in the contemporary seem provincial."[74]

Irving Howe developed a sincere appreciation for the erudition of some of his colleagues, but he was being very modest about the extent and quality of his own knowledge. He was not entirely absorbed in the contemporary nor would anyone describe him as provincial. His literary criticism was historically informed and his general interests impressively wide. Howe demonstrated this consistently in his writing and his teaching. Several students remembered, for example, a public seminar of the English department that began with a reading of James Joyce's three-page story "Araby." A brief pause followed to allow the magic of Joyce to settle. Then an hour of intense discussion ensued among Irving Howe, J. V. Cunningham, and Philip Rahv. They argued about the nature of Joyce's genius, about "realistic fiction," Irish history, and the decline of the West. They were passionate about their differences, Jeremy Larner said, but each "duly conceded, as they went along, the points on which their opponents were better informed," and Howe more than held his own.[75]

Howe was good for Brandeis, and for several years Brandeis was good for him. But even as he came to enjoy his professorial role and the literary life, he hungered for engagement with politics. Howe did continue to include politics and history in his teaching. For example, he often demonstrated, line by line if need be, that a writer's politics, however important to understand, could not in the end, determine the value or power of the story he or she produced. At the same time, he continued to show that all "tastes" imply social and historical assumptions.[76] This was exciting and satisfying, but it wasn't enough "politics" for Irving Howe.

A more explicit public activism beckoned: McCarthyism continued to poison the atmosphere of American democracy; there was a trend toward cultural conformity abroad in the nation; intellectuals were in retreat from radicalism; Stalinist totalitarianism had left a dark, perhaps ineradicable stain on the very idea of socialism; no significant socialist movement existed in the United States and, in all likelihood, none would appear in the near future, especially if socialists failed to reexamine their premises and redefine their goals. Something needed to be done. "When intellectuals can do nothing else," Howe would write twenty-five years later, with some self-deprecation, "they start a magazine." It was more complicated and difficult than that, but in short, that was how *Dissent* was conceived and why it was launched.

6

The Origins of *Dissent*

THE FIRST ISSUE of *Dissent* did not appear until the beginning of 1954, but Irving Howe had been thinking about starting a new anti-Stalinist Marxist magazine as early as 1949. In the spring of that year he had written an article for *Partisan Review* about the absence in America of good, small, politically radical periodicals. At the same time, in a letter to Dwight Macdonald, he mentioned the possibility of starting a magazine with Lewis Coser and others, one that would attempt to reconsider, reformulate, and give new life to socialist tenets and, in the longer run, to reverse the disintegration of the socialist movement in America.[1] Howe told an interviewer in 1977 that he and a number of his friends "who had been involved in various socialist groups and sects" in the late forties had come to feel that they were at a dead end. They wanted to get away from sectarianism and "out of rigid ideologies." But at the same time, they wanted to maintain "the socialist idea, . . . refurbish it, . . . invigorate it."[2]

No serious magazine was doing any of this in the late 1940s: Dwight Macdonald's *Politics*, although always provocative, was little more than a vehicle for the editor-owner's personal and ever-changing outlook, and in any case it folded in the fall of 1949; *Commentary*, founded in 1945, remained liberal and reformist in perspective; *Partisan Review*'s socialism, without the prospect of an activated revolutionary working class, had dissipated early in the 1940s; and Paul Sweezy's *Monthly Review*, which Howe characterized as a journal for "left authoritarians" advocating "the radicalism of the blackjack," was still mired in the mud of 1930s Stalinist fellow-traveling.[3] A new magazine was necessary, Howe thought, one that could stake out a "dissenters" position of independent radicalism between the Stalinists and the increasingly affirmative liberals at *Commentary*; one that could resuscitate socialism and, as important, expose Stalinism abroad and combat Mc-Carthyism and the violation of civil liberties at home.

Irving Howe's staunch and consistent defense of civil liberties began as early as his student days at the City College of New York in the late 1930s. Though a tireless opponent of the Stalinists, Howe, in support of academic freedom, participated in a sit-down demonstration demanding the reinstatement of Morris Schappes, a Stalinist professor of English. And he defended the right of every student group to free speech, even while he was sometimes physically deprived of that right himself by members of the Young Communist League.

Beyond City College and throughout the 1940s, Howe, despite his unflagging and severe critique of bourgeois democracy, continued to admire the ideals of classical liberalism, especially its emphasis on civil liberties. In 1948 he and many of his friends on the anti-Stalinist left "were bitterly opposed to the Progressive Party," which they saw, accurately enough, as essentially a front for the Communist movement. Nevertheless, Howe believed that the Progressive Party had a right to be on the ballot, "to function freely in the country, to say its piece."[4]

Irving Howe also continued to take a principled, virtually absolutist civil-libertarian stand against legislation or procedures that would prevent Communists from teaching. And this at a time in the late 1940s when many eminent figures, including John L. Childs, a professor at the Teacher's College of Columbia University, and the leaders of the American Federation of Teachers, held that the Communist Party (CP) was not a party like other parties but a conspiracy, and that membership was prima facie evidence of unfitness for teaching.

Even Sidney Hook, who was against restrictive legislation, loyalty oaths, and government investigations of teachers, and who believed that the "mere fact of membership" in the CP was not enough to warrant dismissal, saw membership in the party as a "presumption of unfitness warranting inquiry by a committee of a teacher's peers." Hook insisted that he defended the right of teachers to hold Communist views, but in 1949 he was clearly sympathetic to the University of Washington's firing of professors for membership in the CP. And in a letter to Herbert Aptheker, Hook wrote: "My evidence for characterizing the Communist Party as a conspiracy, and its members as professionally unfit to fulfill the vocation of a teacher, has been published many times."[5]

Hook did contend that actual behavior, such as teaching in an ideologically doctrinaire manner (something he thought Communists incapable of avoiding) or engaging in conspiracy, was the only true test for dismissal. But his fierce and frequent denunciations of Communism and the nature of his arguments clearly helped reinforce the atmosphere of suspicion, mistrust, and intimidation around educators who were CP members, and put them in the untenable position of having to prove their "innocence."[6] Moreover, as Irving Howe (as R. Fahan) pointed out in attacking Hook, the argument that Communist professors should be dismissed because they were "doctrinaire" did not make sense unless all doctrinaire professors, observant Catholics, for example, were fired. In any case, in practice, Howe said, Communist teachers behaved pretty much like everyone else, and few were the kind of party-line automatons Hook made them out to be. Stalinists did do damage, Howe admitted. But in the university as elsewhere, he said, "There is only one way to fight them: political exposure and intellectual defeat." In addition, Howe said, students ought not to be sheltered from unpopular ideas. Much later Howe, who understood that nonradical teachers were every bit as biased in their classrooms as their radical colleagues, wrote, "I knew quite as well as Hook that Stalinist professors sometimes propagandized outrageously in the classroom. It seemed better, all the same, to put up with whatever problems this might cause than to endanger the fragile structure of academic freedom by declaring categorical bans."[7]

Howe's basic points were eminently sound, but a follow-up piece he wrote for *Labor Action* (again as R. Fahan) unfairly implying that Hook was moving into an alliance with the Catholic Church was mockingly polemical and ad hominem. Almost immediately he heard that Sidney Hook was furious with him. Hook was particularly incensed that Howe had used a pseudonym in order to "invent facts" and escape "responsibility," and he interpreted the content and style of Howe's article as a personal assault. Howe argued, convincingly, that he had used the pseudonym many times in the past and did so this time "for reasons . . . not unconnected with the Attorney General's proclivity for compiling lists." Although Howe had written mostly under his own name since leaving the army in 1946, he was, after all, in this case defending the right of Communists to teach in the face of ongoing congressional and state investigations of suspected leftists on college campuses.[8]

The political atmosphere could indeed be intimidating. At the federal level, eleven leaders of the Communist Party were convicted of violating the Smith Act (1940), which had made it illegal to advocate or teach the violent overthrow of the government. These widely publicized anti-Communist activities launched by the government were part of a trend that had begun as fears of the Soviet Union increased during the Cold War. In 1947 the House Committee on Un-American Activities (HUAC), originally created in 1938 as a temporary body and resurrected after the war, began conducting hearings on Communist subversion in Hollywood, which then carried over to many other areas of American society. In the same year, President Truman, in response to and partly in order to ward off right-wing extremism, instituted a loyalty and security program for all federal employees that was widely imitated at the state and local levels, and he revived the attorney general's old list of subversive organizations.

In 1948 the Alger Hiss case led to increased fear of Communist subversion and to a demand for repressive legislation. And in the very next year, Karl Mundt and Richard Nixon sponsored a bill to require registration of Communists and leaders of Communist front organizations, the banning of Communists from government employment, and the fining and imprisonment of anyone conspiring to establish a Communist dictatorship. In 1950, Senator Joseph McCarthy began the crusade that would give his name to an era. Falsely claiming to possess evidence that the federal government was pervaded with Communists, McCarthy initiated his own hearings into Communist subversion through his Permanent Subcommittee on Investigations.

In this political context, although Howe himself was probably safe, it was not surprising that he would (even if not consistently) employ a pseudonym for his pieces defending Communist teachers. In regard to the style of his articles, which in the process of defending civil liberties attacked Sidney Hook, Howe wrote: "If [I] was excessive, I regret it since I have fought again and again in the movement" (and in himself he might have added) "against that sort of tone." Only days later, after rereading his essay, Howe sent Hook an addendum admitting that the piece was "unnecessarily nasty" and that some of its conclusions about Hook were "farfetched." Howe apologized yet again and said, "I think my political point of view sufficiently sound not to have used that sort of polemical method. I regret you were the victim of it." And he said the same in an open letter to *Labor Action*.[9]

Hook was not at all satisfied. He angrily characterized Howe's explanation as "extremely disingenuous" and asked facetiously whether it was Howe's politics or his character "which makes it constitutionally impossible for you to do elementary justice to people with whom you disagree." There was yet another pointed exchange between the two, bringing the correspondence to an end but to no resolution, not even on the note struck by Howe in his very first letter: "I strongly believe it should be possible for people in the anti-CP left to maintain decent relations even while sharply disagreeing with each other. I hope it will be possible."[10]

Hook and Howe were both raised in immigrant Jewish households in New York City, had started as Marxists in their teens, became anti-Stalinist socialists in the circle of the New York intellectuals, and were in the late 1940s and early fifties outspoken opponents of both Communism and McCarthyism. But the fact that they were, as Howe later put it, "in almost complete agreement on guiding political principles" did not prevent Howe, the democratic socialist, and Hook, the ex-radical and nominal social democrat, from differing, sometimes sharply, in the responses they made to actual events. They had taken, for example, clashing positions on the Second World War, Howe severely critical and Hook supportive of the Allied effort against fascism. And from that point they tangled with one another sporadically over a period of four decades.

Even when there was apparent confluence between Hook and Howe in the late 1940s and early 1950s, as in their reaction to the confessions of ex-Communist Whittaker Chambers, there were pointed differences between the two men. Among the many repentant former Stalinists who were rushing to atone for their sins, Chambers, a thoroughgoing absolutist who had traded in his Marxism for a new monolithic faith in the God of Christendom, was the most sensational. He had in 1948 provided evidence that former State Department aide Alger Hiss was guilty of spying for the Soviet Union, and in both his testimony before Congress and his 1952 memoir *Witness*, Chambers indicted not only Communists and fellow-travelers but all liberals and leftists as morally complicit in Hiss's guilt.[11]

Both Howe and Hook accused Chambers, justly, of absolutism (to which, at times, they themselves had been prone) and of irresponsibly lumping together progressives, New Dealers, liberals, and socialists with Communists.[12] Particularly galling to both men was Chambers's characterizing as incorrigible, godless, leftist totalitarians all those democratic socialists and left-liberals, like Howe and Hook, who had been fighting the anti-Communist battle all along. Howe was particularly angry that Chambers ultimately portrayed socialists as "allies of communism, even if, in mere fact, they perished resisting it." Members of the independent left, Howe said, had suffered terribly at the hands of men like Whittaker Chambers when Chambers was a Communist, and they were still under attack from Chambers and his ilk now that Chambers had switched sides. Hook, like Howe, also angrily charged Chambers with being deaf to the screams of the victims of Communist totalitarianism and for recklessly ignoring distinctions between "progressives, liberals and men of good will" on the one side and Communists on the other.[13]

Despite the similarities, however, there were important differences in emphasis and implication in the criticisms made by the two men. Hook was more openly admiring of Chambers for his "courage" and "intelligence," and he touted the public repentance of ex-Stalinists as a tool to expose and deflate the Communist movement.[14] Hook did not want to see the confessions of former Communists do damage to the democratic left, and he defended the theoretical "privilege" of a radical movement to exist. But, unlike Howe, Hook seemed to wonder whether much on the left was actually worth salvaging. Irving Howe and Harold Rosenberg and other dissenters remained unwavering in their commitment to socialism. Hook, on the other hand, even as he continued to identify as a man of the democratic left, failed to join in advocating any kind of leftist vision.

There were, however, positive moments between Howe and Hook that went beyond politics. In 1961 or 1962 when the two antagonists were at Stanford University, Howe, recently divorced and alone, "was in a rather deep depression," and Hook expressed his genuine concern by persistently asking whether Howe was eating enough. Hook's wife, in a classic Jewish gesture of solace and solicitousness, brought Howe some chicken soup, which moved him, he said, to "speechlessness." Sometime later in the decade, Howe and Hook, though still in disagreement on some things, had begun an occasional exchange of cordial, professional letters. And by the late 1980s, even though Hook remained a fiercely stalwart Cold Warrior, they had come together in relatively friendly embrace in their attempt to save higher education from the excesses of multiculturalism and political correctness.[15]

But in the forties and fifties there was mostly acrimony. Even as Hook and Howe were battling it out over the civil liberties of Communist teachers, they were also at each other over the participation of the Americans for Intellectual Freedom (AIF), Hook's liberal anti-Communist group, at the Waldorf World Peace Conference. In 1949 the American Communist Party, seriously declining in membership, reputation, and influence, made a last major effort, along with sympathetic cultural groups and a number of figures from the Soviet Union, to gather people together at Carnegie Hall and the Waldorf Astoria in New York City in behalf of their views of the Cold War. Some of the sponsors, including Leonard Bernstein, Marlon Brando, Albert Einstein, and Aaron Copland, were neither Stalinists nor fellow-travelers but naive supporters of the conference who sincerely hoped to promote peace. Most of the women and men connected with organizing the event, however, were Stalinists or pro-Stalinist progressives.

The conference was held only a year after the Soviet-supported Stalinist takeover in Czechoslovakia, and an open justification of Soviet behavior would have alienated even long-term fellow travelers. The Communist Party, therefore, kept discreetly in the background, defending Russian policy only indirectly. The anti-Stalinist liberals of AIF, however, attempted to deflate the conference by publishing materials disclosing its true sponsorship. The AIF also challenged the participating Russians' claim to be free intellectual agents and pointed out that the conference organizers failed to include any known anti-Stalinists among their speakers. The organization did not, however, make its presence at the conference forcefully felt, nor did it identify itself with *socialist* anti-Stalinism explicitly.

In his report on the conference for *Labor Action*, Howe, apparently attempting to imply that the AIF had been too quiet at the Waldorf, made a point of saying that most of the anti-Stalinists who spoke out in criticism, including himself, Dwight Macdonald, Mary McCarthy, Robert Lowell, and Norman Mailer (a sponsor of the conference), were not officially connected with "the Hook opposition."[16] This remark caught Hook's attention and moved him to characterize Howe's article as an example of "the pattern of distortion, invention and omission" in Howe's writing. But Howe's report and another he did for *Partisan Review* one month later, while not uncritical, were quite fair to the AIF. Howe credited the organization and many of its members who were at the Waldorf Astoria with at least disturbing the "conference's sense of unanimity." He also praised the group, on the one hand, for attacking the State Department's denial of visas to Communist delegates from England and France, and on the other, for exposing to the public the fraudulent nature of the conference itself. And he wrote to Hook saying, with some justice, that his references to the AIF were, "as a whole, not hostile, if only because the AIF did a pretty good job."[17]

Part of the tension between the two men, reflective of an important splintering among the New York intellectuals, no doubt stemmed from the fact that Howe's anti-Stalinism was firmly rooted in the socialist camp, whereas the anti-Stalinism of the AIF and of Hook, who was still at least theoretically on the democratic left, was much less clearly connected to a radical vision or to activist socialism. Indeed, Irving Howe accused many intellectuals nominally on the left, including Sidney Hook, of having little or no politics, except what he called the politics of "Stalinophobia." So calcified were the intellectuals, Howe charged, so blinded by their fear and hatred of Stalinism were they, that they could see no other evils nor be moved to act against them. Neither Jim Crow nor poverty elicited a reaction. "Only Stalinism," Howe wrote, "rouses their feelings. Only Stalinism can jolt them into making an occasional political response."[18]

Furthermore and just as important, Howe argued, intellectuals affected by Stalinophobia seemed more committed to fighting Communists and Communist sympathizers than to protecting them and civil liberties in general against the often demagogic nature of congressional investigations. But Howe and other left intellectuals, including Harold Rosenberg, Paul Goodman, Meyer Schapiro, and Lewis Coser, all of whom later helped launch *Dissent*, felt that they—and perhaps they alone—could wage what they considered an indispensable two-front war: on the one hand against Stalinism, and on the other against the Stalinophobia that led intellectuals to overlook or even support violations of civil liberties, as in the case of the University of Washington, and only a little later in the even more insidious and widespread case of Joseph McCarthy's anti-Communist crusade.

Only through this two-front war could anti-Communism be protected against being co-opted by ideological reactionaries. Only in this way could the distinction between left and right anticommunism be maintained, and important social problems beyond Stalinism, like segregation, poverty, and inequality, be addressed. Only in this way could civil liberties be protected. And civil liberties would be a topic of major concern from the very first issue of *Dissent*. But this was still some four years away. In the meantime, there were other magazines, other writers, and other organizations to confront.

Irving Howe and the other "dissenters" were convinced that *Partisan Review* and *Commentary*, despite their liberal anticommunism, were insensitive to the dangers of McCarthyism. But because *Partisan Review* editor Philip Rahv occasionally opposed McCarthyism, if only timidly, *Commentary* was Howe's primary target. Howe suspected that *Commentary* not only acquiesced in but also approved of some of the means and ends of McCarthy's anti-leftism. And his suspicions were reinforced by many statements made in *Commentary* in the early 1950s.

Commentary editors did say that "protecting American institutions from Communist infiltration without at the same time defeating our own traditions of civil liberty" was a "devilishly complex" problem. But ultimately (and especially after the Communist takeover in China in 1949 and during the war in Korea), the magazine found itself in the camp of those liberal anti-Communists who were more worried about the threat of Communism and Soviet expansionism and less about civil liberties, more worried about conspiracy and less about a viable future for the anti-Communist Left in the United States. This was revealed most clearly in an article by Irving Kristol in 1952. Kristol did not approve of McCarthy; indeed, he labeled him an "irresponsible" and "vulgar demagogue." But he went to considerable lengths to disparage the idea that the senator from Wisconsin constituted a serious threat to American liberties. Kristol himself confessed later: "I did not disassociate myself from McCarthy as vigorously as I should have." Instead, he attacked liberals—harshly and directly. Several paragraphs in his essay unjustly called into question the authenticity of the anticommunism of everyone on the liberal Left, including the anti-Stalinists. "Liberals," Kristol wrote, "are convinced that it is only they who truly understand Communism and who thoughtfully oppose it. They are nonetheless mistaken, and it is a mistake on which McCarthy waxes fat. For there is one thing the American people know about Senator McCarthy: he, like them, is unequivocally anti-Communist. About the spokesmen for American liberalism, they feel they know no such thing. And with some justification."[19]

Later in the same year, Elliot Cohen, the senior editor of *Commentary*, underscored Kristol's dismissal of the menace of the Wisconsin demagogue. Senator McCarthy, Cohen wrote, "remains in the popular mind an unreliable second-string blowhard; his *only* support as a great national figure is from the fascinated fears of the intelligentsia." Nathan Glazer, an associate editor, did attack McCarthy more than once in the pages of *Commentary* in the early fifties. Indeed, in March 1953, in order "to repair the damage" to *Commentary*'s liberal reputation created by Irving Kristol's article, Glazer wrote an excellent analysis of McCarthyism; but the the conclusion of the piece seemed logically unconnected to everything that went before it:

> All that Senator McCarthy can do on his own authority that someone equally unpleasant and not a Senator can't, is to haul people down to Washington for a grilling by his committee. It is a shame and an outrage that Senator McCarthy should remain in the Senate; yet I cannot see that it is an imminent danger to personal liberty in the United States.[20]

These statements by Cohen and Glazer constituted, in Howe's words, "a kind of backhanded apology . . . for McCarthyism." Nathan Glazer himself admitted later that he was uneasy with the positions he and other *Commentary* writers took on McCarthyism. The *Commentary* crowd's "attack on Communism," he said, "was so forceful" that they failed to face fully the danger to civil liberties, and failed to understand the nature, or the appeal, of the people attacking those liberties.[21] McCarthyism unfortunately was not, as editor Elliot Cohen would have it, simply a figment of the imagination of the intelligentsia. It was no "reign of terror," but, McCarthyism had, for a time, significant support in America that cut across regional and class lines and was especially pronounced among old-line Republicans. And it did great damage to persons, to civil liberties, and to the American justice system generally.[22] Even Norman Podhoretz, a third-generation New York intellectual and long-term editor of *Commentary*, who went from left of liberal in the 1950s and early 1960s to neoconservatism by 1970, said in 1998 (long after he had dropped the "neo"), that combating Stalinist "ideas and activities through demagogic congressional investigations, and . . . putting people in prison or throwing them out of work, was disgraceful and disgusting." And "it was finally true," he said, echoing Irving Howe's words of a half-century earlier, "that the hard anti-Communists around *Partisan Review* and *Commentary* in the early 1950s had been more concerned with fighting against the ideas of the Communists and their liberal fellow-travelers than with defending them against their congressional inquisitors."[23]

There was, particularly before and during the Second World War, a genuine threat to national security posed by Communists who took their orders from a Moscow intent on destroying its ideological enemies. But there were many American Communists who were not spies and who did no harm and yet suffered by going to jail or losing their jobs, their reputations, their marriages, or their health. Moreover, by the early 1950s, when Senator Joseph McCarthy got around to charging that there were several hundred card-carrying Communists in the State Department and even more in other "vulnerable" institutions, the Soviet espionage effort had come to a virtual standstill. At that same time, Communism in America had lost most of whatever influence it had once possessed.[24]

One of the great ironies of this period of the Cold War is that at the very moment when the issue of Communist espionage became a dangerous political obsession for Americans, it had already become a question better left to students of the past than to manipulative and opportunistic politicians. Perhaps it is even more ironic that in such a context of Communist weakness some American intellectuals allowed their hatred of Communism to become so strident and indiscriminate as to deflect them from an adequate resistance to McCarthyism. Some of these intellectuals, including Sidney Hook, were members of the American Committee for Cultural Freedom (ACCF), which was founded in 1951 to counteract pro-Communist propaganda.[25] Not invited to join the organization, however, were Irving Howe, Lewis Coser, Meyer Schapiro, and Philip Rahv, all of whom were more absolute about the protection of civil liberties than most of the members of the ACCF.

Irving Howe and his friends were well aware that American Communists, even in their period of decline, could constitute a threat to the security of the United States, and they had in any case "no fondness" for American-bred Stalinists. "Politically," Howe said later, "we were bitter opponents, but we took, in the 1950s, a strict civil libertarian position."[26] Howe's group, unlike the ACCF, vigorously opposed the undiscriminating, heavy-handed persecutions of Communists and fellow-travelers. Repression, Howe felt, played directly into the hands of the Communists by creating sympathetic martyrs. Even more important, the persecutions, which ran roughshod over civil liberties, were "a violation of American traditions and principles."[27]

Howe was aware that in regard to civil liberties, the ACCF was a "mixed bag," with James Burnham and Max Eastman, outspoken defenders of Joseph McCarthy on the right, and with Arthur Schlesinger, Jr., and David Riesman, strenuous critics of McCarthyism, on the left. But all four men ultimately resigned from the organization, leaving a liberal middle whose anticommunism, according to Howe, "was too blunt . . . too crude" and kept most of the members from fully recognizing "the danger to civil liberties which the government-sponsored—and McCarthy-inspired—hysteria was creating at home." After Schlesinger resigned, he wrote a piece for *Partisan Review* that said in part:

> I cannot go along with those who profess a belief in cultural freedom, on the one hand, and refuse to condemn McCarthyism, on the other—those who argue, apparently, that McCarthyism is a genial excess of political zeal, a Washington matter with no larger reverberations in our culture. The real *trahison des clercs* lies, in my judgment, with those who collaborate with the foes of the mind—whether they are the demonic foes of the mind, like Hitler and Stalin, or the gangster foes, like McCarthy and McCarran. We cannot hope to preserve cultural freedom and cultural pluralism in a society where political freedom and political pluralism become impossible.[28]

There were members over the years who did recognize the dangers to which Howe and Schlesinger had referred, including Ralph Ellison, James Farrell, Diana Trilling, and Norman Thomas. Even ACCF chairman Sidney Hook, admitted, unlike some in his group, that McCarthyism was as dangerous as Communism. He publicly and repeatedly denounced the "irresponsible and morally scandalous methods of McCarthy," and in 1953 he published a long letter to the *New York Times* condemning McCarthy and calling for a national referendum to retire the senator from public life. The organization itself in 1954 sponsored the publication of a book by James Rorty and Moshe Decter attacking McCarthy. But on the whole, Irving Howe was right in his description of the ACCF as ambivalent. The group, in its characteristic style, had considered a resolution introduced in 1952 by two of its officers, Daniel Bell and Irving Kristol (both classmates of Howe at CCNY), condemning Communism *and* "certain types of anticommunism," but it was tabled—and never resubmitted.[29]

Had Irving Howe and other anti-Stalinist socialists like Lewis Coser and Meyer Schapiro been invited to join the ACCF, they would, Howe said, "of course have refused." Howe needed a group on the left which would take as unequivocal a position against McCarthyism as against Communism, and one whose anticommunism would aim not only to expose, discredit, and repulse Communists, but to salvage the possibility of democratic socialism. *Dissent* was the vehicle, Howe thought, to make this happen.[30]

By the early months of 1953, while Howe and his growing family were still living on Grover Avenue in Princeton, he took important steps to make the magazine a reality. His energy and enthusiasm for politics and literature, and his need to move back and forth between the two, as well as to make them meet, appeared to be unbounded. Howe had only recently completed his book on Faulkner and was in the midst of his Princeton University lecture series on politics and the novel, as well as his work with Eleazer Greenberg for the *Treasury of Yiddish Stories*, when he asked a small number of important potential *Dissent* supporters and writers to meet.

Among the group gathered at the Nassau Tavern on Palmer Square, one of Princeton's favorite watering holes, were Dennis Wrong, the Princeton political sociologist and Irving's friend whose anti-McCarthyism was as pronounced as his own; Joseph Buttinger, who had been a leader of the young socialists in Austria after they were forced underground following the fascist coup in 1934; and Muriel Gardner, Buttinger's wife, an eminent psychologist in her own right who had risked her life in the 1930s to rescue endangered Austrian radicals. Gardner was a wealthy heiress but had strong socialist convictions, and Howe hoped she and her husband would donate significant sums of money for *Dissent*.[31]

Soon after this meeting, Howe drove up to Wellesley to see Lewis and Rose Coser, both of whom had been involved from the very start, indeed as early as 1949, in the planning of a new socialist journal. The three talked at length about the future "glory" of their projected magazine, to which Lew had given the name *Dissent*, and how it would be "unhampered by the cowardice and caution of what passed at the time for the left-of-center press."[32] A short time later, the original group of Princeton and Wellesley planners was joined by several others, including Stanley Plastrik and Emanuel Geltman, Howe's friends who, like him, had been members of Max Shachtman's Independent Socialist

League; Bernard Rosenberg, sociologist and independent radical who was Coser's colleague at Brandeis; and Norman Mailer, the author of the celebrated World War II novel *The Naked and the Dead* (1948) and dozens of provocative articles published in *Partisan Review* and *Esquire* magazine.[33]

More friends were needed, not so much for planning as for writing and for donations to help launch *Dissent* and keep it afloat. About fifty people, many of them former followers of Max Shachtman, responded to Howe's call for a meeting, and most were enthusiastic about the project even though they were asked to contribute money and to write articles for no pay. Meyer Schapiro, the great art historian and socialist, never fulfilled his promise to write, but he did join the editorial board, lending it stature, moral support, and intellectual eminence. "It mattered," Howe said, "that Meyer Schapiro attended some board meetings, speaking in his passionately lucid way about socialism as the fulfillment of the Western tradition." Perhaps as important, Schapiro persuaded some of his wealthy friends in the art world to contribute money. In addition, several Abstract Expressionists, whose work often reflected the kind of cultural critique of capitalism offered by Schapiro and Howe, donated paintings to be auctioned in support of *Dissent*, and over the years many artists, including William de Kooning and Robert Motherwell, continued to help sustain the democratic socialist journal.[34]

In the spring of 1953, Howe wrote Dwight Macdonald and asked to use the old *Politics* subscribers list to solicit funds for *Dissent*. Howe explained that he and his friends were trying to start "a socialist magazine: non-party without a 'line,' but with a general radical outlook." They planned, Howe said, to run the venture "on a shoe string, if we can get the shoe string." He reminded his old friend and erstwhile protagonist that they had not seen one another for years. "Right now," Howe said, "I'm tied up with a new baby, but we must really meet sometime . . . to talk." In the meantime, Macdonald sent Howe the subscribers list as well as a prospectus for a periodical (*The Critic*) that Macdonald himself was planning. Howe found the prospectus "interesting," and thought there was "no real conflict" between the two magazines. *Dissent*, Howe confessed, was "on a much more modest scale," and in any case "people writing for one could write for the other, if they cared to." More important, Howe said, given the difficulties of funding, neither project was likely to "pan out."[35]

Despite Howe's fears, the dissenters did manage to scrape together more than a thousand dollars, mostly from friends. The Buttingers matched this amount at the end of 1953, making it possible to dream at least of a full year's run of the new quarterly. Joseph Buttinger and Muriel Gardner continued, over the years, to give generously, often making up more than half of *Dissent's* annual deficit. According to many who had served on the *Dissent* board, the couple never tried to control the magazine, nor, as Howe put it, did they act as "mere dispensers of largesse but as true comrades."[36]

Howe and some of the other *Dissent* editors tried to persuade Macdonald to write for their magazine, but he was not particularly interested. By the time *Dissent* published its first issue at the start of 1954, Macdonald was busy writing for the *New Yorker* (transformed in the fifties by editor William Shawn into a serious magazine) and was, in any case, apparently worn out by polemics. He would not be attracted to political activism again until the confrontations of the New Left captured his attention in the 1960s. Although Macdonald himself did not accept the invitation to write for *Dissent*, many who agreed to be contributors had once written for Macdonald's *Politics*, including Coser and Howe themselves, C. Wright Mills, Harvey Swados, and Paul Goodman. There were other similarities, too, between *Politics* and Howe's new journal. Just as *Politics* had been formed in the mid-1940s to take over the dissident role that *Partisan Review* had begun to abandon, *Dissent* was created in the mid-1950s to become the vehicle for radical conversation and analysis that was lost when *Politics* collapsed in 1949.

In a statement of intentions published in the first issue of *Dissent*, Howe and the other editors committed themselves to combating conformism and promised to "defend democratic, humanist and radical values," and to confront and expose the evils of totalitarianism "whether fascist or Stalinist." As important, they also expressed a desire to initiate "a frank and friendly dialogue with liberal opinion" as well as to reassess "socialist doctrines," especially in light of American political and cultural life. Although they announced that the magazine would be open to "a wide arc of opinion," their statement, by excluding not only Stalinist and "totalitarian fellow-travelers" but also "those former radicals who have signed their peace with society as it is," actually invited participation from a rather narrow spectrum of political opinion.[37]

Nathan Glazer, reviewing the first issue of *Dissent* for *Commentary*, excoriated the new editors for their exclusions and characterized

Howe's magazine as representative of the self-righteous isolation of "the left wing of socialism." One of *Dissent*'s own editors, Harold Orlans, also criticized the statement of exclusion, and before the third issue, the magazine dropped the offending sentences from its declaration of purpose, which continued to appear inside the front cover for a number of years. Glazer, however, objected not only to the statement of exclusion. He thought "the whole thing . . . an unmitigated disaster." And he told his *Commentary* readers, "If this is socialism, no further explanations are required for its failure to catch on in America."[38]

Glazer, who was particularly offended by *Dissent*'s hostility toward *Commentary*, seemed to expect the new magazine, in a single issue, to spell out with intricate specificity its goals, its case against conformism, what it meant precisely by the term socialism, and how it intended to promote and implement its political vision in a resistant America. His attack was rambling and excessive (even as he accused *Dissent* of carrying on "the unpleasant tradition of vituperative intemperance begun by Marx"); but he did point up some deficiencies of that first issue, which even Howe described later as "a mixture of academic stuffiness and polemical bristle."[39] Glazer focused, for example, on the apparently naive, and certainly vague statement that the *Dissent* staffers "share a refusal to countenance one man's gain at the expense of his brother," noting that some of those staffers also wrote for profit-making magazines and held academic posts at prestigious institutions (including Howe and Coser). And he was particularly bothered by Howe's reductionist notion that "former radicals" had "sold out" rather than had changed their outlook after reexamination, or in response to changing conditions. Glazer rejected what he called "the perpetual vulgar ascription of material motives to explain intellectual positions"—a fault he now saw "writ large in *Dissent*."[40]

Glazer was certainly on target in some of his criticism, but he was asking a great deal of the first issue of *Dissent*, or of any magazine. Moreover, he was himself guilty of vagueness and distortion. For example, although Glazer claimed that the socialist editors of *Dissent* were pacifists, several, including Howe, had served in the army during World War II, had acquiesced, even if nervously, in the Western military response to the crisis in Berlin in 1948, and supported the use of armed forces in Korea against Stalinist expansionism. One of Glazer's nastier accusations was that the alleged pacifism of the *Dissent* socialists would lead to the Soviets becoming "comfortably established" throughout the world. Glazer not only exaggerated the importance of what a small group of leftist intellectuals, far from the centers of power, thought about the Cold War; he seemed to take the position that the primary responsibility of intellectuals was to determine how to keep the Russians out of Rome, Paris, London, and Hanoi.

Glazer's charge also neglected the fact that Howe and several other dissenters, in addition to backing the American military effort in East Asia, had made proposals about foreign policy that they thought might help stop the spread of Communism, without resorting to an atomic war. They had supported, for example, the liberal anti-Communist forces in Italy and France, and they had backed the Marshall Plan for rebuilding the economies of Western Europe.[41] Some of the *Dissent* editors, even as they touted these potential alternatives to a militarized containment of Communism, had to remind Glazer that the democratic socialism they were reformulating and promoting was not only something they thought just, but also very much part of an anti-Stalinist strategy. "Socialist Norway," it was argued, by way of example, was NATO's outpost in Scandinavia, and "socialist Britain" was America's most important ally in Europe and Asia.[42]

Perhaps if Nathan Glazer had given Howe's magazine the benefit of a number of issues before he wrote his "review," he would have demonstrated his more characteristic openness of mind instead of a narrow and impatient dismissiveness. In any case, in the very month that Glazer was attacking *Dissent* for its blind adherence to "left-wing socialism," Hal Draper of the Independent Socialist League (ISL) published an acerbic critique of Howe's magazine in *Labor Action*, charging the editors, particularly Howe, Stanley Plastrik, and Emanuel Geltman (all former members of the ISL) with backsliding "from socialism to liberalism." Draper mocked the fact that Howe in the very first issue of *Dissent* raised "the question of whether it would not be better today to abandon the word socialism." And the ISL actually went so far as to pass a motion prohibiting members from writing for *Dissent* without "special permission."[43] Although outraged by these negative assessments, especially Glazer's, Howe was also pleased. Getting attacked from right and left simultaneously "delighted us," Howe said later, "since the one thing a new magazine needs is attention."[44]

What both Glazer and Draper missed was the fact that *Dissent*'s announced task was to carve out a viable and respectable position somewhere between the ideological absolutism of Communism (which they steadfastly rejected) and an emerging affirmative pragmatism (which they also resisted). Or, as Howe put it only a little later in a letter to Lewis Mumford, *Dissent* was "seeking to find a radical path between Stalinist totalitarianism on the one hand and the *de facto* acquiescence in capitalist society that has become the policy of most intellectuals on the other."[45] In his attack, Glazer failed to mention the fierce anti-Stalinism of Howe and the others, or *Dissent*'s promise "to reassert the libertarian values of the socialist ideal," and Draper neglected, or purposely ignored, Howe's emphatic statement that "the accent of *Dissent* will be radical. Its tradition will be the tradition of democratic socialism."[46]

The Dissenters wanted to examine recent history, discuss past political visions, and identify "what in the socialist tradition remains alive and what needs to be discarded or modified." In light of the dissipation and fragmentation of the socialist movement in the United States in the postwar period, Howe and others at *Dissent* flirted with the idea of working within the "left wing" of the Democratic Party and had even voted for Adlai Stevenson in 1952. But Eisenhower, in a landslide victory, had been elected president, and the Republicans had captured control of Congress. And *Dissent*'s initial editorial statement in 1954 reflected the editors' disappointment. They swore off all political organizations, and their expectations of momentous political change, via democratic socialist activism, were minimal. "As for significant social or political struggle," Howe asked Draper, "Why not be honest? You're out of it, I'm out of it, almost all socialists in the U.S. are out of it."[47] More important, at least for the moment, according to Howe, was a willingness to recognize common aims with those radicals and liberals who did not consider themselves socialist.[48]

Despite Howe's criticism of "the dominant school of liberalism" (in which he included Sidney Hook, David Riesman, and Lionel Trilling, among many others) for its dogmatic antidogmatism, he came very close, through the 1950s, to arguing for a synthesis of liberalism and socialism. Howe and many others at *Dissent*, especially Coser and the economist Ben Seligman, had traveled from Marxian socialism to democratic socialism and had come to see the benefits of decentralization of power, of a society organized along pluralistic, participatory lines, and of the pragmatic and practical over the ideological.[49] Howe came to believe that the socialist imagination, at its most serious, was in a dialectical relationship with classical liberalism: cooperating on the one hand in defending and expanding the boundaries of freedom, and on the other, critical of a system that failed to extend fully its democratic concerns from the political to the economic arena. "At the very time when it was becoming fashionable to sneer at liberalism," Howe said nearly a quarter century later, at *Dissent*, "we wanted to bring socialist politics and liberal values," especially devotion to equality, tolerance, openness and experiment, "closer together."[50]

With the liberal values of *Commentary*, however, Howe wanted nothing to do. The "sophisticated liberals" who wrote for and read *Commentary*, Howe said, once again were unaware of or seriously underestimated the threat to civil liberties posed by Joseph McCarthy. The most distressing development, Howe insisted, was not that the McCarthyites and other "reactionaries" attack, but that the *Commentary* "liberals hardly remember how to counter-attack." The writers grouped around *Commentary*, who considered themselves "hardheaded liberals," did, after all, "dislike" McCarthyism, but "what really stirred their blood," Howe said, was doing battle against those few remaining dissenters whom Sidney Hook labeled "knee-jerk liberals." Hook and the *Commentary* crowd, Howe insisted, worried less about McCarthy, and more about the "anti-anticommunists"—those leftists who gained credibility and stature from the struggle against McCarthy's violations of civil liberties.[51]

There was some truth to Howe's charge against the *Commentary* liberals, as we have seen, but all too often, in *Dissent* and other political writings, Howe, at least until about 1956 or 1957, displayed little of the complexity of vision and sensitivity to nuance that marked his literary pieces. He may have been aware of this himself. His saturation in literature in pursuit of "a world more attractive," may even have functioned for him, in part, as a way of ameliorating his "attack mode." In any case, Howe's attack on Hook in particular was not entirely fair. It is true that Hook suffered from what Howe called "Stalinophobia" and that he was much more focused on anti-Communism than on civil liberties, but he was openly, strongly, and explicitly anti-McCarthy. And some eight months before the appearance of Howe's *Dissent* piece attacking Hook and his *Commentary* followers, Hook had published his long letter in the *New York Times* calling for a nationwide movement to remove McCarthy from power permanently.[52]

Howe continued, in Dissent and elsewhere, to denounce McCarthyism and what he saw as a conformist, submissive liberalism right up to McCarthy's censure by the Senate in December 1954. In fact, just as Dissent was making its first appearance, Howe published in Partisan Review one of his most provocative and wide-ranging assaults, "This Age of Conformity."

7

The Age of Conformity

IRVING HOWE'S "This Age of Conformity," published in 1954, was a stridently aggressive critique of American society and culture. Essentially an extension of his critical response to the complacently affirmative tone of "Our Country and Our Culture" (the intellectuals' symposium printed in the pages of *Partisan Review* in 1952), the new, longer critique was primarily the result of Howe's continued musings on the culture and politics of the torpid fifties. But it also came directly out of his relationship with Philip Rahv, the editor of *Partisan Review*. After Howe started teaching at Brandeis in the fall of 1953, he came to New York City every two months or so and regularly spent time with Rahv. They took long walks through Manhattan, the kind Howe and his radical CCNY friends had taken in the late 1930s, and they talked about many things, including "the rightward turn" of their intellectual friends, especially those associated with *Commentary. Partisan Review* was itself surrendering to the postwar trend of complacency and conformity. But Howe could not bring himself to say this, especially after Rahv, late in 1953, asked him to take on those intellectuals who had retreated from progressive politics. Rahv particularly wanted his friend Irving "to smash" the New Critics, whose conservative social outlook both he and Howe abhorred. Howe was troubled. He had, after all, felt closer to the New Critics than to the "radical" critics during his short teaching stint at the University of Washington in Seattle, and he was hesitant to promote a victory for politics over literature; but, after some arm twisting from Rahv, Howe agreed to write "This Age of Conformity."[1]

Howe claimed that the essay was not designed "to berate *anyone*," but, as he confessed with some embarrassment a quarter-century later, he had ended up writing a "scatter-shot piece" attacking "almost *everyone*"—mostly other New York intellectuals—for their increasing attachment to established institutions, and "for the growing conservative mood of the moment."[2] Sidney Hook was attacked (again) for discovering "merit" in the Smith Act; Irving Kristol, for minimizing the McCarthyite threat to civil liberties; Mary McCarthy, a former editor of *Partisan Review*, for failing to see that vast material and social inequalities scarred the land she called, without irony, "America the Beautiful." Lionel Trilling was criticized for praising the wedding of intellect and power, and for pronouncing the contemporary cultural situation distinctly improved compared to three decades earlier. David Riesman, Arthur Schlesinger, Jr., and, by implication, Daniel Bell and John Kenneth Gailbraith, were brought to task for not criticizing American culture and society with nearly enough political rigor. Howe also attacked Bertrand Russell and Simone de Beauvoir for their "malicious and ignorant" description of postwar America as suffering under a McCarthyist "reign of terror," and he continued his attack on *Commentary* (in which he had published more than a dozen pieces between 1946 and 1952), as an apologist for American capitalism and middle-class values. Howe even attacked the editors of *Partisan Review*, the magazine in which his essay appeared, for having abandoned the combination of literary and political radicalism that was once its founding principle.

The essay was an attempt to explain "the power of the conformist impulse in our time," and to show that somewhere between the wrongheaded ideas of those who saw in the current moment only "terror," and the indifference of those who saw only health, there was a "simple truth: that intellectual freedom in the United States was under severe attack and that the intellectuals," comfortable with their new postwar opportunities in government, publishing, and the universities, "have, by and large, shown a painful lack of militancy in defending the rights which are a precondition of their existence."[3]

One of the chief culprits in all of this, Howe thought, was conventional centrist liberalism. He agreed with Lionel Trilling's statement that liberalism had become the dominant, perhaps even the only, intellectual tradition in the United States. This prevalence, Howe argued, did yield substantial benefits: it made Americans properly skeptical of fanaticism and absolutism; and it permitted the hope "that any revival of American radicalism will acknowledge not only its break with liberalism, but also its roots in the liberal tradition" of democratic freedoms and civil libertarianism.[4] But at the same time, through its ability to homogenize all political tendencies, through its nearly total support of capitalism, and by its emphasis on moderation, centrist liberalism contributed significantly to complacency and conformity among intellectuals. Indeed, Howe said, "in America there is today neither opportunity nor need for conservatism (since the liberals do [what is] necessary themselves.)" This was especially the case, Howe argued, in regard to *Commentary*, which, he said, skillfully and systematically promoted liberalism as a strategy for conforming to established institutions, and for adapting to, and benefiting from, the American status quo.[5]

The conformity piece, as Howe admitted later, was "a little unfair . . . a little excessive . . . a little overly strident." But it correctly identified the conformist trend in the intellectual world of the 1950s, the new postwar disposition to see mainly virtue in the American model, and it focused on the essential need for the intellectual to be a critic, to stand apart from the governing institutions of society, to cry out "that the fish stank," since as Howe said, "many of the fish did stink."[6] Howe sympathized with those who had often felt frustrated by their inability to implement their ideas, but he argued that intellectuals, in attaching themselves to the seats of power, inevitably surrender their freedom of expression, thereby becoming even more powerless. When intellectuals "become absorbed into the accredited institutions of society," Howe wrote, "they not only lose their traditional rebelliousness but to one extent or another *they cease to function as intellectuals.*"[7]

The conscious hungering for power was not Howe's main target, however. Nor was the materialism or greed of the all-too-human intellectuals his main concern. There was nothing wrong, Howe said, about the fact that he, and many other intellectuals, had begun in the fifties to achieve a modest material success by teaching, by writing articles and books of literary criticism, or by publishing stories in the *New Yorker* or *Esquire*. That Irving and his wife, Thalia, could plan a summer trip or put wine on the table when company came for dinner may have astonished these children of the depression, and may even have caused them some "unease," but as Howe said, it was "nothing to shoot anyone for."[8]

Ideology, Howe argued, much more than money, prompted the rejection of radicalism in the forties and an embrace of conservatism in the fifties. "When intellectuals turn bad," Howe wrote later, "it's always through large ideas rather than small amounts."[9] He did say that "some intellectuals" had indeed "sold out," but the thrust of his critique was directed at "the far more prevalent and far more insidious . . . attrition which destroys one's ability to stand firm and alone." The slippage into conformity and conservatism, along lines demanded by the Cold War, Howe wrote, paraphrasing Arthur Koestler, "is often a form of betrayal," a betrayal that occurs piecemeal, by way of "a chain of small compromises." Given the suffocatingly pro-American *Zeitgeist* which presses down upon us, Howe said, and given "the need to earn one's bread," it was difficult, even for those like himself who had tried to remain critically apart from institutions, to avoid becoming "responsible, moderate," and "tame."[10]

This tendency, Howe maintained, was reinforced by the inclination of intellectuals to see mostly improvement and positive value in the United States, the country which had, after all, emerged as the great liberal counter to totalitarianism, beginning in the 1930s with Nazi Germany and then, in the 1950s, with Stalin's Soviet Union. The proclivity to emphasize the legitimacy and elemental fairness of capitalism and the American socioeconomic system generally, Howe thought, was either the result of a blindness—to how much yet needed to be done in terms of economic and racial justice—or of "a weariness" that had overcome intellectuals, a lethargy stemming from the yearning "to remove themselves from the bloodied arena of historical action and choice" and settle more deeply, or comfortably, into the American center. In these ways, Howe contended, "established power and dominant intellectual tendencies" had come together in harmony. And this, he said, made "the temptation of conformism all the more acute," especially because the rewards (or "carrots," as he called them)—positions of apparent influence in government, publishing, and academia—were for once "real."[11]

Howe argued against this temptation. With a passion perhaps intensified by his own "descent" into institutional attachment at Brandeis University, Howe called for "a total estrangement from the sources of power and prestige." And in an overwrought sentence he no doubt later regretted (given his negative take on the "Beats"), Howe predicted that "even a blind unreasoning rejection of every aspect of our culture, would be far healthier [than attachment] if only because it would permit a free discharge of aggression."[12]

In a number of essays in the 1950s, the Columbia University historian Richard Hofstadter (on the periphery of the New York intellectual group and a future dear friend of Howe's), took issue, at least obliquely, with Howe's "anti-institutionalism." And later in *Anti-Intellectualism in American Life*, Hofstadter attacked Howe head on. Tweaking Howe by referring to him as "Professor Howe," Hofstadter named him as one of those "prophets of alienation" who measure intellectual merit by "the greatest possible degree of negativism." He scorned Howe's belief that the intellectual's primary responsibility was to make an assertion against society rather than to enlighten it or be enlightening about it. And although he shared Howe's concern about the domestication of the avant-garde, Hofstadter dismissed the notion that "accredited institutions" inevitably corrupt intellect.[13] The relationship between intellectuals and power was more complex than Howe had it, Hofstadter insisted. And, in any case, the only alternative to institutional support for intellectuals, he argued, "is the creation of a frustrated cultural lumpen proletariat." Hofstadter, like Howe, did counsel intellectuals against the tendency to focus only on power, but he also strongly warned them against becoming "more concerned with maintaining [a] sense of their own purity than with making their ideas effective."[14] This warning, from a man whom Howe saw as the personification of the independent public intellectual (despite his institutional affiliation), was one Howe himself would take to heart and heed (with some notable exceptions) beginning in the 1960s.

Howe did admit later that his essay was something of an indulgence in "gloomy forebodings," but in the piece, without giving up his central point about the need for change, he had anticipated some of Hofstadter's criticism. "Our world is neither to be flatly accepted nor rejected," he said, "it must be engaged, resisted and—who knows, perhaps still—transformed."[15] And on the same page as his call for "total estrangement," Howe suggested that in regard to compromising oneself, there was a "qualitative difference" between joining the academy and joining the government bureaucracy or the editorial staff.[16]

Recently appointed to the faculty of literature at Brandeis, Howe may have been engaging here in a degree of rationalization; but he was enjoying his teaching, which, more often than not, afforded him "the pleasure of stirring a young mind to knowledge and thought."[17] He took pleasure too in his interactions with university intellectuals, even with scholars, and he felt generally free of administrative interference. He was also reassured by the fact that his friend C. Wright Mills, an early supporter of *Dissent* magazine and a professor of sociology at Columbia since 1946, was, as Hofstadter put it, "trying courageously in these times of danger and complacency, to confront" from within the walls of the academy "the large issues of the world," and "from a notably rebellious point of view."[18]

Howe was not entirely sanguine about the academy—certainly not as sanguine as Alfred Kazin, who (like Irving, without a Ph.D., but five years older) had, by the mid-fifties, held posts at several colleges, including Harvard, Smith, and Amherst. Kazin, again like Howe, was a child of poor immigrants, a young Jewish intellectual from a Yiddish-speaking home, and a fiercely independent writer unconnected to any school of literary criticism. And he, too, saw himself as "a man of letters," an intellectual rather than a scholar, and neither he nor Howe ever wrote for the academic journals. But Kazin was not particularly political, and even though he disliked the academicism of his colleagues, he was less suspicious of the university, which he saw as a patron—one supporting the creation of literature and allowing the writer and the intellectual to fulfill a role once sought outside of educational institutions.[19]

With the steady decline in the number of serious magazines and the shrinking opportunities for freelance writing in the postwar period, it was increasingly difficult for intellectuals to support themselves outside the academy. Edmund Wilson, a virtual hero of Howe's, was still an "independent," as were Harold Rosenberg and Paul Goodman, but these men were becoming the exceptions. And in time even Rosenberg and Goodman joined university faculties. Irving Howe, like them, faced "the need to earn one's bread." He desperately wanted to escape the "unpleasant hack work" he had been doing for *Time* magazine, and, with his growing family (Nicholas now four months old, and Nina past three) he could no longer be satisfied with the wretched pay scale of the more important periodicals. "I can't do a review for . . . the *New Republic*," he told Granville Hicks, "in less than 2-1/2–3 days, for which I will get . . . about $30. Instead of a source of additional income, [reviewing] becomes a drain *upon* one's income."[20]

Howe, as he confessed to the poet Theodore Roethke, took a full-time teaching position rather reluctantly, and he maintained what he called his "instinctive, probably irrational" suspicion of academic institutions; but at Brandeis, as early as the fall of 1953, he had begun to discover that scholarship done by men and women supported by universities could have "a value and a dignity of its own," and that there were professors who "really cared about ideas."[21] And so Howe came to insist, in his conformity essay, that the university was "different," for unlike many other established institutions, he said, it "is still committed to the ideology of freedom," and "many professors try hard and honestly to live by it."[22] The academy had its problems, Howe said, and it was not "the natural home of the intellect," but it was still the intellectual's "best bet" if she or he cannot subsist independently.

Even as he was becoming more comfortable as a professor, however, Howe managed to maintain some critical distance from the university. This is indicated by what Howe had to say when he turned, in his article, from social and political history to a consideration of conformity in literary life and thought. He called "preposterous" the "academic requirement that professors write books they don't want to write and no one wants to read." And in his effort to convince readers of the continued need for the avant-garde in the world of letters, he condemned the power of the Ph.D. system, which "grinds and batters personality into a mold of cautious routine," and which leads in the literary world to a general rigidity of opinion and taste.[23]

It was true that revolutionary works championed earlier by the avant-garde, like Eliot's *Wasteland* and Joyce's *Ulysses*, were now taught in the universities; but precisely because modernist literature had been made "respectable," according to Howe, it had become little more than a source for "raiding" by a middlebrow culture that opposes "everything that is serious and creative." And in a remarkable passage reflective of Howe's commitment to the continuing need for the experimental, and to the idea that the truly "new and better" is necessarily tied to the very best of the past, in literature as well as politics, Howe said that the central purpose of the avant-garde was "a struggle for literary standards . . . a defense not merely of modern innovation but of that traditional culture which was the source of modern innovation."[24]

Howe also anticipated a position he would develop more fully and espouse more forcefully some thirty years later, when he wrote that students have "a remarkable desire to be 'critics,' not as an accompaniment to the writing of poetry or the changing of the world or the study of man and God, but just critics—as if criticism were a *subject*." Literature, Howe said, had become mere raw material for critics who develop elaborate "schemes of structure and symbol," with no apparent regard for actual human experience.[25]

Howe had never thought the "social approach" to literature self-sufficient, but he had almost always made it an important part of his criticism. It was predictable, then, that he would follow Rahv in taking particular exception to the New Critics who, by emphasizing the text over history and biography, had made literature into a nearly independent category of experience. Howe had earlier credited the New

Critics (as he would again later) for helping to preserve the integrity of literary works, and for recognizing that those works often had an inherent value apart from their ability to illuminate the extraliterary. But Howe charged that in its purist devotion to literature, the New Criticism actually clothed a conservative bias. Despite the New Critics' proclamations of ideological neutrality, they used literary "tradition" to sanction a traditional morality or ideology and to oppose the experimental. And they "forgot" that literary tradition could be seen as the result of "a series of revolts, . . . sometimes more than literary, of generation against generation, of age against age."[26]

Howe's attack on the New Critics had political dimensions of its own, but he was forthright in identifying them. In his attempt, for example, to explain the growing prestige of the concept of "Original Sin" among the New Critics and among intellectuals generally, Howe pointed out how useful the idea of "'man's fallen nature'" was to conservatives and to battle-weary liberals, disillusioned by horrors of the twentieth century. The imperfectability of man, as conservatives and tired liberals liked to argue, made unrealistic the liberal-radical vision of the good society. But Howe, with relative ease, demonstrated through allusions to Rousseau and Marx that the vision of the good society did not depend on a belief in the "'unqualified goodness of man.'" Howe no longer believed, as he had written more than a decade earlier, that "the human being is a *completely adaptable organism*"; but when Eve bit the apple, Howe insisted, she did not predetermine "with one fatal crunch, that her progeny could work its way up to capitalism, and not a step further."[27]

After demonstrating that the liberal-radical vision of the good society did not depend on a belief in the perfectibility of man, Howe went on to connect the literary prestige of the doctrine of Original Sin to what he saw as the withdrawal of intellectuals from the arena of political activism (and even political criticism). This departure and their turn to religion in the search for "roots," Howe said, was a retreat from healthy "alienation" and skeptical autonomy. Modern writers and intellectuals, Howe said, quoting Philip Rahv, had once "'preferred alienation from the community to alienation from themselves.'" It was precisely the "lack of roots," Howe insisted, that had given them their speculative power. But now the pervasive talk about the "'need for roots,'" Howe continued, "veils a desire to compromise the tradition of intellectual independence" and diminishes the self through attachment to a party, a nation, or a religion.[28]

It is interesting to note that at the same moment that Howe was deriding the "need for roots" in the pages of *Partisan Review*, he said elsewhere, in reference to his upbringing by Jewish immigrant parents, that "in retrospect I can see how important this was to my life." It meant, among other things, "a home atmosphere of warm and binding love" and the inheritance of "a valuable tradition and style of life, no matter how I was later to deviate from it."[29] And in the same year as the conformity essay, Howe finished *A Treasury of Yiddish Stories*, co-edited with Eliezer Greenberg. He would produce or co-produce eight more important anthologies of Yiddish literature and letters between 1966 and 1987, and he wrote long, ambitious, historically rich introductions for all of these works, especially for *Yiddish Stories* and *A Treasury of Yiddish Poetry* (1969).[30] These were clearly steps in Howe's reconquest of Jewishness, as he himself recognizes in *A Margin of Hope*, and they were important preludes to *World of Our Fathers* (1976), his towering, popular book on the life of Jewish immigrants from Eastern Europe.

Howe's work on Yiddish was an act of critical salvage and another reflection of a conservative cultural instinct that lived alongside, and indeed fed, his political radicalism. Yiddish literary criticism, once a lively art, was after all on the verge of disappearance. Even in New York City, at the center of American literary circles, there was either condescension or utter indifference to the presence of a small but still "vibrant Yiddish culture that could be found, literally and symbolically, a few blocks away." But in the attempt to rescue Yiddish, or at least to slow its inevitable extinction, Howe was also resuscitating an important part of his own identity. And his collaboration with the older Eliezer Greenberg, whom Howe came to love not only for his charm and erudition but also as a link to the immigrant "world of our fathers," was a joyful and sustaining experience.

There were transforming moments, too, as when Greenberg read to Howe, as if it were a meditative epic, Isaac Bashevis Singer's "Gimpel the Fool." Lazer, as he was known, had said to Howe, "Sit still, be quiet, don't interrupt." But it wasn't necessary. Howe knew in minutes that he was encountering a major "new" writer (although anyone reading the Yiddish *Forward* could have "discovered" him much earlier). Irving immediately grasped "the canny mixture of folk pathos and sophisticated overlay" so characteristic of Singer, and the fact that it made "Gimpel," which begins as comedy but soon ascends to sadness and finally to tragic statement, so brilliant a story.

Lazer was happy that Howe took such pleasure in the story, but he pointed out that while "Gimpel" was *very* Yiddish, it was, at the same time, not *really* Yiddish. Only years later, twenty to be precise, did Howe understand fully what Greenberg meant. In 1973 Singer himself told Howe that the two pillars of the Yiddish tradition were "sentimentality" and "social justice," both of which he deplored. Sentimentality, Singer said, is simply "schmaltz" (literally animal fat, but here meaning excessively, even manipulatively, maudlin). And while he said he was *for* social justice, he wouldn't fight to bring it about. "I am a pessimist," Singer told Howe, "and I believe . . . there will never be any justice in this world," no matter what people do. "The best thing you can do," Singer continued, "is run away from evil" and "not fight it, because the moment you begin to fight evil, you become a part of evil yourself."[31]

Singer drew on an older tradition of Jewish thought and lore that preceded the rise of Yiddish literature. The worldview out of which he wrote was strongly at odds with the humanism and nineteenth-century socialism that were dominant in that literature and which were so attractive to Howe. But as with his approach to Dostoevsky and Tolstoy, or to Joseph Conrad and Henry James, Howe did not let politics blind him to the quality of genius in the writing.

He agreed with Greenberg that "Gimpel" ought to be brought, as soon as possible, to the attention of the English-speaking world. But although Greenberg and Howe together had a good command of Yiddish, they did not want to do this particular translation alone, or perhaps they wanted to share their "find" with someone who would be as intensely appreciative. Howe convinced his friend and Princeton associate Saul Bellow, not yet so famous, to come to Greenberg's apartment on East 19th Street to help.[32] Lazer read out the story, sentence by Yiddish sentence, while Bellow sat at the typewriter occasionally asking about refinements of meaning. Irving watched in "a state of high enchantment." After nearly four hours of translation and revision, Bellow read aloud the version of "Gimpel the Fool" that was published in *Partisan Review* (Rahv having also recognized its special genius) and that has since become famous. "It was a feat of virtuosity," Howe recalled, "and we drank a schnapps to celebrate."[33]

Several months later, Howe met Singer, still known only among Yiddish readers, for the first time. They had lunch on Broadway near 82nd Street at Steinberg's dairy restaurant (now gone). Singer, full of jokes, anecdotes, quotations, and opinions that rolled out between bites of blintzes, left Howe "dizzy with amusement and dismay." He could not decide whether he had met a comedian or a genius. But he knew he was in the presence of a master performer. Soon, very much to the credit of Irving Howe, who included "Gimpel" in *A Treasury of Yiddish Stories* along with Singer's "The Little Shoemakers," a kind of fantastic, nightmarish "poem" commemorating the death of a civilization (which Howe considered superior to "Gimpel"), Bashevis, as he was known to a small circle of friends, would belong to the larger world.[34] But in 1954, still excited by his discovery, Howe wanted to share Singer's work with his Brandeis students. He decided to create a course on Yiddish literature to be taught in the spring semester. And in the fall semester, just before winter break, facing only about half his class in American literature, he said, "I have a present to give you for the holiday"; he proceeded to read aloud Bellow's translation of "Gimpel." Although "Irving was usually a bit reserved," one of his former students told me, "he read that story with sincere emotion, and several of us became Singer fans for the rest of our lives."[35]

Not every experience in the collaboration between Greenberg and Howe (and later the poet Jacob Glatstayn) was so intense. But Howe attached himself, as friend and commentator, to these writers whose Yiddish world was shrinking. And he "found strength in joining their moment of weakness," just as Yiddish literature had found strength in the moment of weakness of the East European Jews when their traditional world, while still coherent and self-contained, was already challenged, indeed under assault, from the modern world.[36] In their work together, Howe and Greenberg focused on the flowering of Yiddish literature in the late nineteenth century, a time when the *shtetl* world was experiencing its "last tremor of self-awareness" as it faced pressure from the outside and disaffection from within.

Poised between two opposing forces—folk tradition and modernism—Yiddish literature reached its climax of expressive power in the late nineteenth and early twentieth centuries not by jettisoning tradition, Howe showed, but by redefining it. Perhaps with his mind on the conservatism of the New Critics (about whom he was writing concurrently), Howe took pains, in writing about Yiddish literature, to draw a distinction between tradition, with its rich complexity and its power to transform itself, and conservatism, with its stubborn insistence on countering innovation. He tried to show that the Yiddish writers, especially Sholom Aleichem and I. L. Peretz, in their literary and cultural innovations defended not only the modern, but also the traditional culture out of which the modern sprang. Yiddish literature, Howe wrote, was essentially a product of rebellion against the old Jewish orthodoxy, but it was also steeped in tradition. When the writers "began to write in Yiddish," Howe argued, they "implicitly acknowledged a desire to communicate with man" but they did not cut off entirely the conversation—or the debate—with God. In this way, Howe said, even as the civilization they portrayed was coming apart, the Yiddish writers created a "modern" literature with a traditional emphasis on communal responsibility and fraternity, especially with the poor, a literature endowed with a moral poise and a set of ethics that assumed the functions of nationality, and even religion, as faith faded further for the old-world Jews.[37]

And it was a literature, Howe said, worth celebrating. Unlike most modern literature, which Howe championed but about which he had always expressed some demurrers, Yiddish literature did not confront at every moment extreme situations, images of catastrophe, or the harsh finalities of experience. The Yiddish writers rejected the notion that evil was the last thing to be said about humanity, and they were instead "writers of sweetness." Without any sense of aesthetic distance, without complacency, and without sacrificing their stringent sense of realism, Sholom Aleichem and Peretz and many of the others somehow faced the "grimmest facts of Jewish life" with secure values and a tone of love. Their sense of fraternity with the poor was palpable. Howe recognized that that sense was not uniquely Jewish; concern about poverty could surface in Chekhov, Silone, or Tolstoy. But he knew, too, that the Jews "have had more occasion to look into the matter."[38]

The hero, or better yet, the anti-hero of the Yiddish writers was *dos kleine menschele* (the little person). And the great theme of Yiddish literature, Howe wrote, was *"the virtue of powerlessness—the power of helplessness, the company of the dispossessed, the sanctity of the insulted and the ignored."* This did not necessarily mean, as some critics have suggested, that Howe and the writers he featured found something particularly positive about victimization. It more clearly meant that the impoverished, beleaguered world of the East European Jews and the writers who portrayed it "made impossible the power-hunger, the pretensions to aristocracy, the whole mirage of false values that have blighted Western intellectual life."[39]

For Howe, the *shtetl* (and to some extent the literature it produced), unlike the modern Western world, was "unified, singular, contiguous." Not yet split into sharply defined classes, the shtetl was governed by nonmaterialist values. Its inhabitants, Howe argued, valued learning over acquiring, and collective life over individual achievement. Howe did not idealize this world. He, like Sholom Aleichem, Mendele, and I. L. Peretz, was fully aware of the misery of shtetl poverty and the greed, unscrupulousness, and hypocrisy it could breed. But Howe's descriptions of shtetl coherence and moral tone, and his contrasts of this little Jewish world with the modern West surely owed much to his enduring socialist allegiance. The shtetl community, while not quite Howe's socialist utopia projected onto the past, contained for him a tradition of fraternity and communal responsibility worth salvaging and promoting.

Howe's interest in the Yiddish writers was intensified by their secular emphasis. His "reconquest" of Jewishness through saturation in Yiddish, then, was not at all a turn to religion, but it was a recognition and affirmation of rootedness in a tradition, albeit one that tended to remake itself. Howe's position is complex, but it certainly seems to imply not so much a rejection of "community" as of "conformity." His earlier work on Faulkner and Anderson and their celebration of organic community and fraternity makes this clearer. And even in "This Age of Conformity," Howe wrote that "to deny our heritage both as burden and advantage" would be damaging. It would, he thought, "deny our possible future as a community."[40]

Howe's emphasis in the essay (and in the *Treasury*) on fraternity and community and his obvious distaste for capitalism elicited from some critics the charge that he espoused an outdated Marxism. But Howe denied being anything like "a thoroughgoing or systematic Marxist." In a letter to Robert Warshow, an editor at *Commentary* who had written a long and relentlessly ad hominem letter to *Partisan Review* attacking "This Age of Conformity," Howe said, quite rightly, that one did not have to be a Marxist to accept the main themes of his essay. The qualified anti-institutionalism, for example, was not especially a leftist argument. It was the philosopher William James, after all, who, reflecting the voices of earlier intellectuals, had said "every great institution is perforce a means of corruption." And the anticapitalism that blossomed here and there in the piece was shared even by some non-Marxists, including the traditionalist New Critics who were a target of Howe's wrath. Marxist terminology, moreover, was almost conspicuously absent from the essay. "I used the rather loose phrase 'conformity,' Howe explained, "instead of a more precise political one simply because I wished to emphasize that my complaint was not that certain intellectuals had abandoned this or that ideology but that they had abandoned the traditional idea of keeping a critical distance from state power, any state power."[41] Indeed, at the very end of the piece, Howe, once again reaching for a synthesis with the best in liberalism, identified himself not as a Marxist but as a "humanist."

Warshow seems to have overlooked some of Howe's more complex arguments and subtle qualifications, a result perhaps of his rush to accuse Howe of hypocrisy. Warshow pointed out that, in charging some intellectuals with the sin of selling out to "institutions," including a number of middlebrow magazines, Howe never mentioned his own work with *Time* magazine. Howe's response, that his employment with the Luce publication from 1948 to 1952 was indeed a compromise but not a sell-out, is persuasive:

> I worked for *Time* for the same reason (at least I hope it's the same reason) that Mr. Warshow works at *Commentary*: to support my family. My arrangement at *Time* gave me the free time to write what I wanted—and not merely books of criticism . . . , but many articles defending civil liberties. (Mr. Warshow shouldn't underestimate my energies.) I was a socialist before working for *Time*; I wrote frequently for the socialist press while working there; and I remain a socialist. A good many of my critics managed without working at *Time*, to shed almost every trace of their radicalism and/or intellectual rebelliousness.[42]

Warshow was hardly the only one irritated by Howe's article. The piece's critical and sometimes mocking references to Lionel Trilling, with whom Howe had had a fairly steady correspondence since 1948, led to a rupture in their relationship that lasted nearly eight years. Diana Trilling exacted some revenge on Howe in a letter to *Commentary* in 1956 in which she characterized *Dissent* as a magazine "whose polemic is based not upon intellectual cogency but upon the intellectual intimidation of its readers." Howe, still unable to transcend his old acerbic style, and too thin-skinned to let incidental criticism pass, responded in kind in *Dissent*: "As a leading official of the American Committee for Cultural Freedom," Howe wrote, Mrs. Trilling behaves not only like a cold-warrior, but like "the 'general secretary' of a radical sect whose main joy in life is hunting for deviations among the other sects and chastising those who stray from the proper 'line.'"[43]

Howe and Lionel Trilling, without reaching a full political consensus, restored an authentic friendship in the 1960s, which continued until Trilling's death in 1975. But Diana Trilling, if we are to believe her 1993 memoir, would continue to count Howe among a very long list of "strange difficult ungenerous unreliable unkind and not always honest people who created the world in which Lionel and [she] shared." Perhaps this was essentially a characterization of a whole generation of intellectuals, not particularly aimed at Howe and including even the Trillings themselves. But toward Howe and the others there is an unforgiving quality in the language and the tone.[44]

Howe, remembering later how his friend Philip Rahv put him up to writing his 1954 polemic for *Partisan Review*, said "the opinions I expressed were my own, but the enemies I made should have been Rahv's too. Anticipating that many people—the Trillings for example, would be annoyed . . . Rahv thought it clever to push me into battle while himself avoiding the return fire."[45] At the time Howe thought that some of that "fire" was returned, not only in the form of pointed criticism, but also as conscious neglect. He told the writer Bernard Malamud, who had asked Howe to write a letter of reference for him to the Guggenheim Foundation, that he would gladly do it but that Malamud might "be better off without it." For ever since "This Age of Conformity" was published, Howe wrote, "I have the sense of becoming somewhat *non grata*." And "I've recently had more trouble getting things printed than ever before. It may be coincidence," Howe said, "it may not."[46]

By writing the essay, Howe had made enemies (some permanent), and over time he recognized and stepped back from some of the contemptuous tone and more extreme implications of the piece. And by 1960, when even the *Reader's Digest* was bemoaning the evils of conformity, Howe was actually complaining that he had unintentionally helped to "make the outcry against conformity into a catch-word of our conformist culture." But he continued to think "This Age of Conformity" was basically sound, and he included it in three anthologies of his writings published between 1963 and 1990.[47] In 1966, he added a somewhat self-teasing subtitle: "Notes on an Endless Theme, or A Catalogue of Complaints." But he also added a short introduction in which he reminded readers that when he first wrote his essay, Eisenhower, "the perfect emblem of the torpor and mediocrity that had settled upon the country," was president; McCarthy was still running wild; and "intellectuals were as a rule not distinguishing themselves through a militant defense of freedom."[48]

Although Howe, as we have seen, exaggerated the lack of anti-McCarthy militancy or progressive vision in some of his liberal adversaries like Hook, Schlesinger, and Bell (whose essays written throughout the fifties and gathered together later in *The End of Ideology* were models of social criticism), he was generally right in his take on the Cold War era.[49] Many intellectuals had withdrawn from the arena of political activism and had succumbed to or embraced a conservative or mildy liberal pro-Americanism. And even some of those who were alarmed at the extent and intensity of "the American celebration" and the apparent dissolution of the political Left had taken little or no action to prevent it. Philip Rahv did worry in the fifties that the intellectual community was abandoning its dissenting role, but he left it to Howe to do the heavy hitting.

Alfred Kazin, too, who had said in the postwar period that he "felt the reaction in America creeping around me like the blast of a cold wind," was, like most of his colleagues, unwilling to do much to combat the situation.[50] For alongside the remarkable similarities between Kazin and Howe, there stood one major difference. As Kazin put it in an interview with me in 1997, he, unlike Howe, "was not political." Too many people, Kazin said, with something less than warmth, mistakenly stitched him together with Howe. But the two critics were not the same, Kazin insisted; they did not respond the same way even when they had similar experiences. And he proceeded to tell the following story. Invited by Howe to lecture at Brandeis in the mid-fifties, Kazin gave a presentation that went quite long, and the questions and the reception afterwards went even longer. By the time it was all over and Howe was ready to show Kazin his room for the night, they had to grope their way across a darkened campus. Kazin, walking slightly ahead of Howe, didn't see a slight parapet right ahead of him and tripped over it. Howe didn't see it either, and he too fell. He got back up very annoyed. Brushing himself off, he muttered, "God damn it, Alfred, why must we always have the same experiences?!" This was the all too familiar line, one Kazin had long disliked in the mouths of others, and now that Howe himself had said it, he "happily" retorted, "Irving, I assure you, we don't!"

Kazin assured me that, like Howe, he had "always been on the left. I saw the same problems Irving did," he said. "I still do—the poverty, the greed, the materialism, the complacency of intellectuals. But Irving had 'solutions,'" Kazin said; "I had no solutions." Kazin's long-standing left leanings are confirmed in his voluminous journals. In one typical entry from the early 1950s that could easily have been written by Howe, Kazin said:

> Horrible *Commentary* dinner last night. Insufferable to be in that gaseous, anxiously self-congratulatory atmosphere of Jewish radicals of the thirties prosperously reappearing in the fifties as ex-radicals. Ideologues in every generation, no matter what their latest cause, they have not the slightest interest in social evidence—in poverty, in race hatred (except when "they" turn on us), in workers found to be "unemployable" by the latest technocratic revolution. And now they have found their latest cause in another ideology they call "America." America is just as unreal to them as the Soviet Union was. [51]

Obviously, Kazin could get angry, and did often. But he was, as he said, "not political." Howe saw Kazin the same way: "Kazin and I are often lumped together," he told an interviewer in 1988, "but we are very different. I am a socialist activist, Kazin was more the individualist romantic. He also wrote more rhapsodically than I did. I am drier. Still we were often on the same 'side.' Often against the same things, even if not always, or even often, *for* the same things."[52]

Kazin had said that Irving Howe had "solutions." There were, however, very few explicit solutions or proposals for change in "This Age of Conformity" or in the early issues of *Dissent*. But Howe did identify in the essay areas of cultural decline and social inequity, and he did struggle, in the magazine, to revisit socialist ideology and to reformulate socialist goals and methods relevant for America. With the essay and the magazine, Irving Howe carried to the intellectual community his fight against the new conformity and complacency, along with his continuing campaign for a more open, egalitarian American society. Soon, in that fight, he would not be so lonely a soldier.

8

The Growth of *Dissent* and the Breakup of the Fifties

THE GLOBAL STRUGGLE with the Soviet Union, especially in the period after World War II, had demanded from writers and intellectuals an uncritical pro-Americanism. But by the late fifties, many observers and critics, some in the universities, were taking a different attitude toward, and reducing their emotional investment in, the American celebration. The sociologists David Riesman in *The Lonely Crowd* (1950) and C. Wright Mills in *White Collar* (1951) were among the first small group of American intellectuals to attack the mood of complacency and compliance that characterized the fifties. J. D. Salinger had done some of the same in his classic novel, *Catcher in the Rye* (1951). By the end of the decade, however, this minor current of opposition to the dominant mood of the day had become a flood of criticism from writers and intellectuals such as Norman Mailer, Paul Goodman, Herbert Marcuse, and others, all of whom were deeply hostile to the oppressive conventionalism of the Cold War era. Even *Commentary Magazine* under the leadership of Norman Podhoretz, its new liberal editor, broadened, for a time, its criticism of American life.

For some of this shift, Irving Howe, who had all along taken issue with the excesses of pro-Americanism while at the same time remaining a persistent anti-Stalinist, could take some credit. But there had also been a gradual decline in the intensity of the Cold War itself that helped even more to dismantle the old affirmative consensus in the cultural sphere. The common enemy no longer seemed so fierce or hostile. Stalin died early in 1953, and the Korean War ended in June. Less than a year later at Geneva, Russia and the United States took their first small steps toward military détente.

The Democratic Party, after having lost its majority in Eisenhower's 1952 landslide victory, had regained control of Congress in 1954. And by the end of that year, enough United States senators had finally worked up the courage to censure their reckless colleague Joseph McCarthy. The Supreme Court, also in 1954, had ordered the racial desegregation of the nation's public schools "with all deliberate speed," and very soon thereafter came a number of other political and social challenges to racial inequality and signs of a new and significant movement for civil rights. In the mid-fifties, too, the labor movement, which had produced a number of important strikes after the war, was showing small signs of potential resuscitation. And there were indications as well of cultural and political disaffection among the young and from the "Beats," a new generation of bohemians based in New York and San Francisco. There were even sporadic activist stirrings on college campuses.[1]

Significant hints of change in the political and intellectual context were beginning to emerge, then, just as *Dissent* made its appearance. Howe and his fellow editors had launched their new journal to rethink, recast, and rejuvenate radical ideology. But, in what they had seen as an inhospitable season for the left, they had only modest expectations for influence in the political arena. They would soon grow more hopeful. In the meantime, however, Howe, along with Lewis Coser, Stanley Plastrik, Manny Geltman, and the others, expressed their "dissent" mainly as a matter of conscience and reinvigoration of the leftist spirit.[2]

They did not give up their shared "intellectual conviction that man can substantially control his condition" if he understands it and has the will to do it, but Howe and his colleagues mostly turned in upon themselves, often questioning their own socialist principles, even as they fought hard against those who wanted to dismiss those principles out of hand. They examined the past and tried to extract practical lessons from radical defeats—lessons to pass on to a future left, whenever it might appear.[3]

Howe and the other *Dissent* editors, in order to salvage the reputation of socialism, continued to hammer away at Stalin's perversion of that ideology, a perversion that had been implemented in the Soviet Union and its satellites and which persisted after the dictator's death. The "radicalism of the blackjack," or what Howe labeled "left authoritarianism," had to be exposed, and decisively rejected, if there was to be any revival of socialist consciousness.[4] At the same time that Howe was critical of the enemies of the United States, however, he avoided becoming a mere celebrant of America. In the pages of *Dissent*, for several years running, Howe took liberals to task for having ignored what he saw as the underside of American prosperity: the "crucial role" of "war production" in propping up the country's affluence; the maldistribution of income and wealth; the absence of adequate health care for far too many families; and the impact of automation on the working class.

Howe angrily attacked sociologists and journalists for presuming that America consisted "exclusively of the middle class." Although he had learned some things from David Riesman and William H. Whyte, and had had his hypotheses about conformity partially reinforced by their work, Howe asked why they, and others, published only middle-class centered books like *The Lonely Crowd* and *The Organization Man*, but not also sequels to James Agee's *Let Us Now Praise Famous Men*. There was after all, Howe argued, much to investigate below the middle class: the monotonous, debilitating exploitation in the lives of southern sharecroppers, for example; the gradual decay of the New England textile mills; and the social disruption of New York City under pressure from Puerto Rican migration and the flight of blacks from the South.[5]

For the early issues of *Dissent*, Howe drew on ideas from a variety of sources. He borrowed creatively from Dwight Macdonald and C. Wright Mills, and even took ideas from Daniel Bell, whose essays of progressive social criticism in the late forties and early fifties, although announcing "the end of ideology," amounted to a kind of incremental "rational utopianism."[6] Howe argued for more cooperatives; greater popular participation in decision making; smaller units of industrial production in which the workers might exercise significant influence; and the expansion and strengthening of grassroots institutions to counter the "concentration of authority."

But, it was not enough, Howe and Coser argued in *Dissent*, for contemporary radicals to fight for economic and political justice only. They also had to find, in "this age of conformity," ways of achieving and promoting a sense of "personal autonomy." Given the homogenizing effect of the mass media, the continuing threat to civil liberties, and the "general alienation" produced by a bureaucratized modern society, a socialist, according to Howe and Coser, had to develop a sense of individual "resistance" as a way of preparing for any wider social activism.

This was not to say that for Howe and Coser private existential protest or personal struggle for radical values was more important than a rousing call for social change. But as Coser put it in the late fifties, an authentic American radicalism of the future would include a necessary and desirable link between one's personal life and one's public life.[7] And as Howe said in writing about Hemingway, a writer with whom he had a surprising affinity, there was always a place for "incitements to personal resistance and renewal." Reading Hemingway, Howe said, "one felt stirred to a stronger sense—if not of one's possible freedom— than at least of one's possible endurance and companionship in stoicism." Although written later, this was as good a way as any to describe the small band of Dissenters in their early years. For they were in a kind of holding action, comparable to the efforts of expatriate writers like Hemingway and Fitzgerald "to find an honorable style of survival in a time of moral confusion."[8]

Personal autonomy and individual resistance, celebrated by Howe and Coser, were qualities that defined a significant portion of the Beat generation in the mid-fifties. But in the minds of the Dissenters, with the notable exception of Norman Mailer, the Beats qualified neither as "companions in stoicism" nor the vanguard of radical reform or even of moderate social change. The anti-establishment stance of Kenneth Rexroth, Allen Ginsberg, Jack Kerouac, William Burroughs, John Clellon Holmes, and other poets and novelists was thought too "incoherent," indeed, "opposed in principle," in Howe's words, "to a clear sense of *anything*."[9] Although they did not write essays on the Beats as condescending and mean in tone as those by Norman Podhoretz and Diana Trilling, most of the Dissenters, and most other serious critics, including Howe, Bell, and Kazin, characterized the Beats as anti-intellectual and therefore not to be taken seriously as either artists or political actors.[10] "For if you shun consciousness as if it were a plague," Howe said, "then a predicament may ravage you but you cannot cope with it."[11]

Unlike the "angry young men" in England, the Beats, Howe insisted, had no program, except perhaps to express hurt feelings, participate in powerless tantrums, and display "contempt for mind." But this, Howe went on, put them at one with "the middle-class suburbia they think they scorn."[12] Howe had a point, especially about their "politics," but the little he wrote about the Beats suggested that he, unlike Paul Goodman in *Growing Up Absurd* (1960), did not take them seriously enough to read them closely or with an imaginative tolerance for the experimental.[13]

Howe was more tolerant, perhaps too tolerant, with Norman Mailer, a writer more talented than most of the Beats Mailer himself openly admired, but just as self-centered. Taken with the brilliance of

Mailer's metaphors and his aggressive hostility toward the dominant conventionality of the day, and perhaps looking for a "scoop," Howe made the mistake (though not without "a twitch of discomfort") of featuring the novelist's bombshell essay, "The White Negro," in a special issue of *Dissent* in the summer of 1957.[14] Mailer's "white Negro" or "hipster" (terms he used interchangeably) was a figure with whom he obviously identified: a nonconforming, sexually unrestrained white male whose behavior and values were "borrowed" from the life-style of blacks.

Mailer's positive reflections on the hipster, who was essentially defined by a lack of social inhibition, directly challenged the rationality and intellectuality of the fifties. For the hipster was the incorrigible "psychopath" (in Mailer's view, an existential hero); he was the new avant-garde rebel, and he needed no "head games," no psychotherapy (except perhaps Reichian). He needed only a woman. For "orgasm is his therapy . . . good orgasm opens his possibilities and bad orgasm imprisons him." Love, Mailer continued, was "the search for an orgasm more apocalyptic than the one which preceded it."[15]

The essay and the "great orgasm debate" which ensued in *Dissent* in the months following were, in their fascination with both sex and psychoanalysis, manifestations of the mood of the late fifties. The exchanges, in the magazine and elsewhere, seemed to indicate that Mailer's reduction of psychiatrists to "ball shrinkers," women to sexual receptacles, and blacks to their sex organs, though troubling to some, was balanced for others by Mailer's "enthralling" proclamation of psychosexual emancipation.[16]

Nearly overlooked in all of this was Mailer's homage to violence in the same essay. The hipster, Mailer calmly assured his readers, "murders—if he has the courage—out of a necessity to purge his violence, for if he cannot empty his hatred then he cannot love." And in sentences preceding his discussion of the search for the perfect orgasm, Mailer mused about the propriety, indeed the possible good, of "beat[ing] in the brains" of a fifty-year-old storekeeper as a way of articulating selfhood. "Courage of a sort is necessary," Mailer explained, "for one murders not only a weak fifty-year-old man but an institution as well."[17]

On the *Dissent* board, of which Mailer was a member, there was apparently no debate about the propriety of publishing the piece, which temporarily tripled *Dissent*'s circulation to an astonishing 14,000 copies. "Only later," Lewis Coser said, "did we see that we had made an error, a big one." Howe, too, admitted that publishing "The White Negro" was "unprincipled," and that at the least he and the other editors should have urged Mailer to drop the most reckless sentences.[18] Two years later, in 1959, Howe concluded that, like the Beats, Mailer, in his emphasis on unrestrained individualism and personal liberation, was in danger of being carried away by his "treacherous powers of self-delusion and self-incitement" and by his "fascination with violence."[19] None of this would do, Howe thought, for either art or radical reform.

In the meantime, Howe looked for opportunities on the American scene "to make even a small dent" in the apparent wall of blindness, or indifference, to the social inequities that remained in the nation. He agreed with those affirmers like Hook and Glazer and Kristol who argued that America had made significant improvement since the 1930s in reducing inequalities and expanding economic opportunities. But Howe thought that the gap between what was possible in this regard and what had been accomplished was far too wide. Without giving up on ideology entirely, by which he meant a coherent structure of ideas rather than a rigid dogma, Howe came close to proposing the kind of "empirical utopianism" posited by Daniel Bell. He became an advocate of changes that could offer immediate relief to the overworked and underpaid, changes that could further reduce the injustices of American society and serve as a platform from which to achieve greater reform in the future.[20]

At the same time, Howe joined Lew Coser in an ongoing discussion, sometimes written, on the idea of socialism as problem and goal. There developed between them an intellectual collaboration, and also a friendship—a relationship made closer by the fact that they saw each other on the Brandeis campus several times a week and lived only a few miles apart, Howe in a suburban home in Belmont and Coser in a Cambridge brownstone. Their first joint writing effort was undertaken partly in response to Nathan Glazer's stinging charge that the premier issue of *Dissent* lacked theoretical depth. For the very next issue, Howe and Coser produced "Images of Socialism," an essay rich in historical allusion and rumination. It was not meant to be a "credo"; it did not try to construct "a new and shiny political system for socialists." Indeed, the lengthy piece (frequently reprinted) asked more questions than it answered. But it was the beginning of a powerful, decades-long reflection on the nature of socialism, which Howe and Coser identified as "the name of our desire."[21]

Socialism, or some other new consciousness by a different name, centering on fraternity and social justice, might not arrive in Howe's lifetime, or ever. But he agreed with the novelist and former Italian Communist Ignazio Silone, whose trenchant and melancholy voice he so admired, that "keeping faith was a better rule than any abstract formula."[22] At the same time, he was committed to making that "small dent." Occasionally, Howe, though not particularly familiar with Hebrew texts, would cite one of the ancient sages who had declared in *Pirke Avot, Ethics of the Fathers*, some two thousand years earlier: "It is not your duty to complete the work; neither are you free to desist from it." He was even fonder of telling a Yiddish story about Chelm, the legendary town of East European Jews where a man had been appointed to sit at the gate and wait for the coming of the Messiah. The man complained to the elders that his pay was too low. "In this, you are right," he was told, "but consider: this is very steady work."[23]

Howe chose the title *Steady Work* for his collection of essays on the politics of democratic radicalism written between 1953 and 1966; and steady work was what he himself continued to do. While the "messiah" tarried, Howe increasingly devoted himself to addressing the torments and immediate needs of the less-than-powerful—workers, the poor, racial minorities—even as he retained and refined a larger vision of the good society. And in *Dissent*, throughout the journal's history, much energy and much space were spent assessing the connection between immediate practical reform activity and the ultimate aims (always in the making) of a socialist movement.[24]

Much energy was spent, too, in defending the magazine against enemies. After the third issue, Howe told a new contributor, "We've had a terrific struggle; every conceivable odd against us; scorn, rejection, downright hatred from the Hookite liberals and ex-radicals; but slowly we have been pushing up hill, winning friends even from among people who don't agree with us entirely."[25] Even more energy was spent getting the magazine out. Howe did the line-by-line editing and rewriting, a drudgery he would not have been willing to abide had *Dissent* not emphasized political reflection at least as much as critical journalism. Coser, with his eye on the long term, was a good partner in this regard; and like Howe he was an indefatigable toiler and "punctual to a fault."[26]

Howe gave Coser lots of credit: "The truth is," he told Lew, "that if you and I don't bear down, the magazine drifts. This isn't vanity, just a fact."[27] But *Dissent* worked mainly because of Howe, who put the journal's life at the center of his own existence. Coser was indispensable, but it was Howe who was running the show. Nearly every day he hammered out a steady stream of notes and postcards and made innumerable—and famously abrupt—phone calls reminding writers of deadlines and suggesting projects. And all this while teaching full-time and helping to raise two children at home, and while the books he wanted to read and the essays he wanted to write lay waiting. Someone had to pay attention to the details, and Howe, dedicated to doing, even if not completing, the steady work of the democratic left, did not believe his intelligence, culture, and accomplishment entitled him to withdraw to a world of contemplative leisure. [28]

In the day-to-day management of *Dissent*, Howe was a sharply critical editor and held writers to high standards. If there were lapses in logic or in sustained argument, or when the language of a piece was clichéd, repetitious, overly complicated, or riddled with jargon, Howe could be editorially ruthless in his insistence on revisions in the name of style and plain speaking. But he was kind and nurturing, too, and helped writers to realize what they knew, inspiring them to make connections they hadn't quite articulated. And after the disagreements, there would be a supportive note or phone call, sometimes a lunch, and almost always an invitation to write again.[29]

When an essay was simply bad, Howe rejected it. Once Howe even turned down a contribution from Edmund Wilson. His initial excitement on receiving the piece turned to depression as he discovered that this was Wilson at his most crotchety. Realizing, with some reinforcement from Coser, that he would not print the essay had it come from someone without Wilson's fame, Howe sat down to the difficult and unenviable task of writing a letter of rejection to a man whom he admired and even emulated. Afterward, Wilson would tease Irving about being turned down by a magazine that didn't even pay![30]

Endlessly reworking other people's prose and constantly alert to possible new contributors, Howe also played a key role in keeping a potentially contentious group of radical intellectuals from each other's throats. Although, over the years, some individuals took their leave, most quietly, there was never a factional war or mass exodus. Having lived through too many sectarian splits in the past, Howe did the necessary calming, and even stroking, to hold the *Dissent* group together. When he disagreed with an essay he said so. But unlike Philip Rahv at

Partisan Review, Howe never competed with his writers or tried to impose an ideologically correct position. He told prospective contributor Waldo Frank that while the *Dissent* crew had "certain parallel intentions and purposes ... we clearly write from different intellectual slants." The "great need," Howe said, "is not for agreement but for intellectual roominess and openness; things must not be allowed to be frozen into petty orthodoxies." This was the genius of Howe's leadership, Norman Mailer remembered. It was intellectual but also diplomatic. Howe was "forceful [and] witty," Mailer said, "a real skipper" who "steered the magazine past many obstacles."[31]

The overall work gave Howe genuine pleasure, even if editing *Dissent* was irksome in some of its technical aspects and often frustrating in the face of financial deficits. Michael Walzer, Howe's former student, who began writing for *Dissent* in 1956 and joined the editorial board near the end of the decade, told me in 1997 that the whole thing was run like a "mom and pop grocery." He pointed out that *Dissent*'s budget was tiny and depended in large part on the willingness of editors, including Irving, to tax themselves.[32] Howe, as early as 1954, was already complaining that *Dissent* "is the most expensive magazine in the world on which to be an editor." And he was not above encouraging writers and readers, especially college teachers, to get their librarians to subscribe; nor did he shy away from saying to new recruits, "If you can chip in a few bucks that would be nice."[33]

Howe told one writer not to visit the *Dissent* office because "it isn't an office, just a mailing address. Who can afford an office?" Certainly not the *Dissent* board. Despite subsidies from the Buttingers and incessant fund-raising by Howe (a task he detested), money was always in short supply. Even after circulation climbed from about 4,000 to nearly 10,000 (temporarily) by the late 1960s, there was no *Dissent* office, nor would there ever be one. Subscription lists were kept in the spare bedroom closet of one of the editors, and editorial meetings were held in the apartments of various board members.

But the magazine, to Howe's surprise, stayed alive. Subscriptions and newsstand sales were increasing, and Howe was pleased that *Dissent* had by 1955 surpassed the circulation of the prestigious *Kenyon Review*. Part of the small but growing readership came from within the labor movement, particularly through the United Auto Workers, where some educational directors of union locals ordered bulk subscriptions for members. Howe had made a favorable impression on the UAW, having coauthored with B. J. Widick in 1949 *The United Auto Workers and Walter Reuther*, a sympathetic book that supported the union's attempt to rid itself of the Communists. After completing the book, Howe maintained his UAW contacts and his interest in the labor movement. He recruited the veteran Detroit socialist and labor educator Frank Marquart, who early became a contributing editor of *Dissent*. And throughout the 1950s, culminating with Daniel Bell's prescient essay "The Meaning in Work," only *Dissent*, among the intellectual quarterlies, paid significant attention to the labor movement and to issues pertaining to the workplace.[34]

Neither Howe nor Marquart, nor Bell, nor Irving's friend the novelist Harvey Swados, a *Dissent* contributor and a former UAW activist who coined the phrase "the myth of the happy worker," was optimistic about the current state of the labor movement or its near-term prospects. And their attention to the economic insecurities of workers, and to the quality of work life, appeared to some to be a preoccupation with the past. But the Dissenters were on to something—the discontents of blue-collar laborers—that others would finally notice only fifteen years later, and then all too briefly.[35]

Howe was aware of the problems early, and he was always on the lookout for more positive signs in the labor movement, hopeful that someday the unions could again, as in the thirties, play a role in the reshaping of American life. But he and the other Dissenters were often disappointed. After the first three or four years of *Dissent*, with no classconscious proletariat emergent, they turned much of their attention to the theory of "mass culture" or "mass society." The general public was depicted by the theory not as a potential force for social change, but as an "atomized" mass made up of inhibited, obedient people whose will to resist the state and the prescribed rules of social behavior were seriously weakened by cultural institutions, especially the mass media.

"Marxism was not working very well," Howe said later about the mid-fifties, "class analysis wasn't that effective, so we moved toward this eclectic view, trying to combine elements of Marxism, the mass society approach, Danny Bell's pluralist theory, whatever seemed to work." Howe didn't write about mass society as much as some of the others, but, as he said, "No one escapes the historical moment."[36] Indeed, since the 1940s, Howe, along with many other observers of American society, including Theodore Adorno, Dwight Macdonald, and Paul Lazersfield, had spoken disdainfully of mass culture.[37] In 1948, when he was in the process of rethinking his attachment to sectarian Trotskyism, Howe wrote a piece for Macdonald's *Politics* disparaging the popular culture that dominated American political life. He called it "safe" and "one-dimensional" and complained that it demanded no "creative response from the audience," unlike the modernist art he favored— Joyce's novels and Picasso's paintings, for example—"intentionally difficult" creations that permitted readers or viewers to reach new "heights of sensibility."[38] Worse even than the political quiescence that resulted from mass culture, Howe insisted, were the irrational psychological impulses generated in the atomized masses. And he went so far as to portray Donald Duck as "a frustrated little monster who has something of the SS man in him." Howe, throughout the essay, seemed to be arguing, post-Auschwitz, that with the collapse of traditional communities, mass culture had permitted, perhaps even encouraged, barbarism over reason and totalitarianism over socialism.

By the mid-fifties, however, with McCarthy gone and with the Polish and Hungarian challenges to Communist control in 1953 and 1956, the fear of totalitarianism's power to stay and to spread dissipated some. The pieces in *Dissent* regarding mass culture became less urgent and original. But even the earlier pieces by Harold Rosenberg, Henry Rabassiere, Lewis Coser, and especially Irving Howe had never taken mass culture theory to the point of dismissing ordinary people. Unlike Herbert Marcuse, Howe's colleague at Brandeis who gave mass culture theory an elitist bias and expressed disdain for democratic reform of the system, Howe did not adopt the apocalyptic view: "All or nothing. If you can't make a revolution, you can't do anything."[39]

If, in the mid-fifties, the idea of socialism was "unreal, mistaken, or very far off," Howe told an interviewer in 1982, "there was still a tremendous moral, political and social value in participating in every day-to-day struggle that seemed desirable: higher wages, civil rights, the whole spectrum of things that people were concerned with." Howe didn't disagree with mass society theory. He thought it had "some validity" and continued applicability even as late as the 1980s. "There are elements of experience in modern capitalist society that class analysis [alone] will not explain," he said, but some writers pushed the mass society idea "too far." Macdonald did, even Coser did, and Howe admitted, "possibly I did."[40]

But ultimately, Howe, who, without sentimentality, never lost faith in the resilience and potential of ordinary people, found the mass culture doctrine inconvenient to the practical things he wanted to accomplish. A society of zombies, after all, offered few prospects for reform, and virtually none for the socialist revival Howe promoted. By the end of the decade, in fact, Howe thought the criticism of mass culture had become the opiate of formerly radical intellectuals, conveniently replacing their criticism of bourgeois society. And he wanted little to do with it. In an introduction to a special issue of *Dissent* in 1959 dedicated to the condition of the labor movement, Howe said, "If a few decades ago, American intellectuals deluded themselves by contriving an image of the American worker as a potential revolutionary, today they are inclined to accept an equally false image of him as someone whose socioeconomic problems have been solved and who is joining the universal scramble for material luxuries." Even earlier Howe had said it was time to stop believing the "nonsense that the American population consists merely of a mass of obedient automatons."[41]

What came to be known as "middlebrow culture" was also, for a time, despised in the world of the little magazines and the avant-garde, even by some at *Dissent*. "Mid-cult," as Dwight Macdonald, its severest critic, labeled it, was a "disease" of the bourgeoisie, the middle-class pretenders to "high culture." It consisted of superficially serious but "intellectually insufficient" movies, television shows, and book clubs. It also included magazines such as *Harper's* and the *Atlantic Monthly*, which often published more accessible versions of the ideas of the New York intellectuals. Instead of being pleased at this kind of mid-cult "trickle-down," some highbrows considered it even more insidious and subversive than unadulterated mass culture. Mid-cult, according to Macdonald, was not mass culture improved, but high culture diluted. In any case, many of the intellectuals resented seeing their thoughts in the better-paying glossies under someone else's name.[42]

But many of those at *Dissent*, such as Harold Rosenberg, Howe, and Bernard Rosenberg, who criticized mid-cult, believed that the bourgeoisie as well as the working classes had higher cultural potential, and that, even without "the revolution," the popular media could be improved and harnessed to help fulfill that potential.[43] Howe, in 1960, wasn't sure that this could work with television, whose very structure might be "incompatible with serious art." He did think TV could be enhanced—by showing the summer's baseball games over in winter—for example. (Howe, who took great pleasure in the "national pastime," was still furious that both the Giants and the Dodgers had left New York in 1957.) But he thought it better certainly to keep the "boob-tube" off most of the time in order to read, talk, visit, or simply enjoy the silence.[44]

Howe may have been unsure about the cultural potential of TV, but he was certain that literature and social and literary criticism would not be viable or worthwhile if they became inaccessible, if they produced "writers without audiences." Modern criticism, Howe insisted, had always, "at its best," been an "'engaged'" criticism, "caught up in a desperate struggle over the nature and quality of our culture." And, as early as 1958, he bemoaned the cultural losses resulting from the contemporary critics' lack of contact with the public. "It would be very useful," Howe advised, "if the critics recognized that a criticism without a lively auxiliary journalism soon runs the danger of becoming both estranged and eviscerated."[45]

He believed that democratic societies simply could not thrive without a public discourse, carried on in general magazines and newspapers, that was intellectually rigorous yet accessible to ordinary citizens. And Howe, who had often thought of himself as both a critic and a journalist, in the mode of Edmund Wilson, stopped believing that writers who appeared in the middlebrow magazines were on a descent into hell. He began publishing there himself, in order both to reach the greater public and to fulfill "a gnawing ambition to write something, even three pages, that might live."[46] As early as the mid-fifties he was doing pieces for the *New York Times Book Review*, and by the sixties for its magazine section as well. He also wrote literary and political essays for *Harper's*. Over a period of about two years from the late sixties into the early seventies, Howe contributed germane and incisive, yet sweeping, pieces on Hemingway, Orwell, Dostoevsky, Saul Bellow, John O'Hara, Edwin Arlington Robinson, Gandhi, and Isaiah Berlin, among others. (In the same period, Alfred Kazin, no friend of mid-cult, was also delivering essays to *Harper's* on Mary McCarthy, Lionel Trilling, Walker Percy, and Bellow.)

Howe's belief that ordinary people could reach new "heights of sensibility" in culture and politics was not simply a way of holding on to "the name of his desire," it had been reinforced by events. He took hope, for example, in the emerging civil rights movement and thought that the black crusade might even infuse labor with something of its militant spirit. In the spring of 1956, *Dissent* carried a piece on the movement in Montgomery, Alabama, and in the same issue Howe predicted, correctly, that "in a few decades" the bus boycott would be "looked upon as a political and social innovation of a magnitude approaching the first sit-down strikes in the 1930s." And Coser, too, wrote that the struggle for human rights for Negroes in Mississippi "may be as meaningful a social act as the more spectacular involvements that marked an earlier period."[47]

Howe thought the civil rights movement so critical an issue, that in the fall of 1956, in the face of the failure of the two major political parties to take a "forthright stand" on this "one burning issue of national conscience," he and many of his fellow editors announced that they would vote for one or another of the socialist candidates or, more likely, would not vote at all. And he brushed aside the predictable criticism that he and the others, by their actions, would make themselves mere bystanders, unable to influence the course of events. Howe pointed to what he called a "profounder truth": because the major parties remain committed to "a society whose fundamental values and assumptions we reject," the more effective way to influence American politics "is by working toward a radical reconstruction of American life."[48]

But the Dissenters, even as they remained socialists, kept shedding more and more ideology, and toward the end of the fifties, most, including Howe, no longer thought of themselves as Marxists. The old inhibitions against supporting "bourgeois" candidates soon began to erode. The process was helped along by what appeared to be a change in the general political atmosphere. The Democrats, despite another Eisenhower landslide in 1956, retained control of Congress, and they picked up yet another fifteen Senate seats and forty-eight House seats in the congressional elections of 1958. In the aftermath of these victories, Howe came to believe that there was in the country a significant change in political mood, a new unrest, "a shift toward liberalism," and that "the decisive political struggles during the next few years will occur in the Democratic party." The Left, Howe thought, could begin to feel a little less beleaguered as the hostility to radicalism, so pervasive in the postwar period, had begun to dissipate. And he encouraged radicals, even while he continued to offer a "long-range socialist perspective," to take advantage of the new opportunity. He urged cooperation with liberals in developing progressive programs and in taking progressive action whenever possible. *Dissent* ceased to reprint its initial editorial statement eschewing political organizations, and it began to sound like a magazine that had found at least a new "mood," if not yet a viable movement, to which it could relate.[49]

This mood was reinforced by the antisegregationist sit-in movement that began in North Carolina in the early part of 1960, and by Michael Walzer's sensitive, hopeful reportage from the front lines in the South. Walzer, while still a student at Brandeis in 1955–1956, had had some indirect experience with civil rights activism as a supporter of the Montgomery bus boycott. And some three years later, while still a graduate student at Harvard, he had been involved in the Northern Support movement, which, in conjunction with what was happening in the South, coordinated picketing at forty Woolworth's stores in the Boston Area. Howe continued to see the civil rights movement as an authentic and effective weapon in the battle for racial justice, as well as a symbol of a new sensibility and a guiding example for a revived American left. And he asked Walzer, on the very first day of the southern black student sit-ins, to go to North Carolina to report on the movement for *Dissent*. The magazine had never before sent a writer to cover so distant a story. For the first time, as Walzer put it to me in 1997, *Dissent*'s radical analysis could now be accompanied by radical news.

Howe felt that Walzer's reports on the southern student rebellion would help dispel some of the lingering pessimism about social change that had prevailed among American intellectuals in the 1950s. Neither Walzer nor Howe believed that the blacks and their white middle-class allies would substitute for the proletariat in making "the revolution"; but they did think they were witnessing a new indigenous American radicalism, one beginning to draw on the commitment and resilience of plain people. This was a radicalism to which they could resonate; it was democratically organized and dealt with practical issues of immediate relevance as well as larger visions of social transformation. With its defense of democratic rights and values, Walzer argued, the civil rights movement demonstrated the possibility of stepping "outside the realm of conventional politics," without fearing that "every spark of enthusiasm" and "every utopian dream" would clear a path to totalitarianism.[50]

Totalitarianism was something that the Dissenters fiercely rejected, and they knew that it had often emerged as the ghastly unexpected consequence of a fanatical enthusiasm. But Howe and his colleagues recognized in the civil rights crusade a movement whose "enthusiasm" was more likely to open society up than to close it down. In pursuing their own antitotalitarian utopian dreams, most of the Dissenters distanced themselves from anything that appeared to be antidemocratic. This created no problem in regard to the civil rights activities of the late fifties and early sixties, but it did lead to some complication and ambivalence in the area of foreign policy.

As early as 1951 Howe had rejected the "third camp" position on international relations, which held that radicals could not choose sides in a contest between imperialist forces, and he had moved in the direction of "critical support" of the West. But he did it on his own terms, moving into what some have called the "second and a half camp." Howe wanted, in principle, to support the United States against the Soviet Union, but in many specific instances he found himself, unlike the "hard anticommunists" around *Commentary* and *Partisan Review*, in opposition to American foreign policy. In 1954, for example, after the overthrow of the radical Arbenz government in Guatemala by the CIA, Howe wrote angrily: "For some years now writers like Sidney Hook have been saying that a fundamental objection to Communists and fascists is that they do not stick by 'the democratic ground rule,' but believe in the use of armed coups by minorities." But now, Howe charged, when America itself has sponsored such an act, Hook has somehow lost his voice, has offered only silence.

Howe would not be silent, however. He dismissed the official arguments for intervention as gross rationalizations. The supposition that the Arbenz government was "on its way" to becoming a dictatorship, Howe insisted, was no justification for American involvement, since "the United States shows no alarm whatever over the regimes in numerous Latin American countries which are already absolute dictatorships (Nicaragua, Paraguay, etc.)." And he thought it was simply "crass expedience" to argue that had the CIA not intervened, Guatemala would have fallen into the grip of the Soviet Union. These exaggerations, or outright lies, by the United States, Howe worried, would corrupt "whatever remains in the world of democratic principles" and would only increase the attraction of Stalinism in Central America.[51]

Only a few months earlier, before the CIA coup in Guatemala, Howe had said that the most effective contribution the American government could make to the containment of Communism in Latin America, or anywhere for that matter, was not to embark on military adventures, but to try instead "to undercut the hold of Stalinism by a genuine appeal of radical democracy." This meant Americans had to undo the injustices that tainted their own nation; it meant they had to share, willingly, material resources with those worse off in other lands; and it meant making a "profound and humble effort to grasp the outlook" of foreign populations. It also meant searching for and supporting, within those foreign populations, what Howe and others called a "third force" (rather than a "third camp")—not the established authoritarian governments or the Communist rebels, but genuinely indigenous revolutionary movements that were also anti-Communist.[52]

Perhaps it was naive to suppose that the United States might one day be persuaded to support home-grown revolutionaries in the so-called Third World as long as they displayed sufficient anti-Stalinism. But this third force idea remained powerfully present in Howe's outlook and in the *Dissent* world for at least another decade. And it seems to have prevented a realistic assessment of the situation in Vietnam. Joseph Buttinger, a major financial backer of *Dissent* and of the International Rescue Committee, traveled to Vietnam in 1954 to help settle refugees fleeing from the newly established Communist zone in the North. He grew close to South Vietnamese leader Ngo Dinh Diem, whom he saw as a potential coordinator of a third force, and he served as a publicist for Diem in the United States.

In 1958 Buttinger published *The Smaller Dragon*, a study of Vietnamese political history that cast a favorable light on Diem. *Dissent* ran an excerpt from the book which stressed the difficulties of the situation in Indochina, but which did not acknowledge Buttinger's overall support of American intervention. In the following year, Buttinger, in *Dissent*, in a review of *The Ugly American* (a novel depicting the gross ineptitude and insensitivity of American diplomats in Asia), argued that American aid policies were succeeding in Vietnam. "By replacing imperialism with policies of aid," Buttinger said, the United States "has stopped the 'Russians' without firing a shot." In an introduction to the piece, Howe seemed to put his own imprimatur on this view by praising Buttinger for his deep concern for the Vietnamese in their struggle to secure freedom "from both French and Communist imperialism."[53]

In 1954 Howe, with great foresight, had written:

It now seems highly probable that Stalinism has achieved a major victory in Indochina. If the West does not intervene militarily, the Viet Minh is almost certain to take complete control of the country; if the West does intervene, there follows the likelihood, not of wresting the country from the Stalinists, but of a long bleeding war. We are paying for decades of imperialist cupidity and obtuseness. As Walter Lippman has put it with classical brevity: "The French lost the war in Indochina, not because they were not brave, but because they failed to win the confidence and support of the Vietnamese nation."

In 1946, when a coalition Vietnamese regime was established in the north of the country under the leadership of Ho Chin Minh but not yet under the domination of the Stalinists, political measures of a bold and imaginative kind might have saved the country. But the French, Howe continued, withdrew their support for this government, thereby driving "many nationalist, non-Communist Vietnamese into Ho's arms," and they "transformed what should have been a domestic political struggle between Vietnamese integrity and Stalinist intervention into a colonial war against a foreign imperialist power."[54]

Howe's analysis has stood the test of time and his predictions proved all too true. But his devotion to anti-Communism and to the corollary idea of a third force apparently blinded him to the possibility that even nonmilitary intervention by the United States on the side of the South Vietnamese and against the popular Ho Chi Minh could be a form of "imperialism" and might serve as a stepping-stone to the "long bleeding war" he had warned against. And it was not until 1968, some three years after explicit, full-scale American military intervention in Indochina, that Howe was able to extricate himself fully from the third force bind.

In the meantime in the late fifties, if Howe was worried about "Stalinist victory" in Southeast Asia, he could take heart from what looked like "de-Stalinization" in Eastern Europe.

9

More Breakups

IN THE SPACE of a half-dozen years, Irving Howe's worlds, both public and private, underwent a number of dramatic shifts. To his delight, Communist totalitarianism, which was seen by many as "the end of history," virtually unbreakable, at least in any foreseeable future, had by the late fifties developed visible cracks. To his chagrin, Howe's family had also developed cracks. And Irving's love affair, beginning in 1959, with the wife of a faculty colleague at Brandeis, led to divorce from Thalia in 1960. Howe left Brandeis permanently in 1961 and spent two troubled years at Stanford before returning East to teach at the City University of New York (CUNY) in the fall of 1963. During those two years, *Dissent*, without Irving at the helm, also went through a number of crises that brought the magazine to the brink of breakup.

Despite the chaos in his private life, Howe managed, as he put it, to stay "afloat."[1] He was buoyed to some degree, as we have seen, by what appeared to be a reemerging progressive politics at home. And he was reinvigorated by the challenge to totalitarianism abroad. Early in 1956 Howe was exhilarated by Nikita Khrushchev's intimations of reform and by his revelations about the horrors of the Stalin regime. The "truth" was out at last, and from the mouths of the murderers themselves. There was shouting and even laughing among Howe's friends, several of whom walked "endlessly" around the loop of lower Manhattan measuring their joy, but also the extent of their continued skepticism.[2]

Two things worried Howe: that those on the American "left" might use the changes in the Soviet Union as an argument for moral as well as political reconciliation with the dictatorship; and that the Kremlin's dissociation from Stalin's butchery might actually be a way to legitimize and even consolidate the power of the upper echelons of the Communist Party.[3] His joy was tempered, too, by the "disclosure" that the Stalin regime had murdered a significant number of Yiddish writers and cultural figures. The *Morgen Freiheit*, the Yiddish Communist daily in New York, had reprinted a report from the Yiddish Communist paper in Warsaw which confirmed the existence of widespread anti-Semitism in Russia and named dozens of Yiddish writers who were killed. "To measure the magnitude of this catastrophe," Howe wrote, "you should imagine a situation in which, for political reasons, Faulkner, Hemingway, Auden and Frost are summarily executed."[4]

Still, Howe thought, life in the Soviet Union could improve. The apparent inclination of the Soviet authorities to back away, even a little, from totalitarian terror and to offer concessions, would, Howe hoped, elicit further demands from below. And with the widespread disturbances in Poland in the summer of 1956 and the uprising in Hungary in the late fall, that hope appeared credible. When the first news of what Howe and Coser were calling the "Hungarian Revolution" arrived, the regular autumn issue of *Dissent* was already on its way to the printer, so they set themselves to getting out a special edition of the magazine and wrote continuously for three days.[5]

What had been proven in Hungary, Howe wrote, "is that neither physical might nor the ideological terror of totalitarianism can break the spirit of a people. No matter what the immediate outcome of the events in Poland and Hungary," Howe continued, "they have already achieved the status of the symbolic and the exemplary." They have, he concluded, "vindicated man in the twentieth century." It was a moment, Coser said, "of buoyant hopes."[6]

Some of that buoyancy dimmed when the Russian tanks rolled into Hungary in early November and smashed the rebels. But Howe remained hopeful. For even in the face of the Soviet crackdown, resistance continued in the form of slowdowns in the factories, sabotage on the farms, restlessness in the cities, and open contempt among the students. Howe thought that "a stubborn instinctive resistance" was manifest in the East Europeans, and that the oppressed nation had formed a tacit pact, "a pact to deny consent." Howe admitted that many revolutions had been crushed in the past one hundred years, "but," he went on to ask, "can anyone remember a revolution in which the spirit of the vanquished remained so high as in Hungary today? It is unbelievable," Howe said. And waxing almost religious he called the events "sublime."[7]

Howe expressed some of this passionate sympathy for the Hungarian rebels on the Brandeis campus, where, on the evening of the Soviet incursion, students and faculty had gathered spontaneously (as they often did during international crises) to discuss the Russian repression. A fierce debate emerged mainly between Howe and Coser on the one side, and their colleague Herbert Marcuse on the other. Marcuse was reluctant to support the Hungarian uprising; he intimated that it had a counterrevolutionary dimension, that there were among the rebels fascists and anti-Semites. And in support of Marcuse, one student shouted out that the street-fighters had said "'We have to hang some Jewish meat.'"[8]

Howe and Coser recognized that people they "didn't like" could take over the revolution, but "that was the risk of democracy," they said. Even if there were protofascists defying the Soviet tanks, Howe roared as the free-wheeling discussion escalated, they were, after all, anti-Stalinists resisting oppression in the name of freedom. They had the right to make that fight for freedom and then to be held to that standard.[9] The people who were dying in the street, Howe said directly to Marcuse, needed brotherly support, not scholarly analysis. At this point, several witnesses remember, Howe and Marcuse had to be physically parted to prevent them from coming to blows.[10] Howe retained his animus toward Marcuse, and not without some justification. Later, when Marcuse opposed Sidney Hook's speaking engagement at Brandeis (because he thought the philosopher was an "informer" who would finger the Communist teachers!), Howe, who seems to have encouraged if not initiated the invitation to Hook, told Coser privately that Marcuse "is really nutty and pretty much a totalitarian to boot."[11]

Despite continued disagreement between Hook and Howe, and intermittent mutual sniping, the two had much more in common than did Howe and Marcuse. Both, for example, recognized the irony that Marxist ideology, the original ideals and vocabulary of socialism, appealed to "progressive" sentiments and was thus particularly dangerous to the autocratic regimes that invoked socialist visions of a workers' democracy. And both men were therefore "cautiously optimistic" about change in the world of totalitarianism.[12]

While all of this was going on, Howe continued to teach his classes at Brandeis and to manage *Dissent*, which was all the more taxing with Lew Coser away on sabbatical leave for the academic year 1957–1958.[13]

He was also trying to raise money for the magazine, whose circulation was steadily increasing but whose finances were still a "terrible burden." At the same time, Howe was working on a number of writing projects, including several important pieces for *Dissent*, a half dozen literary essays for other magazines, and putting the final touches to three books, one of which was *Politics and the Novel* (1957), a collection of essays he had begun writing in the early fifties.[14] An enduring work reprinted twice, in 1987 and 1992, *Politics and the Novel* focused on the question of what happens to the novel when it is subjected to the pressures of political ideology. Howe began by repeating Stendahl's well-known remark that "politics in a work of literature is like a pistol shot in the middle of a concert." But for Howe, the central question was, "When is the interruption welcome, and when is it resented?" Politics in a novel—in any work of art, for that matter—was for Howe not necessarily disruptive or corrosive. He saw a problem only "when the armored columns of ideology troop in en masse" and endanger a novel's "life and liveliness."[15]

What counted most for Howe was the sensibility of the novelist, rather than his or her political point of view. In the earlier controversy over Ezra Pound (1949), Howe had said that a poet should be judged by standards that went beyond "pure" poetry. In *Politics and the Novel*, he was saying that political works of art should be judged by criteria that went beyond politics. Howe had apparently found for himself a fluid position between the socialist realism of the 1930s, which he rejected entirely for its obsession with political correctness, and the New Criticism of the forties and fifties, about whose apolitical posturing he had serious reservations. And *Politics and the Novel* displayed Howe's growing, generous, and imaginative literary sensibility. The essays, reflecting on the ways in which the literary imagination echoes or withstands ideology, constituted a kind of search in selected authors for evidence of *menshlikhkayt*—Howe's Yiddish shorthand for compassion, decency and humanity.

It was clear that Howe more often than not found these qualities in authors like Ignazio Silone, his "favorite living writer," and George Orwell, both of whom, like him, were men of the Left. But equally clear in this book (described by Howe as his best work yet) was Howe's great respect and genuine admiration for the talent and insight of writers whose politics were far removed from his own—Henry James, Joseph Conrad, and William Faulkner, for example.

In the view of some segments of the Left, in fact, Howe demonstrated so much sympathy in *Politics and the Novel* for the works of writers considered reactionary that he deserved to be roundly denounced. Howe told Coser, "my book is subjected to a violent attack in the *American Socialist* on the ground that I praise reactionary writers, including Conrad, who opposed the 1905 Revolution!"[16]

The "reactionary" writer who had the most influence on Howe was Dostoevsky. Howe hailed Dostoevsky's *The Possessed* as a brilliant work of ideological and psychological complexity, a tome that scorned liberalism and rejected radicalism but remained "the greatest of all political novels." In a passage that revealed more than a little regret about his own ideologically sectarian past, Howe wrote: "In all of his novels Dosteovsky shows how ideology can cripple human impulses, blind men to simple facts, make them monsters. . . . No other novelist has dramatized so powerfully the values and dangers, the uses and corruptions of systematized thought."[17]

Serious socialists, Howe imagined, would not be dissuaded from their belief by reading *The Possessed*. But he thought, too, that "the quality and nuance of that belief" would never be quite the same after digesting Dostoevsky's masterpiece. This suggests that Howe's study of Dostoevsky coincided with the erosion of his own political certainties. Something similar might be said about the result of Howe's immersion in the works of Turgenev. When Howe summed up the political wisdom in Turgenev's novels, particularly *Fathers and Sons*, he gave some indication of just how far he had come from the doctrinal absolutes of his youth and how richly complex was his more mature approach to literature and politics. Turgenev, Howe said, "speaks to us for the right to indecision, which is almost as great a right as the right to negation. He speaks to us for a politics of hesitation, a politics that will never save the world, but without which, the world will never be worth saving. He speaks to us with the authority of failure."[18]

This authority of failure, according to Howe, is also what made Andre Malraux's *Man's Fate* successful as a work of literary art. The tension generated between Malraux's "mystique of action" and his awareness of the human waste and defeat in all historical effort seemed to chasten Howe, who came to see the wisdom in Malraux's message that "political struggle is not the true end of man's life." Yet Howe also praised Stendahl's *The Red and the Black* because it suggests, among other things, the price that must be paid when politics is *eliminated*

Irving Horenstein (on the right) at a Fresh-Air or Jewish Charity farm in the Poconos about 1930. *(Courtesy of Nicholas and Nina Howe)*

Howe played the violin, at which he was "pretty good," well into his teens. *(Courtesy of Nicholas and Nina Howe)*

Howe at the time of his graduation from DeWitt Clinton High School in 1936. *(Courtesy of Nicholas and Nina Howe)*

City College of New York, 1930s. *(Courtesy of CCNY Archives)*

The Library at CCNY, 1930s. Here, and in Alcove 1, Howe spent more time than in class. *(Courtesy of CCNY Archives)*

Irving Howe (row 3, third from right), among his classmates at City College, 1940.
(Courtesy of CCNY Archives)

Howe at the time of his graduation from City College, 1940.
(Courtesy of Nicholas and Nina Howe)

Irving Howe as a GI in Alaska, 1943–1945. *(Courtesy of Nicholas and Nina Howe)*

Irving Howe as a GI in Alaska, 1943–1945. *(Courtesy of Nicholas and Nina Howe)*

Thalia and Irving Howe on Grover Avenue in front of their new Princeton, New Jersey, home, 1949. *(Courtesy of Nicholas and Nina Howe)*

Thalia Howe, Richard Blackmur of Princeton University's English Department, and Howe, c. 1950. *(Courtesy of Nicholas and Nina Howe)*

Irving Howe with his children, Nina and Nick, c. 1954. *(Courtesy of Nicholas and Nina Howe)*

Howe with students at Brandeis University, c. 1955. *(Ralph Norman, photographer. Brandeis University Archives)*

Lewis Coser and his never-missing cigarette with Howe at Wellfleet, Massachusetts, c. 1957. *(Courtesy of Ellen C. Perrin)*

In the summer of 1958 Irving Howe was an invited lecturer at the University of Salzburg's American Studies Seminar. *(Courtesy of Nicholas and Nina Howe)*

The Howes, *en famille*. Thalia, Nick, Nina, and Irving before the divorce, 1958. *(Courtesy of Nicholas and Nina Howe)*

An informal presentation by Howe at Colby College in Maine, where Jane Wyman, his Stanford graduate student (seated at his right) was teaching in the early seventies. *(Courtesy of Jane Wyman)*

Nick Howe, Jane Wyman, and Irving in Waterville, Maine, in the early seventies. *(Courtesy of Jane Wyman)*

Irving Howe at Baltimore Hebrew University for a lecture in 1983. *(Craig Terkowitz, photographer)*

20. Irving and Ilana Wiener Howe vacationing at Penobscot Bay in Maine, 1987.
(Courtesy of Nicholas and Nina Howe)

Irving and granddaughter Ana in Montreal, 1993.
(Courtesy of Nicholas and Nina Howe)

from social life.[19] It is this complexity of vision and attitude of political openness and possibility that helped make *Politics and the Novel* a minor classic.

Very soon after the publication of *Politics and the Novel*, and not long after the Marcuse-Howe imbroglio, Howe, still smarting and frustrated, participated in a student-sponsored panel discussion at Brandeis on "politics and the novel." Howard Fast, still a member of the Communist Party, even if only tenuously, was one of the guest speakers. According to Jeremy Larner, who moderated the event, Fast, "belying his name," rambled on and on about "scientific socialism," defended Stalinism, and failed to address the sophisticated literary problems raised by Howe. Howe passed Larner a note asking him how long he was going to "let this thing go on." Moments later, Larner, who had nearly dozed off, was awakened by Howe screaming, "'You have blood on your hands!'" Fast, visibly shocked, finally stopped speaking. Howe rose to his feet saying "I have waited twenty years to be on the same podium with you," and he went on to eviscerate Fast with pointed facts about writers (including Fast himself) who had twisted history to fit the party line. Fast, claiming he had never heard such caustic invective, professed himself scandalized and tried to appeal to the audience's sense of "fair play." But only a few months later, perhaps shaken by Howe more than he cared to admit, Fast announced in the *New York Times* that the Moscow show trials of the 1930s and the Hitler-Stalin pact of 1939 had suddenly become too much for him, and he quit the Communist Party.[20]

Some of Howe's students were also shaken, mostly by what they saw as their professor's failure to temper his scorn in the political arena. They knew Irving Howe from the classroom and from reading his *Politics and the Novel*. Many had learned from him not to judge writers primarily by their ideologies. They had learned to see literature as something larger than politics, as "a mirror and a lamp"—an important reflection and illumination of human experience. And they learned to see reading and the study of literature as a way to "connect," to "respond," to gain a better, more nuanced sense of the human condition.[21] A generosity of spirit, a sense of empathy, an openness of mind, a shaking up of embedded assumptions, a modification and enlargement of the self, all of these were the goals of literature, according to Howe. And all were possible, even with writers whose views were fundamentally different from one's own.

The value of *Politics and the Novel*, and of Howe's critical and class-room approach, lay in an ability to balance a concern about the political issues raised by writers with a mainly dispassionate analysis. When, from the point of view of the students, Howe, in his attack on Fast, an invited guest, violated his own "rules" as well as the rules of general propriety, they were taken aback. Some were vocally critical. "You kicked around a helpless man," they said. Others, failing to understand Howe's anger at Fast, a defender of the Moscow trials, and of the murder of the Jewish poets and writers, asked whether this wasn't just a "tiresome quarrel between equally irrelevant old radicals?" Some professors, including sociologist Rose Coser, who had heckled Fast repeatedly, and political scientist Milton Sachs, challenged the students by asking them pointedly, "If murder and terror in the name of leftism weren't worth strong feelings, what was?"[22]

The debate went on for months. In the end, Jeremy Larner and some of the other students wondered: Could it be, after all, that Irving Howe, a man molded by years of philosophical disputation and by the persistent contemplation of politics and morality, had a more developed sense of "what really finally mattered?" What really finally mattered to Howe were freedom and democracy, even more than socialism and its promise of equality, certainly more than restraint and decorum. Not too long after the Fast affair, the socialist and British Labor Party notable Aneurin Bevan spoke at Brandeis and came off mainly as an apologist for the Soviet suppression in Hungary. Howe "roughed him up" in the question-and-answer period, and a little later he asked Coser, "What does it mean to call oneself a socialist [as we do] when there is hardly a party or a party leader in the world that we can identify with; indeed that doesn't rouse us to contempt, anger or hostility?" That some socialists perpetrate oppression or turn a blind eye upon it, Howe said, "requires us all the more to stress the libertarian, [Rosa] Luxemburgist side of the socialist ethic."[23]

Howe could also be tough on those he considered nonsocialists. After a university talk by Jacob Potofsky, Howe took the labor leader to task for his lack of militancy. He admitted to Coser that he had treated Potofsky with some belligerence, but he was proud that he had included, as part of his attack, the following Hasidic story: "When Reb Zusye went to heaven, God didn't ask him why, in his life on earth, Zusye wasn't Moses, but why he wasn't even Zusye." When Potofsky goes to heaven, Howe said to the audience, "God won't ask, why weren't you Eugene Debs" (leader of the Socialist Party in the early twentieth century and several times its presidential candidate), "but why weren't you even Sidney Hillman?" (militant trade unionist and president of the Amalgamated Clothing Workers of America).[24]

Potofsky may not have been Hillman, but as Howe continued to watch the crushing of the Hungarian revolution, he remained Irving Howe, pondering the issues more deeply than most writers in the late 1950s. Witnessing the brutality heaped upon the East Europeans, Irving quickly came to realize that Moscow was unwilling to acquiesce in changes that were judged too dramatic or that moved too quickly. Howe also knew that while the Communist leaders in the Soviet satellites appeared eager to "wrench free from the Russians," they were just as eager to "keep firm control at home." Sadly, Howe concluded that de-Stalinization, on the whole, had not greatly advanced the prospects for democratic socialism. Still, he proposed a policy of encouraging even the tentative liberalization of the Soviet Union, while at the same time criticizing its shortcomings. Perhaps it was time, Howe suggested, to accept a more complex interpretation of Communism, remembering its historic unbudgeability while recognizing its potential capacity for modification.[25]

This did not mean, however, that the West should temper its "fundamental opposition" to existing Communist regimes. While political "arrangements may have to be made" with the Soviet Union in order to preserve the peace, Howe contended, the West ought not consent to a "moral coexistence" with totalitarianism. Howe's creative "double vision" vis-à-vis Russia, which was a substantial improvement over the anti-Communist intransigence of the Cold War period, proved, at first, too contradictory for most people in the West, many of whom found it simpler either to overlook the totalitarian quality of Soviet life in the interest of avoiding a nuclear war, or to see any "constructive engagement" with Moscow as softness on Communism. But many people, including most intellectuals, even the neoconservatives of the 1970s and 1980s, eventually came around to Howe's shrewd and effective strategy for dealing with the Communist world.[26]

What helped prompt Howe to construct and propose this strategy, and what sustained him in his position, was the "enormously cheering" possibility, manifest in the Hungarian rebellion, that "the typical totalitarian combination of terror and indoctrination [had] left so small a mark upon the consciousness of the east European." Much earlier, in

1950, when Howe was writing a critique of George Orwell's *1984* (1949), he had identified the "animal drives" of humankind as among "the most enduring forces of resistance to the totalitarian state." Influenced perhaps by Trilling, who had seen in "instinct" a refuge from the tyranny of culture, Howe had faith in human resilience. And now in 1957, Howe actually saw men and women resisting, covertly and overtly. Through some inner core, "animal drive" or not, the Hungarians had indeed denied consent to the totalitarian state. Although Howe recognized, as Orwell had earlier, that the power of the state survived, even as belief in it was crumbling, he returned to the idea that by encouraging dissidents—student activists, banned novelists, Marxist revisionists—Communist society might be transformable.[27]

The totalitarian state, Howe thought, could maintain itself for a significant period, but not indefinitely, as Hannah Arendt's famous thesis seemed to imply. In the *Origins of Totalitarianism* (1951), Arendt had captured the murderous insanity that sustained the totalitarian regimes and had argued convincingly that totalitarianism was the driving power of the twentieth century. But Howe thought she had failed to consider that conditions of terror cannot be sustained forever, and that all states eventually run down. The state could buy time, Howe admitted, by moving, as the Soviet Union had moved, from the daily imposition of terror to what Howe called "terror in reserve." And the rulers could move away from the indoctrination of an ideology they no longer believed in to holding power for its own sake. But this, Howe argued, introduced vulnerabilities which rebels and resisters were exploiting.

Torn between the euphoria generated by democratic resistance, on the one hand, and the despondency over brutal suppression, on the other, Howe began, he said later, to reflect more intensely and systematically upon the "nature of humankind" and the limits of human malleability.[28] In 1943 Howe, still very much the radical who believed in "the progressive transformation" of humanity, had written that "[h]uman nature is not a doom; it is an experiment."[29] But twelve years later in 1955, with the Holocaust now never very far from his consciousness, Howe wrote to a *Dissent* contributor: "You talk about 'human perfectibility.' I've put the word into quotes—for what does it really mean; it's just a spectre of nonsense."[30]

And by 1957 in the context of the East European disturbances, Howe came to the tentative conclusion that there was something "intrinsically recalcitrant" about human nature. It could operate as positive force, refusing, ultimately, to be transformed by ideology and terror, as the Hungarian rebels appeared to prove. Still, because of the ruthlessness of the totalitarians bent on holding power simply for the sake of power, Howe had to pay attention again, as he had with the Nazis, to the actuality of "radical evil," a deeply rooted, intrinsically recalcitrant and incorrigible evil that was "part of the nature of things" and not fully explainable through social analysis. In the late fifties, a phrase from Saul Bellow's novel *The Victim* (1947), "Evil is as real as sunshine," kept going through Howe's mind.[31]

That Howe recognized this powerful fetter on human possibility did not mean that he had given up on change. He still believed in significant improvability if not perfectibility, but his ruminations about Bellow's pregnant sentence reinforced a healthy check on his earlier arrogance and overly optimistic radicalism which had affirmed the infinite and positive malleability of human nature. And it put in more favorable perspective for him the "conservative idea" (echoed by radicals like Andre Malraux) that politics ought not to engulf the whole of human existence.[32]

Again, acknowledging the existence of intrinsic evil did not mean acquiescing in the notion that the doctrine of Original Sin forever doomed humanity to society as it is. Rather, it intensified awareness of the limits on human wisdom, which was incomplete and fragmentary, and on human aspiration, which was often tainted in its motives. But Howe, professing a kind of Jewish modification of the fatalistic Christian doctrine, continued to believe in an obligation to act or suffer the consequences of inaction.

A Jewish dimension of Howe's thinking emerged in his 1957 review of Albert Camus' novel *The Fall*. Reading that book, Howe said, "I found myself unexpectedly made aware of my Jewish background, in which the depreciation of pride is utterly common but the wrecking of the self as the price of guilt is quite rare. I found myself thinking of *the traditional Jewish morality of the deed*, and wondering whether Clamance's act of helping that old woman in the street . . . was not in some sense, quite regardless of the uses to which he put it beforehand and after, a good act. It is no small question—for that old woman will always be there in the street."[33]

Howe would continue to be moved by "the traditional Jewish morality of the deed" and would continue to feel an obligation to act to relieve misery and to advance justice. To the very last day of his life, he was promoting the kind of reform that would help that woman in the street in the short run, while at the same time he was advocating the cause of democratic socialism in the United States and the world for the long run. But despite his hope that further liberalization of East European Communism might even lead to democratic socialism, Howe had almost no faith in the reformability of the American Communist Party (ACP). He avoided it and virtually read the party out of the movement for progressive change.

In his book, *The American Communist Party* (1957), coauthored with Lewis Coser, Howe admitted that many individual members of the party had worked heroically and had made painful sacrifices in the hope of advancing progressive causes. He also demonstrated that the Communists in America had at times been capable of acting like an ordinary political party. When, for example, Franklin Delano Roosevelt's policies turned sharply leftward in 1935, the ACP tilted toward the New Deal. But even here the party had been acting on orders out of Moscow, as it had from early in its history. The Communist Party's general political culture and behavior in America had once expressed an indigenous radical tradition, Howe said correctly. But the party was transformed relatively early in its history. It became, he concluded, largely an appendage of Russian power and subsequently played a tragically destructive role in the history of the American Left.[34]

Howe also admitted that the disclosures by Khrushchev of Stalin's crimes against humanity and the events in Hungary had stimulated "factional disputes in the American party between true Stalinists and various kinds of 'revisionists.'" The "public face of the . . . party has changed rather drastically," Howe acknowledged, but these changes, he insisted, were "essentially symptoms of disintegration." Moreover, in his conclusion he reminded his readers that he had had no intention in the book of implying that Stalinism was entirely a thing of the past. Although Howe was convinced that by 1957 the ACP was mostly dead, he suspected that the "scattering of hard-shelled believers" that remained would continue to act (if they operated at all) as a "corrupting influence in American radicalism."[35]

In practice this meant that Howe would not participate in organizations, meetings, or demonstrations with Communists and would express horror when other advocates of democratic socialism did share platforms with them. On May Day 1957, A. J. Muste, a contributing editor of *Dissent*, participated in a rally in New York City with delegates from the Socialist Workers Party, the Communist Party and other radical groups. Howe was appalled and said so. He was not trying merely to maintain a position of political purity, as some of his critics have charged. He was reacting to the spectacle of democratic socialists associating with Communists whose comrades in Hungary had only recently repressed, in brutal fashion, the uprisings of students and workers.[36]

Muste argued in defense of his own actions that American Communists had demonstrated their independence from Moscow by openly denouncing the repression in Hungary in the *Daily Worker*. He also insisted that only by participating in discussion with Communists could one have any chance of influencing them. Howe was unconvinced. When Muste and Sidney Lens, another contributing editor of *Dissent*, helped organize the American Forum for Socialist Education with the same group of radicals who sponsored the May Day rally, Howe along with most other editors of *Dissent* refused to take part in this new organization mainly because Communists were involved. "We regard the CP not as a radical group among other radical groups," Howe wrote, "but as an association of political enemies that has no place in the socialist community." Howe, as always, defended the free speech and civil liberties of Communists, but he singled out Muste and Lens for criticism because the society they helped form lent "a helping hand to the Communist Party by providing it with a kind of privileged sanctuary and protective coloration."[37]

The conflict over these issues between Muste and Lens on the one side, and most members of the *Dissent* board on the other, was so intense that when Lens tried to submit another piece to the magazine on the subject of "associating with Communists" it was rejected. Lens stopped writing for *Dissent* and said later that he was asked by Howe to leave the board. Muste, in an act of solidarity, also resigned.[38] This was no mass exodus, but it was an exception to Howe's masterful handling of disputes among the Dissenters. And it is not surprising that it came over the issue of Communism.

One of the defenses Muste had made in support of his associating with Communists was that many of the students and workers involved in the uprising in Hungary were themselves Communists. Howe had made a similar argument earlier against Marcuse's intimation that there were fascists among the Hungarian rebels. But for Howe it was one thing to argue that we must support Communist revisionists fighting to liberalize an already established Stalinist totalitarianism, and very much another thing to argue that American Communists, with little love for the libertarian tradition, living in a workable, if incomplete democracy, were appropriate partners for democratic socialists.

Another notable breakup within the *Dissent* crowd came in 1959 when C. Wright Mills ended his association with the magazine, also over the issue of Communism. In 1957, during a trip to the Soviet bloc, Mills discovered that there were reasons for hope in the Eastern European world. When he returned home, he was, according to Howe, in a "state of manic exaltation." But unlike Howe, who was exalted by the growing dissidence in that world, Mills was mostly impressed by the industrial achievements of the Communist states. And the sociologist came to regard as obsolete the stubborn anti-Communism of his "old friends" at *Dissent*.[39]

Two years later, in reviewing Mills' *The Causes of World War III* for *Dissent*, Howe argued that his old friend, by calling for a kind of non-judgmental relationship between the United States and the Soviet Union, had gone dangerously beyond the proposal for peaceful coexistence. Howe thought peaceful coexistence not only necessary but indispensable. But Mills was now promoting a "moral coexistence" which Howe regarded as intolerable because it meant surrendering the right to be critical of the continuing totalitarian character of the Soviet state. Mills, from Howe's perspective, had been taken in by the left-wing dictators of the Communist world who had not in fact won the consent of the masses but had exploited a profound yearning of people for a better life and turned it into a grotesque caricature of socialism.[40]

Howe, in his exchange with Mills in *Dissent*, had demonstrated a steadfast anti-Communism and a willingness to support some forms of nonmilitary containment. In the very next issue, a disappointed Mills, as a kind of last act before severing his relations with the magazine, responded with an angry letter to "Dear Irving." Just how, Mills wanted to know, did Irving's position diverge from that of John Foster Dulles? "I . . . thought you had abandoned the foot-dragging mood of the Cold War and were trying to make a new beginning," Mills wrote. "To dissent is lovely. But Irving, as regards foreign policy, from what, tell me, do you dissent?"

Howe did not respond directly to Mills's charge that his views were not very different from the State Department's. Instead, he began by agreeing with Mills that "there are many signs of good in the Communist countries." But he then went on to make a list very different from

Mills's inventory of economic progress. Milovan Djilas, the Yugoslavian dissident writer, Howe said, was good, as was Boris Pasternak, whose novel *Doctor Zhivago* Howe had described earlier as "an act of testimony as crucial to our moral and intellectual life as the Hungarian revolution to our political life." The Hungarian revolutionists, of course, were good, as were the Polish 'revisionists' and the Chinese 'right deviationist' intellectuals, and anyone who wished to emulate Tito's "national" Communism or experiment with a mixed economy. Indeed, "everything in the totalitarian world which helps to crumble the party's monopoly of power and thereby disintegrate the rule of the regime," Howe wrote, "is good." But "the regime itself is evil," he insisted. "And only by ceaselessly attacking it—in our ways, the ways of democrats and socialists—can we give some little aid to our comrades, known and unknown, in the east."[41]

At this time, but on another plane entirely, Howe was in need of a "little aid" himself. As already mentioned, he had become, while at Brandeis, sometime in 1959, deeply involved with one of his graduate students who was also the wife of a colleague, and his marriage was coming apart. It does not seem that Irving acted out of any dissatisfaction with Thalia, whom, according to friends and students, he continued to "love and respect."[42] On the surface their relationship appeared to be rock solid. When Howe's students, Michael Walzer and Judith Borodovko, had dinner with Irving and Thalia in Belmont (a suburb of Boston) in 1956, they "were surprised by the stable, bourgeois quality of the life-style." The Howes "had quite a nice house," Judith said, "with a neat lawn, and two nicely done-up little kids plumped down in the middle of a suburban dining room. Thalia was very elegantly dressed. Despite her middle-classness, we found her somewhat exotic, the teacher of classics, the non-Jew married to Irving."[43]

In the summer of 1957, just after getting his book on the *American Communist Party* ready for publication, Howe traveled to Europe with Thalia and then to Greece to visit with her relatives. And as late as the summer of 1958, after Howe finished a round of lecturing in American Studies at the University of Salzburg in Austria, the couple toured France and Italy with their children. Their daughter Nina, almost seven at the time, still has fond memories of the family on that trip.[44]

But Howe appeared to be troubled as early as the fall of 1957, immediately after his return home from Greece to the United States. In a series of letters to Lew Coser, Howe admitted that he was "finding it terribly hard to get back to work again." Perhaps, he said, "European hedonism has corrupted me." And he confessed that he found himself "really bored with teaching. The kids," Howe complained, "get more distant and uninteresting every year." He asked Coser if there wasn't "something almost inherent in academic life, especially once one has gotten tenure, that makes for slackness and sloth? . . . [E]ven at a place like Brandeis," Howe wrote, "there is an 'air of what does it all matter.'" Even Howe's friends, Cunningham and Rahv, whom he called "very gifted men," were "both, in different ways demoralized." The result, Howe concluded, "is a need to fight off the contagion of their surrender."[45]

Needing a change of pace, Howe took unpaid leave from Brandeis to teach elsewhere for the academic year 1958–1959. Thalia, with her doctorate, landed a position at the University of Michigan, and Irving, without the Ph.D. ended up at the nearby but less prestigious Wayne State University in Detroit.[46] How the couple got along that year it is difficult to know, but it appears that Irving was as dissatisfied with his students at Wayne as he was with those at Brandeis.[47] He fled Detroit and returned with Thalia to Waltham.

Not more than a few weeks later, Howe was drawn to Edja Weisberg, his twenty-nine-year-old graduate student and the wife of Howe's friend Harold Weisberg (a colleague in the Department of Philosophy and a Reform rabbi); and about a year later they were "crazy in love." Joseph Cheskis, a Russian refugee teaching Romance languages at Brandeis who had helped with some translations for Howe's anthology, *A Treasury of Yiddish Stories*, tried to "ride herd" on Irving. Cheskis thought Howe had always had a "loose eye," and with his powerful Yiddish accent and paternal manner he told Irving to "keep his fly buttoned."[48] But it was no use. Edja, a Holocaust survivor from Hungary who had come out of the camps at sixteen and was adopted by a wealthy Boston couple, was by all reports "ravishingly beautiful" as well as smart. Irving was enthralled, as were many others. "All of us were in love with Edja," Joseph S. Murphy, a graduate student at Brandeis in the late fifties and later chancellor of the City University of New York, told me in 1997. "She was stunning," said Murphy, and "she worked at making herself more so. . . . She did things with her make up, her hair, and so on." But "what was really so powerful about her," Murphy remembered, "were those numbers—'the Auschwitz tattoo,' and she used them."[49]

It was not so surprising that the combination of Edja's Holocaust aura, intelligence, youthful energy, and looks attracted Irving. He was close to thirty-nine, a dangerous age, one which, according to D. H. Lawrence, "marks the middle of the journey, raises fears of a decline in strength and potency, signals the end of that animal vigor which is the gift of youth." Even earlier, on his thirty-fifth birthday, Irving had told a friend that he was beginning to "feel very old." And now perhaps the Yeats poem, "Sailing to Byzantium," came to mind : "Consume my heart away/Sick with desire/And fastened to a dying animal/It knows not what it is." But it did strike many as puzzling that Howe, with what looked like the model family, became Edja's lover. And "everyone knew about it," including Thalia, Irving's wife of nearly twelve years.[50] She told a colleague (who was sitting in on one of her Greek language classes) that "Irving's affair would come to nothing" because Edja would not leave her husband and young daughter. In the long term this turned out to be true. But the relationship between Howe and Edja continued well into 1961 and brought Brandeis its first scandal.[51]

He did not move out of his house until 1961, and as late as mid-1960 Howe told his publishers who were reissuing his book on Faulkner that "the dedication . . . should read as in the original: To Thalia."[52] It was clear to everyone by 1959, however, perhaps with the exception of Thalia, that the marriage would not last. With the affair still running hot, divorce proceedings were initiated, apparently by mutual agreement, in 1960. By the end of that year, obviously unnerved by the implications of his seemingly impulsive behavior, the impact this was having on his family, and the lack of support from friends, Irving sank into deep depression.

Separately, he and Thalia and the children entered therapy and by early 1961 Howe was able to tell Coser that he was "getting into better shape" and not suffering "nearly [as] much depression as in recent months." He was even beginning again "to work a little." When Irving complained to Coser that his friends (including Lew, at least by implication) not only failed to comfort him but were also passing moral judgments about him, Coser reminded Howe of his "famous impatience" and its power to alienate. "What you say about my impatience," Howe responded, "undoubtedly is true: I'm aware of my faults. . . . Still there are times," Howe wrote plaintively, "when one can ask friends to be patient." In the meantime, Howe said, his analyst, "a magnificent man," was helping him. "He has kept me afloat through stormy weather,"

Howe told Coser, and went on to assure him that "any time I hear anyone say the usual stupid things about analysts, I will indeed show my famous impatience."[53]

By the end of 1960 Irving began to look for work elsewhere while he continued to try to convince Edja Weisberg to leave the Brandeis area with him. Perhaps wanting to get as far away as possible, he accepted an invitation to be interviewed at Stanford. He liked the people in the English Department there which included the critic Malcolm Cowley (a visiting professor) and the poet Yvor Winters. He confessed to Cowley, however, that he was "a little troubled" by one thing: "the sense of arcadian temptation which the area exudes, as if it were a place where tensions slackened excessively and one simply vegetated."[54] That sense, for Howe, so much the urban man, so much the New Yorker, would be confirmed over the two years he spent on the West Coast. The offer he got was good enough to help him with the long-term expenses of a broken-up family, and he decided to go to California, hoping that as professor of American and English literature he would not vegetate, and hoping, too, that Edja would follow him there.[55]

In the summer of 1961, and just prior to his departure for Stanford, Irving left Thalia, ten-year-old Nina, and eight-year-old Nicholas in Belmont and moved into a Boston residence.[56] Money would remain an issue. Maintaining two households, providing child support, and paying for everyone's therapy was costly. Howe, more than once, pressed Random House, which was reissuing his Faulkner book, for the remainder of his advance on royalties, and he dunned them several times for his photocopying costs.[57] Howe was clearly burdened. But, despite what he had told Coser about his inability to do much work in this period, Howe, between bouts of depression, wrote in great spurts. He produced more than ten essays a year from 1959 to 1961, just slightly less than his usual rate, including sixteen for the *New Republic* (for which he had become literary editor in 1957). There were the usual political pieces for *Dissent* but also a number of literary gems on Singer, Mailer, Sholom Aleichem, James Baldwin, and Philip Roth. And alone in Boston in July 1961 within hours of Hemingway's suicide, Howe wrote a masterful essay about the novelist subtitled "The Conquest of a Panic."[58]

Howe carried something of his own sense of panic to California. But he conquered it temporarily by writing in "hyperactive" stretches between periods of guilt and frustration.[59] He also transported across the continent the continuing and seemingly unquenchable desire to have Edja Weisberg follow him. None of this augured well for Howe's accommodation to California, but his experience there was not nearly as bleak as the "gloomy farce" he made it out to be in *A Margin of Hope*. In the first place, there were Stanford faculty, including David Levin, Malcolm Cowley, and Yvor Winters, who were eager to have Howe on board.[60] Wallace Stegner predicted correctly that Howe would not stay long in what a New York Jewish intellectual could only perceive as "exile." And he was ultimately infuriated by Irving's contemptuous dismissal of his beloved West as "dead." But even Stegner, at the start, was enthusiastic about the addition of Howe to the English Department. In fact, even before Howe arrived at Stanford, he was involved in an administrative controversy, and Stegner helped hammer out a compromise that eased the way for Irving to join the faculty.

Howe had been an interdepartmental committee's unanimous choice to hold the first William Robertson Coe Chair of American Literature and American Studies, but the Coe bequest had specified that the money be used to combat "the threat of communism, socialism . . . and other ideologies opposed to our American system of Free Enterprise." And very late in the day, lawyers for the university declared Howe, who had described himself as co-editor of "a journal of socialist opinion," ineligible. They recommended appointing Irving simply as professor of English. Winters, Levin, and Stegner, the three American Studies professors, insisted that the administration's proposed "compromise" violated Howe's academic freedom. And they felt certain Howe would scorn the demotion. Backed by all the tenured members of the English Department, they said they "would not teach in a program designed to accomplish political ends." With the support of Winters, Levin, and the even better-known and influential Stegner, an arrangement was worked out whereby the Coe money would go to buy books in American Studies for the library, with no ideological restrictions, and there would be no Coe professorship that year. Howe delighted everyone by agreeing to the deal.[61]

On the night Howe arrived in California, David Levin met him at the San Francisco airport. Levin could tell immediately from Howe's dark expression that his expectations were not high. As they entered South Palo Alto, Howe's forebodings grew deeper. It was 9 P.M. on a hot Sunday, and everything in the California Avenue business district was closed for the evening. Howe could not, at that hour, find, within walking distance, a place for coffee. And the dingy hotel in which a frugal friend had advised him to reserve a room did little to improve his mood.[62]

Although Howe did learn to enjoy many things about the Bay Area, his first night as an immigrant in the alien West no doubt left him with an indelible impression of the distance he had traveled from the Northeast. When he later wrote about the California years, it was almost as if he could not get past the depressed state in which he had initially encountered the Pacific Coast. Nor does it seem that he ever got over his negative first impressions, or indeed the anti-California bias he had brought with him. Howe could make it seem as if he had experienced nothing positive in "the second-rate culture" in which he found himself "unmoored." One could come away from A Margin of Hope, for example, thinking that Howe had spent his entire two years in the tiny windowless room in which he spent his first miserable night. But, in fact, the next day, with the help of David Levin's wife, Howe had found a much better place in Palo Alto, and by his second year, a comfortable, well-located apartment on Pfieffer Street in San Francisco.

There were many other things, too, that brought Irving comfort, but he often needed others to help him see them more clearly. Early in his California sojourn he picked up again the therapy he had begun in the East. During his first visit, Howe, apparently wanting to display his "intellectual virtuosity," said that the doctor's name (Kelev?) meant "dog" in Hebrew. When the therapist quickly responded, "You really think you're the first one to notice that?," Howe, relieved by this sample of the doctor's method of "dry mockery," relaxed. But not for long.

Only a week or so later he entered the doctor's office saying he felt so bad, he ought to be hospitalized. The doctor asked Howe what he had been doing since his last visit. He said he "had written a little, though badly, and had had an encounter with a woman, not too bad; still . . . ." The therapist jumped up and into a bit of gleeful mimicry: "A little creativity, a little sexuality—my God, who can stand it?" It was Howe's turn to rise, "white with anger," fists clenched and ready to strike. Suddenly, however, awash with insight and the perspective offered by the therapist, Howe burst into laughter.[63]

Therapeutic, too, were a number of significant friendships Howe made, several with graduate students, that endured long after the Stanford years. Very quickly Howe hooked up with Jane Fowler and Bill Wyman, developing in relatively short order an association that "went well beyond the traditional student-professor relationship." Bill and Jane were soon to become husband and wife, but in the late summer of 1961 both were in failing marriages, as was Celia Morris, another graduate student who joined the Howe "entourage" about a year later. All were searching, individually, in quite the American way, for a second chance, for new opportunity on the California frontier. But, Irving, according to Jane, "was even more adrift than the rest of us in those days." In the absence of a vital communal life, he stumbled along alone, in pain and disarray, trying to determine "what to do with himself." He took "refuge," she said, in the house Jane and Bill owned in the country and even stayed over often in what came to be called "Irving's room."[64]

A self-described "starry-eyed graduate student," Jane took all of Howe's classes and was the research assistant for his edited collection of George Orwell's work. She was serious and bright. Bill Wyman, "a football player in college and a mule-packer from Montana," was certain that it was Jane in whom Irving was really interested. "I was alien to Irving," Bill told me in 1997, and not anything like the New York Jewish students, those "articulate, ironic" students Howe was used to. But the two men "gravitated toward one another." Bill taught Irving to swim. And Irving taught Bill "about ideas." Wyman had not been a very good undergraduate student, as Howe discovered when he saw a transcript of Bill's studded with "D's"; but Irving worked closely with him anyway and helped him get a master's degree in English.[65]

Howe was delighted to learn that Jane, as well as Bill, knew and loved baseball; and quite often the threesome were at Candlestick Park together, usually in the outfield close to Willie Mays. The novelist Alan Lelchuk, then a graduate student at Stanford, also went to games with Howe, as did Harper's editor Willie Morris. One night, with Howe and Morris in attendance, a Giants-Mets ballgame was suspended for more than an hour in the fifth inning because of fog. Howe, apparently remembering again how far he was from New York, said: "This wouldn't happen in the Bronx."[66] But joy could be restored watching the game. For Howe, as for many Americans, ordinary citizens as well as intellectuals, "the diamonds and rituals of baseball create[d] an elegant, trivial enchanted grid on which our suffering shapeless sinful day leans for the momentary grace of order." Ballet, too, especially choreography by Balanchine, would come to play this role for Howe. He would sometimes compare the two "art" forms: "Isn't Willie Mays catching a fly ball," Howe asked rhetorically in an essay for *Harper's*, "as elegant as Nureyev in a *pas de deux*?"[67]

The solace of baseball and friendship, however, were not enough to keep Howe from sporadic rounds of despair. Late in 1961 he told Lew Coser that "no one can be more severe in passing judgments about me than I can: that's part of the trouble. And as for my sins, crimes, and derelictions, all I can say is that I have paid heavily, very heavily, and continue to each day." Later he told Coser that he knew he had inflicted pain on Thalia, and that he felt guilty about his behavior "in regard to [her] and the kids," but not for anything "beyond that." And he continued almost daily right through the summer of 1962 to call East in his unwavering and desperate attempt to persuade Edja Weisberg to come to California. His phone bills were almost as bad, Howe told a colleague, as his bills for the psychiatrists for himself, his ex-wife, and his children.[68]

According to a story told by Philip Rahv to several Brandeis colleagues, sometime in July 1962 Howe called the Weisberg residence very late in the night. From bed, Harold answered, but Irving insisted on talking to Edja, whom he described as "a free, grown-up woman." It would take until August for Howe to realize that this free woman was not going to leave her husband (who by this time was quite ill). Edja, the survivor of the Holocaust, had, as Joseph Murphy put it, "a greater capacity for suffering—for guilt and pain—than for love," and perhaps she chose to stick with that suffering rather than pursue the possibilities of happiness with Irving.[69] There may, of course, have been a more prosaic reason: Edja's own sense of responsibility to her husband, and her feeling that it was immoral to leave him, affair or no affair. But Howe convinced himself finally that he had been "used" by Edja "in some psychological way"; used, he told Coser, "for the enactment of a fantasy strongly desired, yet not risked."[70]

Irving shared his misery with others, including his old Princeton friend Dennis Wrong who was across the bay at Berkeley for the summer of 1962. "Irving talked to me often about Edja," Wrong said, "because I myself had left my wife, at Brown, planning to marry the young wife of a junior colleague."[71] Howe, in jettisoning his wife and seeking a new one, appears to have been acting very much like his peers. This behavior among middle-aged men (or those approaching it), especially among the New York intellectuals, was widespread. Saul Bellow has had five wives, Kazin four, Mailer six.

Howe also continued to confide in Coser (who had only one wife), sometimes writing as often as twice a week. "I continue to feel bruised," he told his friend Lew, and "I'm not really working."[72] Although David Levin, whose faculty office was next door to Howe's, thought Howe was typing all the time and "at a rate of what seemed like 500 words a minute," Howe did not in fact deliver his normal barrage of essays in the California period. But he did write a handful of political pieces for *Dissent* and more than a dozen literary articles for other periodicals.[73]

The writing could bring respite. No doubt Irving thought about Edmund Wilson, who himself had experienced a "sort of nervous breakdown" in 1929, but who, by giving literary expression to his "internal conflict and ranklings" could "thumb his nose at the world." "Well," Howe said later, "at least for a while."[74] If Howe's writing did not bring complete or long-term relief, it did produce a number of wonderful essays, including one on Robert Frost.

Frost's "lyrics speak of the hardness and recalcitrance of the natural world," Howe wrote, "of its absolute indifference to our needs"; but also "of the refreshment that can be found through a brief submission to the alienness of nature." Howe, who could feel the starkness of the Pacific Coast and the "calming grandeur of the red-woods," seemed to be reflecting his own grudging surrender to California's natural environment. But grudging it was, and temporary, too. Howe fully sympathized with Frost, the "modern poet who shares in the loss of firm assumptions and seeks, through a disciplined observation of the natural world and a related sequel of reflection, to provide some tentative basis for existence," some "'momentary stay' as [Frost] once remarked 'against confusion.'" But, again in sympathy with Frost, Howe offered a qualification: "always provided one recognizes the need to move on."[75] These sensitive and moving lines of Howe's are all the more impressive when we learn that they were produced while he was sitting on the floor of the Wymans' living room with Bill's two-year-old son running around, and with Jane making a racket with pots and pans in the kitchen. With a piece of plywood propped up on his knees for support, Irving thought and wrote about Frost, and "absolutely nothing distracted him."[76]

In this period also, but not under the same conditions, Howe wrote his long piece on T. E. Lawrence, a profound, searching and self-revealing essay. Lawrence, an amateur archeologist and undistinguished staff captain in British Military Intelligence, rapidly became a leader of the Arab revolt against the Turks during World War I. A cluster of tribes that had neither nationalism nor a unified politics, the Arabs were notoriously inconstant and divided, and virtually leaderless. Lawrence had seen the necessity of breathing "a vibrancy of intention" into the revolt by stirring the Arabs into behaving *as if* they were a nation. But he needed to avoid directly provoking the Turks, an enemy capable of destroying the uprising, and he wanted to "go around" the British, an "ally" that would disarm it. He hoped to help make the Arabs a free people, not through full-scale war for which they were not ready, but by rebellion, by a kind of "national strike." This was a task and a challenge Howe thought "worthy of a serious" and "ambitious man."[77]

Lawrence was riddled with tensions and seeming contradictions. A dynamiter of railroads and bridges, he was also an intellectual, a literary man who read Mallory between raids. An ingenious military leader who sensed in the Arabs an unformed yearning for dignity, Lawrence could also turn himself into an ordinary recruit tending the "shit-cart" of his camp. He was troubled by ambition and guilt, even worried about the shape and rhythm of the sentences in the book he would later write, but he was, as Howe believed, a hero "in the tangle of modern life . . . struggling with a vision he can neither realize nor abandon."[78]

Torn, like Lawrence, between the rival attractions of action and withdrawal, Howe saw the wary but dedicated desert warrior as a paradigmatic modern man, the "prince of our disorder." And he read Lawrence's memoir, *The Seven Pillars of Wisdom*, with its "series of broken reflections upon human incompleteness" as a "modern" book, as necessary for comprehending the twentieth century as the work of Brecht or Kafka or Pirandello.[79] Howe did not admire Lawrence as an agent of British imperialism, of course. And he was not uncritical of Lawrence's overzealous feats of military bravura and physical endurance. But Howe valued the bourgeois Victorian-become-Arabian-adventurer as a man who had, like himself, learned to live with both uncertainty and commitment, and indeed, to make a kind of heroic triumph out of the tensions between the two. He admired him for leaving "the settled life of middle-class England which seemed to offer little but comfort and destruction"; for abandoning "the clutter of routine by which a man can fill his days, never knowing his capacity for sacrifice or courage"; and for breaking with "the assumption that life consists merely of waiting for things to happen."[80]

The essay on "Lawrence of Arabia" by the "boy from the Bronx" was what Lionel Trilling might have called an act of moral imagination, a dedication to Howe's own unwavering socialist ideals and to his own ambitious tasks and tensions. Shortly before writing his piece on Lawrence, Howe wrote a review about Faulkner that imparted a variation on these themes: "What matters in Faulkner's world is neither success nor failure, happiness nor misery, but the constant readiness to live out the requirements of a man to exhaust, even destroy himself in the effort to fulfill his humanity."[81] Although closely matched to some sense of his own recent personal experience, these ideas expressed more importantly for Irving, as for Lawrence, a persistent yearning to stamp "intelligence and value upon a segment of history."[82] In Howe's case, this meant having a role to play, indeed a heroic role, in transforming America in the long run into a fairer, more fraternal, more pervasively democratic society. In the meantime, the Lawrence essay, Howe told Coser, was "something I'm proud of." And it helped his damaged ego, he said, "when people respond to some abstraction called 'IH' which they know from print."[83]

In a different sphere, it helped Irving's ego, too, that he was often surrounded by women. "It's curious," Howe wrote Coser, "that being unmarried, one suddenly begins to think of oneself as somehow an object for persuasion and contemplation by the opposite sex." Socially, Irving was invited everywhere, David Levin told me, and "everywhere he was always in the company of attractive women." This puzzled many, who knew that "Irving was smart all right," but wondered what other "social charms" this brusque character from the East possessed.[84]

At parties Howe often looked bored and distracted, even badly troubled. He could get lively, Levin said, when the conversation turned to politics or intellectual matters, but he rarely initiated such conversation when the talk turned "small." Howe's colleague, Wilfred Stone, said Irving was the rudest guy he'd ever known. He would often walk out of a cocktail party without saying good-bye, Stone complained. It was as if Irving were saying "if the world isn't going to make itself interesting to me, the hell with it." Howe himself admitted later that even before he got to California, the upheavals in his personal life had made him grow "disdainful of the routine passage of existence, the ordinary exchanges of courtesy and commonplace."[85]

Yet despite (because of?) his manner, his seeming pride in his own misery, Howe was rarely without a woman at his side. Over the two-year period, Irving had sustained relationships with several intelligent and attractive younger women, including Susan Sahl (the former wife of comedian Mort Sahl) and a woman remembered by Howe's associates only as Esther. He was also seen from time to time with "a blonde from Berkeley" who had introduced him to Erik Erikson and who accompanied Irving to parties and luncheons.[86]

There was a very close association, too, with Kay Seymour House, a Cooper scholar and teaching assistant hired at Stanford at the same time as Howe. Thirty-five and the single mother of two, House, like Jane Wyman and later Celia Morris, served as Irving's research assistant, as well as an informal adviser about "practical things": lightbulbs, mothballs, seatbelts, and so on. Like many brilliant people, House said, Irving lacked "common sense" about the quotidian.[87] Despite this "flaw" in Irving, Kay, who was traveling in the summer of 1962, took the risk of renting her house to him for the month of August. Howe's children, Nina and Nicholas, were coming out to visit, and Irving, "excited and nervous about" the "very new situation for all of us," needed a larger place.[88] Kay did insist, however, that Irving keep her cleaning woman. We have no record of what he thought, as a socialist, of hired household help.

Kay helped out in other ways as well. Although in his teaching Howe was a master of organization and presentation, he didn't always have the inclination or the time for rigorous preparation. Returning from a trip East one Sunday night, he called House saying he had to do a class on *The Adventures of Huckleberry Finn* the next day, and had not put anything together. House dutifully handed over a paper she had done in a graduate course. Irving reworked it, creatively, and delivered it as a lecture on Monday morning that brought the students to their feet applauding. And then, having "made it his," he kept on using it.

On another occasion, when Howe was teaching a Faulkner seminar "full of Ivy League students and one nun," he dragged Kay House in as a "mouthpiece." Irving told her that only the nun was understanding any of the sexual innuendo in Faulkner, and she couldn't say anything. (This was before the nuns had "kicked their habit," as Herb Gold has put it.) So House found herself (unknown to the other students) a last-minute addition to the seminar as the secret spokesperson for "Sister Sam." Kay was impressed by Irving's sensitivity to the nun's predicament, and by his sensitivity in teaching generally.[89]

Howe never talked about the specifics of his teaching at Stanford in his letters to Coser. He could take occasional pleasure in it, however, and from time to time was surprised by the quality of some of the students. He told David Levin he was "amazed" to discover that some of the suntanned young men who tossed around a football on the front lawns of their fraternity houses could also write decent responses to poetry. And at Stanford, as at Brandeis, Howe developed an excellent reputation as a teacher and a supportive mentor. Jane Wyman, who went on to teach American literature at Colby College, and Bill Wyman, now a writer as well as a mule-packer, testify to this, as does the writer Celia Morris, who said that she would never have completed her doctoral dissertation if Irving hadn't told her more than once to "stop kvetching, and do the footnotes."[90]

As a graduate student at Stanford, Gerald Graff, who went on to make his own distinctive mark in literary criticism, was "in awe of Howe." Graff called him "a stickler for evidence, for logical reasoning, and for felicitous style." And, with apparent good feeling, he also recalled that Howe was a "challenging" teacher, one of the few who would argue with you, but who was also "willing to change his mind." Alan Lelchuk, later the author of several well-received novels, also had "great respect for Howe's sharp mind and energetic New York style." Lelchuk had fond memories, too, of Irving's first public talk at Stanford. "Everyone came," Lelchuk said; "there were 250 people in attendance, unheard of for literary events." Howe, the first Jewish tenured full professor at Stanford, lectured "unabashedly on a Jewish subject," dealing with Singer and Sholom Aleichem in a serious, analytical way. The reception by the faculty was very good, Lelchuk recalled, and the "small bunch of Jewish students from the Bronx and Brooklyn, including me, who had come up through the public higher education system were delighted."[91]

Howe continued to inspire students to literary careers and to give public lectures on a variety of topics. And he elicited enthusiasm from a small following. But, he found the majority of his students intellectually dormant. He once asked a class full of "bright-cheeked, good-hearted innocents" whether the questions raised in *The Brothers Karamazov* seemed to them deeply relevant. "Not many," Howe said later, could answer "Yes" with real honesty. The dull students said "No" with ease, the brighter ones "No" with some discomfort. Recognizing that for most of his students neither literature nor the past existed outside of the classroom, Howe said he would try to persuade them, excite them, bludgeon them, if necessary, into believing that Ivan Karamazov's words were burningly important to them. Apparently the students, by their expressions and body language, implied that that attempt threatened the suburban California way of life they had chosen. "My dears," Howe remembered saying, "you are right."[92]

Howe concluded, partly from experiences like these and partly from preconceived notions, that moral introspection and intellectual excitement were not "natural" to California. Nor, he thought, was political activism, except perhaps on the right. Having seen a fair-sized minority of conservative students at Stanford and elsewhere in the state, Howe found it "hard to understand" or "cope with" their "rationalized hardness of spirit." They used Russell Kirk, Barry Goldwater, and Ayn Rand, Howe said in 1962, to confirm their ideology, and to convince themselves that America had few real problems and that the poor didn't really exist. At least in the thirties, Howe pointed out, the children of the rich "still knew something about poverty." His affluent suburban California students, however, had learned to brush "every unpleasantness beneath the social rug," like too many other prosperous Americans.[93]

Ignorance of literature and history, Howe insisted, allowed his students to assume that they, and everyone else, were totally free, that through mere exertion of will and intelligence people could make anything they wished of their lives. The central task, then, of the intellectual in the university, Howe believed, was "to validate the past, to insist upon its organic relationship with the present, to deny that America is exempt from history." After all, Howe asked, of what can the new and better world we seek be made if not—"together with the work of the future—the conserved heritage of the past?" And Howe did continue to seek a new and better world outside as well as inside the classroom.[94]

David Levin spoke for several other colleagues when he said later that the main contribution Howe brought to Stanford, even beyond the impact of his intellect and the range of his interests, was politics. Levin did not mean that Howe was trying to convert students or faculty to some version of socialism. He meant that Howe brought to the campus the quality of "engagement." This showed up often in class, as we have seen, and in more public arenas as well. In the spring of 1963, for example, during the campaign against segregation in Birmingham, Alabama, a small number of students and teachers including Howe organized a rally, the first in many years on the sleepy Stanford campus, to declare support for the civil rights movement. The novelist James Baldwin spoke, concluding with an appeal for funds. Hundreds of students, Howe said later, "moved by that belief in 'fairness' with which some Americans still grow up," came forward and began making contributions. But student marshals also came forward to enforce a long-standing rule against political fund-raising on campus. Before any confrontation between the two groups could take place, however, Irving Howe reached out his long arms, and over the heads of two or three students grabbed the basket of money. "I'll take the responsibility," he said, and the marshals withdrew. Drawing upon his memories of leftist soap-box speakers in Manhattan and the Bronx, Howe made a further appeal for funds, and bills and coins continued to drop into the basket.[95]

Politics in its broadest sense was still at the center of Howe's being. And New York, which was political in ways that Howe believed California could never be, continued to beckon. The "action" was there, and of course, so was *Dissent*. The magazine was almost always in his thoughts, so much so that he sometimes exaggerated its importance. He was, for example, "astonished" that the Stanford library did not subscribe. Howe continued to contribute his pieces to *Dissent*, and he even did some fund-raising, but he knew he could not direct the journal from San Francisco. He told Coser to put Michael Walzer in charge. That didn't sit particularly well with some of the other editors, especially Plastrik and Geltman, who thought that Walzer was too young and inexperienced. And for a while it looked as if *Dissent* might sink in Howe's absence.[96]

The crisis at *Dissent* was clearly one of the reasons Howe wanted to get back East. He also missed, personally, the general atmosphere of political commitment and reflection around the magazine. As early as August 1961, Howe told Coser somewhat desperately, "If we give up *Dissent*, that means giving up any sort of politics for the rest of our lives, and I don't think we really want to do that." [97] And despite his graduate student friends, his lovers, and even Willie Mays, there was still too much that Howe disliked about the mind-softening, "self-satisfied and self-adoring" state of California.[98] Like other New York Jewish intellectuals—Leslie Fiedler, for example, who had poked malicious fun at the "cowboys" he encountered at the University of Montana, or Bernard

Malamud, who had lampooned his fly-fishing colleagues at Oregon State University—Howe persisted in an attitude of contempt for everything Western.

He also persisted in his deep need for New York. Howe had written Samuel Hux that the city was "in [his] blood, like a poison." And New York was the place, he said a little later, where he could talk with the likes of Meyer Schapiro, Harold Rosenberg, and Lionel Abel. "They usually disagree with me," Howe said, "but they put me on my mettle." Outside of New York, in a small town, Howe said, he could be a "big cheese." But the trouble with big cheeses, Howe admitted, is that they are "probably full of holes," and "I want to be near people who can point them out." Howe was consistent in this kind of expression. After a disappointingly small audience turnout (consisting only of English faculty) and a tepid response to his guest lecture on T. E. Lawrence at Wabash College in Indiana in 1962, Howe asked his host how he had ended up in such a "godforsaken place," and told him that intellectuals "need to be working near people you envy or are afraid of."[99]

In the same period, Howe told Coser that he still had aspirations and that he "never had more ideas for things to do." This was partly in response to a remark Alfred Kazin had made about Irving's having gone West "to die." A "decidedly irritat[ed]" Howe wanted his friend Lew to assure Kazin and "whoever else" was making these comments "that these bones still live, and will I hope live long enough to make these bastards envious and uncomfortable." Howe's ambition was still intense, even if partly diverted by personal setbacks. He was clearly itching to be back in the thick of the New York action.[100]

Howe's favorite song in the California years, one he sang out loud while driving and played on the juke box every time he met Jane or Bill or Celia for a coke and a burger, a coffee or an occasional beer, was Ray Charles's "Hit the Road Jack." Howe was ready to do just that as early as the end of his first year at Stanford. Robert Preyer had written him about coming back to Brandeis, but Howe became depressed at the thought of returning to Waltham. He was a candidate for a position at Harvard for the fall of 1962, but that fell through. And then in November "the providence in which [Howe] disbelieved . . . proved merciful." A job offer for fall 1963 arrived from the City University of New York. "I'm tremendously excited by the whole thing," Howe immediately wrote Coser, "because I want to get back east [and] it will be very good for *Dissent*."[101]

Howe wanted to use *Dissent* to examine and exploit what appeared to be opportunities for social transformation in the late fifties and early sixties. The liberal rhetoric of John Fitzgerald Kennedy, with its encouragement of fresh thinking and its challenge to "the image of well-being and assurance," suggested that complacency was now out of date in Washington. And the president's words, if not yet his actions, had generated a hopeful activist glow, especially among the young. And for all Howe's skepticism about mainstream politics, he was encouraged by the string of Democratic victories in this period.[102]

Michael Harrington's *The Other America* (1962) had dramatically increased awareness of the chronic problems of poverty, urban decay, and political powerlessness. Richard Chase's *The Democratic Vista* (1958), a severe critique of the fifties and a perceptive anticipation of the new politics of the sixties, was also beginning to get more attention. And the social and cultural analyses of progressive writers like C. Wright Mills, Paul Goodman, and John Kenneth Galbraith were being translated into political action: a new, small, but growing and articulate student left was emerging; civil rights demonstrations were expanding; and the antinuclear movement was burgeoning, especially on college campuses. Howe's protégé, Michael Walzer, had written in 1961 that "there is an openness to new ideas probably unlike anything since the thirties."[103] That, Howe thought, was even more true in 1962 and 1963. He struggled, therefore, to prevent his private turmoil from thwarting hopes for public life and action. It was a "plastic hour" and time for Irving Howe to return home.

10

The Turmoil of Engagement

The Sixties: Part I

DESPITE HIS PERSONAL troubles, Irving Howe began the decade in a buoyant mood, expressing considerable confidence in the openness of the newly launched Kennedy administration and the liberal rhetoric of the early sixties. He and many of his friends were also attracted to the radical critique of American society voiced by the young leftists who were increasingly visible on college campuses. The Dissenters not only shared many of the values and goals expounded by the students, they admired their energy, commitment, and idealism. "Just about all of us who had experienced the debacles of the thirties and the dryness of the next two decades," Howe remembered later, "were tempted to seek renewal through forming ties with the insurgent students."[1] In 1963 Howe was optimistic enough to write that "as a mood, if not a movement, radicalism is beginning to revive." He even allowed himself to think that significant socialist activism was possible in the United States, and he went so far as to suggest that *Dissent* "venture a little into hypothetical 'program-making.'"[2]

Howe's hopefulness was not entirely unjustified. The decade, as a direct result of democratic organization and pressure, was witness to significant and enduring social progress on racial justice, women's equality, cultural diversity, environmental protection, and consumer rights—progress that continued into and through Richard Nixon's first term as president. But the turbulent political and countercultural activities of the sixties also bequeathed an undesirable dimension of anti-intellectualism and anarchic normlessness, as well as "culture wars" that continue to seethe. Furthermore, the unconscionable war waged by the United States in Southeast Asia for most of the period not only decimated a foreign nation and its people, it left festering wounds in a badly divided American body politic and an understandable distrust of government and politicians.

Moreover, at the end of the decade the critical issues of urban poverty and decay remained unsettled. There was a growing conservative backlash and even an armed reaction as factions of the youth rebellion and the black and antiwar movements turned authoritarian, violent, and apocalyptic. And the United States was still deeply engaged in the folly and tragedy of the Vietnam War, which continued to undergird and inflame all the issues. By the late sixties, Howe's desire for a fraternal community seemed hopelessly naive and his socialist vision far from fulfillment. Looking back on the decade, Howe wondered in a decidedly unoptimistic tone "whether the United States will survive as a democracy." For the first time since the early 1930s, Howe wrote, "one keeps encountering the fear that our social problems may turn out to be intractable, or, what is perhaps even worse, that solving them might not be an adequate solution to the malaise creeping into our bones."[3]

None of this kept Irving Howe from trying. At the end of the sixties, his involvement persisted. He was sobered, more cautious, but nevertheless still genuinely committed to his vision of democratic socialism. Along the way, his "reconquest of Jewishness," partly connected to that same vision, was promoted and even more powerfully defined by a variety of "events," including the publication of Hannah Arendt's *Eichmann in Jerusalem* (1963) and the Six-Day War in the Middle East (1967).

It was mainly the civil rights movement that moved Howe to see the early sixties as "great and stirring days in America." The freedom rides, the marches, and the sit-ins in both the North and the South inspired hope. The awakening of a new consciousness about racial injustice among many whites gave Howe confidence that blacks were "on the way up to freedom." And he was feeling "profoundly glad" and full of hope for "racial fraternity."[4]

Howe was an "integrationist," a position considered much too mild by those on the left who believed that only revolutionary change could bring racial justice. But Howe called the movement for racial equality "revolutionary," and he was not using the term loosely. Like his friend and colleague Bayard Rustin, the radical pacifist and organizer of Martin Luther King's massive March on Washington in 1963, Howe knew that the integrationist movement could not be victorious without a thoroughgoing social transformation. It required radical programs for vastly improved education, decent housing, and full employment through job training, job creation, and new definitions of work and leisure. Howe sincerely looked forward not only to an authentic "racial fraternity," but also to the kind of grand and enduring refashioning of the political economy "that would indeed be a revolution."[5]

The successful completion of the "Negro Revolution," as Howe labeled it in 1963, was so central, he thought, that the survival of the country depended on it. "If the Revolution fails, if it is balked by the racists and abandoned by pusillanimous liberals, this country," Howe prophesized, "will not be a fit place to live." And right through the sixties, Howe and *Dissent* provided encouragement and support. There was "something exhilarating," Howe wrote, "in being able to help a movement which has brought new luster to the old American rhetoric of freedom."[6]

Although Howe neither marched nor sat-in himself, he was stirred by the heroism of the students who risked their lives working for the movement in the Deep South. He was persistent in calling on liberals such as Americans for Democratic Action, the leaders of the unions, and the editors of left-leaning weeklies to encourage mass participation in the civil rights movement, and to press the Kennedy administration (which had "not shown the necessary kind of urgency and dedication") to do more to foster racial justice.[7]

Howe also gave support and encouragement to black scholars and writers such as Randall Kennedy, who went on to become a professor of law at Harvard; Jervis Anderson, a social and literary critic who later joined the staff of the *New Yorker*; and Richard Wright, the author of *Native Son* (1940) whom Howe had made a contributing editor of *Dissent* in 1959.[8] Howe was much taken with Wright's work. Indeed, he thought that with the appearance of *Native Son* American culture had been "changed forever." The novel, Howe argued, in all its "crudeness, melodrama, and claustrophobia of vision . . . brought out into the open, as no one ever had before, the hatred, fear and violence that have crippled . . . our culture." Its clenched-fist militancy was, Howe wrote, "a blow at the white man," which forced him to recognize himself as an oppressor, as well as a blow at the black man, which forced him to recognize the cost of his submission.[9]

Howe agreed with the idea that Wright's "humanity found itself only in acquaintance with violence and in hatred of the oppressor."[10] But Howe, who had learned much since the flap over Norman Mailer's seeming encouragement of murder in "The White Negro," was hardly inviting an easy acquiescence in violence. He was, rather, trying to point up the psychological dynamics and historical conditions which he believed shaped the attitudes of black writers. Howe's abhorrence of violence and of the apparent call for violence in the writings of blacks became clearer in his response to the "poetry" of Le Roi Jones (now Amiri Baraka).

Jones could write "We want poems/like fists beating niggers out of jocks/or dagger poems in the slimy bellies/of the owner-jews," or "Another bad poem cracking/steel knuckles in a jewlady's mouth." As literary and cultural critic Morris Dickstein has said, such "poems," unlike some other good work Jones has done, "do not even marginally belong to literature," but they were "a point on a compass." And Howe recognized in them the literal threat and humorless viciousness of a "racist hoodlum."[11] He also took Jones to task for his response to a question about Andrew Goodman and Michael Schwerner, the two Jewish men killed along with James Chaney, a black civil rights worker, in Philadelphia, Mississippi, in the summer of 1964. Jones had said he didn't care about the white boys. "Absolutely not. These boys were just artifacts, artifacts man. They weren't real. If they want to assuage their leaking consciences, that's their business." Jones, who was too busy practicing verbal violence and fantasizing about an international race war, said, "I won't mourn for them." And Howe, rightly, labeled him an irresponsible "pop-art guerrilla warrior."[12]

Howe was clearly no friend of violence, but he did strongly encourage activism. In his essay "Black Boys and Native Sons" (1963), Howe, perhaps under the spell of the first clear manifestations of a civil rights revolution, used Richard Wright's racial ferocity to chastise two other black writers, James Baldwin and Ralph Ellison, for their apparent refusal to accept "protest" as an inevitable obligation of the "Negro writer in America." Howe said that black writers, even Ellison, who had been mostly silent about the civil rights struggle could not help being entangled with the social predicament of blacks, and certainly could not help "being caught up with the *idea* of the Negro." And he called on Ellison to recognize and embrace this reality.[13]

Howe admired Ellison's work and had, a decade earlier, reviewed *Invisible Man* (1952) favorably, saying "no other writer has captured so much of the confusion and agony, the hidden gloom and surface gaiety of Negro life."[14] But he had taken issue with the novel's beleaguered black hero who "discovered" that his "world had become one of infinite possibilities." Howe thought this assertion of absolute individuality vapid and naively ignorant of the social barriers to freedom, especially for a person born black in America.

In "Black Boys and Native Sons," Howe expanded on this theme, arguing that "freedom can be fought for, but it cannot always be willed . . . into existence." He deplored Ellison's comment on receiving the National Book Award for *Invisible Man* in 1953 that he tried "to see America with an awareness of its rich diversity and its almost magical fluidity and freedom." Howe, uncharacteristically imprisoned in liberal stereotypes, implied that unrelieved suffering rather than "magical fluidity" was the "real" Negro experience. And like Jean Paul Sartre, whom he had criticized for his reductionist position on Jews, Howe seemed to lock Ellison and black writers generally into their "situation."

James Baldwin had said as early as 1961 that "to be a Negro in this country and to be relatively conscious is to be in a rage all the time." He did not mean to say, however, that blacks could write about nothing else. But Howe, in his role of activist, departed from his usual literary sensitivity and asked, or more nearly shouted, "How could a Negro put a pen to paper, how could he so much think or breathe, without some impulsion to protest?"[15] Howe's misbegotten essay led to a sharp, searing exchange with Ellison (Baldwin remaining mostly out of it) in the *New Leader* that carried over into 1964. Ellison appeared to support the autonomy (but not the disconnectedness to experience) of art, an idea that Howe himself had often promoted. "To deny," Ellison wrote, "in the interest of revolutionary posture, the possibilities of human richness" for Negroes, even in Mississippi, "is not only to deny us our humanity but to betray the critic's commitment to social reality." The black man, Ellison continued, "is no mere product of his socio-political predicament. He is a product of the interaction between his racial predicament, his individual will, and the broader American cultural freedom in which he finds his ambiguous existence."[16]

Ellison's argument was rich and self-searching and defies decent summarization. But in his responses he seemed to underscore several of Howe's points about black writers and the inescapability of both ethnic identity and the theme of protest. Ellison showed how tied up he actually was with the "Negro question" by insisting that he was "enlisted for the duration" in the "Negro Freedom Movement" merely by being a black writer. His novels, political or otherwise, he said, were a form of protest, just as his reply to Howe's essay was "a necessary action" in the struggle for black equality.[17] Ellison also admitted that he wanted to "see others distinctly." He made a "positive distinction" between "whites" and "Jews," he said, and saw Howe as a "Jewish intellectual" and not the "white intellectual" Howe called himself. This ought to have made it difficult for Ellison to object to Howe's having seen Ellison "distinctly," that is, not only as a writer, but as a black writer in a social predicament.

Ellison's position was complex, and Howe's position, too, was more complex than it appeared in his essay. Howe knew that no one, black or white or Jewish, could fully put aside the formative experiences of one's life. But he also knew that one could choose at times to write above and beyond ethnic identity. Like many other New York Jewish intellectuals, Howe, early on, in his quest for universalism and cosmopolitan modernism, had tried to evade the stubborn residues of his own ethnic experiences. But finally he had come to see the value of that identity as well as its inevitable durability. A human being, Howe concluded, cannot simply will away life's powerful seminal influences, those enveloping forces of experience and tradition "that shape us before we can even think of choices."[18]

In his reply to Ellison, Howe used the examples of Abraham Sutzkever and Jacob Glatstayn to reinforce this point. The two poets had begun as rebels against the predominant social emphasis of their Yiddish tradition, the first by commemorating nature, and the second by playing with personal introspection. But the horrific anti-Semitic events of the twentieth century "forced them to turn back to the 'plight and protest' of their people." There were literary disadvantages in this turn, Howe admitted, but also enormous gains. "The great themes of writers," he told Ellison almost as if he were lecturing him, "are not those which they choose, but those which choose them."[19]

But in his earlier work Howe had also shown that he admired the dignity, restraint, and irony of Sholom Aleichem and I. L. Peretz as well as their identification and sympathy with the travails of the Jews. He did not chide them, as he chided Ellison, for occasionally quelling their outrage at the poverty, fear, and oppression that engulfed the shtetl world or for writing about other things besides Jewish suffering. Howe was also very taken with the fact that Yiddish poets like Manny Lieb, a shoemaker, Zishe Landau, a house painter, Moishe Lieb Halpern, a waiter, and other Jewish proletarian artists could dismiss the social muse and turn to impressionism and symbolism in their literature.[20]

Howe, like Ellison, clearly recognized the possibility of at least a dimension of freedom for writers, even writers who, along with their people, had suffered violence and degradation. And Ellison, like Howe, recognized that he could not help being caught up with, as distinct from obsessed with, "the *idea* of the Negro." In the late 1940s, prior to writing *Invisible Man*, Ellison, at a gathering of New York intellectuals, told *Partisan Review* editor William Phillips that "literary quality" was more important to him than "ethnic politics." But at the same time he kept insisting that "black experience is always distinct from white experience and always shapes black thinking."[21]

Ellison and Howe, then, were not as far apart as they first appeared. But in 1963 each stressed different, but important, portions of familiar truths. And ultimately both recognized their mutual error of overstatement. In reprinting his replies and rejoinders nearly a year later, Ellison wrote: "There is unfortunately, too little space here to do justice to Howe's arguments, and it is recommended that the interested reader consult Mr. Howe's book of essays, *A World More Attractive*—a book worthy of [the reader's] attention far beyond the limits of our exchange."[22] Howe admitted to associates at the time that Ellison had had the better of the quarrel. Later, in 1982, long after he and Ellison had become friends, Howe publicly granted "some validity" to Ellison's case. And by 1990 he wrote in a postscript that while he still thought "protest as a literary theme" was probably inescapable for black novelists, he had "underestimated the capacity of oppressed peoples like American blacks to create a vital culture apart from social protest."[23]

In his exchanges with Ellison, Irving Howe never explicitly identified himself as a Jew, and oddly, given the point he was trying to make about the ineradicable quality of ethnic experience, he continued to insist that he had not been arguing from any Jewish perspective.[24] But several things suggest otherwise, not the least of which was the fact that Jewish leftists and liberals were deeply moved by black suffering and were disproportionately attracted to the civil rights movement. Howe's use of Yiddish poets to make his case about black writers is also revealing. And during his embroilment with Ellison, Howe was simultaneously involved in another controversy—over Hannah Arendt—which seems to have intensified Howe's identity as a Jew.

The publication of Arendt's *Eichmann in Jerusalem* early in 1963 had a powerful effect on Howe and was a searing event among the New York Jewish intellectuals generally.[25] Arendt seemed to say that the Jewish leadership of Nazi-occupied Europe was passive and inept, and that they had even "cooperated" with the bureaucratic machinery of the Final Solution; therefore they were responsible for the deaths of millions of Jews. Arendt apparently did not intend to indict the Jewish communal elite as conscious collaborators, but the aloof tone of the book cast the leadership and the murdered Jews of Europe in a very unfavorable light and seemed to reduce one of the most tragic human dramas in history to an abstract philosophical debate.[26]

Howe objected mightily to Arendt's thesis and further bemoaned the fact that the work was serialized in the *New Yorker*, where "hundreds of thousands of good middle-class Americans," reading between the slick advertisements for furs and diamonds, will "learn" that had "the Jews not 'cooperated' with the Nazis," many fewer would have been killed. "No small matter," Howe wrote, "and you will forgive some of us if we react strongly to this charge."[27]

Perhaps in an unconscious compensation for their failure to respond during and immediately after the Holocaust, many Jewish intellectuals did indeed in this instance react strongly. When the controversy first erupted, Hannah Arendt was in Basel to participate in a celebration of the eightieth birthday of Karl Jaspers, with whom she had studied. Her husband, Heinrich Blucher, wrote from New York: "Many phone calls are flooding in for you. You should be glad that you are not here."[28]

In addition to calls, there were many angry letters and essays, including Howe's withering critique in *Commentary*. But Howe felt the need to go farther, and he organized, under the auspices of *Dissent*, a public forum on the Eichmann book. The literary critic Lionel Abel, who had written a passionate attack on Arendt for *Partisan Review*, and Marie Syrkin, the veteran Labor Zionist writer, agreed to be on the panel.[29] Hannah Arendt declined Howe's invitation to speak, as did Bruno Bettelheim. In order to achieve "some balance," Howe then turned to sociologist Daniel Bell and political scientist Raul Hilberg to "represent" Arendt's view.[30]

Hundreds of people crowded into a hall at the old Hotel Diplomat in midtown Manhattan to participate in the forum. Able and Syrkin spoke against Arendt as expected. Bell, as he put it to me in 1998, "tried to explain Hannah's work rather than to defend her directly," and Hilberg, a scholar upon whom Arendt had leaned heavily for the Eichmann book, spoke more or less in favor of her thesis.[31] The general debate from the floor was fierce and turbulent, marked by frequent interruptions. The place was afire with urgent exchanges. Vladka Meed, a hero of the Warsaw ghetto uprising, vigorously attacked Arendt's views in Yiddish, while Howe as chair rapidly translated. Holocaust survivors stood up, showed their tattoos, and lambasted Arendt's few defenders.[32]

Howe asked—twice—for more speakers who might support her thesis. None rose, and Howe declared the debate over from the floor. Alfred Kazin, who had entered the hall very late and quite tipsy, leaped to his feet after Howe's announcement to speak in Arendt's favor. Reports that he was shouted down and ushered out are clearly erroneous. Kazin himself and two other witnesses, Daniel Bell and Dennis Wrong, told me that Howe allowed Kazin to speak his piece in full, although he was interrupted by sporadic jeering.[33] "My defense . . . was personal," Kazin recalled in a 1976 interview. "I did it [for] Hannah" as a "friend," he admitted, but "it wasn't too much later when I read the book more objectively, that I realized [it] was . . . dangerous and glib." In his journal, well after the *Dissent* forum, Kazin wrote that "Hannah [has] made me suffer because of the tone she has taken to the doomed people," and for "gleefully confid[ing] to me that the *New Yorker* paid her twenty thousand dollars for its version of 'Eichmann in Jerusalem.'"[34]

Howe believed that the forum, overall, had served a useful role, even if some of it was "ugly." The most "judicious words" in the entire debate, Howe thought, were spoken by Norman Podhoretz, the then liberal editor of *Commentary* with whom Howe, in 1963, still had a very good working relationship. Podhoretz saw Arendt's book rightly, Howe thought, as an example of that strong need among some Jewish intellectuals to make "inordinate demands" that

> Jews be better than other people . . . braver, wiser, nobler, more dignified. But the truth is—must be—that the Jews under Hitler acted as men will act when they are set upon by murderers, no better and no worse; the Final Solution reveals nothing about the victims except that they were mortal beings and hopelessly vulnerable in their weakness. . . . The Nazis destroyed a third of the Jewish people. In the name of all that is humane, will the remnant never let up on itself?[35]

Despite Howe's favorable citation of Podhoretz's view in *A Margin of Hope* in 1982, literary critic and editor Midge Decter, Podhoretz's wife, reviewed Howe's intellectual autobiography very unfavorably. A neo-conservative who despised Howe for his socialism, Decter in a nasty ad hominem footnote called the *Dissent* forum a "lynching" and described Howe as a man whose "Trotskyite training" and habits of "radical activism" had prepared him to participate in acts of "public brutality." Howe was not bothered by being called a "lynch-mob leader" by a "hack" as "predictable" as Decter, but he was distraught because he felt that the honor of *Dissent* was at stake. "In our sporadic forums over the years," he told Marie Syrkin, "we've given the floor to anyone—genius or nudnik—who wanted it. We pride ourselves on our democracy. To have the meeting so maligned really infuriated me."[36]

Decter not only mischaracterized the meeting chaired by Howe, she misunderstood the important consequences of the scorching series of events that began with the publication of Arendt's thesis and continued through the *Dissent* forum and beyond. The emotions tapped by the debate demonstrated just how sensitive an issue Jewishness remained among New York intellectuals. Although most, including Irving Howe, had given up on pure universalism and had been working out their own personal sense of Jewish identity in the years following World War II, they had not completely resolved questions about "authenticity," or about Jews in society generally. Did Jews, religious or not, continue as a group to possess and display distinct ethnic traits? Or were individual Jews Jewish only insofar as they were connected with a rich collective past? And if Jews did constitute an identifiable social grouping, what did they owe one another as distinct from society in general?

The nature and style of the arguments surrounding the publication of *Eichmann in Jerusalem* made it clear that the parochial, or the particularistic, continued to assert itself in the lives of many of these Jewish men and women despite their commitment to cosmopolitanism. William Phillips was disheartened to see that "the question whether one was Jewish or Gentile" had become part of the intellectual dynamic, but there it was. The Gentiles who joined the fray, including Mary McCarthy, Dwight Macdonald, and Robert Lowell, took very different positions from most of the Jews involved, including, finally, Alfred Kazin.[37] Daniel Bell had been very fair in his assessment of Arendt's work, but ultimately he, too, rejected it at its core, and he understood very well why his fellow Jews did the same. "It is [the] tension between the parochial and the universal that explains the furious emotions over Miss Arendt's book," Bell wrote. "For she writes from a standpoint of a universal principle which denies any parochial identity. . . . [B]ut the Jews remain a people, and the shaping elements of the race are the shaping elements of one's identity." Bell openly confessed to the overriding importance of his Jewish ties. It all "goes back to the root of one's identity, and one's root conception of the world," Bell said. And he insisted that one could not "exclude the existential person as a component of . . . human judgment. . . . In this situation, one's identity as a Jew, as well as a *philosophe*, is relevant." [38]

Howe, too, was affected in this way. The dispute over the Eichmann book, Howe told an interviewer years later, "played an enormous role in my consciousness, in *our* consciousness. And though I still have just as sharp an objection to that book, I also feel unwittingly it served a great purpose. The book was like a therapeutic session where you discover that, welling up within you, there is a great mass of feeling that you have not known." It was not just an outpouring of suppressed grief to which Howe was referring, but also to a further recognition and deepening of his identity as a Jew. "Some people taunted us," Howe recalled, "'Ah, you've suddenly become Jews.'" But "those people who had been involved [all along]," Howe admitted, "had a right to taunt us." Marie Syrkin, "a dear friend, had teased me in a gentle way about this and laughed." But she was pleased, Howe said, "that I could be bothered."[39]

While deeply engaged in political and intellectual disputes, Howe was nonetheless desperately lonely, especially for steady female companionship. Except for his years in the army, he had never been without a woman partner for any significant length of time. Married to Thalia Phillies from 1947 to 1960, heavily involved with Edja Weisberg from 1959 to 1961, and in very close relationships with several women at Stanford from 1961 to 1963, including Susan Sahl and Kay Seymour House, there was no absence of women for Irving Howe that lasted more than a few months. And by 1964 he would be married again, to Arien Mack, an extraordinarily bright and very attractive thirty-two-year-old graduate student and widow with two children, Lisa and Jonathan, about the same ages as Howe's own Nina and Nicholas. In the spring of 1963, Howe had flown into New York on one of the several trips he took to the city during his sojourn in California. He conducted some *Dissent* business, looked for an apartment (and found a "ratty" one on Barrow Street in the West Village). He also had a "blind date" with Arien set up by a mutual acquaintance. During dinner they "talked incessantly" about other mutual acquaintances, including Philip Roth, Norman Podhoretz, and the poet John Hollander. They even talked that very first evening about Irving's relationship with Edja Weisberg, and about Arien's relationship with philosophy professor Sidney Morgenbesser.

When Howe moved back to New York in the fall and started teaching at CUNY's Hunter College at 63rd Street and Park Avenue, a "courtship" developed relatively quickly. Irving courted, Arien Mack said, "by sending me reprints of his articles." But there was also romance, and in less than a year they were married (men and women raised in the 1930s and 1940s, even intellectuals, married) and living in an upscale apartment at 90 Riverside Drive near 81st Street.

This marriage lasted ten years, and for seven of those years, for Irving at least, it seemed a match made in heaven. Arien was intelligent, relatively young, and good-looking. And not unimportant at this time in Howe's life, she was Jewish. He paid "amiable attention" to Arien's children, and, happily, they got along well with his children when they were all together on Cape Cod for several weeks every summer through the sixties.[40] In 1970 Howe dedicated a collection of his essays on modernism, *Decline of the New*, to "Arien and Lisa and Jonathan."

Arien was "not especially political," but she leaned very much in Irving's left-liberal direction. Raised in a family whose "Stalinist fellow-traveling" she essentially ignored, Arien found it both ironic and funny, even touching, that Irving, so fervent an anti-Stalinist, could sit across the table from her parents for her sake. "They simply did not talk politics," she said. Beyond ideology, Arien and Irving shared many other intellectual interests, particularly in literature, both being great admirers of Saul Bellow. Indeed, in 1964, when they got hold of the page proof for Bellow's *Herzog*, they were so eager to devour it that they read it side by side, one rapidly handing over completed pages to the other.[41]

During their relationship, Irving continued to be enormously productive putting together selected pieces for *Steady Work* (1966) as well as for *Decline of the New*. He also completed his book on Thomas Hardy (1967) and wrote several rich and enduring essays, including "Culture of Modernism" and "The New York Intellectuals." In 1969 he co-edited the *Treasury of Yiddish Poetry* and had begun to work on his monumental

World of Our Fathers. Arien also accomplished much during this period. She earned a Ph.D. at Yeshiva University, got a job as an associate professor at the New School for Social Research in 1966, and held a one-year visiting fellowship at Stanford University in the late sixties. In 1970 she became editor of the influential journal, *Social Research*, and two years later, chair of the Department of Psychology at the New School. And like Irving, Arien, too, was prolific, publishing a dozen articles in professional journals between 1965 and 1972.

Although by 1971 Arien's busy scholarly and administrative schedule distressed Irving, in the early years the marriage appeared to be quite good for both of them.[42] This was especially true for Irving, who depended on the love, solace, and respite he could derive while he was politically embattled. For throughout his years with Arien he was deeply embroiled over the tactics, strategies, and goals of social change with the growing New Left, especially the Students for a Democratic Society (SDS), as well as with old friends like Max Shachtman, Harvey Swados, and Philip Rahv. Some, but not all, of the disputes stemmed from the reintensification of the Cold War, the escalating hot war in Vietnam, and arguments about how and at what cost to end American involvement in the Southeast Asian conflict.

A ferocious and continuous clash between Irving Howe and his friends, on the one side, and the New Left, on the other, was not necessarily inevitable. But portents of what was to come in the relationship between the Old Left and the younger radicals were evident from the beginning, particularly at two very different events and venues in the early sixties. The first was at the AFL-CIO camp in Port Huron, Michigan, in the summer of 1962, where SDS issued its declaration of values and goals. The second was the initial meeting between *Dissent* editors and SDS leaders at Joseph Buttinger's elegant four-story home on the upper East Side of Manhattan in October 1963. Here, mostly without success, two generations of the Left "fumbl[ed] to reach across the spaces of time" and across the gap of their radically dissimilar political experiences.[43]

SDS had begun as the rejuvenated "student department" of the League for Industrial Democracy (LID), a nearly moribund organization of mainly social democrats interested in fighting Communism and celebrating trade unionism. LID, whose executive board included socialists such as the venerable Norman Thomas and the young Michael Harrington, wanted an intellectually active and energetic "junior wing" that could impress the unions, especially the ILGWU, which helped fund LID. But most of the leaders of the parent organization, scarred by the political battles of the thirties and forties and fused together by the fires of anti-Communism, did not want "radicalism." Nevertheless, they ended up, mainly through the efforts of student activist Al Haber and his small circle of friends at the University of Michigan, including Tom Hayden, with SDS: a youth affiliate, based on college campuses, that saw itself as a force for sweeping change.[44]

In the *Port Huron Statement*, a fifty-page document hammered out over many days and sleepless nights, the SDS tried to define itself. Written by the sons and daughters of the troubled, fragmented American middle class, the manifesto devoted almost as much space to human values and relationships as it did to politics. It emphasized the need for honesty and fraternity and promoted "participatory democracy" as a way to both overcome isolation and estrangement and to produce progressive political change. The statement was steeped in communitarian values, yet it also reflected the search for "human independence" and personal salvation through resistance. As much as it promoted cohesion, even a kind of human fusion, the document was wedded to libertarianism and radical individualism, staples of the American utopian tradition.[45]

The LID board paid little attention to the "values section" of the draft document, but they were worried about what appeared, to their anti-Communist eyes, to be a pro-Soviet bias. And given the Communist Party's history of infiltration and destruction of once-viable left-liberal groups, they were equally worried about the presence of a number of "red-diaper babies" at Port Huron, and the decision taken by the overwhelming majority to allow a member of the Communist Party's youth group to be seated as an observer.

Michael Harrington, a third-generation New York intellectual from the Midwest and a protégé of Irving Howe's as well as a member of the *Dissent* editorial board since the late fifties, was LID's representative at the SDS convention. "The oldest young socialist alive," as he sometimes jokingly called himself, Harrington, thirty-four at the time, was a "one-man stand-in" for radicalism's "missing generation": men and women in their thirties who would have been engaged in systematic activism on the Left had there actually been a viable socialist movement in postwar America. Harrington, who was increasingly becoming Howe's more politically active alter ego, was one of the very few people who might have been able to mediate across the gap that divided the *Dissent* elders from the young radicals. A drinking buddy of Tom Hayden's, seen by the SDS as someone clearly "involved in changing the status quo," Harrington appeared to be a good choice. But Harrington was horrified, as Howe would be later, that the draft document included statements implying that the United States was the primary source of evil in the Cold War. He bridled at those sections which explicitly let Russia off the hook with sentences like "[the] savage repression of the Hungarian Revolution was a defensive action rooted in Soviet fear that its empire would collapse."[46] He was also unnerved by the students' view of themselves as somehow fighting the same battle as the Cuban revolutionaries.

Harrington worried, too, that the draft was excessively critical of liberals and labor unions—and not only because he was fearful of LID's reaction. Like many of his *Dissent* colleagues, including Howe, who were veterans of the wasteful sectarian battles on the Left in the forties and fifties, Harrington was interested in building a united left-liberal coalition with both labor and the middle class at its center. Who else could realign the Democrats into a more liberal party? How else, he wondered, would there ever be "a majority coalition that could transform the most powerful and imperial capitalist power in human history?" At some level the "participatory democracy" that SDS hoped would bring people "out of isolation and into community" in order to "find meaning in personal life" seemed to Harrington irrelevant and even antithetical to the substance of realignment politics, which required less searching for individual "authenticity" and more searching for coalition and compromise.[47]

Shortly before the SDS convention, Harrington had offered Howe and his *Dissent* colleagues and readers advice about dealing with some of the "wrongheaded" ideas of the young radicals. Democratic socialists, he wrote, were going to have to handle certain issues with great sensitivity, especially the popularity of the Cuban Revolution among the adherents of the New Left. The attraction to Castro, Harrington argued, was more a "complex feeling" among the young than the product of a "finished ideology." And while this feeling "must be faced and changed," he insisted that this could not be done by "regaling the newly radical students with facts of the past." Persuasion must come, rather, from someone with social activist bona fides "who has a sympathy for the genuine and good emotions which are just behind the bad theories."[48]

But, as Harrington latter admitted, at Port Huron old habits surfaced, and he literally harangued the students about what he regarded as the many faults and shortcomings of their draft, and he lambasted them for their decision to admit a Communist Party observer. After Harrington left the convention, changes were made to satisfy him. The final document contained an important statement celebrating democracy and Western-style liberties, including a free labor movement. Communists and fellow-travelers were excluded from membership, and there was strong criticism of the Soviet Union and Communist parties throughout the world. But the Port Huron Statement did continue to maintain that the Soviet Union was not inherently expansionist, that it was not the aggressive ogre conjured up by Cold War orthodoxy. And it retained a critique of what Tom Hayden called "unreasoning anti-Communism."[49]

Harrington believed that SDS had responded quite generously to his criticism. Howe, too, liked the final product. But the LID board, biased by Harrington's harsh initial report on the draft document and his attack on the SDS leaders, rushed to negative judgment about the finished statement, and in a panic, grossly overreacted. After a convoluted process in which LID held inquisitorial hearings, fired SDS staffers, sealed records, froze budgets, and locked offices, a compromise was reached. But for many in SDS the distrust of liberals and even socialists was confirmed.

When leaders of the student organization met, then, about a year later with Irving Howe and other members of the *Dissent* board, they brought with them an ambivalent attitude toward the Old Left, a sense of reverence and antagonism combined. The Dissenters, too, were conflicted, yearning for alliance and affirmation from the young but worried about their "insincere anticommunism" and the pronounced dimension of anti-intellectualism among them. *Dissent's* initial response to the New Left in the late fifties and early sixties was full of support and praise. Many of the writers and editors thought a movement had finally begun to emerge that could, perhaps, take the best that the old anti-Stalinist Left had to offer and build on it in the more promising social and political atmosphere of the sixties. Indeed, it looked to some of the Dissenters, including Howe and Michael Walzer, as if the final Port Huron Statement with its emphasis on participatory democracy, although more amorphous than anything in *Dissent*, could have been written largely out of the journal's pages. For in the late fifties and early sixties, article after article in *Dissent* had stressed the central significance of democracy, civil liberties, decentralization, and citizen activism in a politics of opposition, and some even called for a radical movement based on personal autonomy.[50]

But as early as 1960 the same *Dissent* articles also contained reservations about the young radicals themselves. The students, it was charged, were not receptive to "programs," for example, or to the "resolutions" and "machinations" necessary for coalition politics. Even Michael Walzer, the youngest Dissenter, who maintained his organizational connection with SDS and was friendly with Tom Hayden until the mid-sixties, pointed out a certain "organizational naiveté" in the New Left. And Howe and Lewis Coser, who were pleased enough with the Port Huron Statement to invite leaders of SDS to write for *Dissent*, were quite apprehensive about the New Left's lack of commitment to anti-Communism, its lack of concern with analytical criticism, and its romance with Third World revolutionaries.[51]

The Dissenters, then, like the SDS, brought to their meeting in Buttinger's "mansion" on Fifth Avenue and 87th Street (where the Dissent board held its monthly meetings) hope as well as skepticism, and a thirst for connection as well as a wary impatience. Sociologist Todd Gitlin, who was at the meeting as a relatively new SDS leader, said that Howe, writing later, set the scene nicely:

> Two generations sat facing each other. . . . We were scarred, they untouched. We bore marks of 'corrosion and distrust,' they looked forward to clusterings of fraternity. We had grown skeptical of Marxism, they were still unchained to system. We had pulled ourselves out of an immigrant working class, an experience not likely to induce romantic views about the poor; they, children of warm liberals and cooled radicals, were hoping to find a way into the lives and wisdom of the oppressed.[52]

When the discussion began in earnest, Howe almost immediately had trouble with the way the SDS leaders were explaining what they meant by "participatory democracy." Earlier, Howe had thought that in the concept of "participatory democracy" there was an effort by SDS, "a little naive to be sure," but nonetheless an effort, to discover ways to allow people to participate more directly, actively, and steadily in political life.[53] But when Howe heard Hayden and some of the others contrast their envisaged "participatory democracy" to the less than perfect "representative democracy" in which they all lived, as if "somehow the two were contraries," he winced. It pained Howe and the other Dissenters to hear something that "sounded a little too much like the fecklessness of our youth, when Stalinists and even a few Socialists used to put down 'mere' bourgeois democracy."

Even worse, Howe thought, "was the readiness of the SDS people to excuse the lack of freedom in Cuba, a country that seemed to them the home of a better or more glamorous kind of communism." [54] Hayden lauded and promoted Castro's revolution, partly out of sincere admiration, partly out of a growing "anti-anti-Communism" which was becoming the hallmark of the New Left's political identity. The Dissenters saw anti-Communism as an essential component of a genuine democratic radicalism. But the SDS, especially in light of the failed attempt by the United States to overthrow the Cuban revolution at the Bay of Pigs in 1961, the saber rattling over Berlin in the same year, and the Cuban missile crisis in the very next, wanted a fresh start—a break with the reintensifying Cold War and all its vestiges, including anti-Communism, of whatever variety. None of this boded well for the relationship between the generations.

At the same time that Hayden praised Castro's student-led revolution, he also waxed enthusiastic about Gandhi's nonviolent resistance. Howe thought Hayden was brilliant, the "most intellectually gifted of the group," but he failed, with good reason, to understand Hayden's attempt to weave pacifism and moral rectitude together with violence, and was rattled by Hayden's hammering him with both. "I don't mind being attacked from the right and I don't mind being attacked from the left," Howe said, "but when one person attacks me from both sides at the same time, it gets on my nerves." [55] And Howe, by his language and posture, made his state of mind clear. In turn, the young radicals made quite clear their distaste for Howe's "rigid anticommunism" and for the Dissenters' lack of responsiveness to their new moods and styles.

Howe admitted later that he and Stanley Plastrik, as well as Emanuel Geltman and the other Dissenters, handled the meeting badly. Having become somewhat "fixed in our ways," Howe said, "all of us" except Walzer, Howe's former student at Brandeis and Gitlin's former teacher at Harvard who was a literal link between the two groups, "were too impatient." Wanting to influence the young SDS people but also hurt by their assaults and perhaps even fearful of rejection by a growing student movement that did not appear to need them, several of the democratic socialists, especially Howe, scolded or made long windy speeches.[56]

Gitlin and Hayden, and Walzer too, thought the *Dissent* people missed an opportunity on that October day. Howe agreed. He wouldn't recognize until later that he had been sectarian in his very opposition to sectarianism.[57] But he did conclude at the time that he and his older friends were guilty of a "tactical incapacity." Even though Hayden was "hard" and "fanatical," the Dissenters should have played it "more quietly," Howe said, "more calmly." The Dissenters were not wrong to have voiced, in all candor, "their differences with Tom," but, Howe admitted, they should not have made it into "an immediate ideological confrontation."[58] In the next few years there would be other sharp exchanges between Howe and the New Left, especially with Tom Hayden—fierce clashes of generation, personality, and ideology.

In New York in May 1965, Howe and Hayden faced each other on a panel at yet another meeting, this one on the theme of "New Styles in Leftism." Hayden, wearing an old sweatshirt and speaking in what Jack Newfield reported in the *Village Voice* as a "tense staccato voice," denounced socialists like Bayard Rustin and Michael Harrington for having "sold out to the Establishment." He attacked mainstream labor, the church, and civil rights organizations as bureaucratic shells that failed to respond to their own constituencies. And he specifically rejected the theory that social change is achieved by compromise, coalition, and the liberal realignment of the Democratic Party.

Howe, wearing a suit and tie, vehemently disagreed, of course, and in turn went after Hayden for his attitude toward the puppet states of the Soviet bloc, which Hayden had stubbornly refused to label totalitarian.[59] "What, then, *would* you call them, Tom?" Howe asked with what many witnesses characterized as withering scorn. And toward the end of the "discussion," Howe said, "Tom, you talk about participatory democracy, and criticize America for its absence; would you also criticize the so-called socialist countries for the same lack?" Hayden, visibly upset, snapped back: "I won't be red-baited." Irving was insistent, and loud: "I want to know what you mean, Tom—do you have one standard or two?" Hayden, apparently filled with rage, "stormed out of the hall, blinking back furious tears."[60]

Newfield, who had sympathies on both sides of the conflict, was saddened by the growing estrangement of the New Leftists from the "handful of radicals who fought so bravely through the 1950s." But in *The Nation* he described Howe inaccurately and indistinctly as a "revisionist liberal" who had only contempt for the young radicals. Howe wrote an angry reply rejecting the charge and the label, insisting that his sympathies were "strongly with the students." Howe was not always sensitive to what his friend Bernard Avishai called "filial vulnerability," and he had hurt Hayden badly. But Howe's sympathies remained with the youth movement, which he thought might yet become a genuine exercise in democratic radicalism. Even at the end of the decade when SDS slithered into revolutionary, apocalyptic rhetoric and splintered into warring Marxist-Leninist factions, Howe, with little hope of reconciliation, still refrained, as we shall see, from an absolute, total denunciation of the New Left.[61]

Had he been "nicer" in his confrontations with the young radicals, Howe thought later, it might have made a difference with some in the SDS, but "it would not have made a fundamental difference in the way things turned out."[62] In the period from late 1963 through 1965, Howe, not wanting to give up on the New Left despite the bad taste that lingered from *Dissent*'s confrontation with SDS, had attended a number of SDS meetings, including some on the national level. And he continued to see the Port Huron Statement as "a fresh exposition of an American democratic radicalism." But at the meetings, Howe had listened to "endless chatter" about participatory democracy and about aiming at "consensus" without the "encumbrance" of formal democratic procedures like voting. He saw the "manipulative dimensions" of these ideas and techniques which could enable the schemes of tight little authoritarian factions, and he grew increasingly impatient.[63]

That participatory democracy as practiced by the SDS could have "manipulative dimensions" was also attested to by many in the SDS itself, including Gitlin and writer Paul Berman, who said that over time participatory democracy, by dispensing with the formalities and organizational dynamics of representative democracy, had become a formula for demagoguery and chaos.[64] It had had great appeal. It promised "identity and authenticity" through direct involvement in a society in which bureaucratic elites seemed to be making too many decisions without any substantive democratic debate. Michael Walzer was attracted to SDS for this very reason. But he, too, saw instances of the "manipulative dimensions" of participatory democracy, especially in the behavior of his friend Tom Hayden. Walzer shared several examples with me in 1997—one of which is worth repeating here. Hayden, working hard and long in 1965 on the Newark Community Union Project (NCUP) and "living with the rats" (as he told Howe's fourteen-year-old stepson with defiant pride), used to come to Walzer's house in Princeton for rest and relaxation. Walzer, on Hayden's invitation, decided one evening to attend an NCUP meeting to "test" Tom's claim that the movement was being led by community people. But it was "perfectly clear" to Walzer that Hayden had, in fact, "run the meeting from the back of the room. Nothing was done without Tom's approval, and everyone got a crick in the neck from turning around to look at him sitting in that last row."[65]

Howe had described Hayden as a "Bolshevik type" and a "future commissar." But, young Walzer, "caught in the middle" ideologically if not quite generationally, still wanted Dissent to be more open to the New Left. He even encouraged Howe to tone down his criticism of Hayden. Walzer later confessed, however, that although he knew Hayden longer, Howe knew him better.[66] Howe came to regret some of his acrimony; his prophecy, however, about the growing authoritarianism of Tom Hayden and the SDS, Walzer admitted, was chillingly accurate. Irving saw in SDS's anti-anti-Communism something more than just the refusal by New Leftists to recite the catechism of the old democratic Left. He saw a group of young people, ignorant of the past and unwilling or unable to learn from other people's experience, who "were going to be seduced by the likes of Che Guevara," and who were going to repeat the mistakes of the Old Left. They were heading in a direction that would make it extremely "difficult for them to be independent and authentic . . . radicals," as difficult "as it had been for leftists in the Soviet Union."[67]

Although they turned out to be mostly right in the long haul, Howe and other older Dissenters, especially Lewis Coser, were still in some ways arguing with their 1930s contemporaries rather than with the new crop of young radicals. Castro's Cuba was not at the start a totalitarian clone of the Soviet Union. Yet even before the Cuban revolution abandoned its freewheeling style for Stalinist stolidity and before it closed down opposition newspapers, Howe and Coser, worried about incipient authoritarianism on the island, misread the New Left's fascination with Fidel. In the beginning, Castro was less an ideological inspiration for the New Left's emerging radicalism, and more a symbol of their infatuation with the triumph of a popular movement over a brutal American-sponsored dictatorship. But if this early passion was relatively innocent, the eventual wholesale ideological embrace by SDS of Third World Communists like Castro and Mao and Ho Chi Minh was far less so.[68]

It is possible that the SDS in its excesses was acting out of its own obsession with anti-anti-Communism. Believing it was born unencumbered by a past and could simply will freedom into existence, the youth movement was following the path of its own roots in the politics of "naive democracy" ("We can say and do anything we want!"), latent authoritarianism, and the quest for personal salvation. But the movement was certainly reinforced in its arrogance and its turn away from the rhetoric of coalition and reform by the events of the late summer of 1964.

The Mississippi Democratic Freedom Party, an alternative to the segregationist Democratic Party in the South, sent elected black delegates to the Democratic Convention in Atlantic City in August. They were denied seats. This shook further many young people's faith in the liberalism of the Democratic Party and in the constitutional process itself. It seemed far less possible to them now that the immense inequalities of American society could be alleviated simply by electing the right politicians and passing the right laws. In the same month, and much more important in its impact on the young Left and on American social stability, Congress in response to an alleged attack on a U.S. battleship in the waters off North Vietnam passed the Gulf of Tonkin Resolution— a giant step on the road to full-scale American military intervention in Southeast Asia. "The Vietnam War," Howe rightly said later, "was decisive. It generated an intensity of response, a polarization of opinion." And in the opinion of many radical young people, Vietnam was in large part the liberals' war. For not only were many liberals crucial in pursuing and defending the war, but the rationale for American intervention came directly from the Cold War liberalism of the forties and fifties, a liberalism that accepted the mission of "containing" Communism wherever it might emerge, in whatever form.

The youth of the New Left, having taken America's dream and its progressive rhetoric seriously, believed they were watching liberalism sacrifice itself on the altar of race prejudice and the Vietnam War, and they quickly, too quickly, felt betrayed. And again too quickly, they began to search for a new Utopia in some revolutionary land elsewhere. Without the example of an older generation engaging systematically in the politics of the Left, the young people were too desperate and too inexperienced to accept and adopt Irving Howe's commitment to "steady work" and his "heroism of patience," and they headed, instead, for another familiar American cycle of revolutionary enthusiasm, disillusionment, and ultimate dissolution.

In 1965 and 1966, the SDS, still refusing to distinguish between the very different anti-Communism of the right and the Cold War liberals on the one side and the anti-Stalinist socialists on the other, unfortunately fulfilled some of Howe's reluctant but nonetheless dire predictions. They dropped from their charter the sections on "Anti-Communism" as well as the Communist exclusion clause and the antitotalitarian clause. By these changes, the SDS made itself vulnerable to penetration by breakaway veterans of the old Communist Party youth movement, newly reorganized as the Progressive Labor Party (PLP). The opposite of everything the SDS initially stood for, the PLP, a rigidly authoritarian faction proposing to refashion the U.S. itself into a Maoist state, gained prominence if not ascendancy over the next few years.

At about the same time, the SDS added Ho Chi Minh to its roster of Third World Communist heroes, and it promoted not only American withdrawal from the war in Vietnam, but a victory by the Viet Cong. [69] The war, Howe said, "drove the whole country nuts." In his own way, Howe said, he "went a little crazy too." Deeply distressed by the overseas conflict and angered by the irresponsible behavior of some elements of the New Left, a movement he had longed for, worked for, and continued to have hope for, Irving found himself fast becoming a polemicist. This was a posture and behavior he thought he had long since left behind. But he "played the role," and throughout the late sixties Howe wavered between feeling beleaguered and unhappy, and taking "some strange gratification" in being "the socialist the SDS loved to hate the most."[70]

11

Escalation and Polarization

The Sixties: Part 2

BY THE LATE sixties at some American colleges, it took little more than Irving Howe's presence at a podium to elicit a loud chorus of jeers. Some of "the New Left claque," Howe complained, "started booing me before I even opened my mouth." Howe had reason to be annoyed that the shouting often began before the talking, but his reputation for acerbic criticism of the new generation of radicals preceded him. By 1965, as a result of his bitter public exchanges with younger political opponents and his published diatribes against the New Left, Howe was perceived as an enemy.[1]

In more than one essay, but especially in "New Styles in Leftism," a long piece appearing in *Dissent* in the summer of 1965 and often reprinted elsewhere, Howe assaulted segments of the New Left for an "unearned impatience" with systematic thought and an "extreme, sometimes unwarranted hostility toward liberalism." He took some of the leaders of the movement to task for their crude, unqualified anti-Americanism, their growing identification with Third World authoritarianism, and for what he called "a vicarious indulgence in violence."[2] Before and after the essay's publication, Irving delivered it as a talk at many colleges around the country. He claimed to be speaking in support of the students and also for sober rationality. But in fact he had a hard time controlling his temper or curbing his sarcasm when responding to his audiences.[3]

Howe's anger, some of his critics charge, was a case of unrequited love. As the prime mover of a socialist journal for more than a decade, Howe may have hungered for acknowledgment as a leader of any emerging radical movement. But he and his democratic-socialist views were mostly ignored by the New Left. Howe later admitted that having set himself the role of mentor to the young, he was by 1965 literally "reeling from blows of rejection." He and other Dissenters had, after all, been waiting a long time for a new radicalism, "almost as long," Howe quipped, "as Beckett's pair for Godot." But if all Howe had wanted was the admiration of the young, he, "at some expense to [his] convictions," could have told the New Left what it wanted to hear. Instead, and despite warnings from Michael Harrington and Michael Walzer to temper his criticism, he overreacted and got emotionally entangled in harsh and strident disputes. Howe told himself that he "was one of the few people who took the New Left seriously enough to keep arguing with it." But in the end he found this "cold comfort."[4]

Howe did take the young radicals seriously. In his articles and talks he expressed his hope that the "rebellious students [would] provide a new social energy . . . , a new source of ideas and commitment for a revitalized democratic radicalism." He agreed with many of the student criticisms of the university, and even quoted Tom Hayden favorably on the bureaucratization and undemocratic nature of higher education. The new crop of radical students, Howe said with some delight, was a tonic. But he worried about that element of the New Left that was increasingly antidemocratic. For radical politics to make a deep and lasting impact on American society, Howe insisted, "it must be rooted in democratic values." It must "set to work *patiently*," alongside liberal allies (labor, church, black, and academic groups) to intensify and extend the democratic qualities of American society. And it must also therefore avoid "submission to the lure of charismatic leaders and authoritarian ideologies."[5]

Although distressed by the apparent contempt for democracy blossoming among the leadership of the young radicals, Howe in 1965 continued to believe, correctly, that the majority of campus liberals and leftists was devoted to a democratic politics.[6] He continued to be sympathetic to the students. His criticisms of their ideological and confrontational excesses were offered in the hope that SDS would recover its freshness, its richly diverse internal life, and its full commitment to democratic left-liberalism. But all this was lost in the generational divide and the mutual polemics. Tom Hayden admitted later that if the "elders could see us only through the distorting lens of the past, it was true as well that my infatuation with 'the new' made it difficult to sift out what made sense in their paranoid critique." And, as Hayden argued, the excessive criticism by democratic socialists, including Irving

Howe, left him "numb to the potentially valuable lessons of their experience."[7]

The divisive rhetoric and name calling that occurred between left-liberal New York intellectuals and promoters and practitioners of "the new" in the sixties hid their similarities. The New Left (and the Beats before them) shared the intellectuals' negative attitude toward conformity and popular culture. Both groups were concerned with the alienating monotony of contemporary work, the ironically dispiriting effects of prosperity, the dangers of bureaucratization, consolidation of power, and atomic extinction. The New Left may have placed more importance on the value of "personal resistance," but older radicals, including Howe and Coser, had focused on this too, and both groups believed in the significance of political opposition.

In the sixties, Howe gave a nod of recognition to the similarities, but except for the much younger Michael Walzer and Michael Harrington, the Dissenters refused to acknowledge explicitly that the New Left enthusiasts of the counterculture were in some ways their spiritual offspring. The "new bohemians," however, were equally unwilling to recognize that the socialist intellectuals were their spiritual progenitors. And so, as historian Richard Pells put it, "the battle for cultural supremacy that began in the late 1950s and intensified in the 1960s was waged with all the hysteria one would expect to find in a typical family quarrel."[8]

But it wasn't only the generation gap or Howe's fierce recriminations that kept him and others on the anti-Stalinist left from getting their message across. It was also that Howe, despite his hatred of the war, differed significantly from the students on the key issue of how to end the conflict in Vietnam. The New Left, though still some time away from its emphatic and uncritical identification with the Communist side in the Vietnamese conflict, mostly supported an immediate end to American involvement, even if it meant a Communist victory. Whether or not Ho Chi Minh was a Stalinist mattered less to the students and to a growing number of their elders than what they saw as America's violation of its own principle of self-determination. In unleashing its enormous technology of destruction in an undeclared war on a poor divided country some 8,000 miles away, the United States was, in the eyes of the protestors, in murderous defiance of its own liberal ideals.

Howe understood that "the best of the young take the proclaimed values of their elders with a seriousness which leads them to be appalled by their violation in practice."[9] And he agreed with important parts of the New Left's militant antiwar position. In April 1965 in an open letter to Adlai Stevenson, the U.S. Ambassador to the United Nations, Howe, along with several others, wrote: "We have watched in dismay as our government—by its action in Vietnam . . . has clearly violated the UN charter, international law, and . . . fundamental principles of human decency."[10] At about the same time, in the *New York Review of Books* and *Dissent*, Howe called the war an unmitigated disaster, "an evil" that had to be stopped, and he celebrated the antiwar teach-ins and the proposals coming from the universities about ending the war.[11]

In the summer issue of *Partisan Review*, Howe, the lifelong anti-Stalinist, went so far as to say that "[o]ur policies in Vietnam," which have required "self-defeating military involvement," are not justified by the American goal of "preventing a Communist takeover."[12] Later in the year, Howe, along with Harrington, Rustin, Coser, and Penn Kemble, chair of the New York SDS, published a letter in the *New York Review of Books* which, while expressing a number of misgivings about the course of the protests, called them "legitimate" and predicted yet more of them should the Johnson administration continue to pursue the war and to react with a "mixture of hysteria and foolishness" to vigorously expressed dissent about America's Vietnam policies.[13]

One might take all this to mean that Howe, like many of the younger antiwar protestors, was for immediate and unconditional withdrawal. But, Howe, although he had wavered over the years, still seemed to harbor a slim hope that a "third force," democratic or at least anti-authoritarian, might yet come alive in South Vietnam to take on both the American-supported military regime and the Communist Vietcong. Howe called for a general cease-fire, but he feared that an immediate American withdrawal could only mean a Communist victory and a slaughter of the opposition before his elusive third force could emerge. He hesitated, then, to demand a complete or abrupt end to the war and called instead for "negotiations."[14]

In 1964, when there were fewer than 20,000 U.S. troops in South Vietnam, Howe had said that "if continuing the present policy means a hopeless attrition of the Vietnamese people, it must be stressed that simply for the U.S. to pull out of the country would mean something quite as inhumane." And still hoping, perhaps, to gain time for the emergence of a non-Communist nationalism in South Vietnam, Howe called for a last-ditch injection of economic aid and land reform, as well as a U.S.-brokered nonaggression pact between the North and South.[15]

But America continued to intensify its military role. In 1965, the bombing of North Vietnam began and U.S. troop strength in the South rose to an astounding 200,000. In the face of this escalation and the increasingly urgent calls for immediate withdrawal, only Howe's lingering obsessive anti-Stalinism and his fear of a Communist takeover in the South can explain his insistence on a continued U.S. presence in Vietnam. Calls for immediate withdrawal came even from within Howe's own circle. Michael Walzer argued the issue with Howe often, sometimes in public. And Howe faced similar pressure from SANE, the antinuclear group in which he had been very active since the early sixties.[16]

Howe resisted these pressures. He continued to talk about the negative consequences of a Vietcong victory and, although with less conviction, a potential democratic "third force." He repeated his warning that calling for immediate withdrawal rather than negotiation meant alienating the popular support necessary to end the war. His colleagues in SANE, Howe said, were "really good people," the kind of "moral absolutists" necessary for any campaign. But he thought there were too many "moralists" in SANE, as in the New Left, and he clashed with them all the time. Some of his friends, Howe believed, cared only about what Max Weber called "the ethic of ultimate ends"—act rightly and leave the results with the Lord. Howe, on the other hand, knew that "the Lord, too often, . . . seems not to be paying attention." He opted instead for "the ethic of responsibility," one which accounts for potentially negative consequences even of action seen as "right." Howe rejected the Thoreauvian notion that "any man more right than his neighbors constitutes a majority of one already." He talked about the need for a more effective and less dangerous "majority" built through organization, compromise, and alliance. In the "fixed moralism" of the SANE people, Howe thought he recognized a touch of selfishness, a need to keep oneself pure. He was not entirely mistaken. But Howe missed that those who pushed for unconditional withdrawal were not only participating in "the politics of rectitude." Many of them also believed, with much reason, that continued American presence in Vietnam would do as much damage as a Communist takeover, and that there would be no "third force" in any foreseeable future.[17]

By the middle of 1965, Irving, too, was increasingly pessimistic about a third force. He saw even more clearly now that the strength of the Vietcong had always rested "upon very considerable indigenous support." He admitted, as he had done as early as 1954, and many times since, that by defeating the French at Dien Bien Phu, the Communists had made their leadership position in Vietnam unassailable. He confessed, too, that the "democratic left" had never been strong in Vietnam, and whatever there was of it had been "repeatedly smashed by the Japanese, the French, the Communists and the Diem government." Howe seemed to recognize once again that Stalinism had already won in Indochina, and that the United States was hopelessly and counter-productively trying to act in the name of a South Vietnam that had crumbled through years of "reactionary and stupid policies" into little more than an oppressive military apparatus.[18]

By fall Howe seemed altogether resigned to the fact that there would indeed be no third force in Vietnam. "It is hopeless," he wrote. "It is too late." Disastrous U.S. and South Vietnamese policies, Howe believed, had destroyed any possibility of a democratic alternative. He insisted that "[w]e have no further moral right to inflict a war upon a people that has suffered twenty-five years of bloodshed." The larger-scale war necessary to defeat the Communists, Howe knew, "would bring consequences far worse than . . . a Vietcong victory." Negotiation, during a bombing halt and a general cease-fire on the ground, was therefore the only "solution," he said, even though he predicted that the final result would be a Communist-style dictatorship for all of Vietnam.[19]

But many in the antiwar movement saw the call for negotiations as a way of hiding from the reality that Howe himself described. Even with a bombing halt and a cease-fire, an unlikely scenario in 1965 or 1966, the inevitably long and convoluted process of negotiation would, it was thought, simply prolong the war and, as Howe himself predicted, with no measurable difference in the outcome. His fear of Stalinism, wherever it might emerge and in whatever form, and his tortured ambivalence about the American role in Vietnam left Howe in an untenable position: in support of continued U.S. intervention and, in the opinion of some, in support of the war itself.

Many young protestors sensed Howe's equivocation. They also believed that he and other democratic socialists like Harrington and Bayard Rustin were more worried about the confrontational tactics of the antiwar movement (including, in August 1965, the attempt by Berkeley students to block troop trains passing through Oakland, California) than they were about the horrors of the war itself.[20] It also made no sense to the protestors that Howe, Harrington, and others on the anti-Stalinist left fretted so much about Communist participation in the movement. Although Howe was chillingly prescient about the pro-Communist factions of the SDS who would later encourage violent street action and even, in a few instances, acts of terrorism, members of the Communist Party in the early antiwar movement proved among the more cautious voices. They did not advocate violence, nor did they burn American flags or wave Vietcong flags. They saw themselves, and were seen by many young activists, as part of a potentially successful coalition, an ideologically diverse group of American radicals committed to ending the war.[21]

Even before Vietcong flags appeared in any significant number at antiwar demonstrations, Howe's deeply rooted fear of Communism as well as his practical wisdom made him, along with Harrington, call for a critique of the Vietcong as well as the United States, lest the American people infer that antiwar meant pro-Communism. Any movement, Howe and Harrington argued, that even appeared to be "a fifth column" for Communist warriors currently doing battle with American troops would have "no chance of winning" the majority of the country, or even a significant minority, to the idea of withdrawal from Indochina.[22] This did not sit at all well with members of the New Left, even those who had thought highly of the democratic socialists. Carl Oglesby, for example, president of SDS in 1965, had been a *Dissent* subscriber in the early 1960s, and he had read with appreciation Harrington's *The Other America*. As a former graduate student in English, Oglesby also had been impressed with Howe's study of *Politics and the Novel*. He had in fact "loved and admired" both Harrington and Howe, but by the fall of 1965, mostly in response to their insistence on "even-handedness," he changed his mind: "Here were these guys I admired so much denouncing me as a Red because I wouldn't criticize both sides [in the war] equally." This was nonsense, Oglesby said, "because both sides weren't invading each other equally, weren't napalming each other equally."[23]

Later in the fall of 1965, in yet another critique, Howe probably did the ultimate damage to his dwindling reputation among the more radical youthful protestors. The antiwar demonstration in April in Washington, for which 25,000 people had turned out, had been surprisingly nonviolent and quite moderate in its slogans. There were few chants of "Ho-ho-ho Chi Minh/the NLF is gonna win," nor were Vietcong flags especially noticeable. Nonetheless, in an October pronouncement coauthored with Harrington, Rustin, and several others on the anti-Stalinist Left, Howe criticized those antiwar protesters (always "a small far-out" but articulate and visible minority) who, at times, did offer "explicit or covert political support to the Viet Cong," and who aimed to transform the movement "into an apocalypse, a 'final conflict' in which extreme gestures of opposition will bring forth punitive retaliation from the authorities."[24] The criticisms in the statement were sound and even prophetic, but the timing and tone of the broadside suggested to the protesters that Howe and his comrades were frozen in the anti-Communist Old Guard with nothing to offer to the cause of peace, except criticisms of those who were actually trying to stop the war.

Staughton Lynd, a young Yale historian who saw himself as a New Leftist and front-line activist against the war, took exception to Howe's call for a critique of both sides in the Indochina conflict. Indeed, Lynd wanted a Vietcong victory and challenged Howe to tell him why that was immoral. Howe's simple reply reflected some of the differences between the anti-Stalinist Left and the younger generation of radicals: "A victory for a Communist or Communist-dominated movement means another totalitarian dictatorship suppressing human freedoms."[25]

Once again, however, the growing alienation between the Old Left, whose average age was above forty, and the protesters, whose average age was under twenty-five, resulted not simply from "tone" or "the generation gap." The radical journalist I. F. Stone, who was nearly sixty in 1965, blasted the New Left at the April antiwar rally for its negative attitude toward liberalism. Indeed, Stone, identifying himself as a "liberal," called some of the young activists at the demonstration ineffective "snot-nosed Marxist Leninists," and over the years he repeatedly criticized "stunt-mongers and suicide tactics" in the antiwar movement. But because Stone, since the early sixties, had consistently argued the case for a U.S. pullout from Vietnam, he unlike Howe, continued to get a respectful hearing in the movement and from the New Left.[26]

Although Howe throughout this contentious era continued to speak and write about the war and about politics generally, he often longed for respite, for "stretches of the commonplace," and for the literary and aesthetic wholesomeness of a "world more attractive." He could not, however, avoid the noise and the heat, or the excitement and moral obligation of politics, even if it sometimes drained his spirit. But Howe, unlike Trotsky, his erstwhile hero, refused to forfeit entirely his intellectual and literary commitments for a life of political action. Instead, he emulated writers like Chekhov and Boris Pasternak, whose strongest devotion was indeed to literature, but "whose sense of responsibility led them . . . to speak out on grave issues."[27] During the storm-laden sixties, this attempt at balancing a life in letters with public activism called on Howe's extraordinary energy and multiplicity of skills for living simultaneously in the several worlds of politics, literature, academia, and family.

In the hope of keeping up with the tumultuousness of the decade and perhaps even of influencing the course of events, *Dissent*, beginning in 1966, went from a quarterly to a bimonthly publication. This kept Howe busier than ever soliciting funds, articles, and writers, as well as doing the additional day-to-day editorial work required by the magazine's expansion. He expressed "a certain sense of being burdened" and told Coser that *Dissent* had steadily become for him "an uphill project." Howe's postcards got even briefer, his phone calls more truncated, but the flood of each continued. And throughout he remained devoted to the journal and to the issues of social justice it emphasized, especially the crusade for civil rights. Between 1965 and 1969, Howe wrote nearly a dozen pieces focusing on racial equality, and another dozen which included substantive discussion of the "Negro movement" and its "unquestionable rightness of purpose."[28]

He also continued to write literary criticism (more than a dozen essays in the second half of the decade in addition to a book on Thomas Hardy), and to teach at the City University of New York. Here students still cared to read Jane Austen and Henry James, even during the nerve-racking days of America's escalation of hostilities in Vietnam.[29] But Howe kept talking as well about the horrors of the military conflict to young people at CUNY and other universities, including Harvard and Yale and the New School. He condemned the war for its devastating impact on the Vietnamese; its wastefulness in terms of American lives lost and resources diverted from social programs; and its role in the polarization of the home front and in the growing desperation and misdirection of the young.[30]

In the summers Irving escaped from much of the polemical atmosphere of the mid-sixties by spending several weeks, together with Arien and their respective children, in Truro and Wellfleet on Cape Cod. Here,

Howe could relax as well as remain productive. Over two summers, for example, Howe worked effectively on his study of Thomas Hardy. He had told Lionel Trilling, with whom he had renewed his friendship in the early sixties, that he had been working on the Hardy project for years, "writing a section now and then only to interrupt it with a host of other things."[31] But, in those benign months at Cape Cod, Howe experienced several "bursts of productivity" and finished his book. The completion of *Thomas Hardy* (1967), Howe's ninth major work, was, as he told Lew Coser, yet "another act of defiance against fate, time, enemies and sloth," but it was also for him "literature regained." This repossession, Howe said later, "brought a purification through detachment." As he worked on Hardy, Howe found that "Tess and Jude, [and] Sue Bridehead . . . were utterly real" to him, while the war in Vietnam seemed very far away. [32]

Howe was attracted to Hardy partly because the English writer, like Sherwood Anderson and William Faulkner (Howe's other book-length subjects), and Howe himself, possessed an image of a more coherent, more communal past, which served as a stimulus for his negative assessment of the dominant culture.[33] Hardy's nostalgia for the rootedness of settled country life, which during his own lifetime was disrupted by the forces of commerce and industrialism, formed a major theme in his novels. His idea of another "earlier" England, "as genuine memory, a romantic assumption or a dramatic fiction," demonstrated brilliantly, Howe thought, Hardy's concern with the loss of community, the decline of fraternity, and the cost of impersonal, alienated existence.[34] Hardy had shown little interest in politics in its narrow sense, but in his depictions of the "modernization" of rural England there was an inherent critique of the accompanying uprooting and subsequent social fragmentation of his world.

But Hardy never yielded to a "tiresome romanticizing of the past." He saw not only accumulated richness but also stagnation in the old and stable culture. Although Hardy said he believed in a "harmonious submission to the natural order," his sympathies, Howe contended, were less with those who surrender to their habitual surroundings, and more with those like Clym Yeobright in *Return of the Native* and Jude Fawley in *Jude the Obscure* "who decide to separate themselves from their environments and pay the price of estrangement."[35] Howe's own mix of early rebelliousness against the constraints of parochial ethnicity and his subsequent embrace of the traditional world of immigrant

Jewry and Yiddish culture helps account for his attraction to the poignant, complex counterpoints in Hardy's work. Howe was also taken with Hardy's search for a new synthesis, a new principle of unity. He appreciated and in some ways replicated Hardy's struggle to create a philosophical structure to replace a religious faith that had lapsed, but to whose ethical center he was still attached.[36]

Hardy's struggle resembled that of his contemporary I. L. Peretz, the classic Yiddish writer, for whom Howe felt the deepest resonance. And it was similar to the attempt by Jewish immigrant socialists of the early 1900s, so admired by Howe, who tried to integrate Jewish ethical premises with progressive secular modernism in a way that would provide a renewed coherence. This was the kind of struggle, Howe said, that intensified Hardy's sympathies "for all those who were fumbling toward some notion or intuition by which to enclose the chaos of events."[37] In tone and temperament Hardy belongs to an earlier time, Howe wrote, but "he can be read as a precursor of modernism's search for a post-Christian rationale for values."[38]

Truro was a good place for Howe to write about Hardy and the nineteenth-century novelist's world of Wessex. Like Cape Cod, with its low-growing pines, bright-colored beach plums, white sands and slower pace, Wessex, in the heart of the English countryside, represented a harmony of nature and society. It was a "place" to which Hardy's protagonists, fleeing the confusions of their modern lives, could return, for a time, for a sense of rootedness, or at least simplicity. Similarly, the Cape was Howe's pastoral, a reprieve from the "chaos of events," a "restorative of sanity."[39]

Literature regained was not the only thing that provided Howe a respite from the urgency of politics. He also enjoyed time with his family at their Cape Cod home, where "all 4 . . . kids," his and Arien's, gathered and "got . . . along well."[40] Howe took genuine pleasure in this, and appears to have played an active and loving role as father and stepfather. Nina Howe recalled that in the summer of 1965 or 1966, when she was fifteen or sixteen, the reconstructed family was sitting around the kitchen table after lunch when someone made a remark that sent Howe in search of a book. He returned to read, in a clear, loud voice, "rich in expressive detail," Ambrose Bierce's macabre short story, "Oil of Dog." The children were spellbound by the ghoulish piece, but also laughed heartily at points, perhaps recognizing the inherent warning about the overzealousness of "capitalistic enterprise" in the satiric tale, or in

Howe's "interpretation" of it. Nina remembered this moment not only because of the "entertainment value of a well-read story," but also because it signified so much about her father's approach to literature: reading was not just a solitary activity; it could be a focus for exchange, a time for sharing feelings and exploring with others "the world of ideas."[41]

Discussion continued at the beaches, which were full of interesting people to talk to. On any given summer day Irving and Arien and their children could encounter Alfred Kazin, or Allen Tate and Isabella Gardner, Robert Jay and Betty Jean Lifton, Daniel Aaron or Philip Roth, all of whom were also at the Cape to write as well as to enjoy the sun and surf. Rumor had it that there was so much important, authoritative composition going on in Truro and Wellfleet that one critic's wife, trying to keep down the noise of the neighborhood children, put her head out the window and, pleading with the kids to be quiet, said: "The professor is writing a book review. I'm sure all of your mothers and fathers have reviews to write too!"[42]

Also at the beach was the Pulitzer Prize–winning American historian Richard Hofstadter, with whom Howe had become quite close. Hofstadter thought that Howe's polemical interactions with the New Left proved that he hadn't yet freed himself from his "youthful delusions." And Howe thought that Hofstadter, an ex-Communist, had "veered too far toward a conservative kind of liberalism." But in Hofstadter, as in Lionel Trilling, Howe had found a friend whose "liberalism of spirit" he wanted to share. Despite a number of differences in their respective approaches to literary style and criticism, Howe and Trilling shared the belief that liberal politics, indeed all politics, needed the imaginative qualities of literature, and that liberalism particularly needed literature's sense of possibility, variousness, and complexity. Trilling and Hofstadter, Howe said, respected his "urgent need for public struggle," but both men had the kind of poise that helped him pull back a little from his "obsessions" with democratic socialism, and from his "life of clamor."[43]

Away from the beach, back in the commotion of New York City, Howe and Arien could go to the ballet, which they had been doing regularly from the beginning of their marriage "as a diversion from [their] harried New York existence." By the mid-sixties Howe began to care more about the ballet as an art form, especially the distinctive qualities of Balanchine's work, and he soon "fell in love with the whole thing."

He found himself remembering a humorous story in which a Trotskyist is "exposed" as a passionate admirer of Jane Austen. "But then again," he asked, "why not?" Why not indeed? For Howe the dance "embodied a union of emotion and feeling, body and spirit, act and suggestion." He appreciated the grace and intelligence of disciplined movement in the dancers as much as he did in professional ball players. Unlike the jerky mannerisms of rock musicians, this kind of movement, Howe recognized, demanded years of training and control, and while the performer's body was an "expressive instrument," it was not merely "letting itself go," in self-delight.[44]

There was also Eliezer Greenberg, yet another friend who helped Howe withdraw temporarily from the din and disorder of politics. By the mid-to-late sixties, Howe had been collaborating with Greenberg for more than fifteen years, translating and editing anthologies of Yiddish literature, and the relationship and the work had become a sustaining experience. "There was a pleasure in doing something absolutely pure," Howe said, whether it was arguing playfully over a difficult phrase, determining the suitability of a Yiddish poem for conversion into English, or simply enjoying again a well-constructed Old World story.

Having felt the allure of Yiddish culture from as early as the 1950s, Howe asked himself later, whether he was attracted to the secular Jewish milieu precisely because it was in its "twilight period." But he decided that this was "not the whole story." Perhaps Yiddish culture was so appealing, Howe speculated, "because it was as close as anything now could be to the world that had given me shape." Perhaps it "stirred" him, he said, "because it seemed to speak back to me as no other culture did." Perhaps for Howe, like the Yiddish poets he immersed himself in—Jacob Glatstayn, Itzak Manger, Kadia Molodowsky, and many others—he simply could not "break past the visible and invisible boundaries of Yiddish." Like them he had, in his youth, asserted his own voice and style and tried to shake off "the burdens of the folk" in order to speak as a cosmopolitan individual. But like them, too, he returned to "the web of Jewish destiny," ultimately making it the very substance of his work. Howe's collaboration with Greenberg, then, was not only another episode in "literature regained" and another day a week away from the Vietnam war and heated exchanges with "leftist ideologues," it was also, like the Hannah Arendt affair, another step for him in "Jewishness reconquered."[45]

Surely it was Howe's newly resuscitated Jewishness that informed his sour review of the 1964 Broadway musical, "Fiddler on the Roof," which he saw as an unworthy dilution and distortion of the Old World stories of Sholom Aleichem. From early in his career Howe had been a champion of Sholom Aleichem, whom he rightly saw as a neglected literary giant. And he may have been fearful that "Fiddler" would further obscure the great Yiddish writer's work, perhaps in the way the 1956 musical "My Fair Lady" had driven Shaw's "Pygmalion" from the serious stage. Irritated by the sentimentality and romanticization of "Fiddler" and its failure to grapple with the construction and oppressions of tradition, Howe, in his passion to salvage the genuine in the world of Yiddishkayt, dismissed the play's depiction of the imaginary Anatevka as "the cutest shtetl we've never had."[46]

Howe's sense of ethnic identity was organically connected to what he saw as authentic in Yiddish tradition. It was intensified, too, by other elements and developments in the larger Jewish world. Howe's Jewishness was reinforced, for example, in June 1967 with the advent of Israel's Six Day War in the Middle East. Egypt, Jordan, and Syria, emboldened by a vast supply of Russian weapons, apparently thought the time was ripe to annihilate the "Zionist entity" in their midst, or at least to draw Israel into a war of attrition that would destroy her over time. Egypt closed the Tiran Straits, and along with other Arab states mobilized forces close to Israel's borders. Faced by a massive disadvantage on the ground and by pervasive rhetoric from across the Arab world threatening the extermination of the Jewish state, Israel, after a significant period of waiting, opened the war by launching a series of preemptive strikes on air bases throughout Egypt.[47] Although Howe had experienced a sense of satisfaction when Israel declared its independence in 1948, he had paid little attention to the Jewish state after that. In 1967, however, his "first reaction" to the potential destruction of Israel was a powerfully felt concern for her survival. Indeed, Howe in *Dissent* that year classified the preservation of Israel as "an urgent moral [and] political necessity."[48]

Sentiment toward Israel on the largely Jewish editorial board of *Dissent*, in the 1950s and early 1960s, ranged from general indifference (there were virtually no articles in *Dissent* on the new state before 1967) to Henry Pachter's distinctly anti-Zionist attitudes on the one side, and Michael Walzer's Labor-Zionist sympathies on the other. And although Howe, mostly under the influence of Marie Syrkin, his friend and Brandeis colleague, had moved from support of a binational workers' state in Palestine (the Trotskyist position) to a two-state solution, he insisted that he was not a Zionist or even a Jewish nationalist.[49]

This was true in that Howe remained a critic of particular policies pursued by various Israeli governments over the years, especially the continued occupation of the West Bank and Gaza Strip and the building of Jewish settlements in those captured territories. But he consistently defended Israel's right to exist. His attitude, he said often and aptly, was very much like that of many Israelis "who see in a vigorous but responsible criticism [a] token of their commitment to democratic Israel."[50] Howe's Jewishness, unconnected, in the main, to religion or nation, was grounded in his devotion to Yiddish literature and the progressive dimensions of Jewish secularism. But after 1967, in his relationship to Israel, he appears to have added a latent dimension of nationalist sentiment to his Jewish identity.

Noam Chomsky, a severe critic of Howe's from the radical Left, thinks Howe made his "post-1967 switch to unthinking Zionist commitments" largely because he needed another weapon against the New Left. Young radicals had indeed begun to attack a relatively democratic Israel in 1967 as an imperialist puppet of the United States. At the same time, faintly echoing Howe's own distant Trotskyist past, they celebrated Arab and other Third World dictators whose suppression of human rights had been justified as "historically necessary" for the economic development of their countries. But Howe had been a relentless critic of the New Left's romance with revolutionary authoritarianism well before 1967. What Chomsky missed was Howe's attraction to Israel for its democracy, its important socialist dimensions, and not least for its Jewishness. For Howe, 1967 was crucial not because of the New Left's denunciation of Israel, but because the Jewish state, "a democratic nation, remarkable for its morale, and composed in significant measure of the victims of genocide," had faced yet another intended Holocaust.[51]

Very soon after the Six Day War, Howe admitted that although it had taken several years after World War II for the enormity of the Holocaust to sink in, there was, finally, for him a stout link between the Nazi mass murder of the Jews in Europe and his turn to Yiddish literature and Jewish themes.[52] In 1954 he dedicated *A Treasury of Yiddish Stories* "To the Six Million," and in 1969 his *Treasury of Yiddish Poetry* "To the Yiddish Writers Destroyed by Hitler and Stalin."

Howe's reawakened Jewish consciousness and his support for Israel, which continued until his death in 1993, had nothing to do with the New Left. But that many of the young radicals, including numerous Jews, merged New Left rhetoric with anti-Semitic sentiments, or that a few even went so far as to collect money for Palestinian guerrillas, added new frustration and bitterness to Howe's well-established antipathy.[53]

Many in the New Left who considered Howe an incipient supporter of U.S. imperialism saw his defense of Israel as consistent with his reluctance to sanction an unconditional American departure from Vietnam. But Howe's position could not be logically classified as "imperialistic" in regard to either Vietnam or Israel. By 1967 he was even more explicit in his condemnation of the war in Southeast Asia, saying the United States, in order to prop up Diem's dictatorship and subsequent authoritarian puppets, had unilaterally intervened in what was essentially a civil war.[54]

In his support of Israel, Howe had never proposed that the United States involve itself militarily in the Middle East, or anywhere else, for that matter. This, despite the fact that from 1967 to 1970 Israel suffered more than four thousand casualties in the so-called "war of attrition" launched by a Soviet-armed Egypt.[55] An American military intervention in the region, Howe feared, meant a potential nuclear confrontation between the USSR and the United States. He was not bound, however, by an "inflexible abstentionism." Howe thought specific situations favored U.S. "intervention" of a kind: economic help for a struggling Yugoslavia; limited sanctions against the racist government of Rhodesia; or, combined with moral sanctions and flexibility in peace negotiations, arms for Israel. But, as Howe argued, in none of these instances could American policy be explained by the Leninist theory of imperialism which was so widely employed by the New Left. If U.S. foreign policy in the Middle East, for example, were based primarily on concern with American investments in the region, the overwhelming bulk of which were in oil in Arab countries, that policy would have to be, Howe insisted, "decisively more favorable to the Arab nations."[56]

Howe's positions on Israel and Vietnam were in fact consistent, not in their alleged imperialist quality, but in their commitment to democracy. The survival of Israel, Howe said, ought to be a major priority for everyone who cared about democracy, and defending her against the enemies of democracy, he argued, was not only desirable and necessary, it was possible—by means short of full-scale American military intervention.[57] On the other hand, when Howe finally recognized that there would be no emergent democratic force in Vietnam in any foreseeable future, he finally called for unconditional American withdrawal. But that took until 1968. In the meantime Howe remained embattled not only with the New Left, but also with old friends.

Howe and Max Shachtman hadn't spoken for almost a decade after Howe left the Independent Socialist League (formerly the Workers Party) in 1952. But in the early sixties the two former Trotskyists began a correspondence largely concerning Shachtman's editing of Trotsky's papers. Their exchanges grew warmer over time, but by 1966 Shachtman had moved significantly to Howe's right and there was yet another split between the two men, this time mainly over the war in Vietnam, which Shachtman had come to support unequivocally.[58]

Shachtman and his faction of the Socialist Party were bent on promoting a political realignment in the Democratic Party, linking liberals and labor to the civil rights movement, and encouraging them to defy the power of the conservative Southern Democrats or Dixiecrats. This was consistent with Shachtman's long-held dream of achieving power for the working class and was not at all alien to Howe, who since the early sixties had endorsed voting for liberal Democrats and cooperating legislatively with the left wing of the Democratic Party. But Shachtman, unlike Howe, defined working-class interests solely in terms of what major union leaders said they were. George Meany, the president of the AFL-CIO, America's largest and most powerful labor organization, and most other union officers backed the war. This meant Shachtman could not permit the Socialist Party to take a strong antiwar position. Indeed, in the summer of 1965, believing "a democratic force" could still win in Vietnam, Shachtman announced that he opposed American withdrawal from the conflict. He was angry at Howe and Harrington and others on the *Dissent* board who, although hesitant to endorse a full, immediate and unconditional withdrawal, called for cease-fire and negotiation. And he was furious at Howe for having said in the spring of 1965, and many times thereafter, that a Communist victory was all but inevitable, and that such a victory would be a lesser evil than a prolonged and wider war.[59]

In 1966 at a private meeting in Bayard Rustin's New York apartment, Shachtman shocked Howe and Harrington and a contingent of other *Dissent* editors when he tried to justify supporting the U.S. war indefinitely. Anything was preferable, Shachtman said, to "Communist victory," even the propping up of the "reprehensible Saigon regime" by an expanded and interminable war. The American military effort, he insisted, simply must continue until the Communists were beaten. When Howe and others vigorously objected, Shachtman attacked them as "a bunch of . . . Gandhian pacifists who were against the use of violence under all circumstances."[60] The political differences between the *Dissent* group and Shachtman widened ever further over time. But as late as 1969, when Harrington and Shachtman were barely speaking, Howe, harking back to the sectarian squabbles and fragmentations of the forties and fifties, asked his former mentor, "What have we learned over all these bitter years if we can't avoid a split?" Shachtman responded by expressing his continuing respect for Howe's talents, but there was no closing the gap between them, and their relationship would soon end.[61]

Howe was not only attacked by old associates now to the right of him, but also by those who saw themselves to his left. By the late 1960s Howe and the novelist Harvey Swados were friends whose worlds had intertwined for decades. The two men first met in the early 1940s in Buffalo where the Workers Party was building a new branch. Both remained socialists to the end of their lives. But Swados could be as impatient and irascible as Howe, and as independent minded, and from the beginning they had their political differences.[62] None, however, were as sharp as over the war in Vietnam. In 1967 Swados took Howe to task for failing to see that his "principle of anti-Communism" leads "*inevitably* to reactionary ends"—like the U.S. intervention in Southeast Asia. He compared Howe's insistence on anti-Communism to the opinions and behavior of Secretary of State Dean Rusk and Secretary of Defense Robert McNamara, whom many on the Left considered "war criminals."[63]

Swados had sent his attack on Howe to the *New York Review of Books*, but he withdrew it after he was persuaded by Richard Hofstadter that it could be construed as aid and comfort to the "young totalitarians" of the New Left in their hate campaign against Howe. He sent Howe a carbon copy, however, and a longer letter explaining his views. He went on to say that Howe could not really call himself a socialist if he persisted in his anti-Communism as a principle of government or international relations, as distinct from a personal commitment to democratic values. Anti-Communism, Swados insisted, was simply a disguise for "the nakedness of U.S. imperialism."[64]

Howe thought the letters were "astonishingly hostile and nasty." He was particularly upset that he was tied to the anti-Communism of Rusk and McNamara. That was as unfair and undiscriminating, Howe argued, as linking Swados to the anticapitalism of Mao and Brezhnev. He agreed with Swados that anti-Communism had been used in reactionary ways and reminded him, accurately, that he had often said so in the past: about the early stages of the Cold War; about the Dominican Republic; and not least, about Vietnam. But he also defended the positive instances of anti-Communism, like the Berlin airlift in 1948 and the Marshall Plan.[65]

In explaining the quality and complexity of his left anti-Communism against the reactionary anti-Communism of the Right, Howe also reminded Swados that, throughout the 1950s, he had fought against those who insisted that Communists should, ipso facto, be denied the right to teach. "I engaged in numerous polemics and suffered considerable attack for taking that position," Howe wrote. "To be sure," he continued, "no one expects the kids to care anything about what happened as long ago as 1954, clearly another century." But, Howe said, at least "Swados should remember."[66] Howe might also have reminded his friend that he was *still* fighting for the civil liberties of Communists, and that as recently as 1963, he had called for repeal of the McCarran Act (1950) requiring the registration of "Communist-action organizations." Citing principle and expediency, Howe had argued that Communists should be allowed to speak freely, and with impunity, as befits confidence in the idea of a free society. For the attorney general's office to hunt down the aging leaders of American Communism instead of "letting them molder in the obscurity in which they otherwise would be," Howe said, is not only "rotten" but "stupid," for "it allows the futile American Communists to pose as—indeed, to be—martyrs."[67]

After yet another exchange of letters with Swados, Howe finally dashed off one of his famous postcards saying "we seem to have reached a dead-end, so let's stop."[68] The correspondence picked up again about a year later, less contentious now, more social and literary. Howe had brought the earlier political communications with Swados to a halt because, while wanting and needing to be engaged in the general debate over the war and the politics of the New Left, he felt the futility of repetitious arguments and wanted to turn more of his energy to writing. He was, in 1967, involved in three projects that would eventually become "signature" pieces for him: his essays on "The Culture of

Modernism" and on "The New York Intellectuals," and his "big book" on Jewish immigrants, *World of Our Fathers*.

Even in these durable and still valuable works of retrospection, however, it was evident that Howe was influenced by the chaotic political and cultural context of the sixties. In *World of Our Fathers*, as we will see, and in essays leading to that book, Howe celebrated secular Jewishness and its manifestation in a Jewish socialism which held to values sadly missing in the "socialism" of the New Left in the late sixties: a "complicated and chastened sense of history, a sharp concern for the actualities of immediate social life, institutions of fraternity and freedom, and a rigorous commitment to democratic values."[69] That the New Left suffered dearly for this lack weighed heavily on Howe as he wrote about the early twentieth century Jewish radical movement that had added a powerful progressive dimension to American politics.

The New Left was also on Howe's mind when he sat down near the end of the decade to write on literary modernism and the New York intellectuals. In both essays Howe indicated a continuing appreciation of the modernist masters. But the general direction of the pieces was toward a critique of some of modernism's consequences—authoritarianism on the one hand, or decadence and nihilism on the other. These were attitudes Howe associated with the New Left and the counterculture generally. He had always had reservations about modern writers like Eliot and Yeats and Pound who were attracted to the forces of reaction. But now in 1967–1968, in the face of disdain for liberalism among the young political and cultural radicals, Howe seemed even more worried that "in every important literature, . . . except the Yiddish, the modernist impulse was accompanied by a revulsion against . . . liberalism."[70] Howe explicitly indicted the literature of the sixties (which included such talented and innovative writers as John Barth, William Gaddis, and John Hawkes) along with the New Left, and what he called the decade's "new sensibility," for being "impatient with ideas" and contemptuous of rationality. This new sensibility, Howe insisted, was tired of nuance and the habit of reflection, and it either wanted the "narcotic of certainty"—literature and music and ideology "as unarguable as orgasm, and as delicious as a lollipop"—or it embraced the nihilism present in modernism but against which the great modernist masters like Mann and Kafka and Joyce had always struggled. Howe feared the new sensibility with its superficiality and its nihilism, he said, because "it despises liberal values, liberal caution, liberal virtues."[71] Some of the new sensibility had appeal, Howe wrote. It captured genuine yearnings of the young, and he admitted, it even has "a vibration" of moral desire, a quest for goodness of heart. Still, Howe warned, "we had better not deceive ourselves. Some of those shiny-cheeked darlings adorned with flowers and tokens of love can also be campus *enrages* screaming 'Up Against the Wall, Motherfuckers, This is a Stickup.'" Howe the erudite rationalist was appalled by the arrogance and lack of constraint this slogan represented. And Howe the socialist, in one of his famous understatements, said it "does not strike one as a notable improvement over the 'Workers of the World, Unite.'"[72] Howe's socialism and the secular Jewishness to which it was linked made him see as inherently unworthy those developments that seemed to stress the emotions and physical pleasure over reason, and personal and sexual fulfillment over social change. He admitted later that he "was naive in much of this." When he had been teaching at Brandeis, Howe said, "there were only glimpses of the counterculture." And when he heard that his student Martin Peretz had smoked marijuana with Norman Mailer in the late fifties, he felt "a shudder of bewilderment."[73]

In his role as a critic, this attitude, this revulsion from the moral and sexual upheavals of the decade, obstructed Howe's appreciation of many of the new art forms and moved him to lump together in a negative package all of the cultural changes of the sixties. He had been able, relatively well, to separate out, from the extremes of the New Left, currents of democratic left-liberalism among young people, but he did little of this in terms of "the new sensibility." Drug users, writer Susan Sontag, the *New York Review of Books*, novelist Thomas Pynchon, rock musicians including Bob Dylan and the Beatles, and theater critic Robert Brustein were all mistakenly tarred by Howe with the same brush—the absence of stylistic, moral, or conceptual controls.[74]

Howe wasn't repulsed simply because the new sensibility emphasized images of sickness, disintegration, and insecurity. He had understood and even celebrated the acuity with which modern writers like Proust, Beckett, and Joyce had honed in on "extreme situations and radical solutions," had focused on "experiment . . . apocalypse and skepticism," on "images of rebellion . . . and nothingness." But he was most taken with those writers who, in grappling with these demons of the modern era, displayed a "dialectical canniness" and stayed powerfully affirmative. He was less comfortable with the hopelessness in the work of Eliot or Edith Wharton than with the lyricism and rhapsodic moments in Joyce or Frost, a modern poet who searched for that "momentary stay against confusion." And he admired Pirandello, the playwright who had a sharp eye for the absurdities of modern existence, but who was far removed from "the view that life is inherently absurd."[75]

Howe's preferred modernist writers were raised in cultures where Christianity still had at least some historical residue. And although religious belief no longer fully survived in those writers, they responded, Howe thought, to religion's echo, to its "call to duties, burdens and limits." Howe, too, raised in a culture informed by religious values though he was not a man of faith, was marked by the Jewish inclination to responsibility and restraint. Howe's secular Jewishness, then, contributed not only to his socialist perspective, it also provided him with an "inner conservatism," which served as a way of balancing his radical public role.

Howe's Jewish "inner conservatism" was part of the reason he responded so positively to Saul Bellow's *Mr. Sammler's Planet*. He called the novel, which first appeared serially in the *New Yorker* in the late sixties, "extremely brilliant," and he praised Bellow as the most gifted and "most serious" of the American Jewish writers, and the "most Jewish in his seriousness." Like Bellow's protagonist Arthur Sammler, Howe found himself reeling from the general incoherence, insensitivity, and vulgarity of personal and social behavior in contemporary America. Like Bellow himself, Howe believed in *menshlikhkayt*—decency, compassion, "that root sense of obligation which the mere fact of being human imposes on us."[76] And it was *menshlikhkayt* that Howe found conspicuously missing in the "new sensibility" and among the young generally.

It is possible too that in his condemnation of the licentiousness of the young, and the decline of "standards" among the not so young, Howe may also have been reacting, in classic Freudian fashion, to his own infidelity at Brandeis in the late fifties and early sixties. In any case, he now sternly rejected what he called the "psychology of unobstructed need," a narrowly selfish, one-dimensional psychology he thought dominated the counterculture and especially the New Left.[77]

Getting back to "steady work" at the typewriter, even if not far removed from the "culture wars," was a tonic for Howe. But only a few months after his private feud with Swados, Irving was involved in an even more furious and ad hominem "conversation," this time in public, with past *Partisan Review* editor Philip Rahv. Although Rahv, too, was a sharp critic of the "new sensibility," he, unlike Howe, differentiated it from the New Left, a movement he defended with great spirit. The immediate provocation for his battle with Irving was a review by Rahv in the *New York Review of Books* (NYRB) of *The Radical Imagination* (1967), a book that drew together essays by Howe and others previously published in *Dissent*. The bulk of Rahv's piece was devoted to an attack on Howe's politics. Howe's use of anti-Communism as the supreme test of political rectitude on the Left struck Rahv as a "terrible blunder." It not only underlay Irving's "equivocation" on the Vietnam War, Rahv argued, but also led him to make "ill-timed thrusts at militant New Leftists" like SDS president Carl Oglesby, who had "rightly" refused to "exhibit or stress his anti-Communism." Rahv charged that Howe's articles were filled with "used-up formulas" and that the most recent essays were characterized by an antirevolutionary attitude. Finally, he accused Howe, "presumably a democratic socialist," of putting such "illimitable emphasis on the word 'democratic' that in consequence his 'socialism' appears wide of the mark."[78]

A month later, the *NYRB* printed "An Exchange on the Left" between Howe and Rahv. "Had I been wise," Howe said later, "I would have ignored the whole thing, perhaps sending Rahv a postcard bearing his favorite tag, 'Who needs it?'"[79] Howe was not wise. He wrote a long reply defending his "social democratic" approach to American politics, but also directly needling Rahv, who after nearly twenty years of painful circumspection and rightward drift had suddenly reawakened on Howe's left to give him "Little Lessons in Leninism." Howe agreed that he was, as Rahv charged, against some current political activities (many of them unnecessarily confrontational) that paraded as "revolution." But, he said, with no mass base in the working class or the middle class or even among the students, these provocations were in no sense a true radicalism. Howe called the "smugly moralistic" posturing of the New Left and many of its older converts who imagined themselves in some kind of "vanguardist" role a "'radicalism' of the attic and the playground." He went on to lambaste fellow New York intellectuals, including the crowd around the *NYRB*, who had joined in with this "corrupt apocalyptic fantasy."

To Rahv's criticism that Howe placed an inordinate emphasis on democracy, Howe responded: "I proudly accept the charge. To me democracy and socialism are unbreakably linked; fifty years after the Bolshevik revolution—with all the blood, all the defeat, all the despair, all the broken hopes that followed it—this is the lesson to which I dedicate my voice."[80]

The tone and substance of most of Howe's piece was neither kind nor meant to be. And it had the effect of provoking Rahv to a forceful rebuttal in which he declared, once more, the bankruptcy of liberalism and social democracy and again celebrated the prospect of revolution. He claimed that Howe had forgotten that "vanguard action is always accomplished by minorities" and that "the fear of alienating the majority is the fear of action itself." He clearly implied that Howe was a coward who was made "nervous" by the mere appearance of revolutionary potential.[81]

More than a decade later, Howe tried to think through what had happened in this "brawl." Without minimizing the differences between Rahv and himself, Howe said that he had been "hurt and angered in ways that went beyond politics. "What troubled me was . . . a feeling that [Rahv] was being personally disloyal, that even if all or some of what he said was true, he should not have been the one to say it."[82] The personal wounds that Howe and Rahv inflicted on each other were so deep that the two men, once truly close friends and colleagues, did not speak again for the remaining six years of Rahv's life. Both were literary people, but in the sixties, Howe said, "in some sense politics counted for more. . . . You could differ on literary issues and maintain a friendship. Not on politics."[83]

Apparently the NYRB editors felt the same way. As a consequence of his exchange with Rahv, Howe was dropped as a contributor for ten years. Irving was not exactly unhappy to be dissociated from the NYRB. He agreed with the magazine's focus in the sixties on America's general "failure . . . in the cities," on black frustration, and on the ensuing disturbances erupting sporadically in many urban areas. He also felt that during "the ghastly Vietnam War" the NYRB was immensely valuable in registering the deep sense of horror, anger, and frustration felt by a large number of intellectuals, and that it published a useful and seemingly inexhaustible series of proposals about what ought to be done to end the hostilities. But he thought that the NYRB, especially in 1967, too often printed materials supportive of the various protest movements at their arrogant, anti-American, and mindless worst. He had in mind several pieces by Mary McCarthy and Noam Chomsky. But Howe was most distressed by the August 24 issue in which Andrew Kopkind, apparently dismissing liberal norms and values and encouraging violence, wrote that "[m]orality, like politics, starts at the barrel of a gun." Worse for Howe was the irresponsible illustration on the cover—a carefully drawn Molotov cocktail graphically depicting all its ingredients.[84]

Howe was no pacifist, but he was clearly repelled by violence, even by what he called the "uncivil" disobedience of "prerevolutionary" gestures—the attempt to stop troop trains or to take over official buildings, for example—which challenged the authority of the state in nonrevolutionary situations. Disobedience that was truly civil was a legitimate tactic, Howe thought, but only in some very limited instances, and only as a last resort. He was rightly worried about the alienation of "middle Americans" and a backlash from the Right, which proved to be one of the more important long-term consequences of the sixties. Howe was most concerned about some New Left statements implying that, in blocking access to corporate recruiters like Dow Chemical, the manufacturer of napalm, it was not only necessary but desirable to violate "bourgeois" civil liberties, including freedom of speech and assembly. "The social order we are rebelling against is . . . anti-democratic," said Carl Davidson, an officer of SDS, in November 1967. And since the institutions of American society are "totalitarian, manipulative, [and] repressive," they "are without legitimacy in our eyes, they are without rights."[85]

Howe despised this kind of rhetorical excess and the violence he believed would inevitably follow from it. He also saw in these "ideas" a grave threat to the liberalism that he had long promoted as the historical and moral foundation for democratic socialism. Whenever American radicalism showed any sign of growth in the past, Howe said, it had largely been in "consort with an upsurge of liberalism." In the course of the radical attacks on liberalism and the attacks on himself as a "liberal," Howe recognized more and more his commitment to its ideals. He told a colleague of Arien's at the New School that "the *values* of liberalism alone make life worth living, no matter what critique one may have of liberal politics or practice." Finally, he dismissed as absurd the notion that "radicalism can grow fat on the entrails of liberalism," and he warned, to the contrary, that assaults on the "vulnerable foundations of democracy" could help bring repressive social forces into play.[86]

Howe, of course, was not only anxious about the incipient violence of the New Left, he was horrified by the very real violence perpetrated by American forces in Vietnam. This combination of agonizing concerns made Howe desperate for a vehicle through which millions of people like himself could register an effective nonviolent opposition to the war they hated. He thought there was such an opportunity in Senator Eugene McCarthy's campaign to win the presidential nomination of the Democratic Party. The forthrightness of McCarthy and the active grassroots participation in his candidacy, Howe told the *New York Times* in December 1967, gave him hope that serious people could work together to force a radical change in America's "disastrous" Vietnam policy. "It's enough," Howe said, "to make one feel that democracy isn't as worn out as the nihilists, desperadoes [and] cynics . . . on all points of the political spectrum keep telling us these days."[87]

McCarthy's chances were soon enhanced by the Tet offensive. On the last day of January at the start of the Vietnamese New Year (Tet), the Vietcong and the North Vietnamese launched a full-scale, many-pronged attack against American forces throughout South Vietnam. The operation was not a glorious military success for the Communists, who suffered very significant fatalities, but it inflicted heavy casualties on the U.S. soldiers and their Saigon allies and sent America into shock. There was a fast-growing, if not sudden, realization, brought home by the incessant TV images of mounting losses, that American policy in Vietnam was grossly ineffective, and that the president and his cabinet officers had lied repeatedly about the course of the war.

Senator McCarthy rode the shock waves to a stunning success in March in the New Hampshire primary, winning 42 percent of the vote against 49 percent for Lyndon Baines Johnson, the sitting Democratic American president. The results were generally interpreted as a rejection of Johnson's Vietnam policies. Howe wrote to Coser that although most current public events depressed him, he was encouraged by the progress of the McCarthy campaign in which he himself had become quite active.[88] Howe called it his first chance for "wholehearted electoral work" since his "undistinguished soapboxing for Norman Thomas." And he even tried to bring the New Left back to coalition politics by urging them to support McCarthy.[89]

It was time, Howe said, for the young radicals to turn from "pseudo-revolutionary posturings . . . to the hard work of radical social reconstruction." Howe did not believe for a moment that the mere election of McCarthy or of Robert F. Kennedy, who had announced his candidacy only days after the New Hampshire primary, was going to solve America's problems. Only an end to the war combined with unremitting struggle in behalf of new radical programs would provide a beginning in that direction. Howe never relinquished hope for a wide-ranging and eclectic Left, one that would make alliances with liberals but one that would also sustain a socialist vision and a radical dimension in American politics. And he called on the New Left to join with the Old in as broad an effort as possible to end the war and to promote social reform at home.[90]

After Tet, Howe further toned down his anti-Communism. He not only said, yet again, "Better peace with the probability of a Viet Cong takeover than a war which can only go on and on," he relinquished his "negotiations now" stance and came over to Michael Walzer's long-held position calling for immediate withdrawal. As long as the war continues, Howe told his friend Harvey Swados, "no conciliation among generations or opinions on the left is possible, especially since the kids now feel, rightly, that it's crazy to get killed just to gain a negotiating advantage."[91]

Still fearful of eliciting repressive responses from large segments of the American population, Howe continued to shy away from the "radical resistance" that systematically advocated that students refuse to enter the armed forces. He did, however, express solidarity with and pledge support to those like Dr. Benjamin Spock and the Reverend William Sloan Coffin, who pursued that course. And he joined Michael Harrington in a public vow to stand behind students who, as conscientious objecters, whether religious or not, refused to be drafted, promising "to provide whatever material and moral aid we can in case they are subject to prosecution."[92] Howe and Harrington concluded their formal "Statement on the Draft" by asking whether this country, in the willful pursuit of an odious war, ought to jail "thousands of its finest young people, precisely the ones who in other circumstances might take the lead in social reconstruction?" The answer they said must be a firm "No!"

The full statement, published in *Dissent*, was signed by a wide spectrum of professors, political activists, and editors, including virtually the entire *Dissent* board, but also Norman Podhoretz, editor of *Commentary*. The American Civil Liberties Union was represented, as were the United Auto Workers and Americans for Democratic Action, Jewish Socialist Youth, and the Young People's Socialist League. But there were no signatories from SDS. The leadership was not interested in joining with Howe and his "liberal" friends even though they called for "popular demonstrations . . . and continued agitation," as well as for work in the primaries and other "bourgeois" electoral activities.[93]

Many thousands of young leftists and liberals flocked to Mc-Carthy and Kennedy. But large segments of the New Left, believing, illogically and insensitively, that things have to get worse before they get better, refused to support either candidate. Tom Hayden even declared publicly that "a vote for George Wallace," the segregationist governor of Alabama who had entered the presidential race, would further the objectives of the radical Left "more than a vote for RFK."[94] Despite these excesses, the New Left, Howe insisted, still "contains precious resources of energy and idealism." And those qualities, he said, "ought to be thrust into the mainstream of American politics."[95] Too many New Leftists were not ready to do that, however, and events seemed to conspire to confirm them in their antiliberalism and anticoalitionism.

The Reverend Martin Luther King, Jr., who had since 1967 become particularly vocal in his opposition to the war in Vietnam, was gunned down on April 4, 1968, in Memphis, Tennessee, where he was leading a major protest against the exploitative wages and working conditions of black sanitation workers. Many young people, not only SDS leaders or its former members, reasserted the connection they had been making since 1964 between the war against the Vietnamese and the violence and oppression perpetrated against black people in the United States. In an atmosphere of racism and murderous violence at home and abroad, they continued to see no hope in liberalism or the politics of coalition. Some even promoted counterviolence.

Howe was grief stricken by King's death but he warned against violence even as riots erupted in 150 cities and towns across the United States. In Chicago the mayhem very quickly moved Mayor Daley to issue a "shoot to kill" order. In Memphis, Harlem, Detroit, and Newark, buildings were afire, and in Washington, D.C., federal troops surrounded the White House. "No one can fail to understand why American Negroes should now respond with rage—or even violence," Howe wrote. There comes a time when people cannot take any more, he said, a moment at which they no longer care to reason but "to strike a blow." But "if we still wish to save this country, we must say with absolute firmness: whoever counsels or acquiesces in violence is totally irresponsible. If we wish to keep American Negroes from being butchered in the streets this summer, we must say with absolute firmness: whoever counsels or acquiesces in violence is helping pave the way for an American fascism."[96]

Despite the gloom and the cynicism in the aftermath of King's murder, Howe still had hope for the McCarthy campaign, especially since President Johnson, at the end of March, had pledged not to run again, an event Howe called "a triumph for democracy."[97] Robert Kennedy won the important California presidential primary in June but he was murdered by an assassin on the very night of his victory. And Vice-President Hubert Humphrey, who had entered the fray in April but had failed to dissociate himself from Johnson's foreign policy, looked vulnerable. There was, however, a long way to go to the election, and in a year in which there had already been a presidential "abdication," two major assassinations, widespread racial violence, and white backlash, more disorienting and destabilizing events were yet to come.

At the end of April student protestors occupied the buildings and offices of Columbia University, and by May radical demonstrations and sit-ins had spread to many other schools. Although they had a number of specific demands, student rebels everywhere seemed to be saying that they wanted to change the university from a bureaucracy training them for slots in a capitalist society into a school for cultural and political revolution. Howe, of course, was deeply interested in the confrontations and particularly concerned about Columbia, on Morningside Heights, not very far from his home on Riverside Drive, and where he had close friends and associates among the faculty, including Richard Hofstadter, Lionel Trilling, and Daniel Bell.

The Columbia administration waited for several days before retaliating against the students, without warning, by calling in a massive police force, which responded with unnecessary brutality. "The kids have just been thrown out bodily," Howe wrote Coser, "the place is in an uproar." He and many others, even some who were furiously angry at the students for forcing what Howe called "a denouement in blood," thought the administration had acted "quite stupidly." Grayson Kirk, the president of Columbia, and Mark Rudd, the president of the campus SDS, Howe said, "are made for each other, symbiotic."[98] The police, Howe thought, ought to be barred from campuses. But he asked the students who were attempting what he saw as a forceful revolutionary transformation of the university if they could logically complain when the powers that be responded in kind.

Howe warned again about backlash. He knew that institutions of higher learning, including Columbia, had been somewhat contaminated by outside interests and believed they should return to their true purpose of teaching and scholarship. In the meantime, by attacking the university, Howe said, the students risked destroying one of the few institutions that was still fairly sensitive to their needs and capable of protecting those who played an adversarial role in society. He told Coser that the rebel leaders "now . . . have the sympathy of the majority of the students and a good portion of the faculty," and "I really feel as if they are going to drag us all down, to some sort of apocalypse, an orgy of destruction. Sooner or later the backlash one senses as being latent in the country will burst out—and then—."[99]

In the immediate aftermath of the Columbia melee, Howe had "a very long talk with Dick Hofstadter," who told him he thought "the university ha[d] been wrecked" and that he was thinking about leaving. The two men admitted the validity of much of the students' criticism, and Howe even took some of the blame for their alienation himself. A factor in all of this, he said, is "surely . . . faculty neglect." Unfortunately, "we went our way," separate from the students, Howe confessed, "while the Maoists nibbled away."[100] Later, although still angry at the way Columbia responded to the student takeover, Howe took the SDS directly to task for inviting repression. Constant assault on widely accepted institutions, he insisted, does not help the Left but the Right, which wins support among the masses for more authoritarianism.[101]

Although Howe was not particularly sympathetic to what the SDS now stood for, he continued to support its original ideals. In October 1968 in a *New York Times Magazine* article he said: "Radical measures" are called for at this terrible time in American politics. "The Vietnam War is a scandal and a disaster," Howe wrote, and "social obligations pile up shamefully in the cities." Militant protest is clearly needed, he said, but in fighting injustice we must not use methods that give the enemies of liberty an occasion for deflecting that battle, or an excuse for destroying the procedures of democracy.[102]

Howe was so busy responding to events in 1968 that he wrote only two or three essays dealing with literature, but a dozen or more on the war and politics. The war and politics—of a sort—were also on the minds of the protestors who went to Chicago in August. They were there to get attention, and perhaps even to disrupt the Democratic convention, which was primed to nominate Hubert Humphrey as the party's presidential candidate. What transpired under Mayor Daley's watch could be classified as a "police riot," but several groups who had come to Chicago were purposefully provocative. They wielded chains and clubs and a variety of other home-made weapons, and some, including Abbie Hoffman, the putative leader of the "Chicago Seven," threatened to pollute the water supply with LSD. Twenty years later Carl Oglesby, the former president of SDS, called the events "horrifying" and rightly said that the student organization and other confrontational groups were much to blame. By their threatening gestures in Chicago, they had put thousands of antiwar innocents and the New Left movement itself at risk.[103]

Oglesby in the 1980s came to realize as true what Howe had said back in 1968, and he called the "Chicago Summer" a fatal error in which the New Left's provocations made the movement, and not the war, the focus of the public debate.[104] Howe was not entirely unsympathetic, however, even to these young people. Indeed, in 1970, he objected to the conduct of the trial for the "Chicago Seven" and to the severity of their punishment. Radical dissent, Howe said, would never be silenced by stiff jail sentences. He admitted that the young defendants intended to stage a political spectacle at their trial rather than a real legal defense. But he thought the court had acted with blatant partiality and vindictiveness.[105]

When the tear gas had cleared from the streets of Chicago, Humphrey was indeed the Democratic nominee who would oppose Richard Nixon in November. Howe, despite his distrust of Humphrey, did not, of course, support Nixon. He would not accept the "reprehensible" and "idiotic" idea that putting the Right in power would have the "progressive" effect of radicalizing its victims. The question for Howe was whether people like him should stay home on Election Day, thereby bringing a left-liberal defection to the notice of the Democratic Party. The hope was that Humphrey would win, but by smaller than expected margins in some major northeastern states. That plan, however, might backfire, Howe told Coser, and help bring "a victory for Nixon" and a special loss for blacks.[106]

By early October, Howe seemed to put that worry aside and announced that he could not vote for Humphrey. Less than three weeks later, however, again recognizing the danger, indeed, the irresponsibility of abstaining, Howe changed his mind. "Millions of people will . . . live . . . worse under Nixon than under Humphrey," Howe wrote, "and most of these millions are black. What I wrote in the last issue [of *Dissent*] was, therefore, wrong. We must try to recognize the difference between a fundamental political commitment and a particular, often uncomfortable choice in the voting booth." This statement, however, appeared in the first issue of *Dissent* for 1969, two months after the conclusion of the election.[107]

Given that *Dissent*'s subscriber list was little more than 4,000, it is unlikely that Howe's new recommendation, had it appeared in time, would have changed the outcome of the presidential contest. In any case, Nixon was elected, the Democrats retained control of the Congress but lost seats, and George Wallace won 13.5 percent of the vote. Howe thought the New Left's behavior, including the actions and rhetoric of the Black Panther Party, had indeed elicited a backlash, which was partly responsible for the ascendancy of the Right. SDS, unconcerned about the alienation of any possible support in the body politic, perhaps even glorying in its near-total isolation, continued its provocative behavior. In 1969 it had split into some three or four factions, including the Progressive Labor Party and the Weathermen, some of whom turned terrorist. By summer, after the infamous violent "days of rage" marking the first anniversary of the Chicago riots, many of the leaders of the SDS were forced to go underground. The membership of this once promising student organization plummeted from about 100,000 to 2,000.[108] A potentially viable movement of youth, Howe said, in the fall, "has sealed its eventual doom [in] an abandonment to factional convolutions and absurdities, and then a surrender to authoritarian ideology"—and then, finally, in its use of violence and outright criminality which played directly into the hands of its enemies.[109]

But despite resistance and frustration, Howe continued to talk to young people and to make his case for democracy and socialism. He was invited in 1969 to speak on foreign policy at the University of Missouri in Kansas City, along with Tom Hayden and Zbigniew Brzezinski, a Columbia professor at the time. He hesitated, knowing that he was not likely to be warmly received by a college audience. But he accepted because they offered him "the astounding sum of $1200," some of which Irving donated to a struggling *Dissent*. There were nearly 1500 people in the auditorium, many of whom began to boo when Howe appeared. Unfazed, he spoke against the Soviet invasion of Czechoslovakia (1968). But Hayden refused to condemn it. "Politically and morally," Howe said later, "this was the last straw—so—I went after Tom, pretty fiercely." When Howe finished, Brzezinski congratulated him, but he did not intervene in the debate. For Brzezinski, Howe said, this battle with the New Left was not real. "For me, on the other hand, it was a painful internal struggle."[110]

What Howe wrote in that same year, 1969, about George Orwell, he could easily have written about himself: "Even when he wanted to pull back to his [writing], Orwell kept summoning those energies of combat and resources of irritation which made him so powerful a fighter against the cant of his age. His bones would not let him rest."[111] Howe did not rest, either. He kept on writing *and* fighting. Together with Allard Lowenstein, the New York congressman and liberal antiwar activist, Howe took on a number of New Left people at a 1969 Harvard forum on protest tactics. Howe and Lowenstein held fast to the principles of nonviolence. Many of the students in the audience were hostile, which didn't surprise Howe. But at one point, Martin Peretz, an old friend and former Brandeis student who gave significant financial support to the New Left as well as to *Dissent*, rose to attack Howe from "the Left." This was "more than I could take," Howe said; "it seemed as if everyone was losing his mind," and "I replied very sharply." Later, Lowenstein told Howe he shouldn't have been "so rough on Marty." But when the congressman saw that Irving was about to "burst out again, either into rage or tears, he quickly added, 'Not that he didn't deserve everything you gave him.'"[112]

The question for Howe was not so much about what people "deserved" as about whether he was changing any minds. If in the late sixties there were few real victories in this regard, Howe did have an occasional personal "success." In 1969 Howe was a visiting fellow at the Center for Advanced Studies in the Behavioral Sciences near Stanford University, where his wife Arien held a postdoctoral fellowship in the Psychology Department. He drove everyday to Stanford to have lunch with her. And while walking on campus he was bombarded, at least a dozen times, "with hooting, hissing, and taunting." It was "hard to know how to react," he wrote to his old friend Max Shachtman. "I'm a middle-aged man, with a pot belly!"[113] But on one of those days when he and Arien were being followed by a group of SDS students chanting hostile slogans and led by a fellow named "Cohen," Howe was asked by what right he called himself a radical. To this he finally responded. He wheeled about and shouted: "Cohen, you know what you're going to end up as—a dentist! And I'll be a radical long after you start pulling teeth." Cohen blanched, Howe remembered later. Perhaps the student was even moved to change his mind about democratic procedure. In the 1990s Cohen, though not a dentist, was a lawyer working within the system. In any case, at the time, the insult was "simply too dreadful" for Cohen, and Howe marched off "in miniature triumph."[114]

Throughout the year Howe did battle, but when necessary he was also a skilled diplomat. At *Dissent*, where editors and contributors differed over how to end the war in Vietnam, it was Howe, Walzer said, who prevented splits. He also defused tensions arising from the magazine's perennial financial difficulties. These grew even worse in the late sixties when *Dissent* ran an annual deficit of nearly $10,000. Some board members, all of whom were expected to make relatively small donations, urged quite strongly a return to quarterly publication. But Howe convinced them that it would be seen "as a retreat." He contributed some of his own money and the entire royalty advance he received for editing *Beyond the New Left* (1970), a book he described as "not a bad thing, but a quickie I knocked together to save the magazine."[115]

There was, however, one split which Howe, despite his best efforts, could not prevent. This arose over disagreements between the League for Industrial Democracy (LID), with which *Dissent* was temporarily allied and on whose board sat several Dissenters, including Howe. In 1969, Tom Kahn, who sat on both boards, presented Hubert Humphrey with LID's Man of the Year Award. Stanley Plastrik and Lew Coser were furious and wanted to break with LID for honoring a man who had never really taken an antiwar position. But Howe, who was equally angry, wanted to "make every effort to prevent splits" among the left-liberals. He printed a letter dissociating *Dissent* from the award, but not from LID itself.[116] Howe did, however, send Kahn a personal note saying that the LID action had created "intense difficulties" for "Mike [Harrington] and me in our little worlds." He told Kahn that the *Dissent* people were "really against the war. . . . It's not just a matter with us, of covering our left flank, or cursing the war because it interferes with domestic needs. . . . We think it is a reactionary war." What LID people thought about the war, however, was unclear to Howe, who asked Kahn quite pointedly, "Are you really for the war but think it inexpedient to say so?"[117]

It took until 1972 for the differences between LID, which had become mostly a lobby for the trade unions, and *Dissent*, which retained its democratic socialist character, to split completely. Irving, however, had long before resigned from the LID board. The turning point for

Howe came when Kahn in the late spring of 1969 asked him to cospon-
sor a conference denouncing the New Left as a threat to academic freedom. Howe declined and chose to make his discomfort with Kahn clear
in a number of private letters. These also show us nicely where Howe
stood at the end of this turbulent decade: "I don't mind you attacking
the New Left," Howe wrote. "I favor it. It is the terms of the attack that
I question," as well as the "tone of unqualified hostility toward student
turmoil. . . . I try to understand [t]he desperation of the students," Howe
insisted, "and I share at least some of [their] motivations. . . . That the
tactics of the New Left segment of the students are appalling, I haven't
exactly been negligent in saying publicly. But I say it," Howe pointed
out to Kahn, from "premises radically different from [yours]. I say it because *I am against the war*, because I fear [New Left] tactics are self-defeating. I also give the students—who represent far more than the New
Left—a lot of credit for getting opposition to the war going."[118] Howe
kept up his own opposition to the war into the early seventies, when
conditions in Vietnam and political pressure at home finally brought it
to an end.

12

Retrospection and Celebration

IRVING HOWE, in his trenchant criticism of New Left excesses, implied that full American withdrawal from Southeast Asia might have come sooner than 1973 if the young radicals had not engaged in alienating and self-destructive behavior.[1] Perhaps he was right. Certainly in the late sixties the irresponsible actions and rhetoric of the most militant elements of the protest movements, white and black, helped move the "silent majority" in America to reassert a set of older values, including patriotism, duty, and self-restraint. Extremism on the Left and the general turbulence of the sixties also encouraged a large part of the younger, more socially mobile middle class to retreat, right through the seventies, from idealism and a community orientation into skepticism, fragmentation, and private refuge.

At the end of the decade, when Howe was writing his intellectual autobiography, he tried to "retrieve the seventies." He came up with a roster of presidents and politicians and a string of public events, but he had difficulty describing the decade's "distinctive historical flavor." Much later, however, it is easier for us to see that a significant social transformation was occurring in those years. Mistrust of government reinforced by the scandalous criminality of Watergate, tax revolts calling for mindless reductions in social welfare spending, racial resentment over court-ordered school busing, the realignment of southern politics with the Republican Party, and the emergence of a reactionary George Wallace as a political force added up to a great shift away from public-spirited universalism and social justice and toward personal self-fulfillment and the sovereignty of freewheeling private enterprise.[2]

There were some signs of hope. At its 1969 convention, Americans for Democratic Action (ADA), a group of 60,000 left-liberals closely associated with the Democratic Party, approved a resolution calling for a "massive redistribution of wealth and power" in the United States. Michael Harrington, who had become an ADA board member in 1970, was relatively hopeful that what he saw as the organization's "closet socialists" would soon become more openly active.[3] Howe, too, was cautiously optimistic in the early seventies. Despite the collapse of SDS and the dissolution of the New Left, he thought perhaps something remained of the earlier "genuine stirrings of moral outrage [and] creditable impulses of social rebelliousness and idealism." But Howe showed some uncertainty about this when he wrote: "It would be very sad if the turmoil of the 1960s were replaced by a torpor of the seventies, the desperate errors of the New Left by a complacent acquiescence of new conservatives."[4] Unfortunately, Howe's worst fears materialized. The seemingly amorphous seventies almost from the start were giving birth to the conservative, narrowly individualistic eighties. And this is what Howe and his circle of democratic socialists faced in the new decade as they tried to make sense of, and learn from, the mistakes of the old one.

Howe spent much time in retrospection, but he also had to deal with important new issues and personal losses. Israel's security became a major concern for him after the devastating Yom Kippur War in 1973; he was divorced from Arien in 1976, and he suffered the death of his father in 1977. Several of his friends also died in the seventies, including Richard Hofstadter, Harvey Swados, Lionel Trilling, and Eliezer Greenberg. Howe continued to be much occupied with *Dissent*, which, while finally returning to quarterly publication in 1972, still took a great deal of his time. He also did a significant amount of writing in the seventies outside the magazine, including three edited anthologies of Jewish writings, another on Israel, a biography of Leon Trotsky, and *World of Our Fathers*, Howe's 700-page celebration of the East European Jewish immigrant community in New York. At the very beginning of the decade he wrote two long essays—one on feminism and one on Philip Roth—both of which partly reflected Howe's political wounds from the battles of the sixties.

In the seventies Irving Howe continued to reflect on and bemoan the failures of the New Left, but he also pointed to the accomplishments of the civil rights movement of the sixties, and to the positive social and cultural changes wrought by the feminist movement at the end of that decade. Yet Howe who, with a sense of urgency, had joined the crusade for black equality as it developed in the middle fifties, did not express, early on, any special sympathy for the women's movement.[5]

Building on the catalyst provided by Betty Friedan's *The Feminine Mystique* (1963) and by the National Organization of Women (NOW) founded in 1966, a second generation of feminists emerged in the late sixties. Coming mainly out of a male-dominated New Left in which women were treated as second-class citizens (and worse) by men who claimed to be progressives, a revivified feminism brought new energy to a nearly moribund left-liberalism. But Howe, at the start, perceived the movement, especially its middle-class element, as "an indulgence." Feminism did not quite meet his definition of "politics" because he thought that, like the New Left itself, it sacrificed an explicit political platform for the sake of ideology or grandiose unfulfillable visions of social change. Howe supported equal pay for equal work, legalized abortion, and day-care centers—"demands that could be won short of revolution or an equally improbable transformation of human character."[6] But as he told Lew and Rose Coser, he thought militant feminism's unrelenting and unqualified attack on the family and "patriarchy" not merely intellectually incompetent but something "new . . . and pretty rotten." He thought, too, that people who might have greeted feminism warmly were put off by those radicals like Shulamit Firestone and Kate Millett who seemed to insist on an implacable and seemingly never-ending battle between the sexes.[7]

Late in 1970 Howe published in *Harper's* a long review essay of Millett's *Sexual Politics*. He sharply criticized the book for its historical, literary, and logical inadequacies, which were indeed legion. Howe was not far off the mark when he said Millett's ideas bore the musty smell of "vulgar Marxism" because they reduced a multitude of social phenomena to the single base of "sexual domination." Nor was he wrong in pointing out that Millett had displayed inordinate ignorance about the crucial role that social class (as well as gender) had played in determining the destiny of women.

It was also justifiable for Howe to defend the family, something "co-existent with human culture itself," as having yielded protection and "certain profound satisfactions" to all human beings throughout history, not merely satisfying "the dominating impulses of the 'master group.'" He concluded his essay by harking back to the world of immigrant Jewish workers and his own family. "Was my mother," he asked, "a drudge in subordination to the 'master group'? No more a drudge,"

Howe answered, "than my father," who also used to come home from work in the factory with blistered hands and feet. He would never have thought to ask, Howe said, whether his mother had been a "sexual object"—Millett's term for all women of whatever class or condition. But in 1970, in the shadow of so much time past, he did ask. And he wrote in response, most likely while smiling, "I should like to think that at least sometimes she was."[8]

We smile, too, in the hope that now and then there were indeed mutual sexual satisfactions in the bedrooms of the East Bronx. Yet Howe misses a different but equally important point about his parents. Contrary to what he thought, his mother may very well have been more of a "drudge" than his father. Both parents worked in the garment industry, but his mother for less pay. Both came home exhausted, but his mother did the cooking, cleaning, and scrubbing. Howe missed something else, too. In zealously criticizing Millett for proposing an end to family (something the vast majority of American women did not desire), Howe overlooked some of the genuine grievances feminism addressed. He also seemed to ignore the similarity between the movement's aim of transforming basic social institutions and even the meaning of equality itself, and his own earlier and oft-repeated call for a redefinition of the structure and meaning of work and leisure.

Several feminists were apparently asked to comment on Howe's review. Vivian Gornick simply scribbled across the first page, "Poor Mrs. Howe!" to which Arien responded, "Vivian Gornick? She should be half so lucky!"[9] Notwithstanding his wife's spirited defense, Howe's essay was an exercise in intellectual overkill. It was intemperate and ad hominem in many places, especially in declaring that "the emotions of women toward children don't exactly form an overarching preoccupation in *Sexual Politics*: there are times when one feels the book was written by a female impersonator."[10] This and other displays of unwarranted anger reveal an unreadiness in Howe to accept women as fully equal to men.[11]

This attitude also surfaced occasionally in his personal correspondence. In a letter to the Trillings in the early seventies, Howe expressed some concern about his marriage. "Nothing desperately wrong," he wrote, "but many small difficulties accumulating." And he reminded Diana Trilling that "you once said to me that militant women have nothing to fear as much as achieving their goals. Well, Arien gets responsibilities, burdens, etc., and it makes life hard."[12] A decade later, Howe confessed that in the seventies he noticed within himself "habits of condescension that women no doubt noticed long before, but were only now combative enough to criticize." Such recognition, Howe said, "I didn't like. . . . I wasn't prepared to admit that in my pure heart—socialist heart of hearts!—there could be so much as a grain of sexual bias. But of course there was."[13]

Needless to say, Howe had no monopoly on this regressive predisposition. It was endemic among men and as much among the New York intellectuals as anywhere else. If a writer in that circle happened to be female—Elizabeth Hardwick or Mary McCarthy, for example—she became one of the "boys." Wives (or "girlfriends"), on the other hand, were treated badly or ignored entirely. Hardwick admitted that "no one," including herself, "paid attention to the wives at the parties; they just sat there while everyone else was drinking cheap whiskey and battling over politics." Women who were not writers and thus not part of the inner circle were in fact "totally invisible," Arien Mack told me. After a typical party on the upper West Side, she complained to Irving that "had I stripped naked and stood at the center of the room, no one would have noticed me!"[14]

Howe's friends and colleagues, male and female, are nearly unanimous in saying that he made "a good faith effort" and grew more sensitive toward women and the women's movement in the last fifteen years of his life. What shook him into recognizing the significance of the new feminism, Howe himself said later, was not its ideology or its more extravagant hopes, "but the depth of anger many women now feel free to release. You simply had to pay attention to this." And Howe did pay more attention, especially after the feminist movement broadened to include women below the middle class and began to focus more clearly on issues of material equality.

Howe's attack on Millett was virtually his last "antifeminist" polemic. He had it reprinted once (with the offensive phrase about "a female impersonator" removed) in 1973, but never again. And by 1982, while not an activist for feminism, nor an aggressive recruiter of women writers for *Dissent*, Howe was from the sidelines giving "two cheers" for women's liberation. "Two cheers," this complex and wary dissenter said, "because no public movement quite merits three."[15]

Kate Millett wasn't the only literary figure with whom Howe tangled in the early seventies. He also took on Philip Roth. In 1959 Howe reviewed Roth's *Goodbye Columbus*, a novella with five other stories including "Eli the Fanatic" and "Defender of the Faith." He said Roth was a skilled, intelligent craftsman with "a unique voice, a secure rhythm [and] a distinctive subject." But Howe also said that the stories were too close to the surface of reality and needed more "imaginative transformation." More important, he suggested that Roth, unlike Delmore Schwartz or Bernard Malamud who had also dealt harshly with middle-class American Jewish life, found almost "no sustenance" in Jewishness. Howe, too quickly, took this to mean that Roth's work signified the end of a tradition of Yiddishkayt and Jewish secularism—"a tradition against which many of us rebelled," Howe said, "but which, by shaping the nature of our rebellion, helped to give meaning to our lives."[16]

Despite Howe's demurrers, his review was mainly favorable. But by 1972, three years after the publication of *Portnoy's Complaint*, Roth's wickedly funny but warmly embracing caricature of an aggressively overprotective Jewish mother, a passive father, and their beleaguered but morally resilient and soulful son Alex, Howe wrote a much longer, much more sharply critical "reconsideration." Howe was not, he said, centrally concerned about the graphic sexuality of *Portnoy*—the masturbation and the oral and anal sex—that helped the book become a best-seller. Nor, despite what he called Roth's contempt for things Jewish, did Howe think the book was anti-Semitic, as many other critics and Jewish community leaders charged.

Instead, he built on points in his earlier review and said that Roth, although focused on Jewish settings, was too ignorant of things Jewish to really be involved in the venerated, "morally serious" practice of Jewish self-criticism and satire, à la Singer or Bellow. Coming at the end of a Jewish tradition which could no longer nourish his imagination, Roth was one of the first American-Jewish writers, Howe contended, who derived no norms or values from Jewish heritage. This was an overstatement, indeed an outright blunder, as Roth's later work would prove. Worse was Howe's unseemly follow-up:

> One reason that Roth's stories are unsatisfactory is that they come out of a thin personal culture. . . . Perhaps this . . . has some connection with [the] free-floating contempt and animus, which begin . . . to appear in Roth's early stories and grow . . . more noticeable in [Portnoy]. Unfocused hostility often derives from unexamined

depression, and the latter . . . I take to be the ground-note of Roth's sensibility.[17]

Perhaps it was Howe's passionate struggle against "the new sensibility" of the sixties and early seventies that led him to perceive Roth as a kind of "cultural New Leftist" and prevented him from seeing the young writer's use of exaggeration and his employment of "schmaltz and schmutz" as part of the long, rich Jewish "literary" tradition in the United States. As Alfred Kazin argued earlier, "Jewish clowns" and "vulgar culture" had from the start supplied America with an "élan that made for future creativity in literature, as well as for the mass products of the 'entertainment industry.'"[18] The consciously grotesque style of Jewish parody is after all found not only in the Marx brothers and Woody Allen but also in Clifford Odets and even Saul Bellow. But, Howe in 1972, deeply and affectionately immersed in the materials of Yiddishkayt, the bedrock of World of Our Fathers, allowed his intensified Jewish sensitivity and moral seriousness to get the better of him as a literary critic. He not only attacked Roth personally, he uncharacteristically missed the significance of his work.

Roth's Alex Portnoy, Howe complained, is crying out to be released from the claims of Jewish distinctiveness and the burdens of the past. He wants, somehow, out of nothingness to create himself as a human being. "Who, born a Jew in the 20th century, has been so lofty in spirit never to have shared this fantasy," Howe wondered. But "who, born a Jew in the 20th century, has been so foolish in mind as to dally with it for more than a moment?"[19] A nice set of rhetorical questions, but they repeat Howe's stubborn misperception of Roth as lacking Jewish identity or moral conscience. Howe seems to ignore in Portnoy, and elsewhere in Roth's work, the ethical striving that is as strong as the sexuality. He failed to recognize Roth's genius in portraying the restless young American Jew, very much like Howe himself, burdened *and* blessed with remnants of an authentic tradition of justice and righteousness, who is forced to live in the superficial, promiscuous, and tawdry world of modern American culture.

As he grew older Howe tempered his negative judgment, and by the late seventies he even contemplated writing a fresh and affirmative piece on Roth.[20] Perhaps he was taken with Roth's newer work, including his richly imagined "Looking at Kafka" (1973), a story resonant with secular Jewishness, grounded in European Jewish history and the Holocaust, and mostly a celebration of the mutual support in Roth's own family. Roth, post-Portnoy, also made several direct positive statements about his own Jewish identity. In 1975 he said: "I have always been . . . pleased by my good fortune in being born a Jew. . . . It's a complicated, morally demanding, and very singular experience. I find myself in the historic predicament of being Jewish, with all its implications. . . . Who could ask for more?" And who could ask for a better definition of secular Jewish identity in modern American society? Not even Irving Howe. Still, even after yet more good work by Roth, including *The Ghost Writer* (1979), which was a virtual tribute to Bellow and Malamud and a sensitive retelling of the Anne Frank story, and perhaps Roth's best book, Howe did no new retrospective—one of his few great errors of omission as a literary critic.[21]

Bernard Avishai, a mutual friend of the two men, told Howe that Roth was deeply hurt by Howe's 1972 critique. "Why should he care that much about one critical review," Howe asked. "He has his fame, his women, his wealth; why does he care about me?"[22] Howe clearly underestimated his stature and influence as a critic and misunderstood again, as with Tom Hayden, the problem of "filial vulnerability." As more than one of Howe's close associates said, "Irving was a little like the uncle we all seem to need"—one who can be critical, but "whose approval we crave."[23] That this was true for Roth was revealed in 1978 when James Atlas, the biographer of Delmore Schwartz and later of Bellow, interviewed Roth for the *New York Times*. Roth proudly showed Atlas Howe's first review and then glumly handed him the second. "Not that he's the only reader in the world," Roth said wistfully, "but he was a real reader."[24]

Apparently still feeling wounded five years later (and eleven after Howe's negative reappraisal!), Roth in *The Anatomy Lesson* (1983) parodied Irving Howe as Milton Appel, a hypocritical "sententious bastard" who had never in his life "taken a mental position that isn't a moral judgment." But as several critics and Philip Roth himself have pointed out, it is Appel who had the best lines in the exchanges with Roth's alter ego, Nathan Zuckerman. Indeed, it seems at times in *The Anatomy Lesson*, as well as in earlier works including *The Professor of Desire* (1977) and *The Ghost Writer*, that Roth is reexamining and modulating his own tone and style, if not exorcising a sense of guilt. "Tilting at yourself," Roth admitted, "is *interesting*, a lot more interesting than winning."[25] Even at less than his best as a critic, then, Howe produced important critical insights with which the most brilliant and creative writers felt it necessary to grapple.[26]

For Howe, critical writing throughout the seventies continued to be a respite from countless editorial, personal, and political tasks. He also still enjoyed teaching at City University where in 1970 he was promoted to Distinguished Professor, the university's highest rank. Although he could sometimes express frustration at student ignorance or impatience with pretentiousness, especially in graduate courses, Howe was mostly relaxed in class, often humorous, and always interesting. He was also supportive of students outside of the classroom. Morris Dickstein, who served as an examiner on a Ph.D. oral exam with Howe and Kazin in the seventies, tells a story typical of Irving. The student, Dickstein said, facing these giants of literary criticism, was "totally paralyzed." But both Howe and Kazin showed genuine sympathy and tried to get the student to talk about what *he* knew and liked. Indeed, Howe asked him, "What have you read recently that moved you." Dickstein was touched by Howe's concern, and the lesson he learned that day, he said, "stayed with me."[27]

For all these reasons, Howe was a much sought after teacher and adviser. Indeed, he even grumbled occasionally about how busy he was at CUNY. He also complained about other "innumerable and exhausting pressures." In 1971 he explained to Harvey Swados that he hadn't written to him in a while because his life at school, at *Dissent*, and in the political arena too, was always "do this, write that, talk to him, help there." The demands at *Dissent* alone got so intense, in fact, that in the course of discussing the magazine's financial problems with Lew Coser, Howe exclaimed, "Oi, vey! How did we get into this business?"[28]

And now and then, "events" just wouldn't let Irving's "bones rest." In 1971 during the riots at Attica State Prison, near Buffalo, New York, Howe wrote to Lenore Marshall, his poet-activist friend, "Sometimes I wish I could lose myself in scholarly work and pay no attention to the moment, to its horrors and foolishness." But it was impossible for Howe to turn away from the "wretched business" of Attica, where "the authorities were itching to kill, and did kill with great brutality." And he spoke out against the troopers, Governor Nelson Rockefeller, and the radical lawyer William Kunstler, who apparently "screwed up the prisoners" and helped drive "the situation to a confrontation." For "those of us" who work for radical reform but "who still want to live by liberal values and freedom," Howe said, "it all bodes badly."[29]

Certainly, the general political situation wasn't very promising. Howe thought there was a "decided swing" on the part of intellectuals, including his old CUNY classmate and former Trotskyist Irving Kristol, toward Richard Nixon, who was reelected president in a landslide victory in 1972.[30] Howe also realized that *Commentary* magazine was drifting further to the right. After he broke with the *New York Review of Books* in 1967, Howe gave most of his pieces to *Commentary*. At first there was no discomfort for him. In the early sixties Norman Podhoretz, much to Irving's delight, had turned *Commentary* in a left-liberal direction. And Podhoretz, like Howe, was an early critic of the Vietnam War. Howe and Podhoretz could also bond to some extent around their shared antipathy to the excesses of the youthful counterculture—the political confrontationalism, anti-intellectualism, and the general life-style associated with hard rock and hard drugs.

But the alliance of Howe and others at *Dissent* with the incipient neoconservatives around *Commentary* was a tentative affair.[31] By 1973 Howe had distanced himself completely from Irving Kristol, the conservative editor of *Public Interest*, to some extent from Nathan Glazer, and to a lesser extent even from Daniel Bell. He was irritated that, in their "analytical" approach, all three tended to assign responsibility for continuing social problems to the malfunctioning of the welfare bureaucracy rather than to moral indifference, social timidity, and racial meanness.[32] And Howe's association with these contributing editors of *Commentary* pretty much came apart as the New Left, the "common enemy," was unraveling in the mid-seventies.

With intellectuals moving rightward, and with Nixon in the White House pledging to dismantle federal initiatives in social welfare and swearing vengeance on his liberal and radical critics, Howe kept wondering, again with some prescience, "whether the New Left phase of the last 6–7 years wasn't a minor interruption of a major trend . . . toward conservatism . . . from the WW II years onward."[33] Despite all, Howe continued to search for new alternatives. Early in 1972 the *Dissent* board met to discuss "the seemingly dramatic breakup of the New Left." Although critical of many of the manifestations of the movement, the Dissenters were not filled "with any joy" over its demise. "Quite the contrary," Howe told the activist historian Christopher Lasch. "We find ourselves distressed by the evident waste of energies, idealism, hope. The question is whether anything can now be salvaged for long-term purposes."[34]

That same question brought Howe and Harrington and other left-liberals together in February 1973 for a week-end-long conference at New York University on "The Future of the Democratic Left." By Sunday, only about fifty of the original one hundred participants remained, and they moved the day's sessions to a run-down welfare hotel on the West Side where the new Democratic Socialist Organizing Committee (DSOC) was born. After this inauspicious beginning, Howe was not particularly optimistic. But DSOC slowly grew, with one campus chapter at a time, an occasional labor union staffer, and here and there a handful of intellectuals. By the mid-seventies there were fewer than five thousand members, but Irving allowed himself a moment of mild enthusiasm. At the bottom of a letter to Harrington, mostly about Michael's work for *Dissent*, Howe scrawled, "Who knows? Maybe we can yet do something."[35]

Alongside DSOC grew the New America Movement (NAM), an organization designed as a successor to SDS—minus the politics of confrontation. Although NAM members no longer cherished notions of revolution, they never entirely eliminated their romance with the Third World. And like the old SDS they regarded DSOC as hopelessly compromised by its social-democratic "illusions," as well as its ties to the Democratic Party and established union leaders. It took until the late seventies for the two groups to consider a merger. In the meantime, the small number of people still on the left remained divided and generally isolated.

Dissent, too, languished. Howe had trouble soliciting good material. His "better editors" were overcommitted, and although some younger people joined the staff, the *Dissent* group, Howe said in 1974, was "not exactly a youth movement." They were more "like a baseball team that can field a pretty good nine," but that was "very weak in reserves." Howe told his board that for the first time in twenty years, "I begin to wonder, in all candor, whether we can or should carry on." Wanting to escape from his "many burdens" and "institutions," he asked Daniel Bell wistfully, "Shouldn't one of the South Sea Islands be reserved for old socialists?" But ultimately Howe concluded, "This seems a crazy time to give up on our kind of magazine," the only "serious democratic socialist journal in the U.S." And the Dissenters carried on.[36]

In the magazine and elsewhere, Howe continued to hammer away at the U.S. government for its perpetuation of violence and authoritarianism abroad. The war in Vietnam was over, but American aid, con-

nections, and complicity were helping to sustain reactionary antidemocratic regimes in Greece, Chile, Portugal, Brazil, and South Korea.
Howe was unrelenting in his argument for democracy everywhere in
the world, even as he pointed out its imperfections and debasements.
And he even began to think about promoting electoral alliances with
Communists in Western Europe, especially in France, Italy, and post-
Franco Spain, where the Communist parties declared themselves eager
to follow the democratic path and to cooperate with other democratic
parties.[37]

Another area of the world very much on Irving's mind was Israel—
especially after the state came close to defeat and potential obliteration
in the Yom Kippur War of 1973. Howe's reactions were "astonishingly
intense," he said. As in 1967, there was something more than political
commitment to a democracy at stake. There was "something else and
deeper," Irving said, something that was "related to his being a Jew."
There were things about Israel that Howe detested: Orthodox Jewry's
disproportionate grip on civil law; the hawkish generals; the Jewish settlements in occupied territory; and the suffering imposed on the Palestinians. But Israel mattered to him, he said, "as a community of human
beings, the home of our survivors."[38]

If the Jewish people voluntarily decided to abandon their tradition
of values and thereby disappeared, that would be, Howe thought, "a
cause for much regret; but not the kind of shattering tragedy signified
by their coming to an end because the world simply refused to let them
live." Howe even joined with Irving Kristol in this sentiment. Howe
and Kristol had long been engaged in ideological dispute, but despite
their "deep political differences" they "experienced the same elemental
response to Israel." Both men recognized that when much of the world
called for "evenhandedness" in a situation in which Israel was surrounded by a half-dozen or more well-armed enemy regimes, the welfare of the Jewish state was not the world's primary concern. "Both of
us are Jews," Howe said, "and both of us have lived long enough to recognize a portion of truth in the sour apothegm: in the warmest of hearts
there's a cold spot for the Jews."[39]

Irving Howe insisted that he had not become a chauvinist, that he
had not lapsed into "uncritical exaltation" of Israel. He was responding
instead, he thought, "to the tragic experiences of our time, the lessons
purchased in blood by my generation." Although Howe later criticized
those who constructed their American Jewishness primarily around an

image of Israel's heroic struggle to build a viable state and to resist annihilation, he apparently did a little of this kind of identity building
himself. Howe's commitment to democratic, Jewish Israel, and his fear
that the state might be abandoned, even by the United States, sacrificed
"to a hope or delusion of détente (if not something much grubbier)," led
him to call for organizing, letter-writing, and lobbying. A time may even
come, he said, "when it will be necessary to turn to more dramatic and
militant methods, perhaps a march on Washington," bringing with us
"the traditional Jewish outcry of *gevalt!*[call of distress]." In the meantime, Howe said, there is "the work of politics, pressure, persuasion."[40]

But Howe clearly demonstrated that he was not the chauvinist he
temporarily feared he had become. Beginning in the early seventies he
was highly critical of the American Anti-Defamation League, the Amer-
ican-Israel Political Action Committee, and other heavyweights of the
Jewish establishment wedded to the notion, "Israel—right or wrong."
He was particularly appalled by the misleading denunciations heaped
upon the Jewish American peace group *Breira* (Hebrew for "alternative" or "choice") by established Jewish organizations who were trying
to muffle dissent about Israel's policies or behavior. Howe was not a formal member of *Breira*, which was organized by a small group of American rabbis, professors, and other activists from the civil rights and antiwar movements of the sixties. But he attached himself, through the
group, to a brand of counterculture subscribed to by young dovish
Zionists and sixties radicals who maintained an overt Jewish identity.
And he agreed with many of their positions and proposals, most of
which reflected those of the Peace Now movement in Israel.[41]

At the beginning of 1974 in the wake of the Yom Kippur War, Martin Peretz, Howe's former student, sponsored a "mission" to Israel for
scholars and intellectuals. Howe, wanting to learn more about the Jewish state by seeing it for himself, went along. He talked with a variety of
Israelis about literature, philosophy, and socialism. But he met mainly
with activists and had long conversations with people who led small
political parties representing the various factions of the peace camp.
Howe immediately involved himself in local affairs, arguing, mostly
unsuccessfully, that left-liberal intellectuals should join the much larger
Labor Party in order to lead it to more radical positions.[42]

During his visit and afterward, Howe, while continuing to defend
the state, remained a critic of many Israeli policies right to the end of his
life. And he persisted in fighting attempts by Jewish leaders in the

United States and Israel to silence dissenting opinions about those policies. Suppression, Howe warned, would mean the abandonment of a healthy Jewish tradition of internal debate, a tradition he thought still alive and well in Israel. Being in the Jewish state, Howe wrote after his return, was "like being back in those heated 'circles' in Crotona Park in the Bronx where uncles debated politics." It would be tragic, Howe thought, to lose this kind of openness to "an atmosphere of conformity and complacence." Howe argued persistently that an atmosphere in which some Jewish opinions, the "official" ones, would be "kosher," while other dissenting opinions would be "*treif*" (unkosher) would do great damage to Israel's democratic character and to world Jewry's rich cultural heritage.[43]

It was also on the 1974 trip that Irving met Ilana Wiener, an Israeli, who would later become his fourth wife. On the long flight to Israel, Howe told Jeremy Larner, his seat-mate and former student, that he and Arien no longer had a "functioning marriage."[44] The troubles had begun as early as 1971 when Irving had difficulty accepting just how busy a professional Arien had become. There were also "problems," Howe had told the Trillings in 1972, with Arien's children, both at college, who were "going through crises in various ways."[45] In the same year, it was widely rumored that Arien was having an affair with a colleague at the New School, which according to Daniel Bell, "Everyone knew about."[46]

Perhaps. But Irving didn't seem to have a clue. Arien initiated the separation in 1975. "It is not a decision I wanted," Howe wrote Lionel Trilling, "and it leaves me . . . feeling pretty bad. . . . But I'm trying to pull myself together. I know I've occasionally fallen into erratic behavior," Irving said, and "probably this was the reason" for Arien's unhappiness.[47] During our interview in 2000, Arien didn't reveal why she wanted the separation and eventually the divorce. But more than once she said she had "no bad memories" of Irving who was "a very sweet and kind man." He was, however, "often terribly distracted." That, Arien said, was "hard on a wife."[48]

The divorce was hard on Irving. Almost immediately, and reflecting a much larger need, he told Arien, "I can't be alone. I can't eat dinner alone." But he ended up living alone and in despair in one room at the Hotel des Artistes on West 66th Street, and his pain went generally unrelieved for nearly a year.[49] He was unable to talk to his good friend Richard Hofstadter, who had died in 1970 and whose "good sense and humor" had kept Irving "from extreme depression and paranoia" throughout the sixties.[50] Nor could Howe lean on his old comrade Harvey Swados, who had died in 1972. And he could no longer write to his confidant Lionel Trilling, who died in 1975 only months before Howe's divorce.

That Irving was able to complete *World of Our Fathers* during this time is nothing short of astounding. He did have a sabbatical leave in 1971 during which he was able to work in earnest on *World*, and he got great help from Kenneth Libo, his primary researcher and virtual co-author, over the six years it took to complete the book. Still, it was a Herculean task. Perhaps it was the only thing keeping Irving afloat. Certainly it was a labor of love. Indeed, *World* was described time and time again by reviewers, and by Howe himself, as "a farewell with love and gratitude" to Yiddish and Yiddishkayt, to Jewish socialism, to Jewish secularism generally.[51] But the book is also something much larger and more complex than a mere death knell. It is an attempt to find enduring meaning in the collective experience of the Jewish working class. And with its sense of intimacy and personal relevance, it is Howe's true memoir, perhaps even more so than his "intellectual autobiography," *A Margin of Hope* (1982).

The sense of intimacy which pervades the book moved some reviewers to ask why the title didn't include "mothers." Howe's sharp but somewhat dismissive responses ranged from, "Without mothers there wouldn't have been fathers," to "'World of Our Fathers' is a title, 'World of Our Mothers and Our Fathers' is a speech." More important than Howe's ripostes is the actual content of the book itself, which paid considerable attention to mothers and to women generally. Indeed, a significant number of cameo portrayals featured women, and in several places Howe seemed to be trying to put some perspective on Philip Roth's "overwrought" depiction of the smothering Jewish mother: "Did she overfeed," Howe asked?

> Her mind was haunted by memories of a hungry childhood. Did she fuss about health? Infant mortality had been a plague in the old country and the horror of diphtheria overwhelming in this country. Did she dominate everyone within reach? A disarranged family structure endowed her with power, she had never known before, and burdens, too; it was to be expected that she should abuse the powers and find advantage in the burdens. The weight of centuries bore down. . . .

[T]he immigrant mother cut her path through the perils . . . of American life. Everyone spoke about her . . . but she herself has left no word to posterity . . . in her own voice, perhaps because all the talk about her "role" seemed to her finally trivial, the indulgence of those who had escaped life's primal tasks. Talk was a luxury that her labor would enable her sons to taste.[52]

There were other sensitive renditions of mothers in *World*, a book which helped commemorate an immigrant community long gone. Published in 1976 when Howe was fifty-six, *World* does not, however, simply evoke a "lost culture"; it represents the culmination of Howe's personal journey from youthful cosmopolitanism and revolutionary internationalism in the late 1930s and 1940s to a substantial Jewishness by the 1970s. Despite what Howe said and wrote both before and after the publication of *World* about the expiration of a recognizably Jewish secular culture in America, and the end of Jewish socialism, this book, his first and only "best-seller," is representative of Howe's long-standing commitment to *tikn olam*—that distinctive moral impulse in Jewish life and values which continues to see the need for improving a far from perfect world. One could even argue, as one reads and rereads this classic, that in *World* lies Howe's hope for Jewish continuity, a continuity partly based on those Jewish values and experiences that first moved him to embrace the politics of left-liberalism.[53]

One could also argue, of course, that Howe need not have lamented the disappearance of Jewishness had he paid somewhat less attention in *World* to Yiddishkayt, labor militancy, and socialist politics, all of which had seen better days; and had he given more attention to traditional religion, which remained a powerful force and had even shown renewed strength beginning in the 1960s and 1970s. But Howe's limited attention to Judaism was not completely inappropriate. Orthodox Jews did build some vibrant institutions in the period about which Howe was writing, but their impact on larger trends within the American Jewish world remained small. And Howe did successfully demonstrate that *secular* Jewishness was indeed the more powerful influence in the Jewish community, infusing immigrants and their offspring with a commitment to liberalism and tolerance and a belief in rationality. Howe portrayed the Lower East Side Jews as dedicated to the idea and reality of progress, as possessing a growing cosmopolitanism, and as holding fast to "a diffused this-worldly messianism" which aimed at producing in the "here-and-now" a culture of democratic secular humanism.[54]

But Howe also admitted in 1990 that *World* was "an intensely personal book. For I wrote it not as an alien visitor to, but as a son of, the world of our fathers—and, yes, our mothers too."[55] Even earlier, Howe had said, "My father had become for me a representative figure of the world from which I came [and] I suppose a good part of *World of Our Fathers* is no more than an extension of what I knew about him," a hardworking but hopeful man who was *"no longer strictly observant in faith or behavior,* but whose life was colored and defined by *Jewishness"*—as was Howe's own.[56]

It was not only Howe's research and reading, then, but also his relatively nonreligious upbringing and general social and political experience that left him committed to the idea that secular Jewishness was the most important animating and sustaining force in Jewish culture.

Indeed, Howe said *World* was not only his father's story, but also "my story, the secular socialist segment of the immigrant community as the sons and daughters moved into the intellectual world."[57] And in *World* Howe used his "own story" more than once, turning fragments of his personal life into source and text for a social and cultural history of his people. He mined his own experiences and memories of the Jewish community—the community which produced an idealistic, militant labor unionism, a vital socialist movement, and which built "layer upon layer of protective institutions, agencies of self-help, charity, education, [and] mutual benefit."[58]

Howe celebrated all of this, but *World* was no exercise in nostalgia. He knew that Jewish slums in the 1880s, 1890s, and into the early decades of the twentieth century bred Jewish "crime . . . wife desertion . . . juvenile delinquency, gangsterism, and prostitution . . . probably more than the records show or memoirists tell."[59] And in *World* Howe not only described appalling scenes of hunger and destitution, he explicitly cautioned against nostalgia as a proper response to poverty, fatigue, and occasional despair.[60] For Howe, the immigrant neighborhood with all its dimensions of *gemeinschaft* was a paradise of a kind but, he insisted, "a paradise we have left behind because we had to leave it, a paradise lost forever."[61]

Howe had neither hope nor desire for the re-creation of the "world of our fathers," but in writing *World* he was doing two very important things. He was paying tribute to the Jewish labor and socialist movements and to the self-educated workers, "the glory of the immigrant world," who filled the ranks.[62] In addition to honoring those women and men who had exhibited a "grandeur of aspiration," Howe was also pointing to the positive qualities of community and fraternity in the immigrant world that might be tailored, and thereby salvaged, for his own time.[63]

Howe's abiding interest in community and fraternity showed powerfully in *World*, just as it had in Howe's studies of Sherwood Anderson, William Faulkner, and Thomas Hardy. If *World* was an exercise in lamentation written about a moment when cultural echoes and cultural erosion occupied the same unstable space, so are novels like *Winesburg, Ohio*, *The Sound and the Fury*, *Absalom, Absalom*, and *Jude the Obscure*. Each of the three writers in Howe's book-length studies had an "image of a better or at least a simpler past" which fueled their "criticism of the dominant culture."[64] These words, written about Hardy, could apply as easily to Faulkner or Anderson, or to Howe himself. Although the values of Hardy, Faulkner, and Anderson differed significantly from Howe's democratic socialism, they derived from a rooted culture, similar in important ways to the world of immigrant Jewry, and they provided a foundation and a perspective for missions of retrieval and rescue of rooted culture, like the writing of *World*.

Over a twenty-five-year period, in many printings and various editions, *World* found its way into nearly every Jewish home in America. Jews hurried out to buy the book, Howe guessed, the way African Americans rushed out to purchase Alex Haley's *Roots*, published the same year, as a "turn back— . . . 'with pride'—to look for fragments of a racial or national or religious identity" no longer fully available.[65] Readers of *World*, now some distance from the old neighborhood, may have been able to reconnect to a time of struggle and idealism they had long put behind them, but for Howe the success of the book indicated a readiness on the part of Jewish Americans "to say farewell in a last fond gesture—an affectionate backward glance at the world of their fathers before turning their backs forever and moving on, as they had to." *World*, he said, "was not a beginning, it was still another step to the end."[66]

On the very last page of *World*, however, where Howe tells us that "the story of the immigrant Jews is all but done," he also intimates that the powerful moral impulse of secular Jewishness has not yet reached a point of exhaustion. In 1974, while deeply immersed in the work for

World, Howe wrote in *Dissent* that "the Messiah has still not come. . . . The world still cries out with its torments. Ours is a time (when has it not been?) for compassion and commitment." And he expressed confidence that "those deep impulsions of value and care that have drawn many Jews toward the liberal-left, regardless of whether it seemed to be in their personal interest—those impulsions remain."[67]

He implied the same in a commencement address at Queens College in the summer of 1977. Howe was critical of the chauvinism, particularism, and social shortsightedness in the "rise of the unmeltable ethnics" evident in the 1970s. He told the graduates that the "great weakness of the turn to ethnicity is that it misreads or ignores the realities of power in America." The central problems of our society, Howe said, have to do with economic policy and class relations, "with vast inequalities of wealth, [and] with the shameful neglect of a growing class of subproletarians. . . . Toward problems of this kind and magnitude, what answers can ethnicity offer? Very weak ones, I fear. . . . [M]ajor movements for social change require alignments that move past ethnic divisions." But he went on to say that there is no reason in principle why ethnic groups could not "move from a reconquest of identity to union with other plebeian communities in behalf of shared needs, thereby helping a little to right the wrongs of our society." And he concluded by admitting that this is

> not just a problem in social strategy; it has also to do with human awareness and self-definition. We want to remain, for the little time that we can, whatever it was that we were before they started pressurizing us in those melting pots. So let's try, even if the historical odds are against us. But there is also another moral possibility, one that we call in Yiddish being or becoming a *mensch.* The word suggests a vision of humanity or humaneness; it serves as a norm, a possibility beckoning us. You don't have to be Jewish (or non-Jewish), you don't have to be white (or black) in order to be a *mensch.* Keeping one eye upon the fading past and the other on the unclear future, enlarging ethnic into *ethic,* you can become a man or woman of the world.[68]

Three years later, as part of a *Commentary* magazine symposium on "Liberalism and the Jews," Irving Howe questioned the editors' assumption that Jewish Americans were pulling back from their commitment to liberalism. He argued that a very large segment of American

Jews—the professional and semiprofessional classes—were deeply enmeshed in the workings of the welfare state and therefore had "an economic and intellectual stake in its flourishing." More important, he went on,

> even if one wished (or thought it possible) to withdraw to a parochial "interest-group" view of Jewish life, it could still be strongly argued that staying with the universalist vision—a belief in a liberal society of steadily accumulating social reforms—remains the best way of defending strictly Jewish interests and an important way of sustaining the inner morale of the Jewish community.

But *most* important, Howe concluded, "social liberalism has been defined as the 'secular religion' of many American Jews, the precious salvage from their immigrant and East European heritage, the embodied value of a major segment of Jewish experience."[69]

Irving Howe did wonder if, in the long run, even this liberal commitment might be enough, by itself, to maintain "a vital Jewish presence in America." Without the additional dimensions of a renewed, authentic religious commitment (something Howe thought highly unlikely for large numbers of Jewish Americans), a sustained mutually enriching commitment to Israel, or an identification with the Holocaust, Jewish continuity in America was hardly assured; and if assured primarily by "Israelism" and "Holocaustism," with what vitality and meaning?

Despite his doubts, Howe's real hope for the future of Jewishness remained the moral impulse in Jewish secularism and its manifestation in political liberalism. "I am not saying", Howe insisted repeatedly, "that liberalism is 'inherent' in Judaism or that the Prophets were canny enough to anticipate my politics. But as a democratic socialist who cares about Jewish values, I continue to believe that liberalism is our natural home, insofar as we can ever be at home."[70]

While Irving Howe had never "found God" or, despite occasional attendance at synagogue on High Holy Days in his later years, ever really felt comfortable with religious institutions, it is equally clear that his "secular" democratic socialism had "religious" dimensions.[71] Not long after *World* was published, a neoconservative critic chided Howe for a socialist attachment that was "religious," in that it was kept alive by a leap of faith, unchallenged by historical example, empirical evidence, or practical consideration.[72] Visibly irritated but far from devastated, Irving told his friend Bernard Avishai, "The annoying thing is that the observation is, in a way, right." It was not that Howe believed in the moral supremacy of socialism over other political convictions, or that his politics reflected an absolutist "theology" or a "faith" in a preordained course of history. Rather, his socialism was "religious," Howe said, because with all of its nuances and limits it was "a faith for rational men and women" that "had to be grounded in the desire to do right by another person," and especially grounded in the desire to protect the powerless from the powerful.

One of Howe's favorite writers, Ignazio Silone, confessed that as a young boy, he had once laughed at the sight of a working-class man being hauled away by the police. His father scolded him harshly, telling Silone never to make fun of any man who has been arrested. "Because he can't defend himself. And because he may be innocent. In any case he is unhappy." Howe found these sentences "overwhelming" and pregnant with moral power, for at the center of Howe's long intellectual and political career there was indeed something "religious," a quality of decency, a sense of outrage about the hurts suffered by people without influence, a basic sentiment the rabbis describe as "for the sake of heaven."[73]

In *World* Howe had written: "A good portion of what was best in Jewish life, as also what was worst, derived from . . . secularized messianism as it passed from generation to generation." Worst, Howe thought, was the kind of messianic radicalism of his Trotskyist youth, and later of the New Left, which seemed to insist on complete and immediate perfection of society. Best was messianism transmuted into *tikn olam*, a powerful moral impulse to mend the world even while recognizing the eternal durability of its imperfection. This more modest version of messianism flowered in America with the "first rush of fresh air," Howe said, "appearing first as socialism, then as Zionism, or the two together."[74]

Howe recognized that these political movements among the Jews "received nutriment from the very faith they had begun to displace." We make distinctions, he wrote in *World*, "between religious and secular ideologies, and we are right to make them; but . . . the two had a way of becoming intertwined." Irving Howe thought they had been intertwined, for Jews at least, in democratic socialism. He had no reason to suppose that there would "ever occur a revival of Jewish socialism in quite the forms it took during the first decades of the century." But near the very end of *World*, Howe asked, "Has American society shown itself to be so splendid and so solicitous of its members that the views of the Jewish socialists no longer retain an edge of truth?" And he expressed "a margin of hope" that the Jewish moral impulse still has something to teach America.[75]

One of the great ironies about *World*, Howe's invocation to socialism, is that it made him a wealthy man. He had published many books before, but the total income from all of them was less than a year's salary for an average toiler in academia. That modest amount paled even further in the face of the money that came in from *World*, not only through royalties, but also from the prestigious National Book Award, speeches at synagogues, Jewish centers, and national Jewish organizations, and from appearances on TV talk shows.[76] Howe basked a bit in the public limelight but he wearied of the pressures. He even told a colleague he was getting somewhat "crazy" from his new role as the "itinerant *magid*" (preacher) going from place to place representing Jewish "ethnicity."[77] It was especially troubling for Irving to find himself at meetings with middle-class Jews more intent on tracing their own genealogies than on learning something about their people's history. Or worse, at "pageants" which re-created the Lower East Side of New York, complete with pushcarts, pickles, and onion rolls, but with no sign of the "tubercular garment worker spitting blood from his years of exhaustion in a sweat shop."[78]

Still, Howe said, it was not unpleasant to anticipate fees and royalties that could provide more than a spaghetti dinner. The money, Howe's occasional disclaimers notwithstanding, also brought more substantial happiness. He bought an up-scale apartment on 83rd Street and Fifth Avenue, only feet from the Metropolitan Museum of Art, and was able to pay for the graduate school educations of his children, Nina and Nicholas.[79] Both eventually earned Ph.D.s. In 2002 Nicholas was a full professor and the Director of the Center for Medieval and Renaissance Literature at Ohio State University at Columbus, and Nina was a full professor of psychology and a member of the Centre for Research in Human Development at Concordia University in Montreal. That he was able to help his children was a genuine pleasure for Howe, and apparently one he was reluctant to give up. When Nicholas found a teaching job in 1978, it was the first time in twenty-five years Howe did not have to support a child. Although apparently proud and relieved, Irving

Howe, the Jewish father through and through, told a colleague that he was also a bit unnerved by the end of Nicholas's dependence on him.[80]

World brought a touch of fame as well as money. There were many glowing reviews and a spot on the best-seller list for some weeks. But celebrity was fleeting. In America, as Andy Warhol said, "everyone will be famous for fifteen minutes." While Howe was dining out, soon after publication of his book, a stranger approached him for an autograph, but it never happened again. Sitting down some weeks later in the same restaurant, he said, "I am [once] again simply a stoop-shouldered man with a bald spot. The fifteen minutes are over."[81]

Other things changed for Howe as well in the late seventies. Very much on the positive side was his marriage at the age of fifty-seven to Ilana Wiener, a forty-two-year-old with degrees in clinical psychology, whom he described to Marie Syrkin as "a lovely Israeli woman."[82] To Howe's delight his new wife was deeply interested in Israeli literature and she filled their apartment with Hebrew writings and sometimes even Hebrew writers. And together she and Irving edited *Short Shorts*, a collection of the shortest stories translated from many different languages, including Yiddish.[83] But there were losses too. In 1976, Howe's daughter, Nina, an attractive and very bright student at the University of Western Ontario, married and moved to Alberta, which for Irving, the New Yorker born and bred, seemed a terribly distant and alien place. Eliezer Greenberg, with whom Howe had just completed *Ashes Out of Hope: Fiction by Soviet Yiddish Writers* (1977), died in the late spring of 1977, cutting Irving's last significant contact with the old Yiddish world. At the end of the same year, Howe's eighty-five-year-old father died.

Howe and his father had never been very close. Like many Jewish parents, David Horenstein had complained that his son didn't call or write enough, and that when he deigned to visit occasionally he usually let his wife Arien do the talking while Irving sat in a corner and read the *Forward*.[84] But Irving had always done his filial duty. After his father had been mugged twice in the late sixties, Irving practically forced him to move from the East Bronx into CO-OP city. And he took care of him when he grew ill, even if without much generosity of spirit. He told his friend Marie Syrkin, "It's hard to write. I'm harassed by having to take care of my father, who is very . . . sick and cranky. I do my duty," Irving said, "perhaps better than I might have expected, but I don't do it with much grace: for which whoever does the forgiving may yet forgive me.

But it's hard." Near the end, as he admitted with painful honesty, Howe could not speak words of love; but he was "overwhelmed by emotion" remembering his father's suffering and endurance. And when he heard his dying father praise his work, Howe did finally weep. He also smiled when he heard that his father had told Nicholas that Irving had been "a good son." [85]

Howe was also a good father. His own children, with whom he stayed quite close over the years, appear to have forgiven his leaving them in 1960 and speak of him with great kindness. Nina and Nicholas, raised primarily by Thalia, apparently developed no Jewish identity, but they remained quite loyal and loving to Irving throughout their adulthood. They were proud of their father's writings and wanted "copies of everything" he published. Nina even relied on Irving to guide her in her reading, and she still keeps a copy of his picture on her desk at school. And Nicholas, who was a graduate student in medieval literature at Yale in 1977, cheerfully shared an apartment with his father while Irving was a visiting fellow for a semester at the National Humanities Institute in New Haven. [86]

Around that same time, Howe had "a big offer" to teach at Yale. But despite CUNY's dreadful financial problems in the late seventies, Howe turned Yale down in order to remain in Manhattan. To some it may seem an odd decision, for Howe was in despair over the deterioration of New York City. When he would walk along 42nd Street to get to class at the Graduate Center between Fifth and Sixth Avenues, Irving was constantly struck by "the sheer moral ugliness" of the scene—the drug dealers, the homeless beggars, the porn shops. He remembered Trotsky's expectation at the end of his book, *Literature and Revolution*, that humankind would someday rise to the levels of Goethe and Beethoven. But he asked himself how that expectation could be reconciled with "seeing what one sees" on the streets: the utter "waste and distortion . . . of human capacity?" [87]

Still, Howe, though no longer in love with the "metropolis," remained hopelessly attached to it, and not just to New York, but to the idea of "the city." He was fond of quoting Lewis Mumford's definition: "a place designed to offer the widest facilities for significant conversation." He knew how far we were from living in the "City of the Just," a phrase, he wrote, which "rings a little hollow now." He knew that we were not yet at ease in the kind of city conceived by the poet Wallace Stevens, a place where "One's grand flights, one's Sunday baths/One's tooting at the wedding of the Soul/Occur as they occur." Yet he wanted to stay in New York, the city which molded him, and where he could still hear a Haydn concert or a reading of Colette or watch in awe the choreography of George Balanchine at Lincoln Center. And in New York, Howe believed, he could be part of a movement to build genuine cities, truly just cities, vital civilizations. If we don't, he warned, "we shall perish."[88]

Howe was dejected about the cultural and material degradation not only of New York but of American cities generally. He was also appalled at the increasing de facto "resegregation" of the urban areas of the United States. In the late seventies he had visited Detroit several times, once in 1977 to lecture at Wayne State University. Howe was deeply distressed by the general decay, the lack of hope, and the sense of abandonment that permeated the city. The urban crisis, he wrote, signified a new version of apartheid, and he employed the rhetorical device of inviting President Jimmy Carter, who needed to have his eyes opened, to walk with him through "the rotting core" of Detroit.

Howe blamed the emergent American Right, with its mean-spirited attack on the cities and on the welfare state (a hidden form of racism and anti-Semitism), for much of the problem. But he recognized, partly from his father's experience and partly from his own observations in Detroit and New York, including the widespread looting during the 1977 power failure, that "crime in the streets" was no illusion. And he understood that "white flight" was not merely racism or a product of the "irrational fears of elderly white people." He knew, too, of course, that the outcry against crime could raise "the specter of . . . reactionary diversions," but he would not pretend there was no issue. His primary response, however, was a call for municipal rehabilitation, a program of federally sponsored employment and job training and generous loans to small businesses run by blacks.[89]

Railing against the "Right Menace," Howe not only opposed the dismantling of social programs, but supported the extension of the welfare state. An increasing interpenetration between state and economy was inevitable in the modern world, Howe argued. The important question, however, was not whether there ought to be "government involvement," but whether a growing partnership between state and economy would serve the interests of corporate hegemony or would be "modulated politically in behalf of democratic and egalitarian values." Some of Howe's critics charged that the extended welfare state he called for was a threat to democracy. On the contrary, he said, the erosions of our liberties have come not from left-liberal activists for economic reform, but from political misconduct by those elements of society like the McCarthyites, the FBI, the CIA, and the Right generally, who bitterly oppose the welfare state and its advocates. And he pointed to Sweden, the Netherlands, Denmark, and England, whose more comprehensive welfare states experienced no concurrent erosion of political freedoms.[90]

Howe knew that political conditions in America made unlikely the emergence of a mass socialist or labor party on the European model. But that did not mean, he said, "that socialism cannot exert significant political influence."[91] And here Howe would stand for the remaining fifteen years of his life—defending the extension of the welfare state both as a just construct in its own right and as a foundation for some future democratic socialism. What that might look like was unclear. But it certainly didn't mean state ownership or highly centralized planning and coercive management. Howe had made that clear many times in the past, and he did so again in yet another retrospective, his new book on Leon Trotsky published in 1978.

Howe had praise for Trotsky, especially for the last dozen years of the exiled revolutionary's life during which his revelations about Stalin and his denunciations of the Communist dictatorship made Trotsky a moral hero. But Trotsky was a political failure, Howe said, who refused to rethink revolutionary Marxist-Leninism even in the face of its ugly realities. Trotsky's insistence on state ownership of the means of production and distribution and his dismissal of bourgeois democracy as a screen for class domination blinded him and many others to the most precious values of modern society—individual liberties and freedom from coercion, without which there could be no socialism. Until the mid-1940s or so, Howe had been devoted to one or another version of Trotskyism. He had said farewell in stages several times, and in this book he declared in no uncertain terms that for very many years Trotskyism, in contrast to the immigrant Jewish socialism Howe had portrayed and championed in *World*, had been "without political or intellectual significance: a petrified ideology."[92]

In *Leon Trotsky*, Howe apologized, indirectly, for his own sectarian political past. But unlike some former radicals among the New York intellectuals, including Sidney Hook who voted for Nixon as the "lesser evil" in 1972, or Irving Kristol who had become a Republican and a spokesman for corporate America, Howe was repelled by conservatism and remained on the liberal left. "There is conservative thought," Howe said, "that is traditional, serious, and worthy of consideration." But that was not what we had in America now, he contended. We have instead, he said bitterly, "the start of a crude . . . class struggle by some of the haves against many of the have-nots." And at the Democratic Socialist Organizing Committee's National Convention in Chicago in 1977, Howe in a keynote address called, without great hope, for a return to a more egalitarian ethic.[93]

Howe's dark mood over the political and social atmosphere in the late seventies was not ameliorated by the approach of his sixtieth birthday. For almost a quarter century Howe had grumbled about aging. Even in 1955, when he was not quite thirty-five, Howe told several colleagues and friends that he was feeling "very old." And by the early seventies (at age fifty-two) he was complaining to the sixty-seven-year-old Trilling that being middle-aged meant having to fight "against erosion and seepage of the spirit."[94]

Howe did, however, find ways to reduce his gloom. In 1978 he started working in earnest on his intellectual autobiography. That helped, but he found even more solace by plunging back into Yiddish literature. With Ruth Wisse he co-edited an anthology of Sholom Aleichem stories, and he told Marie Syrkin that his marriage to Ilana, who was introducing him to Hebrew writers, was "round[ing] out [his] return" to Jewishness. In the next decade Howe would continue that never-ending process of recapturing and redefining Jewish identity. In the course of that search, and in important ways tied to it, he would also try again to find a meaningful and viable radical politics, one recognizing that without some form of socialism, "democracy tends to be limited in scope," and that "without democracy, socialism is impossible."[95]

13

Sober Self-Reflections
Democratic Radical, Literary Critic, Secular Jew

FOR THE PERIOD from about 1970 to 1985, Irving Howe wrote mostly about his own past and the political milieu in which he grew up. *World of Our Fathers* (1976) and *Leon Trotsky* (1978) dealt in good part with Howe's Jewish identity and democratic socialist perspective. By 1982 he had completed *A Margin of Hope*, his intellectual autobiography, and by 1985 *Socialism and America*, a historical and personal retrospective. But Howe also remained deeply interested in literary criticism and returned to it with renewed vigor, especially after his retirement from City University in 1986. In that year he produced an important piece, "Writing and the Holocaust," as well as *The American Newness*, a book-length essay based on lectures he gave at Harvard on Emerson and radical individualism.

For several years he worked with great enthusiasm on small pieces, *shtiklakh* he called them, about Tolstoy, Dickens, George Eliot, Virginia Woolf, and other writers of fiction, which were published posthumously by his son Nicholas as *A Critic's Notebook* in 1994. Throughout these years, Howe remained committed to *Dissent* and loyal to the Democratic Socialists of America (DSA). He saw these as small but important weapons in the fight against Reaganism's "moral-cultural counter-revolution." And his love of Israel, a country he visited almost annually, grew even as he became a severe critic of Menachem Begin and his "hawkish" Likud coalition.

In the late eighties and early nineties, as Communism crumbled in Eastern Europe, Howe reassessed once again the future of socialism. At the same time, though his health was seriously deteriorating, Howe battled to save the literature he loved from the postmodern academic theorists and the advocates of a narrowly conceived "political correctness."

273

He also continued to pay attention to Jewish secularism, the subject of his last public talk, six weeks before he died in May 1993.

There was a moment at the beginning of the eighties when Howe's confidence in his ability to maintain *Dissent* wavered temporarily as it had once or twice before in the previous three decades. Early in 1981, Stanley Plastrik, Howe's friend for forty years and his collaborator and "gyroscope" at the periodical for a quarter century, suffered a massive stroke and died a few months later. "Everyone wants to keep the magazine going," Howe said, "but I am very shaken and don't know."[1] It didn't take very long, however, for Howe to recommit. Although emotionally heartsick over Plastrik's passing and himself suffering from "back trouble" and an "excruciatingly painful knee inflammation," which kept him from the typewriter for long periods, Irving not only stayed on board at *Dissent*, but very much at the helm.[2]

He told Daniel Bell, who had remained a good friend and confidant, that he guessed at sixty-one "we should . . . expect physical troubles and be grateful they aren't worse than they are." But Howe insisted he was not grateful, he was "willful." He not only wanted to keep going at *Dissent*, but also to do at least "one more book, one more article."[3] And as soon as he could get back to the typewriter he wrote the final chapters of *Margin of Hope*. The book was, as advertised, very much an intellectual autobiography, with only few and fleeting references to private life. But in several places Howe was brutally honest about personal matters: his youthful rejection of Jewishness; his infatuated embrace of ideological sectarianism; his occasionally intimidating teaching style; his therapy sessions in California; his too frequently expressed impatience; and his inability to speak words of love to his dying father. In other places, Howe was less than fully candid even about public matters. This, as we have seen in chapter 3, was especially true about his alleged "critical support" of the Allies in World War II. But overall, reworking a number of previously published retrospective essays, Howe wrote a compelling memoir as illuminating of his times as of his intellectual and political commitments. With a sharp clarity and in much detail, Howe traced and interpreted his journey from revolutionary Trotskyist to democratic socialist and "partial Jew."[4]

The book was relatively well received though, as expected, it sold far fewer copies than *World of Our Fathers*. In the critical community, *Margin* was treated favorably by much of the liberal media including the *New York Review of Books* and *The New Republic*, less so in the more radical *Nation* and *Guardian Weekly*, and it was slammed in the *Wall Street Journal* and by the neoconservatives at *Commentary*.[5] Howe told Marie Syrkin he was cheered by a great number of "letters from old friends and readers," but was "somewhat taken aback by the virulence of the neocon attacks," especially Midge Decter's "vicious reactionary and philistine" assault upon Irving and his socialist politics. He was particularly saddened that Irving Panken, an old Trotskyist colleague and friend about whom Howe had written warmly in *Margin*, had "rushed into print" in support of Decter's review. He told Panken that this sort of back-stabbing by someone "with whom my connection goes back 45 years" marked the "final decay of socialist solidarity, or even personal solidarity," which in this case might easily have been met, Howe said, by "silence."[6]

Howe had also written warmly but ambivalently in *Margin* about his old adversary, Sidney Hook. Though they were in basic agreement about some fundamental things including the enduring value of liberalism, the tragedy of Bolshevism, and the inefficacy of revolution, the two men had continued over the years to disagree sharply on particular political policies. And apparently Howe could not bring himself to write a fully sympathetic profile of the philosopher. He concluded that Hook demonstrated a "formidable brilliance" but that something crucial was ultimately missing in him, "some depth of sensibility."[7] Months after *Margin* was published, Irving sent a more affirmative note to Hook on his eightieth birthday saying, "I've learned from you (perhaps not enough you'll say) and I've disagreed with you; but I am glad to have been your . . . almost friend. . . . Stick around a long time and keep writing, meanwhile *mazeltov!*"[8]

Hook in reply, and perhaps in response to what he thought was Howe's unflattering portrayal of him in *Margin*, was polite but not especially accommodating. He accused Irving of disingenuousness and said that his literary criticism had always been more nuanced than his political criticism, and "therefore fairer to those with whom you disagree."[9] Years later, in his own memoir, *Out of Step* (1987), Hook was more explicit in his condemnation of Howe and *Margin*, a book he thought "replete with barefaced inventions." Hook was particularly miffed at the depiction of him as having been, in postwar America, hard on college teachers who were active members of the Communist Party and soft on McCarthyism. Howe, as we saw in chapter 6, had in fact, in the fifties, understated Hook's resistance to McCarthy, and he did so again in *Margin*. But Howe was quite accurate in the case of Hook and the Communist teachers. Hook's strident anti-Communism and his persistent denunciatory rhetoric in the late forties had indeed helped reinforce the atmosphere of wariness, fear, and intimidation around Communists in higher education, and had put them in the shaky position of having to "prove their innocence" in order to keep their jobs.[10]

One of the long-standing differences between the two men was that Hook's liberalism was relatively abstract and often boiled down to one-dimensional anti-Communism, whereas Howe's political philosophy generally translated into an activist promotion of democratic socialism. Even while writing *Margin*, which at the time he called his "real work," Irving, in the face of the Reagan "counterrevolution," could not "keep to his attic." He stayed active in the Democratic Socialist Organizing Committee (DSOC) in the late seventies and early eighties and played an important role in 1982 when DSOC, a group filled with many old anti-Stalinist leftists, merged with the New American Movement (NAM), many of whose members had been in SDS or were sympathetic to it. Howe originally opposed the merger. But NAM agreed to give strong backing to the state of Israel, and also to adopt DSOC's position that Communist nations not be considered socialist. When a DSOC majority responded by voting for the merger, Howe convinced the minority to abstain in order to begin the newly created Democratic Socialists of America (DSA) without factionalism.[11] By 1983 the organization had seven thousand members, making it the largest democratic socialist group in America since the 1930s. This was a promising start. But by 1987 there were only five thousand members. It was difficult to attract younger people who were busy building families and careers. And some people were driven away by tensions within the group. While factionalism did not become full blown, there were "constituencies" in the organization—feminist, environmentalist, Hispanic, black—which engaged in a "politics of identity" and created an atmosphere of fragmentation that put a damper on "common dreams." Howe was "bored" and irritated at this development. He remained in the organization and was active on the DSA speaking circuit, but he attended meetings only occasionally.[12]

The hoped-for "movement" had still not materialized. In the meantime, Irving tried to keep *Dissent*, which continued to have financial problems, afloat. In addition to his usual pleas for funds, Howe accepted Woody Allen's invitation to appear, along with Susan Sontag, Saul Bellow, and Bruno Bettelheim, in a "talking-head" role in the film *Zelig* (1982). Howe, who liked Allen, was not only "flattered and amused," he was paid handsomely and gave much of the money to the magazine. But when Howe told friends in his joking way, "From now on I'm only taking romantic leads!" they understood he planned to use his time for more important things.[13]

Howe began to work more closely with liberals and occasionally he was even out in the field campaigning for Democratic candidates. But mostly he fought with his typewriter against what he called the reactionary politics of the Reagan administration. During the eighties he wrote nearly two dozen diatribes directed at the president and his policies. Howe assailed Reagan for breaking the air controllers' union and for the ludicrous invasion of Grenada. He ferociously criticized the Republican Party's "utter indifference to the plight of blacks" and its support of supply-side economics which generated the largest budget deficit in American history.[14]

Howe also attacked the Reagan Republicans for favoring constitutional amendments to make abortion a crime and to allow prayer in the schools. He thought the "streak of bigotry and intolerance" he saw in Reaganite policy was not only dangerous generally but particularly bad for Jews. He wondered if those Jewish intellectuals and organizational leaders who had "slunk into Reagan's camp" felt any discomfort in the company of the "Moral Majority fanatics"—those enemies of the separation of church and state, a principle to which American Jews had historically been committed.[15]

Not all was doom and gloom for Howe. He was buoyed in 1984 by the Democratic Party's nomination of Geraldine Ferraro for vice-president of the United States. He thought it was "an event of major importance in American political life" that a woman was running for high office as the candidate of a major national party. And Howe's increasingly positive view of feminism was reflected in his remark that the Ferraro nomination was "a triumph, and well-deserved too, for the whole feminist movement." It also confirmed his long-held view that sustained, organized political activity yields positive results.[16] He was encouraged as well by the voter registration drives in the mid-eighties that brought a large number of blacks into American politics. And he was delighted that some of his old friends and associates like Nathan Glazer and Daniel Bell not only refused to relinquish their identities as Democrats and "liberal critics of liberalism," but that Bell, unlike Podhoretz and Kristol, increasingly distanced himself from neoconservatism in his attacks on the social and economic policies of the Republican Party. Howe was also relieved to find that despite some of the *Commentary* crowd's infatuation with Reaganism, Jews continued to vote steadily and disproportionately for liberal Democrats.[17]

Jews and Jewishness were very much on Irving's mind in the eighties. He continued to worry a little about a rightward turn among some segments of the traditionally liberal Jewish community, but much more about what he saw as a general Jewish American "hawkishness" on the question of Israel. Howe's interest in the Jewish state had been sparked by the Six Day War in 1967 and it intensified sharply in 1973 during the Yom Kippur War. He visited in 1974, and then again, as we have seen, almost every year after his marriage to Ilana in 1977.

In 1978, after a month in Israel touring the lower Galilee and the *kibbutzim*, Irving was not only "overwhelmed by the beauty and the work that ha[d] been done," he was impressed with the peace movement. "*Shalom Achshav* ["Peace Now"] seems promising," he told his Zionist friend Marie Syrkin. "The kids running it . . . some [of them] beribboned veterans of the Yom Kippur War," were "hard-headed," Howe thought, and free of the romantic and apocalyptic "nonsense" that had ruined chances for significant reform in America in the late sixties. Perhaps this group, Howe hoped, could promote a wider movement to reverse what he called Begin's "major blunders"—building new settlements, extending Israel's hold on the occupied territories, refusing to countenance talk about a Palestinian State, and resisting full negotiations with the Egyptians.[18]

Upon his return to the United States in April, Howe, along with Marie Syrkin, Bellow, Meyer Schapiro, Daniel Bell, and thirty-two other New York intellectuals, signed a statement supportive of Peace Now that appeared in the *New York Times*. The statement called on Israel to show greater flexibility in negotiations with Egypt and greater sensitivity to the plight of the Palestinians. The statement also expressed opposition "to those aspects of American policy which threaten to diminish Israel's security." Although not explicit, one presumes Howe and his friends were referring to what they saw as premature pressure on Israel to return to pre-1967 borders.[19]

Despite the balanced quality of their statement, Howe and the other co-signers found themselves under attack in several quarters, and especially by the publicist and well-known expert on Soviet Jewry, Moshe Decter. Once a severe critic of Joseph McCarthy, Decter stooped to McCarthyite tactics in his assault. In order to deflect attention from the views of the dissidents, Decter called Howe and several of the others "Trotskyists" who had never had any real love of Israel. Howe feared that Decter's response suggested the existence of an atmosphere in which "loyalty" to Israel is measured by "knee-jerk approval of whatever Begin's government does and says, even if many people are secretly heartsick about it."[20]

Although he had complaints about Israel's "dreadful politics," Howe told several friends that if he were forty instead of sixty, and if he knew Hebrew, he'd probably settle in the Jewish state—"not out of Zionist persuasions but just because it's such a good place . . . a great achievement."[21] He was a little less enthusiastic in 1982, a year in which the beleaguered state of Israel retaliated in a very powerful and "disturbing" way against the Palestinian Liberation Organization (PLO) for its blatant violations of repeated cease-fires and for its ongoing terrorism against Israelis at home and abroad. In June, Israel decided to invade Lebanon, which was still a chaotic puppet state of Syria, harboring the PLO and a number of other active anti-Israel terrorist groups. This time, however, unlike the defensive invasion in 1978, troops went well north, driving the PLO into the capital city of Beirut, which Israeli forces then bombed and besieged. The PLO was indeed forced from Lebanon, but at significant cost in civilian lives. And in September, in the wake of the organization's departure, the Israeli-supported Christian Phalange perpetrated massacres at the Palestinian refugee camps of Sabra and Shatila.

Howe felt it necessary to speak out even before those atrocities occurred, and at the end of June he joined Nathan Glazer, Seymour Martin Lipset, and nearly seventy other Jewish intellectuals "concerned with Israel's survival and great name" in a public statement sponsored by American Friends of Peace Now that appeared in the *Times*. The statement deplored "Israel's excessive use of force in Lebanon," but Howe and the other signers, including Syrkin, Walzer, and Rabbi Joachim Prinz, by their proven commitment to the existence of the state and by the evenhanded tone in which they chose to couch their dissent, distinguished themselves from dissidents like I. F. Stone and Noam Chomsky, who had signed much less friendly statements. They took heat nonetheless from many American Jewish communal leaders, heads of Jewish organizations, and the Jewish press.[22] Howe did get implicit support, however, from some Jewish institutions. The Reconstructionist Rabbinical College, for example, honored him in 1983 with the *Keter Shem Tov* Award, a tribute "bestowed upon persons of academic and communal distinction" in the Jewish world.[23]

Howe continued to gauge the mood in the American Jewish community and to watch events in Israel with "a kind of terrified fascination" and confusion. He was appalled at the behavior of the Israeli government and irritated by continued U.S. financial support despite announced American objections to Begin's policies. But not wanting to reduce U.S. aid to Israel per se, Howe, as he told Marie Syrkin, was "in a trap."[24]

In April 1983 Howe traveled again to Israel, where he experienced his usual mixed feelings during a five-week stay. He was quite proud of Israel, a democracy that could produce an official report on Lebanon critical of the Begin government, and which held Ariel Sharon indirectly responsible for the massacres in Sabra and Shatila, effectively forcing him to resign as defense minister.[25] But Howe, still distressed by the "hawkishness" abounding in some segments of the American Jewish community, was further pained by ugly scenes in Israel where "doves" and "hawks," on the verge of violence, shouted nasty slogans at one another in the streets.[26] He was also unnerved by the enclave of "ardent young settlers" he observed in Hebron encircled by a silent but bitter mass of Arabs. And he wondered what it was about the Jewish experience or psyche that prompted "so bizarre a re-creation of the ghetto," the claustrophobic ghetto Jews had struggled to escape from for centuries. The fanatics have locked themselves in, Howe said, "surrounded by hatred" and in need of protection by Israeli forces. "Is this what Zionism meant," Howe asked, "when it proposed to make Jewish life 'normal'?"[27]

Howe, who remained what he called a "warm friend of Israel" and an "open critic" of Begin and Sharon, felt that he and his Peace Now friends in Israel and the United States were in the midst of a struggle between the democratic liberal Zionist vision represented by Chaim Weizmann and the ultranationalist Zionist vision of Vladimir Jabotinsky. This was a "struggle," Howe said, "over the character of Jewish life both in Israel and the diaspora."[28] He called for negotiations with any Palestinians who openly recognized the legitimacy of the Jewish state. He looked forward to a settlement between Israel and its Arab neighbors that would secure Israel's borders without requiring it to hold on permanently to all of the occupied territories. Twenty years later, and nine since Howe's death, there was as yet no such settlement in sight.

Despite his disappointment over the political situation in Israel, Howe continued to travel there. He told Syrkin in 1985 that he was off again to Jerusalem where "it sometimes seems . . . I have more friends . . . than in New York." He was looking forward to sitting in the sun, reading, and perhaps writing a little "in the home," as he had once put it, "of our survivors."[29] In Israel the Holocaust was rarely far from Howe's mind. He had once remarked, in his distinct style of serious joking, that "Israel had become the religion of Jewish-Americans with the Holocaust as its liturgy." Now, in his later years Howe himself had become preoccupied with these issues.[30] On this trip to Jerusalem he wrote his searching and sensitive essay, "Writing and the Holocaust."

Ten years earlier, Howe had acknowledged in *World of Our Fathers* that memories of genocide "pressed deep into the consciousness of Jews." He concluded, however, that "there was nothing to do" about the unprecedented horror except remember, "and that was best done in silence." In seeming support of silence, even as late as 1985, Howe could quote the Yiddish poet Aron Tsaitlin, who wrote shortly after the Holocaust, "The Almighty Himself . . . would maintain a deep silence. For even an outcry is a lie, even tears are mere literature, even prayers are false." But Howe added: "We also know that it has proved impossible for most writers to remain silent. Nor did Tsaitlin himself, even as he excoriated his need to 'cry out.'"[31]

Howe was in a dilemma similar to Tsaitlin's. He respected silence in the face of so radical an evil as the Holocaust, but he thought, ultimately, that it ought not to be a "prohibited" topic for writers. Perhaps novelists and short-story writers, and even memoirists, could "succeed," he said, if they approached the enormity tangentially, through strategies of indirection, or if their focus were on the time just before or after rather than during the Holocaust. Here he had in mind especially Primo Levi's haunting account, *If Not Now When?*; Aaron Appelfeld's extraordinary novel, *Badenheim 1939*; and Chaim Grade's stunning story, "My Quarrel with Hersh Rasseyner." But even as Howe wrote about employing the literary techniques of "oblique symbols" or "circuitous narratives," he questioned his own role, wondering whether "the whole apparatus of literary criticism with all its nice discriminations and categories," might not "seem incongruous, even trivial . . .

before so intolerable a subject." He was inclined to think there were no easy answers, perhaps none at all.[32]

This was not timidity on Howe's part, nor only a response to the unimaginable; it was also an openness, a self-questioning that had become increasingly characteristic of Irving's life and work since the sixties. Creative tentativeness showed itself in his literary criticism as well as in his political writings, including *Socialism and America* (1985). Howe intended the work "as a modest contribution toward the renewal of socialist thought," and the book is less filled with answers than with "inconclusive conclusions" and probing questions. How, for example, do democratic radicals reconcile their vision of a fundamentally transformed world with the practical day-to-day issues relevant to the needs of workers? This was for socialists "a seemingly insoluble problem" in the 1930s. Perhaps, Howe said, "it still is."[33]

Howe challenged Daniel Bell's argument that socialists were inevitably and immutably "in the world but not of it"; that is, that they *consistently* preferred to hold to their own ideological purity rather than engage in mundane politics. Howe agreed that some socialists ignored American political reality and too often acted in the "tradition of moral testimony," putting individual conscience above community. Such behavior, as in the case of the socialists' unmodulated stand against World War I, Howe said, promoted repression by the U.S. government and factionalism within the group. The movement itself, therefore, Howe said, must assume a portion of responsibility for its own failure.[34]

But Howe did not think socialists alone or primarily were to blame for their hapless fate. The general American electoral process and especially the two-party system were inhospitable, he said, to the prospects of newly emerging ideological parties. And the ethnic heterogeneity of the American work force, along with property mobility and the relative prosperity of American workers, fettered class consciousness. The ideal of progress and opportunity through hard work, Howe admitted, "rests on a measure of historical actuality," but it has also taken on a power independent of social reality. Here, Howe said, "we enter the realm of national psychology and cultural values," values which pretty much eliminate the working class as the main agent of social change.[35] Moreover, in trying to explain the absence of a mass socialist movement in the United States, Howe wrote, we should be reminded that the "terrifying rise of Stalinism" led to a nearly "fatal besmirching of the socialist idea."[36]

Howe made it clear here, as he had many times before, that he had long ago given up on socialism as historically inevitable. Indeed, it was just as logical to ask, he said, "why socialism anywhere?" as it was to pose the question, "why no socialism in America?" It looked as if Howe might have been saying yet one more farewell, as he had, for example, in *World*, to Jewish secularism, or in his many anthologies, to Yiddish. But as in those cases, so with socialism, Howe proved not quite ready to write a requiem, to say a final and definitive good-bye. Something could be salvaged, Howe seemed to hope, in each instance, and here it was socialism as a "regulative idea."

Retaining a utopian image of the long term even if one assumes that the long term will never be reached, Howe suggested, regulates one's principled engagement in the day-to-day world. Socialism had become, for Howe, not so much a blueprint as a personal persuasion, a moral influence, a way of measuring changes in America against a vision of a better and redeeming future. Howe had argued that democratic socialists could work closely with liberal cousins for incremental reform and still keep an eye on the larger prize.[37] In this way, as Howe and Lew Coser had said more than thirty years earlier, socialism operates not as "a controlling day-dream" that can freeze into a "fantasy of static perfection," but rather as a vision that "gives urgency to . . . criticism of the human condition of our time." This socialism, Howe said, as he had in 1954, "was the name of our desire."[38]

Among the many barriers to the fulfillment of socialism's longer-term dream that Howe emphasized was the deeply internalized American belief in individualism. And this, in *Socialism and America* and again in *The American Newness* (1986), he identified with Ralph Waldo Emerson's vision of man as a self-creating and self-sufficient being deriving fulfillment through a direct personal relation to God and nature.[39] But Howe, drawing on his literary knowledge and sensitivity, did not, like other socialists, try to demolish the whole of Emersonianism as a threat to collective purpose. Instead, he engaged Emerson in intellectual and moral struggle and in the process discovered a redeeming value in the nineteenth-century philosopher's ideology of individualism.

In the seventies, Howe had written that even as a schoolboy he had been turned off by Emerson and his naive "American delusions" about self-reliance, because they rubbed roughly against Howe's Jewish "heritage of communal affections and responsibilities." So he and many other left-leaning boys and girls of his generation "abandoned Emerson even before encountering him." But in later years there was deeper and wider reading, more experience with the dangers of attacking individualism too broadly, and a new set of reflections that allowed Howe to "establish amiable diplomatic relations" with Emerson, even if not a complete rapprochement.[40]

Howe continued to argue in *American Newness* that there is something unsatisfying in the stress on absolute self-sufficiency and general withdrawal from the public arena, something impoverished in the view "that contents itself with individualism as an ideology." To speak of a self-generated individual, separated from time and circumstance, he argued, suppresses life's complexities, necessary entanglements, and possibilities. And he continued to point out the greater "social thickness" in Emerson's contemporaries Hawthorne and Melville, both of whom evoke a "sharing of travail that . . . [the Emersonian] cult of self-reliance is ill-equipped to grasp." Howe loved to teach Hawthorne's "My Kinsman, Major Molineaux," a sharp critique of cunning selfishness, and Melville's *Moby Dick*, which among other things is a brilliant portrait of obsessive, aggrandizing individualism.[41]

Yet Emerson has appeal, Howe said, mainly because he asked very large and "radical" questions about a still "new" post-Revolutionary America: Could it give fresh life to religion and art? Could it fulfill humanity's moral and intellectual needs? Or, preempting Trotsky, "Could it create and maintain in the mass of mankind those habits of mind which had hitherto belonged to men of science?"[42] These kinds of questions, Howe insisted, are responsive to nascent "social possibilities and political moods," and "represent the strongest voice of dissent in American culture." Emerson in the mid-nineteenth century, Howe told an interviewer in 1988, was asking that "the American Revolution . . . be deepened, brought nearer completion." And now, as then, Howe said, Emersonianism provided a fundamental basis for an adversarial posture, "for a deep critique of capitalism and materialism."[43]

Howe hardly thought Emerson a socialist, and he knew, of course, that concentrated capital and multinational corporatism in the late twentieth century needed something more powerful than an Emersonian critique. Howe agreed more with another of Emerson's contemporaries, Orestes Brownson, who said that strenuous "efforts of individuals to perfect themselves" may indeed remove imperfections that are "purely individual." But "the evil . . . inherent in . . . our social arrangements cannot be cured without a radical change" in the structure of society. Having witnessed some of those structural changes in other countries which brought "neither greater freedom nor relief for the laboring classes," Howe was more inclined to "reject a simple dichotomy between social transformation and individual regeneration." He insisted instead on their interdependence. "I still believe in community activity and political organization," Howe said, "but I also see value in the Emersonian figure of rectitude" who creates necessary and productive moral tensions.[44]

"Simple Emersonians we can no longer be," Howe said. But he hoped "the newness" would come again, perhaps in the form of a "mixture of social liberalism and a reaffirmed and critical sense of self." In the meantime, he told a Harvard audience in 1986, he would be patient. Yes, patient, even after the many years of disappointment and the bone-deep knowledge of lost opportunity. Emerson's voice still rang clear for Howe: "Never mind the ridicule, never mind the defeat; up again, old heart!—it seems to say—there is victory yet for all justice."[45]

While Howe fought for justice consistently, he also struggled with the conflict between communal obligation and personal desire. He therefore sympathized with Emerson's hesitations and uncertainties about leaving his attic to "fight the good fights" of the nineteenth century. Howe knew, many years after his battle with Ellison (another Ralph Waldo), that responding to the urgencies of the moment could mean abandoning or compromising one's true vocation or values. But even for his beloved literature Howe could not forgo his commitment to public activism.[46]

There would, of course, be no support from Howe for narrowly ideological "crusades" like those that erupted in the late sixties, and for which, in any case, there were no viable constituencies. But even in the "gloomy eighties" there would be "campaigns," unexciting but necessary struggles against the dismantling of the welfare state, and for incremental democratization of the polity and the economy. We have seen before that Howe had a genius (a Jewish genius?) for being gloomy and optimistic at the same time, a trait essential for a visionary socialist engaged in the world "as it is" on a daily basis. A conversation that took place in the seventies between Howe and the Yiddish writer Isaac Bashevis Singer is illuminating. Singer suggested that although Howe wrote in English he was closer than Singer himself to the Yiddishist tradition, a tradition powerfully influenced by socialism. Singer said, that he, unlike Howe, was no socialist. He had "lost the illusion" that things can change. On the other hand, Singer told Howe, "*You* still have hope." "I don't always have that hope," Howe responded, "I have it sometimes." "Yes," Singer said with a sense of weariness, "but sometimes."[47]

Irving Howe never got weary enough to give up hope completely. In the mid-eighties he told an interviewer that the Reagan crowd had played retrogressively but brilliantly on a deep sense of nostalgia in America, but that they would not remain permanently in the saddle. And despite the post–World War II trend among intellectuals toward conservatism, Howe continued to think that the nation as whole was more comfortable with a New Deal type liberalism.[48] Hungry to be right, Howe said in 1987, "not yet visible impulses of renewal may be gathering. The days of Reagan are coming to an end."[49]

Actually, for this Howe would have to wait several years longer. In the meantime there was life to be lived and other issues to face. Irving continued to spend time with his grown children, even trekking out to Nina in Canada where, together with Nina and her husband, he enjoyed watching Balanchine at Les Grands Ballets Canadiens or the Montreal Expos playing the Mets at Olympic Stadium. And when Nina was diagnosed with cancer in 1988, "Daddy was right there," she said, helping her every step of the way, "holding my hand"—and at the same time expressing admiration for Canada's free universal health care plan.[50]

Irving visited his son too, even when Nicholas was teaching medieval literature in Norman, Oklahoma, and together they took a trip to the wildlife refuge in the Wichita Mountains, about two hours from the university. On the drive, Howe, forever literary, remarked that the flat, windswept prairie with its scattering of cottonwood and black oak trees was "straight out of Flannery O'Connor." Nicholas felt that with that "delicious" sentence his father had given him the story that helped him live more comfortably in the alien landscape. Howe himself also found "delicious" (a favorite word of praise) the irony that in the wildlife refuge there was a vast herd of buffalo descended from a small number shipped out to Oklahoma in 1905 from the Bronx Zoo![51]

With his two children and their spouses, Irving relaxed and enjoyed himself thoroughly. Undoubtedly there were also political discussions, including exchanges on the question of Israel, which in the late eighties was very much on Howe's mind. Beginning in the last days of 1987, the Palestinians in the West Bank and Gaza Strip mounted an *intifada* against the Israeli forces in the territories. This uprising, Howe believed, grew out of justifiable frustration and would not be destroyed or suppressed unless Israel was willing to resort to mass slaughter. Howe thought this improbable, especially after returning in September 1988 from a trip to Israel, where he was convinced "moral constraints still work . . . especially within the Israeli army command."[52]

Three months later he was less optimistic, but still hopeful that "Israel as a democratic state will finally agree, with all due precautions, to accept the same national rights for the Palestinians that it fought to gain for itself."[53] Howe remained a sharp critic of Israeli policies and hoped the Israeli government would change its posture on the territories, but he knew that Israel was "surrounded by real enemies and must therefore maintain its military strength (for which American aid is crucial)."[54] And he was sharply critical of Yasir Arafat, the head of the PLO, a "wretched opportunist" who sanctioned terrorism and refused to entertain seriously a recognition of Israel's right to exist.[55]

When the *intifada* was a year old, Howe told a mostly Jewish audience at a conference sponsored by the left-liberal magazine *Tikkun* that "the Israeli-Palestinian conflict is of such overriding importance that we have to give it our major attention." He feared, however, that American Jews would not be able to bear much criticism of Israel, especially from other Jews. Israel, he said once again, had become the "religion" of the American Jews, the last hope for Jewish identity and continuity. It was simply too difficult, Howe said, for large numbers of Jews to become openly critical of Israeli policy, because then "they would feel there is nothing left."[56]

Depressed by the situation in the Middle East and by the sullen solidarity on "Israelism" among American Jews, Howe complained that Jewish Americans constituted a community "drained of its animating passions and energies." And despite much evidence to the contrary, he insisted that Jewish secularism as well as religiosity had grown "thin, lukewarm," had slipped into a "philistinism without much faith or knowledge."[57] Howe was no doubt right that in 1988 there was greater difference of opinion in Israel itself over the Palestinian question than there was in the American Jewish community. And undoubtedly too, "Israelism" was an important pillar of Jewish identity in America. But it wasn't the only one.

Howe was too far removed from organized Jewry and middle-class Jewish life to see that there was still great vitality within the American

Jewish community. Orthodox Jews, for example, have remained stead-fast in their adherence to tradition and Jewish learning, and few in America, even in the twenty-first century, believe any longer that Orthodox Judaism is so out of touch with currents in modern life that it will soon disappear. The Orthodox are only about 10 percent of the Jewish population in the United States, but since 1945, and especially since the late 1970s, there has been a renewed emphasis on traditional observance even among Reform and Conservative Jews, the vast majority of affiliated American Jewry. Skullcaps, prayer shawls, Hebrew usage, and kosher meals have reappeared. Religious circumcision, bar and bat mitzvah, and the marriage canopy have grown increasingly popular. Indeed, a scholarly conference held in Los Angeles in the year 2000 on "The Reappearing American Jew" drew thousands of Jews.[58]

Secular Jewishness too manifested a certain vibrancy, especially in literature. Howe had predicted as early as 1977 that American Jewish fiction, because it drew so heavily from the immigrant experience, had depleted its resources and was for all intents and purposes finished. But some writers appear to have blissfully ignored Howe's pronouncement that their literature was dead. Pearl Abraham, Melvin Bukiet, Myla Goldberg, Rebecca Goldstein, Allegra Goodman, Alan Isler, Lev Raphael, Thane Rosenbaum, Steve Stern, and so many more young authors, immersed in a postimmigrant, postassimilationist, post-Holocaust context, are still writing, not only as Jews, but directly about their redefined Jewishness, religious as well as secular.[59]

Although these men and women do not write in Yiddish, the spirit and sensibility of Yiddishkayt continues in their work. Moreover, even the Yiddish language itself, though hardly making a comeback as a lingua franca, is being taught at a number of colleges around the country and is being refreshed or learned for the first time in innumerable Yiddish-speakers' clubs from coast to coast. And secular Jews, as Howe himself acknowledged, also continue to be heavily represented in liberal political and cultural organizations and movements like the American Civil Liberties Union, People for the American Way, Planned Parenthood, Americans for Democratic Action, and Democratic Socialists of America.

In 1993, the last year of his life, Howe himself may have recognized that there was more to contemporary secular Jewishness than Israelism. He did say in his final public talk that "those of us committed to the secular Jewish outlook must admit we are reaching a dead end." But the conclusion of his talk, "The End of Jewish Secularism," was less absolute. "*If* I am right," Howe said,

> in supposing that a *phase* of Jewish history is now reaching its end,
> then the least we can do is say farewell with love and gratitude. The
> sense of natural piety toward an honored past is not very strong in
> modern culture, but without it, no sort of Jewish life is conceivable.
> This is the world that made us; this is the source of our aspirations and
> values; this is the stamp—in our speech and in our style, in our
> thoughts and in our delusions, in the very shrug of our shoulders—
> that will remain to our very last day.

And since he did predict that "fifty years from now American Jews . . .
will still be discussing the problem of identity," one would like to think
that here Howe meant more than his, or his own generation's, "very
last day."[60]

Howe's complaint about the absence of a strong "sense of natural
piety toward an honored past" could have applied to the state of literature in the universities as well as to the quality of secular Jewishness in
America. Beginning in the mid-eighties, the pervasive and intense academic attack on the "canon" of Western literature for its alleged gender,
class, and racial bias made Howe "very angry." And it drew him and his
"almost friend" Sidney Hook, now in his late eighties and ailing, into a
new alliance against single-minded "political correctness" and into a
warmer, more supportive and more enduring correspondence.

"Those of us who have been or are teachers," Howe wrote Hook,
"get these . . . kids," most of whom come poorly prepared from the high
schools. And "for a short while . . . we have a chance to expose them to
. . . Sophocles, . . . Hume, an essay by Freud, a poem by Keats, whatever
. . . has survived through sheer power of mind and language—and our
[Marxist] colleagues tell us that this is imperialistic or racist or sexist or
whatever."[61]

Howe knew well that there had always been a tradition of "know-nothingism" in America, but what especially infuriated him, he told
Hook, was that anti-intellectualism was now being advanced in the
name of socialism or Marxism. Did current literary academics not know
that Marx, and Trotsky too, were steeped in the culture of the past,
Howe asked, and that both respected, indeed, "adored the Greeks and
Shakespeare." Irving thought Hook would be amused "to know that in

discussing this whole matter with a younger 'leftist' colleague I mentioned in passing that Marx had admired Balzac. He refused to believe it! *Geh zei a khokhem!* [So go be a teacher!]"[62]

Howe, who continued, after his retirement in 1986, to supervise doctoral dissertations at CUNY and to deliver guest lectures at various universities, thought that many of his liberal colleagues were "gutless." They recognized the value of the traditional curriculum but were unwilling to defend their convictions against attacks by "guerrillas with tenure" and challenges by newly "radicalized" students. But Howe told Hook, who was already embattled at Stanford, that he saw a fight coming on the issue in the Northeast. "And," he said, "I mean to get into it as soon as I can."[63] In the course of their shared struggle, both Howe and Hook became more aware of their minority position in the academic world. Hook told Howe "it is really a lonely world for me." For Howe there was no public self-pity, but he did grumble some about his apparent displacement from the college speaking circuit and he told a colleague he thought his "place" as a literary critic was being eclipsed. He also complained to Hook that even among *Dissent* readers (at least among those who wrote letters) almost no one took his side despite his balanced position in the battle over the curriculum.[64]

Although Howe, as we saw in chapter 11, was relatively conservative in his literary tastes, he had long appreciated the fact that the canon was not "handed down from Sinai." A fixed and unalterable "list" of great writers, or some unimaginative interpretation of excellence, Howe knew, was stultifying to creativity, to literature, and to education generally. He called for "certain expansions," suggesting, for example, the "eloquent" writings of Frederick Douglass, and W.E.B. Dubois's "wonderful" autobiography. He even implied that some books could be dropped because they had grown stale or, as important, were nearly impossible to teach without wholesale historical annotation.[65]

It was irritating enough that the self-proclaimed Marxists had replaced the traditional goal of taking over governments with the new one of taking over English departments. But their dismissal of Tolstoy, Dickens, Jane Austen, and Emily Dickinson as mere instruments of class oppression was for Howe the height of arrogance and ignorance. Many writers in the canon, including Chekhov, Balzac, George Eliot, and Melville, were critical of their own societies. Moreover, even those great writers who had not directly confronted the social ills of their time were important to read, Howe argued, so that students "may learn to enjoy the activity of mind, the pleasure of forms, the beauty of language—in short, the arts in their own right."[66]

Howe had entered the fray in behalf of this literature and in opposition to the new breed of literary theorists who seemed to hate fiction and to write about poetry and prose in such mind-boggling "verbal opacity" that they could barely be understood even by their own colleagues. The "Marxists," Howe said with bitter humor, seemed to refuse to "speak in English, a language that for some time served criticism well." The new critical theories and the impenetrable jargon in which they were couched surely alienated the educated layperson. Indeed, Howe's "common reader" was left entirely in the dark. And so were most students, especially since their politically correct teachers, if and when they actually got down to teaching literature rather than theory, Howe said, tended mostly to "expose" writing as a weapon of class, gender, and racial domination—or, they used it as a tool to raise students' self-esteem.[67]

"Is there not something grossly patronizing," Howe wondered, in using literature to raise self-esteem by having black students, for example, read only black authors, or Latino students, Latino authors? Are only white middle-class students, he asked, capable of appreciating diverse literary works? And he reminded readers that Richard Wright had found sustenance in Theodore Dreiser; Ralph Ellison in Hemingway; and Chinua Achebe in Eliot. Perhaps, Howe suggested, there are other yet unknown young Wrights, Ellisons, and Achebes in the universities "who might also want to find their way to an individually achieved sense of culture?"[68]

What the new "Marxists" propose to do in the classroom in order to raise self-esteem, Howe insisted, will have the effect of denying to the masses of ordinary people a common human heritage and will train large segments of the population into "the stupefaction of accepting, even celebrating, their cultural deprivations." This, Howe said, is what true radicals had struggled against for centuries. Genuine radicalism, and certainly democratic socialism, he argued, had fought cultural dilution and dispossession, and had stressed instead enrichment and accessibility through universal education.

Not only socialists, but liberals and democrats, had battled hard to make learning available to everyone. Howe was quite ready to admit that winning that battle had created difficult problems in teaching. But he had always been ready to help students rise to the level of the classics (even as he extended the definition of the term) rather than assume that ordinary young people needed something easier or more "relevant." Even while shaken by the extent of student ignorance, Howe was "often moved by their willingness to work."[69] As early as 1982 he said that "the socialist idea contains the expectation that the plebes, the common workers, can gradually rise to articulation and authority." If you deny that idea, he warned, "you threaten not only the hope of socialism but the basis of democracy." To underscore his egalitarianism, Howe was fond of telling a story about "Big" Bill Haywood, the leader of the old Industrial Workers of the World who was once, in the early 1920s, seen smoking 25-cent cigars. When journalists teased the union head about this indulgence, Haywood replied: "Boys, nothing's too good for the proletariat."[70] For Howe, that definitely included an education in the best that human culture had to offer.

With the "common reader," if not the proletariat, in mind, Howe had, over the years, worked to remake his own writing style. He tried to move from a dazzling virtuoso prose, full of polemical thrusts, to what he called the difficult "discipline of the plain style," from the self-conscious brilliance of the New York intellectuals to greater and greater lucidity in his own voice.[71] In the pieces he did on Milan Kundera, Nadine Gordimer, Gabriel Garcia Marquez, and others, for a revised version of *Politics and the Novel* (1992), and in the short essays he wrote in the 1990s on Dickens, Chekhov, Tolstoy, and Kipling, which were gathered together by Nicholas Howe in *A Critic's Notebook* (1994), Howe achieved a language less adorned and more luminous. The "spare style" of these essays, all of which originate from a passion, a moral striving, and an abiding faith in the common reader, was meant, Irving intimated, "as a political challenge to the obscurantist prose of academic criticism." The substance of his *shtiklakh*—on the novel, the self in literature, characterization, anecdotes, and tone in fiction—is imaginative and provocative. The affectionate "morsels" record the pleasure of thinking about novels and suggest "that there should be no last words on writers and subjects we love."[72]

Howe also felt that there should be no last words on the idea of socialism. He continued during his final years to rethink "the name of his desire," especially in the context of the fall of Communism beginning in 1989. As early as September 1988, Howe and others at *Dissent* suggested that the Communist movement, in deep trouble economically and politically, had everywhere entered a profound and "perhaps final crisis." There was reason, Howe thought, to look forward to the 1990s as a time of some reform in the more industrialized Communist countries and to new social and intellectual currents in Eastern Europe—and "by ricochet" in Western Europe too. "It's rather good," Howe said, "to be alive."[73]

He was delighted with the direction of reform in Gorbachev's Soviet Union. He took heart, too, in June 1989 from the spontaneous uprising of Chinese students at Tiananmen Square, as well as in November from the fall of the twenty-eight-year-old wall separating Communist East Berlin from the western half of the city. He was more convinced now that totalitarianism did not *absolutely* exclude political movement in the form of "action from below or reform from above," an idea he explored further in "Totalitarianism Reconsidered" (1991), a brilliantly original essay and another example of Howe's willingness to change his mind.[74]

By December 1991, astonishing as it still seems, that precise combination of "action from below" and "reform from above" dismantled the Soviet Union completely and liberated the satellite states. From the beginning of the three-year process, Howe had looked forward to a not-too-distant time "when a socialist left in Europe and elsewhere" no longer has to "carry the burden of being (mis)identified with communism."[75] In this he was disappointed almost from the start. Instead of validating the anti-Communist democratic socialists, the continuing events in Eastern Europe elicited a widespread and "loud cacophony" from people proclaiming the "failure of socialism" and embracing the "free market."[76]

These developments depressed Howe and added to the gloom he was still feeling over the untimely death of Michael Harrington in 1989. In November of that year, in the very week the Berlin Wall had fallen, Howe, burdened by his own newly diagnosed heart condition, gave the keynote presentation at the Democratic Socialists of America convention in Baltimore. Irving was stooped at the podium, the little hair he had left had turned white, and, according to several observers, he "looked not just travel-weary but grief stricken." In his address, a morose, chiding speech, Howe told the democratic socialists that they had to work diligently and relatively quickly to reconstruct their group, to make themselves into tireless activists and the kind of experts on social policy that Harrington had been. "Or else," he said, "the DSA would become a collection of nice, irrelevant people who like to get together once a year or so."[77]

One member of the audience claimed that the collapse of Communism, which was happening at that very moment, would mean a revival for democratic socialism all over the world. "My friend," Irving said, in seeming contradiction to his relatively recent hopefulness, "you are living in a dream."[78] But as usual with Howe, who never gave up hope entirely, this negative mood also passed. As popular uprisings emerged against Communist dictatorships in East Germany, Bulgaria, Czechoslovakia, and other parts of Eastern Europe in the winter of 1990, Howe saw "a possibility that a new generation of thinkers will emerge to give the idea of democratic socialism a new urgency and strength. Meanwhile as we watch the events . . . with amazement and hope, there is plenty of work to do."[79]

Howe did not deny for a moment that socialism was "in a state of crisis" all over the world. Indeed, just as he had in 1954 when he started *Dissent*, Howe said, that as an idea and as a movement, socialism needs reconsideration and even "reinvention." For some time it "will probably exist primarily in the sphere of thought and vision." But "even in that limited form," Howe argued again in 1991, socialism can be a "valuable guide to human action." And he hoped that in the coming years social-democratic movements would "contribute significantly to determining in Eastern Europe, *though not there alone*, the social content of a resurgent liberal society."[80]

Here Howe stood until he died two years later. He did show some renewed interest in the concept of "market socialism," a decentralized hybrid system in which the most important means of production and distribution are owned by worker cooperatives or public communities, but where a market mechanism gauges demand and sets levels of production and distribution as well as prices. For the most part, however, Howe pushed for an extension of the welfare state, while at the same time envisioning and working for a much more egalitarian society for the long term. That we speak about "immediate needs," he insisted, by no means eliminates "the need for a larger socialist perspective."[81]

Irving's last years, from 1991 to May 1993, were filled with the things he had always valued—socialist politics, Yiddishkayt, reading, writing, music, ballet, baseball, friends, and family. He stayed relatively active with DSA, where he helped to groom new leadership. He continued his work with *Dissent*, editing, writing, and recruiting younger contributors, including former members of the SDS. He also wrote more than two dozen literary and political essays. There were trips with Ilana to Israel and Paris, and for rest and relaxation they went to the town of Blue Hill on Penobscot Bay in Maine. Howe continued to spend time with his children, and by 1993 with two grandchildren, Nina's Anastasia and Nicholas, in whom he took great delight.[82] From 1990 on, however, illness increasingly brought him face to face with his own mortality.

Even in the early eighties Howe had confessed to thinking frequently about death, not so much in fear of a sudden fatal heart attack as frightened by the idea of "eternal extinction."[83] After "a rattling period of physical infirmity" in 1990 and 1991, death became less of an abstraction.[84] But Howe did not seem unprepared. "Something happened to me in Paris that you might understand," Howe told his friend Leon Wieseltier on a gray September morning in 1991. "I was in the garden at the Rodin Museum. For a few minutes I was alone, sitting on a stone bench between two long hedges of roses. Pink roses. Suddenly I felt the most powerful feeling of peace, and I had the thought that death, if it means an absorption into a reality like the one that was before me, might be all right."[85]

Howe's physical condition grew even worse in 1992, when he had three successive operations—for his heart, for an abdominal aneurysm, and for an enlarged prostate. Through it all and into 1993 Howe battled crankiness and depression, but he remained committed and involved, even giving a number of public talks. As late as March 1993 he spoke at Hunter College on the future of American Jewish identity, and he was scheduled to talk in July at the DSA youth conference in Ohio.[86] He even sat for a series of interviews with filmmaker Joseph Dorman for "Arguing the World" (1997), a documentary about the New York intellectuals in which CCNY graduates Howe, Bell, Glazer and Kristol (going from Left to Right!) are featured.

Bell and Kristol had been close for a time in the sixties, as Dorman's film shows. But a little later, Bell, and to some extent Glazer too, cut their ties with Kristol and others on the Right. Howe had recruited Kristol into Trotskyism at CCNY in 1937, but he had long since distanced himself from his increasingly conservative college classmate. Unlike Howe, Kristol had come to blame "permissiveness," "secularization," and "welfare dependence" for the decline of American life and culture without ever indicting corporate greed and destructiveness for America's social problems. On screen Howe said, "There is a tie that binds all the people that fifty years ago were in Alcove 1 at City College. With people like Danny Bell . . . and even someone like Nate Glazer . . . I do feel very strong ties." But with Kristol, who has become "a spokesman for corporate interests, I feel no . . . tie whatever. . . . I look at him as a political opponent. . . . I wish him well personally, a long life," Howe said with an impish smile. "With many political failures, I hope."[87]

During these very last months, Howe also finished his revisions for *Politics and the Novel* (1992), and most of his short essays for *A Critic's Notebook* (1994). In one of those pieces, on Tolstoy, Howe could easily have been writing about himself:

> Reading the aged Tolstoy stirs the heart. He will not yield to time, sloth and nature. He clings to the waist of the life force. Deep into old age, he battles the world, more often with himself, returning in his diaries, fictions, and tracts to the unanswerable questions that torment him. . . . "And what truth can there be," [Tolstoy] demands of Chekhov, "if there is death?" Death will not pass him by, and its certainty dissolves all claims to meaning. . . . Yet a need for meaning allows him no rest, and finally it overcomes, provisionally, the absurdity in which he thinks all must end.[88]

Howe certainly shared Tolstoy's restlessness of mind and "need for meaning," and he continued until his final days to search for and find meaning in key places. In his very last (nonposthumously) published piece, for example, Howe recognized the significance of physical resistance to the Nazis and showed renewed respect for forceful struggle against compulsory segregation and murder. In 1944, from the army, Howe had written to Al Glotzer about the Warsaw ghetto uprising of 1943 saying, "how nobly and heroically did the Jews fight, for once!" Now, nearly fifty years later, he was reading, over a period of several months, about the "extraordinary" young men and women who mounted the uprising. From a military point of view, Howe concluded, the event was of little importance, but from what he ventured to call "a human point of view, its significance is beyond calculation." These "kids," Howe said, had become for him "an abiding part of consciousness."[89]

In the early nineties Howe also found meaning in his reawakened "utopian thinking." As always he found abhorrent those versions of utopia based on coercion or terror. And he continued to insist that "the communist movement" meant the destruction of entire generations and an enormous waste of human resources. But he reminded himself that not all utopians were thugs or villains. In "Two Cheers for Utopia" (1993), an essay remarkable for its candid reappraisal, Howe, the lifelong anti-Communist, admitted that for many ordinary people Communism had burned with the flames of idealism and hope. And he himself persisted in envisioning a better society, one that transcended the "nasty, brutish and short" existence promoted by unmitigated competition, one grounded in fraternity and equality as well as liberty.[90]

Howe understood that there is an inescapable tension between liberty and equality. Try to enforce equality by coercive methods, Howe said, and liberty suffers; allow sufficient liberty and society will become increasingly inegalitarian. "Surely if we had to choose between liberty and equality," he predicted, "we socialists would choose liberty." Not only is liberty the very medium of civilized life, Howe insisted, but with it the struggle for greater equality becomes possible; while without liberty, as we have seen too often "in Russia, China, and Cuba, the only kind of egalitarianism is one imposed by an authoritarian elite, which is to say, no egalitarianism at all." But so stark a choice is not necessary, Howe thought. Indeed, as his writings over four decades make clear, he believed that liberty and equality were not only compatible but interdependent. He agreed with Michael Walzer, who said, "[T]he case is exactly as socialists have always claimed; . . . liberty and equality are the two virtues of social institutions and they stand best when they stand together."[91]

In democratic socialism, Howe saw the potential for the two virtues to stand together in fuller realization of liberal values. He was far from certain that socialism would ever be more than a marginal phenomenon in America. But he believed that some form of democratic radicalism was necessary in order to achieve greater human fulfillment. To give up this kind of utopian vision, Howe thought, would not only leave many injustices unchallenged, it would be a failure of the imagination. It would turn against the entire experience of humanity, which needs the dream of community and egalitarianism, Howe argued, as much as it needs the reality of bread and shelter.[92]

Meaning, for Howe, was derived too from his "entanglement in difficulty." He could, for example, puzzle over novels like Dostoevsky's *The Possessed*, which he judged "both a great work of literature and also ... a distorted even malicious treatment of its subject." Dostoevsky was himself entangled, Howe thought, in an ideological dilemma. The great Russian writer professed a kind of primitive Christianity at odds with radicalism, but his background and temperament, Howe said, moved him to identify at least subconsciously with the repressed political radicals of his day. Critical of both the establishment and the underworld, Dostoevsky in *The Possessed* spared no character his ridicule. His rich, intricate psychological portraits created a brilliant novel, Howe thought, "entirely subversive in effect." It was also a beautifully rendered work of art. And Howe could read it, he told Mitchell Cohen at lunch the Sunday before he died, with nearly "unalloyed joy" as well as with a sense of its inherent complexity and a powerful awareness of the aesthetic difficulty it created. This "tangle," Howe said, is "exactly where I want to remain, since I believe it is faithful to the actual experience of reading such novels."[93]

Howe was also still creatively entangled in the early nineties with the definition of his own Jewishness. Leon Wieseltier remembers many breakfasts with Irving, at "Leo's" on East 86th Street, which were taken up with discussions about the "decline of secular Jewishness." Howe was without nostalgia, Wieseltier said, but not without anguish over the eclipse of Yiddish and of the "world of our fathers." To the end, even in his last public lecture, Howe wrestled with the question of Jewish identity, concluding ultimately that the wrestling itself was "the very mark" of that identity.[94]

Irving Howe was a man of ardent loyalties—to the secular Jewish tradition, represented mainly by Yiddish culture and the pursuit of social justice; to socialism, both as a fulfillment of that tradition and as a profound extension of democracy; and to liberal arts education, as both a way forward and a stout link to the past. He was committed to literature as a dynamic force in society, not just in politics, but in the heart and conscience. And he never gave up on the imagination as an active element in human affairs. In the days before his death from a burst abdominal aneurysm, Howe was still passionately engaged with the next article, the next lecture on literature, the next speech for an audience of socialists.

In late April, only a week before he died on May 5, 1993, Irving and Ilana were out to lunch or dinner with friends several times. Irving seemed much improved and conversed, unsurprisingly, about politics and literature. He talked about the late works of Tolstoy, that "blessed old magician . . . free of literary posture and the sins of eloquence," and about Walt Whitman, a poet Howe "loved for his egalitarian sympathies and his New York stories."[95] Howe's creative imagination and curiosity were still alive. He asked many questions and sincerely courted opinion. And he waxed eloquent about the value of commitment and comradeship. Complaining a little, too, Howe talked about the state of "higher education" and the frayed intellectual quality of current socialist thinking. But he continued to explore possibilities for rebuilding the movement. Like Tolstoy again, Howe could have said, "It's time to die and I'm still thinking things up." And like Walt Whitman, Howe, too, was "loth to depart," and "garrulous to the end."[96]

His family, friends, and colleagues thought that after three operations Irving's health was stable, and they were shocked by his sudden passing. He is still sorely missed by them. In the literary and political world at large, many feel the loss of his integrity, his luminous intelligence, his radical imagination, his abiding *menshlikhkayt*, his skillful editorial diplomacy, and his consistently critical but supportive spurs to productivity and creativity.[97]

Years after his death Howe's name continues to circulate in segments of society interested in literature and still dedicated to "repairing the world" and improving the human condition on all levels. And around the table at *Dissent* meetings, through the late nineties and into the new century, writers and editors, in periods of discouragement, reminded one another that Irving Howe would have told them to stand fast for social justice and for faith in the intellect. Perhaps most of all they took heart in recalling Howe's "margin of hope" for a more democratic, more humane future.[98]

Notes

NOTES TO THE PREFACE

1. Todd Gitlin, "Irving Howe (1920–1993)," *Tikkun* 8 (July 1993): 38–39.

2. Irving Howe, *A Margin of Hope: An Intellectual Autobiography* (New York: Harcourt Brace Jovanovich, 1982), 263.

3. Ibid., 287; Howe, "T. E. Lawrence: The Problem of Heroism," in *A World More Attractive* (New York: Horizon Press, 1963), 1–39.

4. Irving Howe, quoted in Stanley Kunitz, ed., *Twentieth Century Authors, First Supplement: A Biographical Dictionary of Modern Literature* (New York: Wilson, 1967), 464; *Margin of Hope*, 9, 13; Howe, *World of Our Fathers* (New York: Harcourt Brace Jovanovich, 1976), 225–229.

5. Sanford Pinsker, "Lost Causes/Marginal Hopes: The Collected Elegies of Irving Howe," *Virginia Quarterly Review* 65 (Spring 1989): 585–99.

6. *Margin of Hope*, 345.

7. Irving Howe, "American Jews and Israel," *Tikkun* 4 (December 1988): 71–74.

8. The title of Howe's essay in *Commentary* 2 (October 1946): 361–367.

9. Michael Walzer, "Irving Howe 1920–1993," *Dissent* 40 (Summer 1993): 275–276; Gitlin, "Irving Howe," 39.

10. Daniel Bell, "Remembering Irving Howe," *Dissent* 40 (Fall 1993): 518.

11. Howe, "Silone and the Radical Conscience," *Dissent* 3 (Winter 1956): 74.

NOTES TO CHAPTER I

1. Irving Howe, interviewed by Susanne Klingenstein (audiotape, December 12, 1988).

2. Alfred Kazin, interviewed by author, May 15, 1997; Daniel Bell, interviewed by author, October 30, 1998.

3. Irving Howe, "The Range of New York Intellectuals," in Bernard Rosenberg, ed., *Creators and Disturbers: Reminiscences by Jewish Intellectuals of New York* (New York: Columbia University Press, 1982), 265; Howe, "Lost Young Intellectual: Marginal Man Twice Alienated, *Commentary* 2 (October 1946): 364.

4. Howe, "The Range of the New York Intellectuals," 285.

5. Daniel Bell, "Reflections on Jewish Identity," in Peter Rose, ed., *Ghetto and Beyond: Essays on Jewish Life in America* (New York: Random House, 1969), 472; "Talk with Lionel Trilling," *New York Times Book Review*, February 13, 1955, 21.

6. Howe, "Lost Young Intellectual"; Howe, *A Margin of Hope: An Intellectual Autobiography* (New York: Harcourt Brace Jovanovich, 1982), 114; Howe, "Range," 279.

7. The theme of filial alienation and shame was pervasive in Jewish American cultural expression in the first half of the twentieth century, especially in Anzia Yezierska's stories of immigrant life collected as *Children of Loneliness* (1923), Henry Roth's *Call It Sleep* (1934), Isaac Rosenfeld's *Passage from Home* (1946), and Saul Bellow's *Seize the Day* (1956).

8. Howe, "New Black Writers," *Harper's* (December 1969), 131.

9. Howe, "New York in the Thirties: Some Fragments of Memory," *Dissent* 8 (Summer 1961): 243, 242; Howe, *Margin*, 112; Howe, interviewed by Susanne Klingenstein (audiotape, December 12, 1988).

10. Howe, "Range," 265.

11. Howe, "Range," 269–270.

12. Howe, interviewed by Joseph Dorman (unpublished transcript, Janaury 1993), 1.

13. Howe, "Range," 239.

14. "Jews of New York," typescript, in Works Progress Administration, Jewish Communities, Box 3632.

15. Beth Wenger, *New York Jews and the Great Depression* (New Haven: Yale University Press, 1996), 91–93; Kate Simon, *Bronx Primitive: Portraits in a Childhood* (New York: Viking, 1982); Ruth Gay, *Unfinished People: Eastern European Jews Encounter America* (New York: W. W. Norton, 1996); Lucy Dawidowicz, *From That Place and Time: A Memoir, 1938–1947* (New York: W. W. Norton, 1989).

16. Howe, "Range," 266–267; Wenger, *New York Jews*, 92.

17. Howe, "Range," 266–267.

18. Ibid., 269; Howe, *Margin*, 2–5.

19. Howe, *World of Our Fathers* (New York: Harcourt Brace Jovanovich, 1976), 256–257. This was true not only for the Jewish children who became storekeepers and garment manufacturers, but also for many of the writers and professors, like Irving Howe. It is no accident that the group known as the New York Intellectuals wrote with polemical ferocity, talked faster than anyone else, and often, in their fervency, used rudeness to attack complacency.

20. Howe, "Immigrant Chic," *New York Magazine*, May 12, 1986, 76–77; Howe, *Margin*, 7; Howe, quoted in Stanley Kunitz, ed., *Twentieth Century Authors, First Supplement: A Biographical Dictionary of Modern Literature* (New York: Wilson, 1967), 464.

21. Howe, "Imagining Labor," *New Republic*, April 11, 1981, 33; Howe, interviewed by Joseph Dorman (unpublished transcript, January 1993), 1.

22. Howe, "Range," 268; Howe, "Imagining Labor," 33.

23. Howe, interviewed by Elenor Lester, *The Jewish Week*, Janaury 4, 1976; Howe, "Range," 267.

24. Howe, Margin, 5.

25. Howe, "Imagining Labor," 33.

26. Howe, "New York in the Thirties," 243; Howe, "Imagining Labor," 33.

27. Howe, interviewed by Joseph Dorman (unpublished transcript, January 1993), 4; Howe, "Range," 270.

28. Ibid.

29. As in the old countries so in America boys far more often than girls were encouraged to stay in school and do well there. Women in the Jewish world, as in many traditional societies, were seen as future wives and mothers; and formal learning, until the middle of the twentieth century, remained the near-monopoly of Jewish males.

30. Alfred Kazin, *Walker in the City* (New York: Harcourt Brace and Company, 1951), 21.

31. Howe, "Of Fathers and Sons," *Commentary* 2 (August 1946): 190–192; Kazin, *Walker*, 21.

32. Howe, letter, to Lenore Marshall, n.d., 1969, Columbia University Manuscript Collections.

33. Ibid., Howe, *Margin*, 7, 4.

34. Howe, *Margin*, 4.

35. Ibid., 5; Howe, quoted in Stanley Kunitz, ed., *Twentieth Century Authors*; Howe, "Range," 269–270.

36. Howe, *Margin*, 7–8.

37. Howe, "New York in the Thirties," 244.

38. Howe, "Range," 269.

39. Howe, *Margin*, 9.

40. Ibid.

41. Alfred Kazin, *Starting Out in the Thirties*, 4; Alfred Kazin, interviewed by author, May 15, 1997; Daniel Bell, interviewed by author, October 30, 1998. Joseph Dorman, *Arguing the World: The New York Intellectuals in Their Own Words* (New York: Free Press, 2000).

42. Howe, interviewed by Joseph Dorman (unpublished transcript, 1993), 1.

43. Howe, *Margin*, 12–14; Howe, interviewed by Joseph Dorman (unpublished transcript, 1993), 4, 2.

44. Howe, *Margin*, 24.

45. Howe, "New York in the Thirties," 241.

46. Howe, *Margin*, 14.

47. Jews voted very heavily for Franklin Delano Roosevelt in 1928 when he ran, successfully, for governor of New York State against a Jewish candidate. On the question of historic Jewish liberalism, see Arthur Liebman, "The Ties That Bind: The Jewish Support of the Left in the U.S.," *American Jewish Historical Quarterly* 74 (September 1984): 45–65; Daniel Elazar, "American Political Theory and the Political Notions of American Jews: Convergences and Contradictions," in *The Ghetto and Beyond*; Stephen J. Whitfield, "The Radical Persuasion in American Jewish History," *Judaism* 32 (Spring 1983): 136–152.

48. Gerald Sorin, *The Prophetic Minority: American Jewish Immigrant Radicals, 1880–1920* (Bloomington: Indiana University Press, 1985); Nathan Glazer, *The Social Bases of American Communism* (New York: Harcourt Brace, 1961).

49. This was very much the case with so-called "Red Diaper Babies." For more on this see Paul Mishler, *Raising Reds: The Young Pioneers, Radical Summer Camps, and Communist Political Culture* (New York: Columbia University Press, 1999).

50. Robert Cohen, *When the Old Left Was Young* (New York: Oxford University Press, 1993), 258.

51. Howe, Margin, 25, 14.

52. Robert Cohen, *When the Old Left Was Young*, 259; Ilene Philipson, *Ethel Rosenberg: Beyond the Myths* (New Brunswick, NJ: Rutgers University Press, 1993), 103, 181, 256–258, 354.

NOTES TO CHAPTER 2

1. Irving Howe, "The Range of the New York Intellectuals," in Bernard Rosenberg, ed., *Creators and Disturbers: Reminiscences by Jewish Intellectuals of New York* (New York: Columbia University Press, 1982), 274.

2. Howe, "New York in the Thirties: Some Fragments of Memory," *Dissent* (Summer 1961): 245.

3. Howe, "The Range of the New York Intellectuals," 275.

4. Howe, "The Value of the Canon," *New Republic*, February 18, 1991, 46; Howe, "The Range of the New York Intellectuals," 280.

5. Howe, "The Range of the New York Intellectuals," 275.

6. Morris Freedman, "CCNY Days," in *City at the Center*, ed. Betty Rizzo and Barry Wallerstein (New York: City College of New York, 1983), 64; Irving Kristol, "Memoirs of a Trotskyist," *New York Times Magazine*, January 23, 1977, 50.

7. Ibid.; Howe, *A Margin of Hope: An Intellectual Autobiography* (New York: Harcourt Brace Jovanovich, 1982), 59–65; Meyer Liben, "CCNY—A Memoir," *Commentary* 40 (September 1965): 64–70; Daniel Bell, "Remembering Irving Howe," *Dissent* 40 (Fall 1993): 517–518; Israel Kugler, "Irving Howe" (unpublished typescript, 1993); Freedman, "CCNY Days," 66–68.

8. Bell quoted in Joseph Dorman, *Arguing the World: The New York Intellectuals in Their Own Words* (New York: Free Press, 2000), 46; Liben, "CCNY—A Memoir," 65.

9. Robert Cohen, *When the Old Left Was Young* (New York: Oxford University Press, 1993).

10. S. Willis Rudy, *The College of the City of New York: A History* (New York: City College Press, 1949); James Traub, *City on a Hill: Testing the American Dream at City College* (New York: Addison-Wesley, 1994), 33–39; Freedman, "CCNY Days," 63, and several other essays in Rizzo and Wallerstein, *City at the Center*.

11. Howe, interviewed by Joseph Dorman (unpublished transcript, 1993), 16; Howe, "Range," 276.

12. Kugler, "Irving Howe."

13. Kristol, "Memoirs," 55. Howe also apparently had relatively long eye-teeth that resembled fangs. Later, he had them filed down.

14. Jeremy Larner, "Remembering Irving Howe," *Dissent* 40 (Fall 1993), 540; Larner, interviewed by author (June 19, 1997); Daniel Bell, letter to author, January 28, 2001; Howe, interviewed by Joseph Dorman, 7.

15. Dorman, *Arguing the World*, 2.

16. Ibid., 2, 51; Israel Kugler, letter to Author, January 24, 2001.

17. Howe, *Margin*, 66.

18. Ibid., 35.

19. Ibid., 34.

20. Howe, *Steady Work: Essays in the Politics of Democratic Radicalism* (New York: Harcourt, Brace and World, 1966), 117–155; Howe, *Leon Trotsky* (New York: Viking, 1978).

21. A "social democrat" is someone who supports a form of capitalism—the better, more humane capitalism of the welfare state, with a redistributive, progressive tax policy, activist unionism, and safety-net legislation, but still capitalism, where there are significant concentrations of power in private hands through control of wealth. A "democratic socialist" is one who looks forward to and works for fundamental changes in the structure of the economy, a different system—a decentralized, democratic system in which there is much more worker ownership and cooperative enterprise, as distinct from coercive state ownership, on the one hand, and excessive concentrations of private ownership, on the other. The goal of the democratic socialist is the continuous extension of the welfare state, toward greater social provision in the hope that there well be an eventual transition—not guaranteed, but desired—toward social fraternity and social equality.

22. Bell, "Remembering Irving Howe," 518; Bell, interviewed by author, October 30, 1998.

23. Howe, interviewed by Joseph Dorman, 11.

24. Howe, "New York in the Thirties," 248–249.

25. Leon Trotsky, *The Defense of Terrorism*, trans. H. N. Brailsford (London: Allen and Unwin, 1921), 35, 60.

26. Kugler, "Irving Howe."

27. Many of the "popular front" students belonged to the American Student Union, which was mainly a by-product of the call for antifascist unity by the Comintern's Seventh World Congress in 1935. Roosevelt, earlier denounced by American Communists as a "social fascist," was now a leader to be praised.

28. Howe quoted in Joseph Dorman, *Arguing the World*, 81.

29. Leaflets (1937–1938), archives of the library of the City University of New York; Kugler, "Irving Howe."

30. Cohen, *When the Old Left Was Young*, 170.

31. After the Nazi-Soviet pact, the Communist student movement, having chosen loyalty to Stalin over loyalty to antifascism, lost whatever small amount of self-direction and sense of political reality it once possessed and became even more dogmatic and Moscow-responsive.

32. Howe, interviewed by Joseph Dorman, 8.

33. Ibid., 17.

34. Howe, "New York in the Thirties," 244–245; Howe, "Range," 278–279.

35. Howe, "Range," 278; Alexander Bloom, *Prodigal Sons: The New York Intellectuals and Their World* (New York: Oxford University Press, 1986), 34.

36. Howe, *World of Our Fathers* (New York: Harcourt Brace Jovanovich, 1976), 384–385.

37. Howe, "New York in the Thirties," 243–244.

38. Ibid.; Howe, "Range," 276. Howe graduated as a Bachelor of Social Science, a degree no longer granted at CCNY.

39. Howe, "Range," 277–281.

40. Howe, "Noah Greenberg," *Dissent* 13 (May–June 1966): 225; James Gollin, *Pied Piper: The Many Lives of Noah Greenberg* (Hillsdale, N.Y.: Pendragon Press, 2001), 7, 35, 41–43; Nicholas Howe, "Remembering Irving Howe," *Dissent* 40 (Fall 1993): 532–533; Leon Wieseltier, "Remembering Irving Howe (1920–93)," *New York Times Book Review*, May 9, 1993.

41. Leon Trotsky, *Literature and Revolution* (New York: Russell and Russell, 1957), 215–255.

42. Kristol, "Memoirs," 57; Howe, "Range," 281; Howe, "Noah Greenberg," 225; Howe, "New York in the Thirties," 242; Howe, *Margin*, 56–57.

43. Nicholas Howe, letter to author, June 7, 2001.

44. Rickie (Kimmel) Flanders quoted in Gollin, *Pied Piper*, 43; Phyllis and Julius Jacobson, interviewed by author, March 17, 1997.

45. Howe, *Margin*, 43–45. On relations between men and women in the 1920s and 1930s, see Paula Fass, *The Damned and the Beautiful* (New York: Oxford University Press, 1977), especially 200–203, 218, and 265–269; and Riv-Ellen

Prell, *Fighting to Become Americans: Assimilation and the Trouble between Jewish Women and Jewish Men* (Boston: Beacon Press, 1999), 1–5.

46. Howe, "Range," 280; Howe, interviewed by Joseph Dorman, 8.

NOTES TO CHAPTER 3

1. Irving Howe, *A Margin of Hope: An Intellectual Autobiography* (New York: Harcourt Brace Jovanovich, 1982), 83.

2. Paul Buhle, ed., *The Legacy of the Workers Party, 1940–1949: Recollections and Reflections* (New York: Tamiment Institute, 1985), 1, 12.

3. *New York Times*, April 23, May 1, May 5, May 20, 1936, and March 6, 16, 17, 1941; Israel Kugler, "Irving Howe" (unpublished typescript, 1993); Kugler, letter to author, May 3, 2001.

4. Howe, "The Frauds of Louis Fischer," *New International* 7 (October 1941): 240–244.

5. Howe, "The Free World of Bankrupts," *New International* 7 (October 1941): 254–255.

6. *Labor Action*, December 15, 1941, 1.

7. Howe, *Margin of Hope*, 88.

8. Howe, letter to Albert Glotzer, February 26, 1945, Glotzer Collection, Box 12, Hoover Institution, Stanford University. Howe was also a member of World War II American Veterans Committee founded by a handful of left-leaning political and intellectual figures, including cartoonist Bill Mauldin, writer Thornton Wilder, labor activist Gus Tyler, and even Ronald Reagan. The future president did not remain in the organization for long. But Howe stayed long enough to help Tyler prevent a Communist takeover of the group. Bernard Bellush, "Writing—and Living—the History of America's Left," *Forward*, October 12, 2001, 2; Bellush, letter to author, October 18, 2001.

9. Howe, "Liberals State Their Program of Bankruptcy," *Labor Action*, December 29, 1941, 3.

10. Quoted in Sidney Hook, *Out of Step: An Unquiet Life in the 20th Century* (New York: Harper and Row, 1987), 302–303.

11. Howe, "Exposing the Merchants of Death/Their Profits Born in Blood," *Labor Action*, May 4, 1942, 3; Howe, "The Dilemma of Partisan Review," *New International* 8 (February 1942): 20–24.

12. Howe, "Was the Spanish Civil War 'Our Cause,'" *Dissent* 34 (Winter 1987): 99; Howe, "George Orwell: As the Bones Know," *Harper's*, January 1969, 98–103.

13. Howe, "World Politics and North Africa," *New International* 9 (January 1943): 15–17; Howe [R. Fahan], "A Work of Major Significance," *New International* 10 (August 1944): 272; Howe, "Blum and Thorez Support Suppression of Indo-China," *Labor Action*, January 6, 1947, 3; Howe, "Paris, Saigon, New York,"

Labor Action, January 27, 1947, 4; Howe, "World Imperialist Role Now Public Policy," *Labor Action*, March, 24, 1947, 3; Howe, "How Partisan Review Goes to War," *New International* 13 (April 1947): 109–110.

14. Howe, "How Partisan Review Goes to War," 125; Howe, "Minnesota Witch Hunt," *New International* 7 (November 1941): 268–269.

15. Howe, "Poison Gas," *Labor Action*, March 18, 1942, 4; *Labor Action*, March 30, 1942, 3.

16. Howe, letter to the *California Eagle*, reprinted in *Labor Action*, May 25, 1942.

17. Howe, *Margin*, 87.

18. Lucy Dawidowicz, "Indicting the Jews," *Commentary* 75 (June 1983): 43; Howe, letter to *Commentary* 76 (September 1983): 5–6. See also pp. 24–28 for Dawidowicz's reply to Howe and other critics.

19. Howe, letter to Al Glotzer, Summer 1983, Albert Glotzer Collection, Box 40, Hoover Institution; Al Glotzer letter to author, March 9, 1997. After Howe left for the army, Emanuel "Manny" Geltman (party name Emanuel Garrett), who had been editor earlier, returned from California and resumed his post. But he, too, was soon drafted and Glotzer became editor in 1943.

20. Howe, letter to Glotzer, November 18, 1944, Glotzer Collection, Box 12, Hoover Institution.

21. Carole Kessner, ed., *The "Other" New York Jewish Intellectuals* (New York: New York University Press, 1994).

22. Bell quoted in Alexander Bloom, *Prodigal Sons* (New York: Oxford University Press, 1986), 139. Bellow told an interviewer in 1991 that one of the few things he regretted in his long life was not having been more mindful of the Holocaust. When he wrote "The Adventures of Augie March" in Paris in the 1940s, Bellow saw Holocaust survivors everywhere. As a Yiddish speaker he had access to the appalling truths they harbored. But, as Bellow put it, he was not in the mood to listen. "I wanted my American seven-layer cake," he said. He did not want to burden his writing early on in his career with the constraining weight of Jewish history. "Augie March," which made Bellow's reputation, begins, cheerfully, "I am an American." Jonathan Rosen, "The Uncomfortable Question of Anti-Semitism," *New York Times Magazine*, November 4, 2001, 51.

23. Kazin quoted in Bloom, *Prodigal Sons*, 139; Saul Bellow, *Mosby's Memoirs and Other Stories* (New York: Penguin Books, 1971).

24. Alfred Kazin, "In Every Voice, In Every Ban," *New Republic*, January 10, 1944, 45–46.

25. William Phillips, "Irving Howe," *Partisan Review* 60 (Summer 1993): 335–337.

26. Howe, *Margin*, 251; Howe, "The Range of the New York Intellectuals," in Bernard Rosenberg, ed., *Creators and Disturbers: Reminiscences by Jewish Intellectuals of New York* (New York: Columbia University Press 1982), 285.

27. See letters from Howe in the Glotzer Collection, Boxes 12 and 40, Hoover Institution.

28. Howe [as R. F.], "'Brothers under the Skin': Racial Problems in the United States," *New International* 9 (December 1943): 345–347.

29. Howe, "Genocide and Socialism," *Labor Action*, December 29, 1946, 5; Howe, "The Concentrationary Universe," *New International* 13 (September 1947): 220.

30. Howe, "The 13th Disciple," *Politics* 2 (October 1946): 329–334.

31. Howe, "Possibilities for Politics," *Partisan Review* 15 (December 1948): 1356.

32. Howe, *Don't Pay More Rent!* (Long Island City, N.Y.: Workers Party of the United States, 1947); Howe, "How Partisan Review Goes to War," *New International* 13 (April 1947): 110; Howe, "A Party with a Free and Alert Internal Life," *Labor Action*, April 7, 1947, 3.

33. Nicholas Syracopoulos, letters to author, April 19, 1997, and May 14, 1997.

34. Kenneth Libo, interviewed by author, January 30, 1997; Phyllis and Julius Jacobson, interviewed by author, March 17, 1997; Alan Wald, letters to author, March 2 and March 20, 1997; Howe, letter to Al Glotzer, September 13, 1945, Glotzer Collection, Box 12, Hoover Institution.

35. Howe, letter to Al Glotzer, February 26, 1945, Glotzer Collection, Box 12, Hoover Institution.

36. Ibid.; Howe, *Margin*, 97.

37. Howe, *Margin*, 93–94, 100–102.

38. Howe, letter to Al Glotzer, September 13, 1945, Glotzer Collection, Box 12, Hoover Institution.

39. Howe, "Civil War in Austria," *New International* 7 (June 1941): 127–128.

40. Howe, "The Dilemma of *Partisan Review*," 20–24.

41. Howe, "Crumbling Ground," *New International* 8 (February 1942): 31–32.

42. Howe, "Steinbeck Goes to Norway," *New International* 8 (June 1942): 160.

43. Howe [as R. Fahan], "Silone on Marxism and Christianity," *New International* 8 (October 1942): 246–248.

44. Howe [as R. F.], "A New Literary Critic," *New International* 9 (January 1943): 3.

45. Howe, interviewed by Enrique Krauze, in *Personas e ideas* (Mexico: Editorial Vuelte, 1989), 36–37, translated from the Spanish by Myra Sorin; Howe, *Margin*, 95–96.

46. "The Significance of Koestler: An Exchange between Irving Howe and Neil Weiss," *New International* 12 (October 1946): 251–252.

47. Albert Glotzer [as Albert Gates], "On the Significance of Koestler," *New International* 13 (July 1947): 155–158; Howe, "A Reply," *New International* 13 (July

1947): 158–159; Howe [as Theodore Dryden], "Periodicals," *Politics* 4 (January 1947): 31.

48. Leon Trotsky, *Literature and Revolution* (New York: Russell and Russell, 1957), 218.

49. Howe, "A Reply," 159.

50. Howe, *Socialism and America* (New York: Harcourt Brace Jovanovich, 1985), 101.

51. Howe, letter to James T. Farrrell, August 18, 1947, Farrell Papers, Charles Patterson Van Pelt Library, University of Pennsylvania.

52. Howe, "James T. Farrell—The Critic Calcified," *Partisan Review* 14 (September–October 1947): 545–546, 552; Howe, "Philip Rahv: A Memoir," *American Scholar* 48 (Autumn 1979): 490.

53. Howe, interviewed by Krauze, in *Personas e ideas*, 36–37.

54. Even Midge Decter, in an otherwise scurrilous piece on Howe, recognized this. "Socialism and Its Irresponsibilities: The Case of Irving Howe," *Commentary* 74 (December 1982): 28.

55. Howe, interviewed by Joseph Dorman, 14.

NOTES TO CHAPTER 4

1. Howe, letter to Albert Glotzer, November 23, 1945, Glotzer Collection, Box 12, Hoover Institution, Stanford University.

2. Howe, *A Margin of Hope: An Intellectual Autobiography* (New York: Harcourt Brace Jovanovich, 1982), 104.

3. Howe, "The Thirteenth Disciple," *Politics* 3 (October 1946): 329.

4. Howe, *Margin*, 105; Howe, "Social Democracy versus Communism," *New International* 12 (November 1946): 285–286; Howe, *Margin*, 110.

5. Howe, *Margin*, 114; Howe, letter to Dwight Macdonald, July 2, 1946, Macdonald Papers, Manuscripts and Archives, Yale University Library.

6. Howe, *Margin*, 115–116.

7. Howe, "The Thirteenth Disciple," 329. Howe [as R. Fahan], "Machiavelli and Modern Political Thought," *New International* 9 (December 1943): 334–337.

8. Howe, letters to Dwight Macdonald, August 1, 1946, August 12, 1946, Macdonald Papers, Manuscripts and Archives, Yale University Library.

9. Michael Wreszin, *A Rebel in Defense of Tradition: The Life and Politics of Dwight Macdonald* (New York: Basic Books, 1994), 107.

10. Howe, letter to Dwight Macdonald, September 5, 1946, Macdonald Papers, Manuscripts and Archives, Yale University Library.

11. Ibid., September 15, 1946, Macdonald Papers, Manuscripts and Archives, Yale University Library.

12. Phyllis Jacobson, interviewed by author, March 17, 1997; Howe [as Dryden], "Periodicals," *Politics* 4 (March–April 1947)): 63.

13. Howe, letter to Lionel Trilling, June 20, 1950, Trilling Papers, Columbia University.

14. Howe, *Margin*, 122–126.

15. Howe and B. J. Widick, *The UAW and Walter Reuther* (New York: Random House, 1949); Howe and Widick, "The U.A.W. Fights Race Prejudice: Case History on the Industrial Front," *Commentary* 8 (September 1949): 261–268.

16. Howe, "William Faulkner and the Negroes: A Vision of Lost Fraternity," *Commentary* 12 (October 1951): 359–368; Howe, *William Faulkner: A Critical Study* (New York: Random House, 1952); Howe, *A Critic's Notebook* (New York: Harcourt Brace Jovanovich, 1994), 69.

17. Howe, *Margin*, 162; Howe, letter to Horace Gregory, March 9, 1949, Syracuse University.

18. Howe, letter to Lionel Trilling, September 25, 1948, Trilling Papers, Columbia University.

19. Howe, letter to Lionel Trilling, June 8, 1948, Trilling Papers, Columbia University.

20. Howe, *Margin*, 164–165; Mark Shechner, *After the Revolution: Studies in the Contemporary Jewish-American Imagination* (Bloomington: Indiana University Press, 1987): 26–28; James Atlas, *Delmore Schwartz: The Life of an American Poet* (New York: Avon Books, 1978), 265.

21. Marshall Berman, spoken comments at "Irving Howe and His World," a memorial conference in New York City, April 15, 1994.

22. For Delmore Schwartz, see Atlas, *Delmore Schwartz*; and for Berryman, Paul Mariani, *Dream Song: The Life of John Berryman* (New York: W. Morrow, 1990). In the early forties, Schwartz had to dissuade Berryman from jumping off a bridge in Cambridge. Berryman may not have been serious, but his threat was an "eerie foreshadowing of his eventual fate." Atlas, *Delmore Schwartz*, 199. Leslie Fiedler characterized Schwartz and Berryman and many of their intellectual contemporaries as Stradivarius violins with strings vulnerable to snapping at any given moment. James Atlas, *Saul Bellow: A Biography* (New York: Random House, 2000), 179.

23. Howe, letter to Lionel Trilling, September 25, 1948, Trilling Papers, Columbia University.

24. Howe, *The Critical Point* (New York: Horizon Press, 1973), 180.

25. Howe, interviewed by Susanne Klingenstein (audiotape, December 2, 1988).

26. Howe, *Margin*, 169.

27. In an interview in 1989, Bellow admitted to praying, saying, "My prayers are acknowledgment prayers. I acknowledge that I owe my life to the existence of a Great One." Marian Christy, "Bellow's 'Pleasure in Imaginary States,'" *Boston Globe*, November 15, 1989, 81. *Humboldt's Gift* is an artful fiction not to be confused with anyone's "life," but it is obvious that Delmore Schwartz

was at least part of the inspiration for Bellow's Von Humboldt Fleischer. James Atlas, suggests that Bellow, in *Humboldt's Gift*, in the guise of a tribute to Schwartz was actually attacking him. See Atlas, *Bellow*, 84, 429–430. But this is a questionable judgment. Would Bellow take "revenge" on Schwartz by writing, "Ah Humboldt had been great—handsome, high-spirited, buoyant, ingenious, electrical, noble. To be with him made you feel the sweetness of life"?

28. Dennis Wrong, "Remembering Irving Howe," *Dissent* 40 (Fall 1993): 548–549; Dennis Wrong, interviewed by author, October 15, 1997; Howe, *Celebrations and Attacks: Thirty Years of Literary and Cultural Commentary* (New York: Harcourt Brace Jovanovich, 1979), 31. Howe's review of *Invisible Man* appeared originally in *The Nation*, May 10, 1952.

29. Howe, letter to Lionel Trilling, August 24, 1948, Trilling Papers, Columbia University.

30. Ibid., October 23, 1948, Trilling Papers, Columbia University.

31. Howe, *Margin*, 112.

32. Ibid., 113. The conflict between children and parents was a core theme in Jewish American literature in the decades preceding Rosenfeld's novel. Henry Roth's *Call It Sleep*, for example, arguably the most important novel about fathers and sons, was published in 1934. And filial alienation is a central focus also of Anzia Yezierska's collected stories *Children of Loneliness* (1923).

33. Howe, "Lost Young Intellectual: A Marginal Man Twice Alienated," *Commentary* 2 (October 1946): 361–362.

34. Ibid.; Rosenfeld wrote often about Passover, a holiday when, as he saw it, families were alternately rebound and torn apart. See Steven J. Zipperstein, "The First Loves of Isaac Rosenfeld," *Jewish Social Studies* 5 (Fall 1998–Winter 1999): 12–13.

35. Ibid., 367.

36. Ibid.

37. Howe, "Philip Rahv: A Memoir," *American Scholar* 48 (Autumn 1979): 489

38. Howe, "Sholem Aleichem and His People," *Partisan Review* 13 (November–December 1946): 592–594; Howe and Greenberg, eds., *A Treasury of Jewish Stories* (New York: Viking Press, 1954), 28, 37–38.

39. Howe, *Margin*, 119.

40. Eric Glaberson, "Historical Humanism in the Work of Two New York Intellectuals: Irving Howe and Alfred Kazin," New York University, Ph.D. dissertation, 1982, 213.

41. Howe, letter to Lionel Trilling, March 22, 1949, Trilling Papers, Columbia University.

42. Glaberson. "Historical Humanism," 213.

43. Howe, *Margin*, 120. Sometime in the seventies, an eager young scholar about to begin research for a doctoral dissertation told Howe he was going to

show that the New York intellectuals had scratched each other's backs, and in this way had made their collective way to broad public acclaim. Howe listened, no doubt impatiently, and then shot back: "Not a bad idea, if you change the word 'backs' to eyes.'" Sanford Pinsker, "Why the New York Intellectuals Still Matter," *Midstream* 48 (September–October 1998): 35–36.

44. Howe, letter to Lionel Trilling, March 22, 1949, Trilling Papers, Columbia University.

45. Several writers were unforgiving if their colleagues were even the least bit critical of their work. Saul Bellow, for example, apparently demanded unconditional adoration; and he held grudges against Lionel Trilling, Ted Solotaroff, William Philips, and Alfred Kazin, among others who failed to wax rhapsodic over one or another of Bellow's novels. Atlas, *Bellow*, passim. Irving Howe very much admired Bellow, but he could also, characteristically, write candidly about what he saw as flaws or shortcomings in the novelist's work. At Howe's death, Bellow wrote the following to Al Glotzer: "I didn't think well of his talents or of his plans for personal advancement. . . . As an editor of *Dissent*, he struck me as rather quaint, like an old-fashioned lady, who still cans her tomatoes in August." Cited in Atlas, *Bellow*, 550n.

46. Howe, *Steady Work: Essays in the Politics of Democratic Radicalism, 1953–1966* (New York: Harcourt, Brace and World, 1966), 118.

47. Trotsky, like a number of other "Old Bolsheviks" assailed during the Moscow Trials, was Jewish. And Sidney Hook wrote some years later that "[a]t the time of the Stalinist-Trotsky feud most non-Jewish Stalinists used antisemitic arguments against the Trotskyists," and fellow-travelers referred to Trotsky's sympathizers as "a bunch of neurotic New York Jews." Sidney Hook "Reflections of the Jewish Question," *Partisan Review* 16 (May 1949): 464–465.

48. James Atlas, "The Changing World of New York Intellectuals," *New York Times Magazine*, August 25, 1985, 70; William Barrett, *The Truants: Adventures among the Intellectuals* (Garden City, N.Y.: Anchor Press/Doubleday, 1983), 24.

49. Howe, letter to Edward Alexander, June 2, 1983, quoted in Alexander, *Irving Howe and Secular Jewishness* (Cincinnati: University of Cincinnati, 1995), 2; Lionel Trilling in "Under Forty: A Symposium on American Literature and the Younger Generation of American Jews," *Contemporary Jewish Record* (February 1944): 16–17. Only two of eleven other respondents in the symposium, David Daiches, the Scottish-born literary critic, and Ben Field, explicitly claimed inspiration from Jewish as well as English sources. And Delmore Schwartz attributed his literary creativity to having been raised in two languages, Yiddish and English. But no one else recognized any affinity for "American Jewish culture." Alfred Kazin and Louis Kronenberg, like Trilling, went so far as to deny the existence of anything that might be called American Jewish culture. Kazin praised the work of the great Yiddish writers Sholom Aleichem, Peretz, and I. J. Singer

but traced his own literary influences to Blake, Melville, and Emerson. See "Under Forty," 18–35.

50. Howe, *Decline of the New* (New York: Harcourt Brace and World, 1970), 215; Howe, "Mid-Century Turning Point: An Intellectual Memoir," *Midstream* 20 (June–July 1975): 23–28.

51. Howe (as Theodore Dryden), "Periodicals," *Politics* 4 (January 1947): 31.

52. Howe, "Spruceton Jewry Adjusts Itself," *Commentary* 5 (June 1948): 552–558; Howe, letters to Dwight Macdonald, February 14, 1949, and [no date] 1949, Manuscripts and Archives, Yale University Library.

53. Howe, "Religion and the Intellectuals: A Symposium," *Partisan Review* 17 (May–June 1950): 472.

54. Howe, *The Making of a Critic* (Bennington, Vt.: Bennington Chap Book, 1982), 14.

55. Howe, *Margin*, 137.

56. Howe, "New York and the National Culture," *Partisan Review* 44 (Spring 1977): 175–176; Howe, "Foreword," in Delmore Schwartz, *In Dreams Begin Responsibilities and Other Stories*, ed. James Atlas (New York: New Directions Books, 1978), ix.

57. James Atlas, *Bellow*, 40.

58. Leslie Fiedler, "Partisan Review: Phoenix or Dodo?" in *To the Gentiles* (New York: Stein and Day, 1972), 41.

59. Howe, *Margin*, 137–138, emphasis mine.

60. Howe, *Decline of the New*, 244.

61. Howe, "That Aura of Personal Distinction," *New Republic*, July 30, 1962, 28. Howe, by changing "Jewish" to "Catholic" could have said the same about another of his favorite writers, James Joyce.

62. Howe, *Margin*, 251.

63. Daniel Bell, "Reflections on Jewish Identity," in *Ghetto and Beyond: Essays on Jewish Life in America*, ed. Peter Rose (New York: Random House, 1969), 472.

64. Howe, "An Exercise in Memory," *New Republic*, March 11, 1991, 29–31; Howe, *Decline of the New*, 218.

65. It was not until the 1963 edition of Eliot's work, that "jew" was changed to "Jew."

66. See Anthony Julius, *T. S. Eliot, Anti-Semitism, and Literary Form* (Cambridge, U.K.: Cambridge University Press, 1995), for an intelligent and revealing "adversarial reading" of Eliot's work.

67. T. S. Eliot, *After Strange Gods: A Primer of Modern Heresy* (New York: Harcourt Brace, 1934), 20. Richard Levy makes an interesting distinction between "casual prejudice" against Jews and anti-Semitism, which he defines as organized, ongoing, public action to diminish the influence of Jews. If we define

writing and public speaking as "action," Eliot certainly fits somewhere in between "casual prejudice" and anti-Semitism. Richard S. Levy, *Antisemitism in the Modern World: An Anthology of Texts* (Lexington, Mass.: D. C. Heath, 1991).

68. Howe, "An Exercise in Memory," 31.

69. Karl Shapiro, *In Defense of Ignorance* (New York: Random House, 1960), 35; Cynthia Ozick, *What Henry James Knew* (London: Jonathan Cape, 1993), 16–17; Fiedler quoted in Alexander Bloom, *Prodigal Sons* (New York: Oxford University Press, 1986), 147.

70. Leslie Fiedler, *Fiedler on the Roof* (Boston: David R. Godine, 1991), 63; Howe, "An Exercise of Memory," 31; Howe, *Decline of the New*, 224.

71. In 1991 in "An Exercise of Memory," Howe admitted that the New York intellectuals had been much too easy on Eliot in this regard.

72. Howe, "An Exercise of Memory," 31.

73. Tate quoted in Howe, "The Case of Ezra Pound," in idem, *The Critical Point* (New York: Horizon Press, 1973), 113.

74. Macdonald, letter to Howe, May 21, 1949, Macdonald Papers, Manuscripts and Archives, Yale University Library.

75. Howe, "The Stranger and the Victim: Two Stereotypes of American Fiction," *Commentary* 8 (August 1949): 147–156; Howe, "The Jewish Writer and the English Literary Tradition," *Commentary* 8 (October 1949): 364–365.

76. Howe, "The Jewish Writer," 365–366.

77. Howe, "The Case of Ezra Pound," 109; Howe, "Mid-Century Turning Point: An Intellectual Memoir," *Midstream* 20 (June–July 1975): 24.

78. Joseph Reino, *Karl Shapiro* (Boston: Twayne, 1981); Karl Shapiro, *Reports of My Death* (Chapel Hill, N.C.: Algonquin Books, 1990).

79. Howe, *Margin*, 155; Howe, "Mid-Century Turning Point," 32, 25.

80. Howe, *Margin*, 254–255.

81. *Commentary* 7 (January 1949): 8–18.

82. Ibid., 13.

83. Howe, *Margin*, 256.

84. Carole Kessner, ed., *The "Other" New York Jewish Intellectuals* (New York: New York University Press, 1994), 9–10.

85. Howe, "Range of the New York Intellectuals," in Rosenberg, Bernard, ed., *Creators and Disturbers: Reminiscences by Jewish Intellectuals of New York* (New York: Columbia University Press, 1982) 286; Howe, *Margin*, 260, 276.

NOTES TO CHAPTER 5

1. Howe, "Mid-Century Turning Point: An intellectual memoir," *Midstream* 20 (June–July 1975): 25.

2. Howe, "Reviewing 'The New Course': A Critical Reevaluation," *New International* 12 (September 1946): 210–213. Emphasis mine.

3. Howe, "A Note on Content with a Letter on Tone," *Internal Bulletin* [of the WP] 2 (September 12, 1947): 9–12.

4. Howe, "Observing the Events: Czechoslovakia," *Labor Action*, March 8, 1948, 4.

5. Labor Action, April 5, 1948, 1, 2; *Internal Bulletin* 3 (April 24, 1948); E. R. McKinney, letter to Max Shachtman, Shachtman Papers, Tamiment Library, New York University, cited in Alan Wald, *The New York Intellectuals* (Chapel Hill: University of North Carolina Press, 1987), 311.

6. Howe, "Masaryk: His Suicide Marks End of Road," *Labor Action*, March 22, 1948, 3.

7. Howe, letter to Dwight Macdonald, August 27, 1948, Dwight Macdonald Papers, Manuscripts and Archives, Yale University Library.

8. Howe, *Margin*, 59.

9. *Labor Action*, November 15, 1948, 4.

10. Howe, "Possibilities for Politics," *Partisan Review* 15 (December 1948): 1359; Howe, "What Future for American Socialism?" *Labor Action*, March 7, 1949, 3.

11. Howe, "Porkchoppers Prefabricated," *Anvil*, Fall 1949, 14–19.

12. Howe, "Philip Rahv: A Memoir," *American Scholar* 48 (Autumn 1979): 489.

13. Howe, letter to *Commentary* 12 (October 1951): 388.

14. Howe, *Margin*, 80. New work, much of it based on recently opened Soviet archives, confirms the suspicions of Howe and many of his colleagues. Stalin was no aberration, but an heir of Bolshevik ideology and system. Lenin's positions on dictatorship and terror were central to Stalin's thinking. And it was Lenin and his coterie who had bequeathed to their Stalinist successors the instrumentalities of centralized control: the one-party state, the elimination of internal party dissent, as well as banning of elections, erecting slave labor camps, a secret police, puppet courts, and a mass media with one narrow ideological position. See, for example, the many publications of Martin Malia, and also Helene Carrere d'Encausse, *Lenin* (New York: Holmes and Meier, 2001) and Robert Service, *Lenin: A Biography* (Cambridge: Harvard University Press, 2001).

15. Maurice Isserman, *If I Had a Hammer: The Death of the Old Left and the Birth of the New Left* (Chicago: University of Illinois Press, 1993), 57; Paul Buhle, ed., *The Legacy of the Workers Party, 1940–1949: Recollections and Reflections* (New York: Tamiment Institute, 1985), 1.

16. *Internal Bulletin* [of the Worker's Party] 3 (January 14, 1949): 30–32; Julius and Phyllis Jacobson, interviewed by author, March 17, 1997; Henry Judd, letter to *New International* 14 (September 1948): 223.

17. Peter Drucker, *Max Shachtman and His Left: A Socialist's Odyssey through the "American Century"* (Atlantic Highlands, N.J.: Humanities Press, 1994).

18. R. Fahan and H. Judd, "The New *Labor Action*," *Forum* (March 1951): 19; Simone Plastrik, interviewed by author, May 8, 1997. The wife of Stanley Plastrik and herself a radical activist, Simone Plastrik emphasized the desire of Howe and Plastrik "to have more impact, a larger audience, things possible only outside of a sect."

19. Irving Howe and Henry Judd [Stanley Plastrik], "Statement of Resignation from the ISL," *Forum* (January 1953): 4–6. Emphasis mine.

20. Julius and Phyllis Jacobson, interviewed by author, March 17, 1997; Howe and Judd, "Statement," 5; "Statement from the Political Committee on the Resignation of Irving Howe and Henry Judd," *Forum* (January 1953): 1–3.

21. Emanuel Geltman, interviewed by Maurice Isserman (unpublished transcript, March 19, 1985).

22. Albert Glotzer, "The New York Membership Meeting," *Forum* (January 1953): 8–9.

23. Howe, *Margin*, 232.

24. Emanuel Geltman, "Remembering Irving Howe," *Dissent* 40 (Fall 1993): 530.

25. Howe, "The Sentimental Fellow-Traveling of F. O. Matthiessen," *Partisan Review* 15 (October 1948): 1125–1129; "Possibilities for Politics" *Partisan Review* 15 (December 1948): 1356–1359; Howe and B. J. Widick, "The U.A.W. Fights Race Prejudice: A Case History on the Industrial Front," *Commentary* 8 (September 1949): 261–268; Howe, "Sherwood Anderson and the Power Urge: A Note on Populism in American Literature," *Commentary* 10 (July 1950): 78–80; "William Faulkner and the Negroes: A Vision of Lost Fraternity," *Commentary* 12 (October 1951): 359–368; "Henry Adams: Political Novelist," *New Republic*, September 22, 1952, 25–26.

26. Howe, "The Sentimental Fellow-Traveling of F. O. Matthiessen," 1127, 1128–1129; Howe, "Periodicals," *Politics* (March–April 1947): 63. Wallace, vice-president of the United States from 1941 to 1945, was in 1948 the founder of the Progressive Party, which Howe described at the time as a "completely contrived creature of Stalinism." Whether Wallace was a witting actor or the dupe of the American Communist Party is less important than the fact that he consistently gave Stalin the benefit of the doubt. He advocated abandoning Berlin when Stalin imposed the Soviet Blockade, and he characterized the coup Stalin ordered in Czechoslovakia in 1948 as a necessary and just response to the Truman Doctrine. Wallace not only strenuously resisted Truman's decision to oppose Stalin's expansionist ambitions in Eastern Europe, he also saw Stalin as a man of peace and Truman as the dangerous militarist. He described the Marshall Plan for the reconstruction of Europe as the "Martial Plan." See John C. Culver and John Hyde, *American Dreamer: A Life of Henry A. Wallace* (New York: Norton, 2000), which tries to salvage Wallace's reputation but which provides some

very damaging evidence. For even more, see Ronald Radosh, "Progressively Worse," *New Republic*, June 12, 2000, 44–52.

27. Howe, "Sherwood Anderson and the Power Urge: A Note on Populism in American Literature," 78–80.

28. Howe, *Sherwood Anderson* (New York: William Sloane, 1951), 224.

29. Ibid., 249–250.

30. Ibid., 97–98, 108–109.

31. It is important to note, however, that Trilling was an editor of the American Men of Letters series in which the Anderson book was published, and that Howe wrote in his preface: "The help and encouragement I have received from Lionel Trilling form only one of my debts to him," xii–xiii; Howe had reviewed Kazin's *On Native Grounds* when it first appeared in 1942, and he evinced interest in Anderson at least as early as 1944 by visiting Clyde, Ohio, Anderson's hometown and the model for Winesburg.

32. Howe, *Sherwood Anderson*, 256, 249.

33. Howe, *William Faulkner: A Critical Study* (New York: Random House, 1952), 24–25.

34. Howe, "William Faulkner's Enduring Power," *New York Times Book Review*, April 6, 1954, 1; Howe, "Minor Faulkner," *Nation*, November 12, 1949, 473.

35. Howe, *William Faulkner*, 202.

36. Lionel Trilling, *The Liberal Imagination* (New York: Viking, 1950), x.

37. Howe, "Mid-Century Turning Point: An Intellectual Memoir," *Midstream* 20 (June–July 1975): 27.

38. Howe, *Margin*, 232.

39. Howe, "Liberalism, History, and Mr. Trilling," in John Rodden, ed., *Lionel Trilling and the Critics: Opposing Selves* (Lincoln: University of Nebraska Press, 1999), 150–158 [originally in the *Nation*, May 1950]; Howe, *Margin*, 232.

40. In the several paragraphs above I have drawn in part on Mark Shechner's valuable book *After the Revolution: Studies in the Contemporary Jewish-American Imagination* (Bloomington: Indiana University Press, 1987). "Post-Marxist deconversions" is his phrase.

41. Howe, *Margin*, 197.

42. "Our Country and Our Culture," *Partisan Review* 19 (May–June 1952): 287

43. Ibid., 303.

44. Ibid., 307, 310.

45. Ibid., 299, 301.

46. "Our Country and Our Culture," *Partisan Review* 19 (September–October 1952): 576–580. Emphasis mine.

47. Howe, letters to Waldo Frank, November 18, 1951; March 9, 1952. Special Collections, Van Pelt Library, University of Pennsylvania.

48. Howe, letter to Richard Chase, June 23, 1951, Columbia University Manuscript Collections.

49. Howe, *Margin*, 174.

50. Howe, letter to Robert Heilman, March 21, 1991, quoted in Edward Alexander, *Irving Howe and Secular Jewishness: An Elegy* (Cincinnati: University of Cincinnati Press, 1995), 4.

51. Howe, *Celebrations and Attacks* (New York: Harcourt Brace Jovanovich, 1979), 163; Howe and Lewis Coser, "Images of Socialism," *Dissent* 1 (Spring 1954): 122–138.

52. Howe, letter to Granville Hicks, August 8, 1952, Syracuse University; Howe, letter to Richard Chase, August 14, 1952, Columbia University Manuscript Collections.

53. Information derived from Dennis Wrong, interviewed by author, October 15, 1997, and Wrong's letter to author, November 28, 1997. Wrong was a friend of Irving's in Princeton, an invited guest at the seminars, and eventually a co-founder of *Dissent* magazine.

54. Howe, *Margin*, 182–183.

55. Bernard Rosenberg, ed., *Creators and Disturbers: Reminiscences by Jewish Intellectuals of New York* (New York: Columbia University Press, 1982), 38–39, 50.

56. Howe, *Margin*, 183–184.

57. Howe, letter to Theodore Roethke, September 18, 1953, University of Washington Archives.

58. Howe, letter to Lewis Coser, April 1953, Coser Papers, Box 1, Boston College. Howe, preferring to have the issue thrashed out quickly, also raised the question with Brandeis faculty member Max Lerner. I could locate no record of Lerner's response.

59. Howe, letter to Richard Chase, December 1, 1953, Columbia University Manuscript Collections.

60. Jeremy Larner, interviewed by author, June 19, 1997; idem, "Remembering Irving Howe," *Dissent* 40 (Fall 1993): 539–41; Howe, *Margin of Hope*, 183–184.

61. Judith Walzer, interviewed by author, May 13, 1997.

62. Jeremy Larner, interviewed by author, June 19, 1997.

63. Michael Walzer, interviewed by author, May 13, 1997.

64. Rachel Sugarman, interviewed by author, June 4, 1997; Judith and Michael Walzer, interviewed by author, May 13, 1997.

65. Carole Kessner, interviewed by author, July 26, 1997; Donald Gropman, interviewed by author, October 10, 1997; Gabriella Gropman, interviewed by author, September 30, 1997.

66. Judith Walzer, interviewed by author, May 13, 1997; Rachel Sugarman, interviewed by author, June 4, 1997.

67. Martin Peretz, interviewed by author, August 28, 1997; Jeremy Larner, "Remembering Irving Howe," 539. When Irving Howe found out that Martin Peretz was a descendant of I. L Peretz and that he read and spoke Yiddish, he was delighted. But Peretz told me that Howe was a "little disappointed that I wasn't a socialist, but a Zionist."

68. Howe, *Margin of Hope*, 187. In a review of *Stoner*, a novel by John Williams (1961), Howe quotes with some sympathy Williams's line about a sardonic professor who teaches English "as if he perceived between his knowledge and what he could say a gulf so profound that he could make no effort to close it," and he speaks of "the dry impassioned hostility which often seems a necessary part of teaching." Howe, *Celebrations and Attacks*, 110.

69. Carole Kessner, interviewed by author, July 26, 1997. Kessner, a student at Brandeis in the 1950s and a friend of Marie Syrkin, one of the "other" New York intellectuals Kessner has written about, also tells the following story. Encountering Irving Howe and Philip Rahv strolling on the Brandeis campus in 1953, Kessner asked them something about Syrkin. Rahv replied: "Oh! Marie Syrkin. She's not an intellectual; she thinks *The Great Gatsby* is about bootleggers." Irving Howe just smiled, Kessner said, apparently agreeing with Rahv.

70. Howe, "Interview" with William Cain, *American Literary History* 1 (Fall 1989): 562.

71. Abram Sachar, *Brandeis University: A Host at Last* (Boston: Brandeis University Press, 1976), 143; Bernard Rosenberg, interviewed by Maurice Isserman, October 16, 1983; Howe, letter to Lewis Coser, October 14, 1957, Lewis Coser Papers, Box 2, Boston College.

72. Lewis Coser, interviewed by Maurice Isserman (unpublished transcript, May 3, 1985); Howe, *Margin*, 183–185.

73. Howe, interviewed by Susanne Klingenstein (audiotape, December 12, 1988).

74. Howe, "Mid-Century Turning Point," 26.

75. Jeremy Larner, interviewed by author, June 19, 1997; Judith Walzer, interviewed by author, May 13, 1997; Jeremy Larner, "Remembering Irving Howe," 540–541.

76. This was the way a number of former students I interviewed characterized Howe's treatment of literature. And it conforms with what he says in his essays, especially those included in *Politics and the Novel*.

NOTES TO CHAPTER 6

1. Howe, "Magazine Chronicle," *Partisan Review* 16 (April 1949): 416–427; Howe, letter to Dwight Macdonald, May 8, 1949, Macdonald Papers, Manuscripts and Archives, Yale University Library.

2. Eric Glaberson, *Historical Humanism in the Work of Two New York Intellectuals: Irving Howe and Alfred Kazin*, Ph.D. dissertation, New York University, 1982, 227.

3. Howe, *Steady Work: Essays in the Politics of Democratic Radicalism, 1953–1966* (New York: Harcourt, Brace and World), 296–312.

4. Howe, interview with Joseph Dorman (unpublished transcript, 1993), 22.

5. Sidney Hook, "Should Communists Be Permitted to Teach?" *New York Times Magazine*, February 27, 1949, 7–29; Sidney Hook, *Out of Step: An Unquiet Life in the 20th Century* (New York: Harper and Row, 1987), 504; Hook, letter to Aptheker, December 12, 1952, published in Edward Shapiro, ed., *Letters of Sidney Hook: Democracy, Communism, and the Cold War* (Armonk, N.Y.: M. E. Sharpe, 1995), 211–214.

6. Hook's central arguments can be read in detail in "Should Communists Be Allowed to Teach?" See also Hook, "Academic Integrity and Academic Freedom," *Commentary* 8 (October 1949): 329–339.

7. Howe [as R. Fahan], "Washington Case Raises Civil Liberties Issue: Should Stalinists Be Permitted to Teach?" *Labor Action*, March 14, 1949, 4; Howe, "Intellectual Freedom and Stalinists: Shall Communist Party Teachers Be Prohibited from Teaching?" *New International* (December 1949): 231–236; Howe, *A Margin of Hope: An Intellectual Autobiography* (New York: Harcourt Brace Jovanovich, 1982), 212.

8. Howe, letter to Sidney Hook, March 30, 1949, Sidney Hook Papers, Box 15, Folder 39, Hoover Institution, Stanford University.

9. Howe (as R. Fahan), "Sidney Hook: His New Friends in the Vatican," *Labor Action*, March 28, 1949, 3; Howe, letters to Sidney Hook, March 30 and April 2, 1949, Sidney Hook Papers, Box 15, Folder 39, Hoover Institution; Howe (as R. Fahan), "Letter," *Labor Action*, April 11, 1949, 3.

10. Sidney Hook, Letter to Irving Howe, April 4, 1949; Howe to Hook, April 5,1949; Hook to Howe, April 11, 1949; Howe to Hook, April 12, 1949; Howe to Hook, March 30, 1949, Sidney Hook Papers, Box 15, Folder 39, Hoover Institution.

11. *The God That Failed* (1949), a collection of autobiographical essays by American and European ex-Communists, including Arthur Koestler, Ignazio Silone, and Louis Fischer, preceded Chambers's revelations and accusations but had only a minor impact on the larger intellectual community since it replicated arguments they had been making since the mid-1930s. Irving Howe, "God, Man, and Stalin," *The Nation*, May 24, 1952, 21–23; Sidney Hook, "The Faiths of Whittaker Chambers," *New York Times Book Review*, May 25, 1952, 34–35. Although correct about Hiss's guilt, Howe, given his own powerfully entrenched anti-Communism in 1948, had presumed that guilt "on general probabilities."

He admitted this is an a letter to Al Glotzer, July 27, 1979, Glotzer Papers, Box 34, Hoover Institution.

12. Hook apparently found it ironic that Howe was critical of Chambers's absolutism since Hook believed, incorrectly, that "during this whole period Howe was a Trotskyist—as absolute a Leninist as the Stalinists." Letter from Hook to Neil Jumonville quoted in *Critical Crossings: The New York Intellectuals in Postwar America* (Berkeley: University of California Press, 1991), 107.

13. Howe, "God, Man and Stalin," 22; Howe, *Steady Work* (New York: Harcourt, Brace and World, 1966), 264; Hook, "The Faiths of Whittaker Chambers," 34–35.

14. Hook, "The Faiths of Whittaker Chambers," 34–35.

15. Howe, *Margin*, 212; Sidney Hook Papers, Box 15, Folder 39, Hoover Institution.

16. Alexander Bloom, *Prodigal Sons: The New York Intellectuals and Their World* (New York: Oxford University Press, 1986), 260–261; Alan Wald, *The New York Intellectuals: The Rise and Decline of the Anti-Stalinist Left from the 1930s to the 1980s* (Chapel Hill: University of North Carolina Press, 1987), 279–280; Howe [as R. Fahan], "Stalinist 'Peace' Conference Flops," *Labor Action*, April 4, 1949, 1, 3; Howe, "The Culture Conference," *Partisan Review* 16 (May 1949): 509–511; Joseph Dorman, *Arguing the World: The New York Intellectuals in Their Own Words* (New York: Free Press, 2000), 113. At the end of the conference, Norman Mailer, then a young writer just beginning to be known, rose to say that he regarded the Soviet Union (as well as the United States) as a society declining into "state capitalism." Mailer shocked the conference managers, but delighted Irving Howe and the other dissidents. Howe rushed up to introduce himself to Mailer and almost immediately they launched into a friendly but pointed argument about state capitalism. Howe [as R. Fahan], "Stalinist 'Peace' Conference Flops," 3; Howe, "Mid-Century Turning Point: An Intellectual Memoir," *Midstream* 20 (June–July 1975): 24.

17. Howe [as R. Fahan], "Stalinist 'Peace' Conference Flops," 1, 3; Sidney Hook, letter to Irving Howe, April 4, 1949, Hook Papers, Box 15, Folder 39, Hoover Institution; Howe, "The Culture Conference," 509–511; Howe, letter to Sidney Hook, April 5, 1949, Hook Papers, Box 15, Folder 39, Hoover Institution.

18. Howe, "Intellectual Freedom and Stalinists," 231–236.

19. Irving Kristol, "'Civil Liberties,' 1952—A Study in Confusion," *Commentary* 13 (May 1952): 229; Kristol, quoted in Dorman, *Arguing the World*, 121.

20. Elliot Cohen, "The Free American Citizen, 1952," *Commentary* 14 (September 1952): 229, emphasis mine; Nathan Glazer, "The Method of Senator McCarthy," *Commentary* 15 (March 1953): 266; Dorman, *Arguing the World*, 124.

21. Dorman, *Arguing the World*, 122, 124.

22. For these issues, see Michael Rogin, *The Intellectuals and McCarthy: The Radical Spectre* (Cambridge, Mass.: MIT Press, 1967); Stanley Kutler, *The Ameri-*

can Inquisition: Justice and Injustice in the Cold War (New York: Hill and Wang, 1982); David M. Oshinsky, *A Conspiracy So Immense: The World of Joe McCarthy* (New York: Free Press, 1983).

23. Norman Podhoretz, *Ex-Friends* (New York: Free Press, 1999), 130.

24. Allen Weinstein and Alexander Vassiliev, *The Haunted Wood: Soviet Espionage in America—The Stalin Era* (New York: Random House, 1999). In a 1951 KGB memorandum uncovered by the authors, Soviet spymasters acknowledged to their superiors that they no longer had any inside sources in the American government: "The most serious drawback in organizing intelligence in the U.S. is . . . the lack of agents in the State Department, intelligence service, counterintelligence service, and other most important U.S. governmental institutions," 299–300. Although one could not have known this with any precision in the 1950s, it was clear to some that the "Communist threat" was greatly exaggerated. Only three Communists had important posts in the federal government in the 1940s: Lauchlin Currie, FDR's China adviser; Alger Hiss, who had been in charge of the U.N. desk at the State Department; and Harry Dexter White, an assistant secretary of the Treasury under FDR. All three had resigned by 1946, and all of this became public in 1948, two long years before McCarthy began to exploit the issue of an internal Communist threat. Also see Commission on Protecting and Reducing Government Secrecy, *Report* (Washington, D.C.: United States Government Publications Office, 1997), Appendix A, 37.

25. The ACCF is sometimes confused with the CIA-supported Congress for Cultural Freedom. But the ACCF was formed before the Congress. It did later become affiliated with the larger organization, but it is unlikely that more than a tiny fraction of the membership, if any, knew about the CIA funding.

26. Howe quoted in Dorman, *Arguing the World*, 122. At the end of 1951, in the midst of McCarthy's anti-Communist tirades, and while Howe was still a member of the Independent Socialist League, he criticized E. M. Forster for occasionally subverting "his own liberalism by a display of impatience with abstract ideas," and he quoted Forster as saying, "If I had to choose between betraying my country and betraying my friend . . . I hope I should have the guts to betray my country." Howe responded by saying: "No doubt; but what if the friend had already betrayed the country? It is questions like this that our time poses, and Forster skirts them rather cavalierly." Howe, "Pleasures of Cultivation," *New Republic*, December 10, 1951, 16. In the infamous espionage case of Julius and Ethel Rosenberg, Howe, as he did with Alger Hiss, presumed guilt (again correctly). He did not follow the case meticulously, but he later concluded that "Julius was guilty, the case against Ethel was weak, and the trial and the execution were outrageous." Howe, letter to Albert Glotzer, Glotzer Collection, Box 34, Hoover Institution; Howe, "The Troubles of *Daniel*," *Dissent* 31 (Winter 1984): 123.

27. Howe, quoted in Dorman, *Arguing the World*, 122.

28. Howe, interviewed by Joseph Dorman (unpublished transcript, 1993), 23; *Partisan Review* 19 (September–October 1952): 593.

29. Sidney Hook, letter to Richard Rovere, April 2, 1952, Norman Thomas Papers, New York Public Library; Hook, letter to the *New York Times*, May 8, 1953; James Rorty and Moshe Decter, *McCarthy and the Communists* (Boston: Beacon Press, 1954); Bloom, *Prodigal Sons*, 270.

30. Howe quoted in Powell and Robbins, *Conflict and Consensus* (New York: Free Press, 1984), 43.

31. Dennis Wrong, interviewed by author, October 15, 1997.

32. Howe, "Forming Dissent," in Walter Powell and Richard Robbins, eds., *Conflict and Consensus: A Festschrift in Honor of Lewis Coser* (New York: Free Press, 1983), 62; Lewis Coser, interviewed by author, April 8, 1997; Bernard Rosenberg, "An interview with Lewis Coser," in *Conflict and Consensus*, 39.

33. Simone Plastrik, interviewed by author, May 8, 1997; Lewis Coser, interviewed by author, April 8, 1997.

34. Howe, *Margin*, 237; Lewis Coser, interviewed by author, April 8, 1997; "The *Dissent* Art Show," *Dissent* 8 (Summer 1961): 232; "The Second *Dissent* Art Show," *Dissent* 11 (Winter 1964): 244; David Craven, *Abstract Expressionism as Cultural Critique* (Cambridge, U.K.: University of Cambridge Press, 1999), 3–9.

35. Howe to Dwight Macdonald, March 1 and March 18, 1953, Macdonald Papers, Manuscripts and Archives, Yale University Library. Hannah Arendt, Mary McCarthy, Richard Rovere, and Arthur Schlesinger, Jr., joined Macdonald in the attempt to begin *The Critic*. They collected pledges totaling $55,000, but, according to Macdonald, "since we figured it would take twice that at the very least to carry on [the] mag for [the] first two years, we dropped the project." Macdonald to Alfred Kazin, November 26, 1960, Dwight Macdonald Papers, Manuscripts and Archives, Yale University Library.

36. The Buttingers provided between $1500 and $3000 a year. It was not very much, as Coser pointed out, "compared to the large-scale funds backing journals such as the *Nation* or the *New Republic*, but it meant much to us." Irving Howe, letter to Lewis Coser, November 1957, Coser Papers, Box 2, Boston College; Lewis Coser, "Joseph Buttinger," *Dissent* 39 (Fall 92): 556. Howe, "Forming Dissent," 64.

37. Editors, "A Word to Our Readers," *Dissent* 1 (Winter 1954): 3–4.

38. Nathan Glazer, "Philistine Leftism," *Commentary* 17 (February 1954): 201–206.

39. Howe, "Forming Dissent," 64.

40. Glazer, "Philistine Leftism," 205. Glazer wondered facetiously "what the editors plan to do about Royalists, aristocrats, anti-Semites, and other non-signers of peace with society who decide to take advantage of this implicit invitation," as well as about "all those former radicals who have signed a general

peace, but reserved their position in certain matters, such as the segregated school systems of the South."

41. Henry Judd [Stanley Plastrik], letter, *New International* 14 (September 1948): 223; Irving Howe and Henry Judd, "Statement of Resignation of Irving Howe and Henry Judd from the Independent Socialist League," *Forum* (January 1953): 4–6.

42. Harold Orlans and C. Wright Mills, "Letters," *Commentary* 17 (April 1954): 404, 405.

43. Hal Draper, "A New Magazine Presents Itself," *Labor Action*, February 22, 1954, 3.

44. Howe, "Forming Dissent," 64. Glazer's review continued to bother Howe for at least another decade. What was troubling about the *Commentary* editor's review of *Dissent*, Howe wrote in 1963, "was the fact that an intellectual socialist journal, such as would have simply been taken for granted in any free European country, occasioned such venom and rage, as if somehow a deviation from the standard Cold War sentiments were a scandal, even a kind of treason." "A Revival of Radicalism?" *Dissent* 10 (Spring 1963): 111.

45. Howe, letter to Lewis Mumford, April 15, 1954, Coser Papers, Box 1, Boston College.

46. Editors, *Dissent*, "A Word to Our Readers," 3.

47. Ibid.; Howe, letter to *Labor Action*, February 27, 1954, 3.

48. Lewis Coser and Irving Howe, "Images of Socialism," *Dissent* 1 (Spring 1954): 122–138.

49. Howe, "America, the Country and the Myth," *Dissent* 2 (Summer 1955): 241–244; Coser, "What Shall We Do?" *Dissent* 3 (Spring 1956): 156–165; Ben Seligman, "The Economics of Joseph Schumpeter," *Dissent* 1 (Autumn 1954): 370–374; and "Keynesian Economics: A Critique," *Dissent* 3 (Winter 1956): 62–67.

50. Howe, "Socialism and Liberalism: Articles of Conciliation," *Dissent* 24 (Winter 1977): 22–35; Howe, "Mid-Century Turning Point: An Intellectual Memoir," *Midstream* 20 (June–July 1975): 28.

51. Howe, "Does It Hurt When You Laugh?" *Dissent* 1 (Winter 1954): 4–7; Howe, *Margin*, 215. In the *Dissent* piece, Howe used the example of the ISL, from which he had resigned a year earlier, to reinforce his point about the liberals' neglect of civil liberties: "For six years now a conspicuously powerless group called the Independent Socialist League, in political complexion Marxist and pre-mature anti-Stalinist, has been on the A[ttorney] G[eneral]'s List." But, Howe continued, "the ISL is accused of nothing more than being Marxist and desiring the abolition of capitalism. . . . Does anyone—except to his honor, Norman Thomas—speak up?"

52. Hook, letter to the *New York Times*, May 8, 1953.

NOTES TO CHAPTER 7

1. Howe, "Philip Rahv: A Memoir," *American Scholar* 48 (Autumn 1979): 490.

2. Howe, "This Age of Conformity," in *A World More Attractive* (New York: Horizon Press, 1963), 251–282; originally published in *Partisan Review* 21 (January–February 1954): 1–33; Howe, "Philip Rahv: A Memoir," 490; emphasis mine.

3. Howe, *A World More Attractive*, 273, 265.

4. Ibid., 265, 263. Howe explicitly mentioned champions of that liberal tradition, John Dewey and Alexander Meiklejohn.

5. Ibid., 261–262, 265.

6. Joseph Dorman, *Arguing the World: The New York Intellectuals in Their Own Words* (New York: Free Press, 2000), 26.

7. Howe, *A World More Attractive*, 257–258. Emphasis in the original.

8. Howe, interviewed by Alexander Bloom, in *Prodigal Sons* (New York: Oxford University Press, 1986), 314.

9. Howe, "Mid-Century Turning Point: An Intellectual Memoir," *Midstream* 20 (June–July 1975): 27–28.

10. Ibid., 255–256, 252.

11. Ibid., 272, 267.

12. Ibid., 259.

13. Richard Hofstadter, *The Paranoid Style in American Politics* (New York: Vintage Books, 1965); Hofstadter, *Anti-Intellectualism in American Life* (New York: Vintage Books, 1963), 419. Also see Hofstadter, "Two Cultures: Adversary and/or Responsible," *Public Interest* 6 (Winter 1967): 68–74.

14. Hofstadter, *Anti-Intellectualism in American Life*, 427–432.

15. Howe, *A Margin of Hope: An Intellectual Autobiography* (New York: Harcourt Brace Jovanovich, 1982), 171; Howe, *A World More Attractive*, 255.

16. Howe, *A World More Attractive*, 259.

17. Howe, *Steady Work*, 101.

18. Lewis Coser, interviewed by author, April 8, 1997; Richard Hofstadter quoted in Russell Jacoby, *The Last Intellectuals: American Culture in the Age of Academe* (New York: Basic Books,1987), 85.

19. Alfred Kazin, "The Writer and the University," *Atlantic Monthly* (October 1955): 79–81; Kazin, *A Lifetime Burning in Every Moment* (New York: Harper-Perennial, 1997), 139–165; Howe, interviewed by Susanne Klingenstein (audiotape, December 12, 1988).

20. Howe, letters to Granville Hicks, August 8, 1952, and [?], 1952, Syracuse University.

21. Howe, letter to Theodore Roethke, September 18, 1953, University of Washington Archives; Howe, letter to Richard Chase, August 14, 1952, Colum-

bia University Manuscript Collections; Howe, "Mid-Century Turning Point: An Intellectual Memoir," 26.

22. Howe, *A World More Attractive*, 259.

23. Ibid., 276, 274.

24. Ibid., 278–280.

25. Ibid., 274.

26. Ibid., 269.

27. Ibid., 272; Howe [as R. Fahan], "Machiavelli and Modern Political Thought," *New International* 9 (December 1943): 334–337.

28. Howe, *A World More Attractive*, 260.

29. Irving Howe, interview, in Stanley Kunitz, ed., *Twentieth-Century Authors, First Supplement: A Biographical Dictionary of Modern Literature* (New York: Wilson, 1967), 464.

30. Howe, ed., *Selected Short Stories of Isaac Bashevis Singer* (New York: Modern Library, 1966); Howe and Greenberg, eds., *A Treasury of Yiddish Poetry* (New York: Holt Rinehart and Winston, 1969); Howe and Greenberg, eds., *Selected Stories: I. L. Peretz* (New York: Schocken Books, 1974); Howe and Greenberg, eds., *Yiddish Stories Old and New* (New York: Holiday House, 1974); Howe and Greenberg, eds., *Voices from the Yiddish: Essays, Memoirs, Diaries* (New York: Schocken Books, 1975); Howe and Greenberg, eds., *Ashes Out of Hope: Fiction by Soviet Yiddish Writers* (New York: Schocken Books, 1977); Howe and Ruth Wisse, *The Best of Sholom Aleichem* (Washington, D.C.: New Republic Books, 1979); Howe, Ruth Wisse, and Khone Shmeruk, eds., *The Penguin Book of Modern Yiddish Verse* (New York: Viking, 1987).

31. Howe, *Margin*, 260–263; radio transcript reprinted in *Midstream* 18 (June–July 1973): 32–38.

32. The largest proportion of the stories were translated by Howe and Greenberg. Other translators included Saul Bellow, who did two stories; Anne and Alfred Kazin, who did one; and Isaac Rosenfeld, who did a half-dozen. All worked at the rate of one cent per word.

33. Howe, *Margin*, 261–265; Ken Libo, interviewed by author, January 30, 1997.

34. Howe told Bernard Malamud, whom he was trying to recruit for translation work, that "Little Shoemakers" was "even better than Gimpel." Letter to Malamud, June 6, 1953, Harry Ransom Humanities Research Center, University of Texas, Austin.

35. Howe, *Margin*, 263; Donald Gropman, interviewed by author, September 8, 1997.

36. Howe, *Margin*, 265.

37. Howe and Greenberg, *A Treasury of Yiddish Stories*, 28–32, 42–44.

38. Ibid., 39.

39. Ibid., 38; emphasis in original. Two recent writers who have overstated Howe's inclination to promote the value of victimization are Edward Alexander, *Irving Howe: Socialist, Critic, Jew* (Bloomington: Indiana University Press, 1998), 81–83, and Julian Levinson, "Transmitting *Yiddishkayt*: Irving Howe and Jewish-American Culture," *Jewish History and Culture* 2 (Winter 1999): 42–65. Critics who have focused on Howe's "reductionist" use of the *kleine menschele* figure to represent all of Yiddish literature make a more telling case. Irene Klepfisz has pointed out that Jewish women writers (none of whom appear in Howe's classic) such as Yenta Sedutzky and Dora Schulner rarely used the *kleine menschele* motif, focusing instead on female characters whose struggles made clear some of the *internal* rifts of the shtetl. Their stories were regularly carried by the *Forward* and the *Tsukunft*. And David Roskies has suggested that Howe's emphasis on the *kleine menschele* theme caused him to overlook the fantasy school of Yiddish fiction represented by S. Ansky, David Ignatoff, and Moyshe Kulbak. Irena Kelpfisz, "Introduction," in *Found Treasures*, ed. Frieda Forman, et al. (Toronto: Second Story Press, 1994); David Roskies, "The Treasuries of Howe and Greenberg," *Prooftexts* 3 (1983): 111.

40. Howe, *A World More Attractive*, 261.

41. Robert Warshow, "This Age of Conformity," *Partisan Review* 21 (March–April 1954): 235; Howe, "Letter," *Partisan Review* 21 (March–April 1954): 239.

42. Howe, "Letter," *Partisan Review* 21, 240. Two years earlier, Howe had written to Bernard Malamud about a review of *The Natural* he had written for *Time* but was never published. "Beats me," Howe said, as to why. "I never know. . . . In any case it was a very rudimentary version of my opinion, *Time* being what it is, and my little job there being just a way to feed my family and have some time for my own work." Letter to Bernard Malamud, September 9, 1952, Malamud Collection, Harry Ransom Humanities Research Center, University of Texas, Austin.

43. Trilling and Howe quoted in Edward Alexander, *Irving Howe*, 92.

44. Diana Trilling, *The Beginning of a Journey: The Marriage of Diana and Lionel Trilling* (New York: Harcourt Brace, 1993), 420.

45. Howe, "Philip Rahv," 490.

46. Howe, letter to Bernard Malamud, September 13, 1954, Malamud Collection, Harry Ransom Humanities Research Center, University of Texas, Austin. Howe was most likely referring to his manuscript for *Politics and the Novel*, published finally in 1957. "The political novel book is a sore point with me," he wrote to Victor Walter. It is finished [and] I think, the best thing I've written yet; nonetheless I can't seem to get it published. Everyone talks about a book of essays as a commercial kiss of death. I suppose I'll have to try the university presses, though it isn't a scholarly book. It is galling to find that while I

had no trouble with my previous books, I do with this one now." Letter to Walter, November 18, 1954.

47. Howe, "A Mind's Turnings," *Dissent* 7 (Winter 1960): 31.

48. Howe, *Steady Work*, 313.

49. Bell's essays appeared in various journals, including *Commentary*, *Partisan Review*, *The New Republic*, and *Encounter* from 1947 to 1958. And in 1959 he actually had a piece (not his last) in *Dissent*. Many of his writings were revised and republished in 1961 as *The End of Ideology*. The book was submitted in substitution for a doctoral dissertation when Bell was hired at Columbia University.

50. Kazin, "Letter," *Commentary* 12 (October 1951): 389.

51. Kazin, interviewed by author, May 15, 1997; *A Lifetime Burning in Every Moment: From the Journals of Alfred Kazin* (New York: HarperCollins, 1996), 131.

52. Howe, interviewed by Susanne Klingenstein (audiotape, December 12, 1988). Another difference between Kazin and Howe was their approach to their personal writings and private lives. Kazin's memoirs are filled with intimate information, whereas Howe's autobiography, *A Margin of Hope*, is almost entirely intellectual, with only very rare moments of personal exposure. Kazin, kept many letters he received and copies of most he sent, and late in his life he deposited his voluminous personal journals in the New York Public Library for researchers to use freely. Howe, on the other hand, kept no copies of his letters, and destroyed those he received when he was through with them; and he kept no diary or journal.

NOTES TO CHAPTER 8

1. For a full and perceptive analysis of the rise of a new sensibility see Morris Dickstein, *Gates of Eden: American Culture in the Sixties* (New York: Basic Books, 1977), 51–88. See also the early chapters of Todd Gitlin, *The Sixties: Years of Hope, Years of Rage* (New York: Bantam Books, 1993); George Rawick, "The American Student: A Profile," *Dissent* 1 (Autumn 1954): 393–398.

2. Howe, "Does It Hurt When You Laugh?" *Dissent* 1 (Winter 1954): 4.

3. "A Word to Our Readers," *Dissent* 1 (Winter 1954): 3–4; Lewis Coser, "What Shall We Do?" *Dissent* 3 (Spring 1956): 156–163.

4. Howe and Coser, "Authoritarians of the Left," *Dissent* 2 (Winter 1955): 176–183.

5. Howe, "America, the Country and the Myth," *Dissent* 2 (Summer 1955): 242–244.

6. Howe appears to have been particularly influenced by Bell's "Adjusting Men to Machines," *Commentary* 3 (January 1947); "America's Un-Marxist Revolution," *Commentary* 7 (March 1949); "The Prospects of American Capitalism," *Commentary* 15 (March 1953).

7. Howe and Coser, "Images of Socialism," *Dissent* 1 (Spring 1954): 130–138; Coser, "What Shall We Do?" 161–164.

8. Howe, "Hemingway: The Conquest of Panic," *New Republic*, July 24 1961, 20; Howe, *A World More Attractive* (New York: Horizon Press, 1963), 64.

9. Howe, "Mass Society and Post-Modern Fiction," in *World More Attractive*, 95–96, originally published in *Partisan Review* 26 (Summer 1959): 420–436; emphasis mine. Alfred Kazin went a bit farther, suggesting that the antiestablishment stance of the Beats was a "criminal" posture. "The criminal is the protester," he wrote in his journal. "The real question here is: are they doing anything more than 'protesting'? Is there anything more than a striking of attitudes?" Alfred Kazin Journals, August 31, 1957, New York Public Library.

10. Norman Podhoretz, "The Know-Nothing Bohemians," *Partisan Review* 25 (Spring 1958): 305–315; Diana Trilling, "The Other Night at Columbia," *Partisan Review* 26 (Spring 1959): 214–227.

11. Howe, *World More Attractive*, 95–96.

12. Ibid.

13. Goodman treated the Beats sympathetically but also quite critically. He characterized them as living powerlessly in a fantasy of rebellion, while all the while suffering from shame and "fear of impotence." Most important he pointed out that the new bohemians, who rejected the values and morals of their own bourgeois origins, especially in their racial and sexual nonconformity, had no appeal for the poor or the working classes who, in the main, aspired to middle-class respectability. Goodman, *Growing Up Absurd* (New York: Random House, 1960).

14. Howe, "Forming Dissent," in Powell and Robbins, eds., *Conflict and Consensus: A Festschrift in Honor of Lewis Coser* (New York: Free Press, 1984), 67.

15. Norman Mailer, "The White Negro: Reflections on the Hipster," *Dissent* 4 (Summer 1957): 276–293. The essay may have been, in part, a tribute to Wilhelm Reich, who died in 1956.

16. Ned Polsky, "Reflections on Hipsterism," *Dissent* 5 (Winter 1958): 73–81; Mailer, "Reflections on the Hipster," *Dissent* 5 (Winter 1958): 73–77; Dickstein, *Gates of Eden*, 81; Dan Wakefield, *New York in the 50s* (New York: Houghton Mifflin, 1992), 220–224; Mark Shechner, *After the Revolution: Studies in the Contemporary Jewish-American Imagination* (Bloomington: Indiana University Press, 1987), 174–179.

17. Mailer, "The White Negro," 280, 284.

18. Lewis Coser, interviewed by author, April 8, 1997; Howe, "Forming Dissent," 67.

19. Howe, *World More Attractive*, 128. Here, unlike in 1957, Howe was prescient. Mailer was not only fascinated with violence, he, like "the hipster" he admired, ultimately perpetrated it, directly and indirectly. In 1960, only a year after Howe's warning, Mailer stabbed his wife Adele; and in 1981, he champi-

oned the cause of an actual psychopath, with a degree of literary talent, and won his release from prison. Soon thereafter, Jack Henry Abbot murdered a waiter in a dispute over the use of a men's room. This act of "courage" emancipated no one—not Abbot's victim certainly; not himself; nor Mailer, his sponsor.

20. Howe, "Forming *Dissent*," 62.

21. Howe, *Steady Work* (New York: Harcourt Brace and World, 1966), 271.

22. Ignazio Silone, "Choice of Comrades," *Dissent* 2 (Winter 1955): 17–18.

23. Nicholas Howe, "Remembering Irving Howe," *Dissent* 40 (Fall 1993): 532–533.

24. One intermittent discussion beginning in 1959 involved the concept of "market socialism," a hybrid system in which the major means of production and distribution are owned by worker cooperatives or public communities, but where a market mechanism gauges demand, sets levels of production and distribution, as well as prices, and promotes decentralizaton. Benjamin Seligman was its foremost advocate, but Howe and Coser and many other Dissenters ignored market socialism altogether until the late 1980s. Seligman, "Socialism without Marx," *Dissent* 6 (Summer 1959): 258–266.

25. Howe, letter to Waldo Frank, September 29, 1954, Special Collections, University of Pennsylvania.

26. Howe, "Forming Dissent," 65.

27. Howe, letter to Coser, September 13, 1957, Coser Papers, Box 2, Boston College.

28. Michael Walzer, interviewed by author, May 13, 1997; Bernard Avishai, interviewed by author, April 7, 1997; Maurice Stein, interviewed by author, July 25, 1997; Dennis Wrong, interviewed by author, October 15, 1997.

29. Walzer, "Irving Howe 1920–1993," *Dissent* 40 (Summer 1993): 275–276; Robert Kuttner, "Remembering Irving Howe," *Dissent* 40 (Fall 1993): 538–539; Jeremy Larner, interviewed by author, June 19, 1997.

30. Howe, "Forming *Dissent*," 67–68.

31. Howe, letter to Waldo Frank, September 9, 1954, Special Collections, University of Pennsylvania; Norman Mailer, interviewed by Eric Glaberson, "Historical Humanism in the Work of Two New York Intellectuals: Irving Howe and Alfred Kazin," Ph.D. dissertation, New York University, 1982, 227–228.

32. Michael Walzer, interviewed by author, May 13, 1997.

33. Howe, letters to Victor Walter, November 18, 1954, January 19, 1958.

34. Bernard Rosenberg, interviewed by Maurice Isserman (unpublished transcript, October 16, 1983); Frank Marquart, "The Auto Worker," *Dissent* 4 (Summer 1957): 219–233; Bell, "The Meaning in Work," *Dissent* 6 (Summer 1959): 242–249.

35. Harvey Swados, "The Myth of the Happy Worker," *Nation*, August 17, 1957, 65–68. In the early 1970s, media and academic interest in workers and the

existence of the "blue collar blues" were provoked by the drama of the Lord-stown, Ohio, auto workers' strike, the release of a report by the Department of Health, Education, and Welfare on the quality of worklife, and the publication of Studs Terkel's oral history, *Working*.

36. Howe, interviewed by Maurice Isserman (unpublished transcript, January 24, 1982).

37. See the various essays collected in Bernard Rosenberg and David White, eds., *Mass Culture* (Glencoe, Ill.: Free Press, 1957).

38. Howe, "Notes on Mass Culture," *Politics* 5 (Spring 1948): 120–123.

39. Henry Rabassiere, "Some Aspects of Mass Culture," *Dissent* 3 (Summer 1956): 327–332; Harold Rosenberg, "Pop Culture and Kitsch Criticism," *Dissent* 5 (Winter 1958): 14–19; Howe, interviewed by Maurice Isserman, January 24, 1982.

40. Howe, interviewed by Isserman, January 24, 1982.

41. Howe, *Decline of the New* (New York: Harcourt Brace, 1970), 227; Howe, "A Word," *Dissent* 6 (Autumn 1959): 371; Howe, "A New Political Atmosphere in America?" *Dissent* 6 (Winter 1959): 7.

42. Dwight Macdonald, *Against the American Grain* (New York: Random House, 1962), 32–50; Gerald Graff, *Professing Literature* (Chicago: University of Chicago Press, 1987), 222. For some, even the *New Yorker*, within the pages of which Macdonald lambasted mid-cult, was itself mid-cult. But in the fifties, under the editorship of William Shawn, the magazine had been transformed from a trivial haute bourgeois publication to a serious journal.

43. Rosenberg and White, eds., *Mass Culture*; Harold Rosenberg, *The Tradition of the New* (New York: Horizon Press, 1959), 260–263.

44. Howe, "Symposium on TV," *Dissent* 7 (Spring 1960): 297.

45. Howe, "Modern Criticism: Privileges and Perils," in *Modern Literary Criticism: An Anthology* (Boston: Beacon Press, 1958), 4–5, 37.

46. Howe, *Decline of the New*, 240.

47. Howe, "Reverberations in the North," *Dissent* 3 (Spring 1956): 121; Coser, "What Shall We Do?" *Dissent* 3 (Spring 1956): 156–163.

48. Irving Howe and Stanley Plastrik, "Notes on the Elections," *Dissent* 3 (Fall 1956): 341–345.

49. Howe, "A New Political Atmosphere in America?" *Dissent* 6 (Winter 1959): 5–8.

50. Michael Walzer, interviewed by author, May 13, 1997; Walzer, "A Cup of Coffee and a Seat," *Dissent* 7 (Spring 1960): 118–119; Walzer, "The Idea of Resistance," *Dissent* 7 (Autumn 1960): 373.

51. Howe, "Guatemala and American Politics," *Dissent* 1 (Autumn 1954): 334.

52. Howe, "The Problem of American Power," *Dissent* 1 (Summer 1954): 211–219; see also several articles in *Dissent* 3 (Spring 1956); and *Dissent* 6 (Spring 1959).

53. Joseph Buttinger, *The Smaller Dragon: A Political History of Vietnam* (New York: Praeger, 1958); Buttinger, "Vietnamese Mandarins," *Dissent* 5 (Spring 1958): 138–147; Eugene Burdick and William Lederer, *The Ugly American* (New York: Norton, 1958); Howe, "Introduction," *Dissent* 6 (Summer 1959): 318. Buttinger, by 1962, did a complete reversal of his views of Diem and became a sharp critic of the American role in Vietnam. See his *Vietnam: The Unforgettable Tragedy* (New York: Horizon, 1977), and his review of the Pentagon Papers, "How We Sank into Vietnam," *Dissent* 19 (Spring 1972): 407–441.

54. Howe, "The Problem of American Power," 217.

NOTES TO CHAPTER 9

1. Howe, letter to Lewis Coser, May 15, 1961, Coser Papers, Box 3, Boston College.

2. Howe, *A Margin of Hope: An Intellectual Autobiography* (New York: Harcourt Brace, 1982), 208.

3. Howe, "Notes on the Russian Turn," *Dissent* 3 (Summer 1956): 309–310; Howe, "Communism Now: Three Views," *Partisan Review* 23 (Fall 1956): 527–529.

4. Howe, "Notes on the Russian Turn," 311.

5. Coser, interviewed by author, April 8, 1997.

6. Howe, "The Russian Attack on Hungary," *Dissent* (Special Issue, November 1, 1956): 3; Coser, interviewed by Maurice Isserman (unpublished transcript, May 3, 1985).

7. Howe, "And Still They Fight Back," *Dissent* 4 (Winter 1957): 3–8. Much later, Howe told Maurice Isserman that while Hungary challenged the idea that totalitarianism was "unbudgeable" short of war, it also confirmed it. "We felt a terrible frustration in regard to Hungary. Either you are for peace, or you are for freedom, and in some ways there is a conflict between the two. And while we might rant and rave about Hungary, we were not in favor of starting a world war to save Hungary." Howe, interviewed by Maurice Isserman (unpublished transcript January 24, 1982).

8. Donald Gropman, interviewed by author, September 8, 1997.

9. Ibid.; Howe, interviewed by Maurice Isserman, January 24, 1982; Lewis Coser, interviewed by author, April 8, 1997.

10. Jeremy Larner, interviewed by author, June 19, 1997; Lewis Coser, interviewed by author, April 8, 1997; Donald Gropman, interviewed by author, September 8, 1997; Bernard Rosenberg, interviewed by Maurice Isserman, October 16, 1983.

11. Howe, letter to Coser, November 1957, Coser Papers, Box 2, Boston College.

12. Howe, "Problems of National Communism," 124.

13. Lisa Long (Brandeis University archivist), letter to author, February 22, 2001.

14. In addition to *Politics and the Novel*, Howe in 1957, produced with Lewis Coser, a history of *The American Communist Party* (Boston: Beacon Press, 1957), and with Israel Knox, a history of *The Jewish Labor Movement in America* (New York: Jewish Labor Committee, 1957).

15. Howe, *Politics and the Novel* (New York: Columbia University Press, 1992), 11, 15, 20.

16. *Politics and the Novel* was completed in 1954 but not published until 1957. Howe found the delay in getting into print "the best thing [he'd] written yet . . . galling." Howe, letter to Victor Walter, November 18, 1954; Howe, letter to Coser, September 10, 1957, Coser Papers, Box 2, Boston College.

17. Howe, *Politics and the Novel*, 22, 57–60, 71.

18. Ibid., 22, 120, 132–138. In an introduction to the 1992 edition of *Politics and the Novel*, Howe wrote that the book "was written at a moment when I was gradually drifting away from orthodox Marxism," 7.

19. Ibid., 216, 36.

20. Donald Gropman, interviewed by author, September 8, 1997; Larner, interviewed by author, June 19, 1997; Larner, "Remembering Irving Howe," *Dissent* 40 (Fall 1993): 539–541. Late in the year Howe reviewed Fast's memoir, *The Naked God* (1957), not very favorably. "Fast never explores the crucial question: what was it that held him, and others like him, for so long a time in a condition of intellectual bondage? The question matters not because it may reveal something about his personal psychology or because it comes as a thrust from hostile critics like myself, but because it helps us get at a major political and intellectual problem." He did, however, say, again as much in criticism as anything else, that the book "does contribute a few items to the documentation of the psychopathology of Stalinism. . . . There is Joseph Clark, then foreign correspondent of The Daily Worker telling Fast, "If you and Paul Robeson had raised your voices in 1949, Itzik Feffer [a Yiddish poet murdered by the Stalin regime] would be alive today." Howe, "A Captive Not Quite Freed," *New Republic*, December 16, 1987, 181–189.

21. Howe, ed., *Fiction as Experience: An Anthology* (New York: Harcourt Brace Jovanovich, 1978); Howe, ed., *Classics of Modern Fiction* (New York: Harcourt Brace and World, 1968).

22. Larner, "Remembering Irving Howe," 539–541; Howe, interviewed by Todd Gitlin (audiotape, April 15, 1985); Howe, *Margin*, 189.

23. Howe, letter to Coser, October [5?] 1957, Coser Papers, Box 2, Boston College.

24. Ibid., October [31?] 1957, Coser Papers, Box 2, Boston College.

25. Howe, "The Problem of National Communism," *Dissent* 4 (Spring 1957): 121–127.

26. Howe, "Notes on the Russian Turn," *Dissent* 3 (Summer 1956): 309–310; Howe, "The Problem of National Communism," 127; Howe, "Intellectuals and Russia," *Dissent* 6 (Summer 1959): 299; Howe, "Freedom and the Ashcan of History," *Partisan Review* 26 (Summer 1959): 267, 272. For the views of the neoconservatives on "dealing with the Communists," see *Commentary* magazine from 1975 to 1985.

27. Howe, "The Russian Attack on Hungary," 7; Howe, "1984—Utopia Reversed: Orwell's Penetrating Examination of Totalitarian Society," *New International* 16 (November–December 1950): 360–368.

28. Howe, *Margin*, 203.

29. Howe [as R. Fahan], "Machiavelli and Modern Political Thought," *New International* 9 (December 1943): 334–337.

30. Howe, letter to Victor Walter, July 1955.

31. In addition to a dozen or more articles in *Dissent* from 1956 to 1959 in which, cumulatively, Howe makes his views known, see Howe, *Politics and the Novel*, 22, 36, 57–60, 71–75, 120, 132–138; Howe, "Orwell as a Moderate Hero," *Partisan Review* 23 (Winter 1956): 103–108; Howe, "Of Freedom and Contemplation," *New Republic*, September 8, 1958; Howe, "Silone: The Power of Example," *New Republic*, September 22, 1958, 18–19; Howe, "On Ideas and Culture," *New Republic* February 2, 1959, 17–19.

32. Howe, *Politics and the Novel*, 203–235.

33. Howe, "The Weight of Days," *New Republic*, March 11, 1957, 17; emphasis mine.

34. Howe and Coser, *The American Communist Party* (Boston: Beacon Press, 1957), 233; Howe, "American Communism before Stalin," *Nation*, March 30, 1957, 280–281. The debate about just how much the American Communist Party was defined by the Soviet government is ongoing. For the view that the party was primarily a creature of the Soviets, see Theodore Draper, *The Roots of American Communism* (New York: Viking, 1957); Harvey Klehr, *The Heyday of American Communism: The Depression Decade* (New York: Basic Books, 1984); Allen Weinstein and Alexander Vassiliev, *The Haunted Wood: Soviet Espionage in America—The Stalin Era* (New York: Random House, 1999). For the Communist Party as a manifestation of native radicalism in America, see Maurice Isserman, *Which Side Were You On? The American Communist Party during the Second World War* (Middletown, Conn.: Wesleyan University Press, 1982); Mark Naison, *Communists in Harlem during the Great Depression* (Champaign: University of Illinois Press, 1983); Paul Mishler, *Raising Reds: The Young Pioneers, Radical Summer Camps and Communist Political Culture* (New York: Columbia University Press, 1999).

35. Howe and Coser, *The American Communist Party*, 498–499, 550–554.

36. For another view on this and for an altogether different take on Irving Howe, see Alan M. Wald, *The New York Intellectuals: The Rise and Decline of the*

336 NOTES TO CHAPTER 9

Anti-Stalinist Left from the 1930s to the 1980s (Chapel Hill: University of North Carolina Press, 1987), 311–321.

37. Irving Howe and A. J. Muste, "Two Statements," *Dissent* 4 (Summer 1957): 332–337.

38. Sidney Lens, *Unrepentant Radical* (Boston: Beacon Press, 1982), 222.

39. Howe, *Steady Work: Essays in the Politics of Democratic Radicalism, 1953–1966* (New York: Harcourt, Brace and World, 1966), 247.

40. Howe, "C. Wright Mills' Program," *Dissent* 6 (Spring 1959): 191–196; Howe and Coser, *The American Communist Party*, 552.

41. Howe and Mills, "The Intellectuals and Russia: An Exchange," *Dissent* 6 (Summer 1959): 295–299; Howe, "Of Freedom and Contemplation," *New Republic*, September 8, 1958, 16.

42. Willard Wyman, interviewed by author, October 18, 1997; Jane Wyman, interviewed by author February 26, 2001; Judith Walzer, interviewed by author, May 13, 1997.

43. Michael and Judith Walzer, interviewed by author, May 13, 1997.

44. Howe, letter to Lewis Coser, September 1957, Coser Papers, Box 2, Boston College Library; Nina Howe, "Remembering Irving Howe," *Dissent* 40 (Fall 1993): 534.

45. Howe, letters to Lewis Coser, September 20, [25?], October 2, 12, 1957, Coser Papers, Box 2, Boston College.

46. Howe, letter to Richard Chase, July 21, 1958, Special Collections, Columbia University.

47. Later, for some reason avoiding (or unconsciously denying) his own brief association with Wayne State, Howe told the following story about a "representative" student who had taken a class, not with him, but with the novelist Herbert Gold, Howe's colleague at Wayne: Gold tried to introduce some ideas about the moral problems that have plagued humanity since Socrates. The student, C. A., sat there, "impervious and recalcitrant, the classics bouncing off her like rubber balls off a fence." The Humanities, wrote C. A. in her final exam, "are a necessary additive to any teacher's development worth her 'salt' in the perilous times of today. The West and the 'Free World' must stand up to the war of ideas against the 'Iron Curtain.'" And this in answer to a question about Beethoven and Goethe in the context of German romanticism. C. A. did not earn a passing grade in the course but, Gold told Howe, she was "admitted on probation to the student-teacher program because of the teacher shortage and the great need to educate our children in these perilous times." Howe, "Universities and Intellectuals," *Dissent* 11 (Winter 1964): 11.

48. Joseph S. Murphy, interviewed by author, December 4, 1997; Maurice Stein (a colleague of Howe's at Brandeis), interviewed by author, July 25, 1997. The Cheskis story was confirmed by both Murphy and Stein.

49. Joseph S. Murphy, interviewed by author, December 4, 1997.

50. Howe, *A Margin of Hope*, 287. No less than nine of my correspondents and interviewees confirmed the affair between Edja and Irving, as well as the fact that it was no secret.

51. Victor Walter, interviewed by author, March 4, 1997.

52. Howe, letter to Morris Phillipson, July 11, 1960, Random House Collection, Columbia University Library.

53. Howe, letters to Coser, February 23, 1961, and May 15, 1961, Coser Papers, Box 3, Boston College. Howe's respect for therapy grew during this period and remained solid. In 1971, referring to Freud's famous "Wolf-Man" case, Howe wrote: "Some see in the story evidence of how inadequate Freudian therapy is, since the Wolf-Man had had to keep returning for additional treatment. Yet when one takes into account how immense were his psychic troubles at the time he came to Freud, a more reasonable judgment would be that even his partial ability to function as a normal person for periods of time, to say nothing of his growth in self-understanding, constitutes a tribute to the powers of psychoanalysis." Howe, "A Gathering of Good Works," *Harper's* (July 1971): 88–92.

54. Howe, letter to Malcolm Cowley, January 21, 1961, Cowley Collection, Newberry Library, Chicago.

55. David Levin, interviewed by author, June 5, 1997; Kay Seymour House, letter to author, May 5, 1997.

56. Victor Walter, interviewed by author, June 4, October 22, 1997; David Levin, interviewed by author, June 5, 1997; Dennis Wrong, interviewed by author, October 15, 1997.

57. Howe, letter to Phillipson, April 11, 1961, Random House Collection, Columbia University.

58. Howe, "Hemingway: The Conquest of a Panic," *New Republic*, July 24, 1961, 19–20.

59. Howe, letters to Coser: November 1961, Box 3; August 1962, Box 4; October 10, 15, 25, and November 2, 1962, Box 4, Coser Papers, Boston College; Howe, *Margin*, 287.

60. David Levin, *Exemplary Elders* (Athens: University of Georgia Press, 1990): 123–125. Levin told me that he had been "warned to expect a not very generous representation of the California episode in Howe's memoir." Even so, he said, "I was astonished by the brevity and simplicity of Irving's dismissal." Levin, interviewed by author, June 5, 1997.

61. Ibid.; Jackson Benson, *Wallace Stegner: His Life and Work* (New York: Penguin Books, 1997), 338–340. The Coe Chair was later reintroduced, but administrators promised that there would be no questioning of a nominee's political views. According to David Levin, that promise was kept, and Howe's successors endured not "so much as a hint of political interference." Levin, *Exemplary Elders*, 129. In contrast, the University of Minnesota decided simply to turn down a similar endowment from the Coe Foundation.

62. Howe, *Margin*, 288–289; Levin, *Exemplary Elders*, 127.

63. Howe, *Margin*, 288–289.

64. Jane and Bill Wyman, interviewed by author, October 18, 1997.

65. Ibid.

66. Alan Lelchuk, interviewed by author, June 30, 1997; Willie Morris, *New York Days* (Boston: Little Brown, 1993), 330–331.

67. Donald Hall, "Baseball and the Meaning of Life," in David Plaut, ed., *Baseball Wit and Wisdom* (Philadelphia: Running Press, 1992), 6; Howe, "Ballet for the Man who enjoys Wallace Stevens," *Harper's* (May 1971): 108.

68. Howe, letters to Coser, November 1961, October 1962, Box 3, and Box 4, Coser Papers, Boston College; Kay House, letter to author, May 13, 1997.

69. Joseph Murphy, interviewed by author, December 4, 1997.

70. Howe, letter to Coser, October 1962, Box 4, Coser Papers, Boston College.

71. Dennis Wrong, interviewed by author, October 15, 1997.

72. Howe, letter to Coser, October 1962, Box 4, Coser Papers, Boston College.

73. Levin, interviewed by author, June 5, 1997.

74. Howe, *Celebrations and Attacks: Thirty Years of Literary and Cultural Commentary* (New York: Harcourt Brace Jovanovich, 1979), 223.

75. Howe, "Robert Frost: A Momentary Stay," *New Republic*, March 23, 1963, 23–28.

76. Jane Wyman, interviewed by author, February 26, 2001.

77. Howe, *A World More Attractive* (New York: Horizon Press, 1963): 17. "T. E. Lawrence: The Problem of Heroism" was originally published in *Hudson Review* 15 (Autumn 1962): 333–364.

78. Ibid., 20.

79. Ibid., 29.

80. Ibid., 18.

81. Howe, "Yoknapatawpha County," *New York Times Book Review*, July 22, 1962, 6–7, 24.

82. Howe, *A World More Attractive*, 15.

83. Howe, letter to Coser, November 2, 1962, Coser Papers, Box 4, Boston College.

84. Howe, letter to Coser, June 1962, Coser Collection, Box 4, Boston College; David Levin, interviewed by author, June 5, 1997; Benson, *Wallace Stegner*, 339–340.

85. David Levin, interviewed by author, June 5, 1997; Benson, *Wallace Stegner*, 339–340; Howe, *Margin*, 287.

86. Interviews by author with David Levin, Jane Wyman, and Bill Wyman, as cited earlier; Thomas Moser, letter to author, July 2, 1997.

87. Kay Seymour House, letters to author, May 13 and May 30, 1997.

88. Howe, letter to Coser, August 1962, Coser Collection, Box 4, Boston College; Kay House, letter to author, May 30, 1997.

89. Kay House, letter to author, May 13, 1997.

90. Celia Morris, "Irving Howe: A Memoir" (unpublished typescript), 4, 6.

91. Gerald Graff, interviewed by author, April 14, 1997; Alan Lelchuk, interviewed by author, June 30, 1997.

92. Howe, "Universities and Intellectuals," 11.

93. Howe, "Journey to the End of Right," *Dissent* 9 (Winter 1962): 82.

94. Ibid.

95. Levin, interviewed by author, June 5, 1997; Levin, *Exemplary Elders*, 125–126; Howe, *Margin*, 284.

96. Lewis Coser, interviewed by author, April 8, 1997.

97. Howe, letter to Coser, November 5, 1962, Box 4, August 25, 1961, Box 3, Coser Papers, Boston College.

98. Howe, *Margin*, 289.

99. Samuel Hux, "Uncle Irving," *Modern Age* 37 (Summer 1995): 333; Howe, quoted in Victor Navasky, "Notes on Cult: Or, How to Join the Intellectual Establishment," *New York Times Magazine*, March 27, 1967, 128; Bert Stern, letter to author, January 30, 1997.

100. Howe, letter to Coser, August 1962, Box 4, Coser Papers, Boston College.

101. Ibid., November 5, 1962, Box 4, Coser Papers, Boston College.

102. Howe, "A New Political Atmosphere in America?" *Dissent* 6 (Winter 1959): 5–8; Howe, letters to Coser, November 1961, June 1962, October 1962, November 1962, Coser Papers, Box 3, Box 4, Boston College.

103. Michael Walzer, "After the Election," *Dissent* 8 (Winter 1961): 3.

NOTES TO CHAPTER 10

1. Howe, "Philip Rahv: A Memoir," *American Scholar* 48 (Autumn 1979): 495.

2. Howe, "A Revival of Radicalism?" *Dissent* 10 (Spring 1963): 111.

3. Howe, "The Decline in Democratic Sentiment," *Harper's Magazine*, August 1970, 93–98.

4. Howe, "The Negro Revolution," *Dissent* 10 (Summer 1963): 214; Howe, "The Negro Revolution (Continued)," *Dissent* 10 (Autumn 1963): 304.

5. Howe, *Steady Work: Essays in the Politics of Democratic Radicalism, 1953–1966* (New York: Harcourt Brace and World), 62; Howe, "Why Should Negroes Be above Criticism?" *Saturday Evening Post*, December 14, 1968, 10, 14–15.

6. Howe, "Toward a Free, Multi-Racial America" (unpublished draft, 1963); Howe, letter, *New York Times*, February 16, 1965; Howe, "What Is New

about Selma?" *Dissent* 12 (Spring 1965): 147–149; Howe, "Writer Can't Keep to His Attic," *New York Times Magazine*, December 5, 1965, 43–45; Howe, "The First Generation of SNCC," *Dissent* 14 (July–August 1967): 461–463; Howe, "Where Is the Negro Movement Now?" *Dissent* 15 (November–December 1968): 491–493; Howe, "Nixon's Dream and Black Reality," *Dissent* 16 (March–April 1969): 101–107.

7. Howe, "What Is New about Selma?" 148.

8. Joseph Dorman, *Arguing the World: The New York Intellectuals in Their Own Words* (New York: Free Press, 2000), 199–200; Jervis Anderson, interviewed by author, June 12, 1997; Howe, interviewed by William Cain, *American Literary History* 1 (Fall 1989): 556–564.

9. Howe, "Black Boys and Native Sons," *Dissent* 10 (Autumn 1963), reprinted in Howe, *A World More Attractive* (New York: Horizon Press, 1963), 100–101.

10. Ibid., 107.

11. Morris Dickstein, *Gates of Eden: American Culture in the Sixties* (New York: Basic Books, 1977), 175–176; Howe, "The Return of the Case of Ezra Pound," *New York World Magazine*, October 24, 1972, 20–24.

12. Howe, *Steady Work*, 52–53.

13. Howe, *A World More Attractive*, 98–122.

14. Howe, *Celebrations and Attacks: Thirty Years of Literary and Cultural Commentary* (New York: Harcourt Brace Jovanovich, 1979), 31.

15. Howe, *A World More Attractive*, 100. Baldwin having published, later in 1963, *The Fire Next Time*, a protest essay of some significance, remained mostly out of the debate.

16. Ralph Ellison, *Shadow and Act* (New York: Random House, 1964), 112. Herein Ellison published "The World and the Jug," a combination of two separate essays published in the *New Leader*, December 9, 1963, and February 3, 1964, the first in response to Howe's "Black Boys . . ." and the second in rejoinder to Howe's reply to Ellison's response.

17. Ibid.

18. Howe, "New Black Writers," *Harper's* 239 (December 1969): 131.

19. Howe, "A Reply to Ralph Ellison," *New Leader*, February 3, 1964, 12–14.

20. Howe, "Sholom Aleichem and His People," *Partisan Review* 13 (November–December 1946): 592–594; Howe, "An Unknown Treasure of World Literature: Who Will Make Sholom Aleichem Available?" *Commentary* 14 (September 1952): 270–273; Howe, *Treasury of Yiddish Stories* (New York: Viking Press, 1954), 37–71, 74–76; Howe, *Treasury of Yiddish Poetry* (New York: Harcourt Brace Jovanovich, 1969), 30–31.

21. William Phillips, *A Partisan View* (New York: Stein and Day, 1983), 116.

22. Ellison, *Shadow and Act*, 107.

23. Jervis Anderson, interviewed by author, June 12, 1997; Howe, *A Margin of Hope* (New York: Harcourt Brace Jovanovich, 1982), 258; Howe, *Selected Writings 1950–1990* (New York: Harcourt Brace Jovanovich, 1990), 138.

24. Cynthia Ozick, "Literary Blacks and Jews," in Paul Berman, ed., *Blacks and Jews: Alliances and Arguments* (New York: Delacorte Press, 1994), 74n.

25. Hannah Arendt, *Eichmann in Jerusalem: A Report on the Banality of Evil* (New York: Viking Press, 1963), appeared originally as a series of articles in the *New Yorker*. To get some better sense of the heat generated in the intellectual community and the Jewish community generally and for the various perspectives, see *Partisan Review*, Summer 1963, Fall 1963, Winter 1964; and *Commentary*, September 1963, October 1963, February 1964.

26. Daniel Bell, "The Alphabet of Justice," *Partisan Review* 30 (Fall 1963): 428.

27. Howe, "The New Yorker and Hannah Arendt," *Commentary* (October 1963): 319.

28. Blucher, letter to Arendt, mid-March 1963, in Lotte Köhler, ed., *Within Four Walls: The Correspondence between Hannah Arendt and Heinrich Blucher, 1936–1968* (New York: Harcourt, 2001), 386.

29. Lionel Abel, "The Aesthetics of Evil," *Partisan Review* 30 (Summer 1963): 211–230.

30. Howe, letter to Lewis Coser, September 1963, Coser Papers, Box 4, Boston College.

31. Daniel Bell, interviewed by author, October 30, 1998; Dennis Wrong (also in attendance at the forum), interviewed by author, October 15, 1997.

32. Ibid; Howe, "More on Eichmann," *Partisan Review* 31 (Spring 1964): 260.

33. Alfred Kazin, interviewed by author, May 15, 1997; Dennis Wrong, interviewed by author, October 15, 1997; Daniel Bell, interviewed by author, October 30, 1998. See also Wrong's letter to *Commentary*, February 1983, 6–7. Elisabeth Young-Bruehl, the author of *For Love of the World: A Biography of Hannah Arendt* (New Haven: Yale University Press, 1982), was one of those who misrepresented the Kazin incident, writing that he was "ushered out with a roar from Lionel Abel." Howe did not let this pass: "Since I wanted to lean over backward in behalf of fairness," Howe insisted, "I gave [Kazin] the floor. . . . We of *Dissent* . . . have a cherished record of tolerance and freedom on such matters that we cherish, and I do not take lightly any insinuations that we have behaved otherwise." This was not quite the finish for Howe, who was clearly furious with Miss Young-Bruehl. "I also recall," he continued, "that I indicated to you a readiness to talk about my relations with Hannah, which would have included of course the *Dissent* forum. You chose not to take up that offer. . . . Given what you have in your book, I wonder whether you decided as you did because you

knew only too well how you wanted that page to read." *Dissent* 19 (Summer 1982): 382–383.

34. Kazin, interviewed by Alexander Bloom, October 23, 1976, in Bloom, *Prodigal Sons: The New York Intellectuals and Their World* (New York: Oxford University Press, 1986), 330; Kazin, *A Lifetime Burning in Every Moment* (New York: HarperCollins, 1996), 179.

35. Podhoretz, quoted in Howe, *Margin*, 274–275.

36. Midge Decter, "The Irresponsibility of the Socialists," *Commentary* 74 (December 1982): 31; Howe, letter to Marie Syrkin, January 7, 1983, Syrkin Papers, Jacob Rader Marcus Center of the American Jewish Archives.

37. Phillips, McCarthy, Macdonald, Lowell, et al., "More on Eichmann," *Partisan Review* 31 (Spring 1964): 253–283.

38. Daniel Bell, "The Alphabet of Justice," 428, 417.

39. Howe, quoted in Bernard Rosenberg, ed., *Creators and Disturbers: Reminiscences by Jewish Intellectuals of New York* (New York: Columbia University Press, 1982), 285–286.

40. Jeremy Larner, interviewed by author, June 19, 1997.

41. Howe, "Strangers," *Yale Review* 66 (June 1977): 486–487; Arien Mack, interviewed by author, October 12, 2000; Mack, letters to author, February 8 and 22, 1997; Howe, letter to Lenore Marshall, July 27, 1968, Columbia University, Manuscript Collections; Jeremy Larner, interviewed by author, June 19, 1997.

42. Howe, letter to Lenore Marshall, September 18, 1971, Columbia University, Manuscript Collections.

43. Howe, *Margin*, 291.

44. This section and much of what follows on the SDS and the development of a New Left depends in part on three excellent studies: Morris Dickstein, *Gates of Eden: American Culture in the Sixties* (New York: Basic Books, 1977); Maurice Isserman, *If I Had a Hammer: The Death of the Old Left and the Birth of the New Left* (Urbana: University of Illinois Press, 1987); and Todd Gitlin, *The Sixties: Years of Hope, Years of Rage* (New York: Bantam Books, 1993).

45. *The Port Huron Statement* (New York: Students for a Democratic Society, 1964).

46. Tom Hayden, "Draft Paper for S.D.S. Manifesto," 1962, 20–23, quoted in Gitlin, *The Sixties*, 113.

47. Michael Harrington, *Fragments of the Century: A Social Autobiography* (New York: Dutton, 1973), 146–147.

48. Harrington, "The American Campus," *Dissent* 9 (Spring 1962): 164–166.

49. *The Port Huron Statement*, 24–25.

50. Michael Walzer, "Dissent at Thirty," *Dissent* 31 (Winter 1984): 3–4.

51. Arthur Mitzman, "The Campus Radical in 1960," *Dissent* 7 (Spring 1960): 142–143; Michael Walzer et al., "The Young Radicals: A Symposium,"

Dissent 9 (Spring 1962): 129–163; Lewis Coser, "The Young Radicals," 159–162; Howe and Coser, "New Styles in Fellow Traveling," *Dissent* 8 (Fall 1961): 496–498; Coser, interviewed by Maurice Isserman, May 3, 1985; Michael Walzer, interviewed by author, May 13, 1997.

52. Gitlin, *The Sixties*, 172; Howe, *Margin*, 291–292.

53. Joseph Dorman, *Arguing the World*, 139.

54. Howe, *Margin*, 292.

55. Howe, interviewed by Todd Gitlin (audiotape, April 15, 1985).

56. Todd Gitlin, interviewed by author, March 18, 1997; Howe, interviewed by Todd Gitlin (audiotape April 15, 1985); Dorman, *Arguing the World*, 143.

57. Howe, "Notes from Jerusalem," *New York Review of Books*, September 29, 1988, 14.

58. Howe, interviewed by Todd Gitlin (audiotape April 15, 1985).

59. Since the early sixties, Howe had called for supporting liberal elements even if they were associated with the Democratic Party. In 1965, only months after his encounter with Hayden, Howe wrote: "In Texas, there is a coalition of labor, liberal, intellectual, and minority groups (Negro, Mexican) within the Democratic Party—and by all accounts a pretty good coalition. Can one say, as if all wisdom were bunched into our fist, that such a development should not be supported simply because it grows up within the framework of a major party?" *Steady Work*, 66.

60. Jack Newfield, "New Styles in Leftism—Round Two," *Village Voice*, May 13, 1965, 9; Todd Gitlin, interviewed by author, March 18, 1997; Jeremy Larner (who was on the panel), interviewed by author, June 19, 1997; Michael Walzer, interviewed by author, May 13, 1997.

61. Newfield, "Revolt without Dogma: The Student Left," *The Nation*, May 10, 1965, 494; Howe, Letter to *The Nation*, May 24, 1965; Bernard Avishai, interviewed by author, April 7, 1997.

62. Howe, interviewed by Todd Gitlin (audiotape April 15, 1985).

63. Ibid.; Howe, *Margin*, 293.

64. Todd Gitlin, interviewed by author, March 18, 1997; Paul Berman, interviewed by author, October 8, 1998.

65. Walzer, interviewed by author, May 13, 1997; Arien Mack, interviewed by author, October 12, 2000.

66. Walzer, interviewed by author, May 13, 1997.

67. Ibid.; Walzer in Dorman, *Arguing the World*, 143–144.

68. Isserman, *If I Had a Hammer*, 119–122; Gitlin, *The Sixties*, 117–121.

69. Gitlin, *The Sixties*, 174–192; Isserman, *If I Had a Hammer*, 202–219; Paul Berman, "Democracy in the Streets," *New Republic*, August 10 and 17, 1987, 28–35; Berman, interviewed by author, October 8, 1998.

70. Howe, interviewed by Maurice Isserman (unpublished transcript, January 24, 1982); Howe, interviewed by Todd Gitlin (audiotape April 15, 1985).

NOTES TO CHAPTER II

1. Howe, interviewed by Todd Gitlin (audiotape April 15, 1985); Michael Walzer, interviewed by author, May 13, 1997; Arien Mack, interviewed by author, October 12, 2000.

2. Howe, "Berkeley and Beyond," *New Republic*, May 11, 1965, 63; Howe, "New Styles in Leftism," *Dissent* 12 (Summer 1965): 295–317. The essay was included in Howe's *Steady Work: Essays in the Politics of Democratic Radicalism, 1953–1966* (New York: Harcourt, Brace and World, 1966); *The Radical Imagination: An Anthology from Dissent* (New York: New American Library, 1967); *Beyond the New Left: A Confrontation and Critique* (New York: McCall Publishing, 1970), and *Selected Writings 1950–1990* (New York: Harcourt Brace Jovanovich, 1990).

3. Marshall Berman, "Remembering Irving Howe," *Dissent* 40 (Fall 1993): 519–520.

4. Howe, interviewed by Maurice Isserman (unpublished transcript, October 21, 1982); Howe, *A Margin of Hope: An Intellectual Autobiography* (New York: Harcourt Brace Jovanovich, 1982), 315.

5. Howe, "Berkeley and Beyond," 59–62; Howe, "New Styles in Leftism," 295.

6. Howe, "Berkeley and Beyond," 63.

7. Tom Hayden, *Reunion: A Memoir* (New York: Random House, 1988), 92.

8. Richard Pells, *The Liberal Mind in a Conservative Age* (New York: Harper and Row, 1985), 380.

9. Howe, "New Styles in Leftism," 300–301.

10. Howe et al., "Declaration to Ambassador Adlai Stevenson," *New York Times*, April 18, 1965, 22.

11. Howe, "Vietnam: The Costs and Lessons of Defeat," *Dissent* 12 (Spring 1965): 151–154; Howe, "I'd Rather Be Wrong," *New York Review of Books*, June 17, 1965, 8.

12. Howe, "Vietnam: The Costs and Lessons of Defeat," 154; Howe et al., "On Vietnam and the Dominican Republic," *Partisan Review* 32 (Summer 1965): 397–398.

13. Howe et al., "The Vietnam Protests," *New York Review of Books*, November 25, 1965, 12–13.

14. Howe, "Last Chance in Vietnam," *Dissent* 11 (Summer 1964): 275–278; Howe, "Vietnam: The Costs and Lessons of Defeat," 151–154.

15. Howe, "Last Chance in Vietnam," 275–278.

16. Howe and Walzer "formally" debated the Vietnam question in *Dissent* 12 (Spring 1965): 151–156. SANE, a grassroots citizens' organization, had lobbied successfully for passage of the partial nuclear test ban treaty in 1963.

17. Howe, interviewed by Todd Gitlin (audiotape October 15, 1985); Howe, quoted in the _New York Times_, October 20, 1967, 9; Howe, _Margin_, 299–301.

18. Howe, "Vietnam: Costs and Lessons of Defeat," 154; Howe, _Steady Work_, 199–201. As early as April 1965, in a letter to the activist group Artists and Writers Dissent, Howe, said he saw "the military victory of the Vietcong [as] a disaster," but one that "it would be best to accept," since the only available method for avoiding a Vietcong triumph is a wider, deeper war. Michael Harrington Papers, Tamiment Library, New York University.

19. Howe, "Response," _Partisan Review_ 32 (Fall 1965): 628–629.

20. _New America_, April 30, 1965, 5. Howe was less worried about the participation of Communist Party members in marches and rallies than he was about their public sponsorship of the demonstrations. He was even more worried about people like M. S. Arnoni, a pro-Communist editor who allegedly urged Berkeley students to volunteer for the Vietcong, and who in other ways expressly worked for a Communist victory in South Vietnam. Howe, letter to "Artists and Writers Dissent," April 1965, Michael Harrington Papers, Tamiment Library, New York University.

21. Maurice Isserman, _The Other American: The Life of Michael Harrington_ (New York: Public Affairs, 2000), 256–264.

22. Michael Harrington, _Fragments of the Century: A Social Autobiography_ (New York: Dutton, 1973), 157–160.

23. Carl Oglesby, interviewed by Maurice Isserman, April 20, 1993, quoted in Isserman, _The Other American_, 258.

24. The full text of the statement appeared in _New America_, October 31, 1965, 5.

25. Philip Nobile, _Intellectual Skywriting: Literary Politics and the "New York Review of Books"_ (New York: Charter House, 1974), 35.

26. I. F. Stone, "Daydreams and Suicide Tactics," _New America_, June 18, 1965, 5. For more on Stone's involvement with antiwar protest, see Robert C. Cottrell, _Izzy: A Biography of I. F. Stone_ (New Brunswick, N.J.: Rutgers University Press, 1992), 238–259.

27. Howe, "Writer Can't Keep to His Attic," _New York Times Magazine_, December 5, 1965, 43–45.

28. See especially "What Is New about Selma?" _Dissent_ 12 (Spring 1965): 147–149; "The First Generation of SNCC," _Dissent_ 14 (July–August 1967): 461–466; "Where Is the Negro Movement Now?" _Dissent_ 15 (November–December 1968): 491–493; and "Nixon's Dream and Black Reality," _Dissent_ 16 (March–April 1969): 101–107.

29. Many of the essays are collected in _Decline of the New_ (New York: Harcourt Brace and World, 1970) and _The Critical Point_ (New York: Horizon Press, 1973).

30. Marshall Berman, "Remembering Irving Howe," *Dissent* 40 (Fall 1993): 520.

31. Howe, letter to Lionel Trilling, June 23, 1966, Trilling Papers, Columbia University.

32. Howe, letter to Lewis Coser, September 1967, Coser Papers, Box 8, Boston College.

33. Howe, *Thomas Hardy* (New York: Macmillan, 1967), 2, 21, 45.

34. Howe, "On Ideas and Culture," *New Republic*, February 2, 1959, 17–19.

35. Howe, *Thomas Hardy*, 2, 23–24.

36. Howe, "On Ideas and Culture," *New Republic*, February 2, 1959, 17–19.

37. Howe, *Thomas Hardy*, 30.

38. Howe, "The Short Poems of Thomas Hardy," *Southern Review* (Autumn 1966): 879.

39. Howe, *Margin*, 322; Howe, *Thomas Hardy*, 30.

40. Howe, letter to Lenore Marshall, July 27, 1968, Manuscript Collections, Columbia University; Arien Mack, interviewed by author, October 12, 2000.

41. Nina Howe, "Remembering Irving Howe," *Dissent* 40 (Fall 1993): 533–534.

42. Arien Mack, interviewed by author, October 12, 2000; Alfred Kazin, interviewed by author, May 15, 1997; Kazin, *New York Jew* (New York: Alfred Knopf, 1978), 237.

43. Arien Mack, interviewed by author, October 12, 2000; Howe, letter to Lionel Trilling, November 1970, Trilling Papers, Columbia University; Howe, *Margin*, 323–325.

44. Howe, "Ballet for the Man Who Enjoys Wallace Stevens," *Harper's* (May 1971): 102–109; Morris Dickstein, *Gates of Eden: American Culture in the Sixties* (New York: Basic Books, 1976), 275.

45. Howe, *Margin*, 284–285; Howe, "Introduction," in *A Treasury of Yiddish Poetry*, ed. Howe and Eliezer Greenberg (New York: Holt, Rinehart and Winston, 1969), 61; Howe, "Introduction," in *The Penguin Book of Modern Yiddish Verse*, ed. Howe et al. (New York: Viking Penguin, 1987), 47.

46. Howe, "Tevye on Broadway," *Commentary* 38 (November 1964): 73–75.

47. There have been attempts by revisionist historians to shift a major part of the responsibility for the war to Israel. See especially Benny Morris, *Righteous Victims: A History of the Zionist Arab Conflict, 1881–1999* (London: J. Murray, 2000), and Avi Shlaim, *the Iron Wall: Israel and the Arab World* (New York: W. W. Norton, 2000). Whatever the merits of these accounts, Israel, in the late spring of 1967, understandably perceived that its existence was at stake. In mid-May, Egypt announced the closing of the Tiran Straits, massed troops on its border with Israel, successfully encouraged Jordan and Syria to do the same, and got Iraq and Saudi Arabia to mobilize as well. Only days earlier, government-controlled Cairo radio announced: "This is our chance, Arabs, to deal Israel a mor-

tal blow of annihilation, to blot out her entire existence in our holy land." And on May 30 the station declared that Israel will either be strangled to death economically or "perish by the fire of the Arab forces encompassing it from the South, from the North and from the East." Similar announcements were made by Egypt's President Nasser and leaders of other Arab states. Still, Israel waited from May 15 to June 5 before it launched a preemptive strike. Martin Gilbert, *The Arab-Israeli Conflict: Its History in Maps* (Jerusalem: Steimatzky, 1990), 65–67; Walter Laqueur and Barry Rubin, eds., *The Israel-Arab Reader: A Documentary History of the Conflict* (New York: Bantam Books, 1985), 175–189.

48. Howe and Stanley Plastrik, "After the Mid-East War," *Dissent* 14 (July–August 1967): 387–390.

49. Henry Pachter, "Troubles of a Jewish Conscience," *Dissent* 14 (July–August 1967): 485–486; Michael Walzer, interviewed by author, May 13, 1997; Howe and Plastrik, "After the Mid-East War," 387.

50. Howe, "Introduction," in Howe and Carl Gershman, eds., *Israel, the Arabs and the Middle East* (New York: Bantam Books,1972), 1–2.

51. Howe and Plastrik, "After the Mid-East War," 389.

52. Howe, "The New York Intellectuals: A Chronicle and a Critique," in *Decline of the New*, 245, originally published in *Commentary* 46 (October 1968): 29–51.

53. Howe, "Political Terrorism: Hysteria on the Left," *New York Times Magazine*, April 12, 1970, 25–27, 124–128; Howe, "Vietnam and Israel," *Dissent* 17 (September–October 1970): 404.

54. Howe and Plastrik, "After the Mid-East War," 389.

55. Nadav Safran, *Israel: The Embattled Ally* (Cambridge, Mass.: Harvard University Press, 1981), 226.

56. Howe, "Vietnam and Israel," 404.

57. Howe, "Introduction," in Howe and Carl Gershman, eds., *Israel, the Arabs and the Middle East*, 2.

58. See letters from Howe to Shachtman from August 1961 to June 1963, microfilm reel 3379, Max Shachtman Collection, Tamiment Library, New York University.

59. Peter Drucker, *Max Shachtman and His Left* (Atlantic Highlands, N.J.: Humanities Press, 1994), 280–281, 300–301; Howe, "Vietnam: The Costs and Lessons of Defeat," 151–154; Howe, "Open Letter," *Dissent* 14 (January–February 1967): 107; Howe et al., "What Can We Do?" *Dissent* 14 (July–August 1967): 399.

60. Isserman, *The Other American*, 271.

61. Howe to Shachtman, May 3, 1969, and Shachtman to Howe, May 13, 1969, Shachtman Collection, Reel 3379, Tamiment Library, New York University.

62. Howe, "Harvey Swados, 1920–1972," *Dissent* 20 (Spring 1973): 149–150.

63. Harvey Swados, letter to the *New York Review of Books*, March 1, 1967, Harvey Swados Papers, University of Massachusetts at Amherst.

64. Harvey Swados, letter to Howe, March 13, 1967, Harvey Swados Papers, University of Massachusetts at Amherst.

65. Howe, letter to Harvey Swados, April 7, 1967, Harvey Swados Papers, University of Massachusetts at Amherst. Swados's charge that Irving's anti-Communism helped sustain American behavior in Vietnam was echoed only a few months later when Howe participated in a *Commentary* magazine symposium that asked liberal and left anti-Communists if they felt any responsibility for U.S. policy in Southeast Asia. Most respondents were absolute in their denials, including Howe, who said, "None whatever." He explained that he and his allies in the fifties had criticized both extremes—the Stalinists and the overzealous McCarthyite anti-Communists. "We had the choice," Howe said, "of telling the truth . . . knowing it might be exploited by the reactionaries, or of keeping silent and thereby not merely acquiescing in horrible events but allowing the reactionaries to exploit the truth all the more effectively." He thought there was no logic to the idea that leftist anti-Communism had to lead straight to the Cold War strategies of John Foster Dulles or Dean Rusk. This was just as simpleminded, he said, as the notion that opposition to capitalism had to lead to Stalinist terror. Howe et al., "Liberal Anti-Communism Revisited: A Symposium," *Commentary* 44 (September 1967): 31–79.

66. Howe, letter to Swados, April 7, 1967, Harvey Swados Papers, University of Massachusetts at Amherst.

67. Howe, "The Prosecution of U.S. Communists," *Dissent* 10 (Winter 1963): 12.

68. Howe, letter to Swados, April 10, 1967, Harvey Swados Papers, University of Massachusetts at Amherst.

69. Howe, *Steady Work*, xiii.

70. Howe, *Decline of the New*, 15–17.

71. Ibid., 30–33, 255.

72. Ibid., 257.

73. Howe, interviewed by Todd Gitlin (audiotape, October 15, 1985).

74. Howe, *Decline of the New*, 252–260; Morris Dickstein, *The Gates of Eden*, 9–10.

75. Howe, *A World More Attractive: A View of Modern Literature and Politics* (New York: Horizon Press, 1963), ix; Howe, *Celebrations and Attacks: Thirty Years of Literary and Cultural Commentary* (New York: Harcourt Brace Jovanovich, 1979), 144, 124.

76. Howe, "Fiction: Bellow, O'Hara, Litwak," *Harper's* (February 1970): 106, 114.

77. Howe, *Celebrations and Attacks*, 124; Howe, *A World More Attractive*, 273; Howe, *Decline of the New*, 253.

78. Philip Rahv, "Left Face," *New York Review of Books*, October 12, 1967, 10–13.

79. Howe, "Philip Rahv: A Memoir," *American Scholar* 48 (Autumn 1979): 497.

80. Howe, "An Exchange on the Left," *New York Review of Books*, November 23, 1967, 36–39.

81. Philip Rahv, "An Exchange on the Left," *New York Review of Books*, November 23, 1967, 42.

82. Howe, "Philip Rahv: A Memoir," 497–498.

83. Howe quoted in Andrew James Dvosin, "Literature in a Political World: The Career and Writings of Philip Rahv," Ph.D. dissertation, New York University, 1977, 207, 179.

84. Howe, *Decline of the New*, 263; Michael Walzer, interviewed by author, May 13, 1997; Dennis Wrong, interviewed by author, October 15, 1997; Dennis Wrong, "The Case of the New York Review," *Commentary*, November 1970, 54–59; *New York Review of Books*, August 24, 1967; Philip Nobile, *Intellectual Skywriting: Literary Politics and the "New York Review of Books*," 50.

85. Howe, "A Word about 'Bourgeois Civil Liberties," *Dissent* 15 (January–February 1968): 10.

86. Howe, "Notes on the Here and Now," *Partisan Review* 34 (Fall 1967): 581; Howe, letter to Benjamin Nelson, September 26, 1967, Benjamin Nelson Papers, Columbia University; Howe, *Decline of the New*, 40–41, originally published as "Beliefs of the Masters," *New Republic*, September 16, 1967.

87. Howe, letter to the *New York Times*, December 17, 1967.

88. Howe, letter to Coser, March 1968, Coser Papers, Box 8, Boston College; Howe, letter to Harvey Swados, July 12, 1968, Swados Papers, University of Massachusetts at Amherst.

89. Howe, *Margin*, 312.

90. Howe, "Collapse of a Myth," *Dissent* 15 (March–April 1968): 199.

91. Ibid; Howe, letter to Swados, July 12, 1968, Swados Papers, University of Massachusetts at Amherst.

92. Howe, "Draft Statement on the Draft," March 1968, Albert Glotzer Collection, Box 34, Hoover Institution, Stanford University.

93. "Statement on the Draft," *Dissent* 15 (May–June 1968): 193–196.

94. *Village Voice*, May 30, 1968, 1.

95. Howe, "Introduction," in *Beyond the New Left: A Confrontation and Critique* (New York: McCall, 1970), 14.

96. Howe, "In This Moment of Grief," *Dissent* 15 (May–June 1968): 197.

97. Howe, "A Triumph of Democracy," *Dissent* 15 (May–June 1968): 198–199.

98. Howe, letter to Lewis Coser, May 1, 1968, Lewis Coser Papers, Box 8, Boston College; Howe, letter to Christopher Lasch, June 1, 1968, Lasch Papers,

University of Rochester; Howe, "Confrontation Politics Is a Dangerous Game," in *Beyond the New Left*, 40–54. The article originally appeared in the *New York Times Magazine*, October 20, 1968.

99. Howe, letter to Lewis Coser, May 3, 1968, Coser Papers, Box 8, Boston College.

100. Ibid., May 7,1968, Coser Papers, Box 8, Boston College.

101. Howe, *Beyond the New Left*, 45–46.

102. Ibid., 54.

103. Jonah Raskin, *For the Hell of It: The Life and Times of Abbie Hoffman* (Berkeley: University of California Press, 1997), 146, 251.

104. Ibid.

105. Howe, letter to the *New York Times*, February 20, 1970, reprinted in *Dissent* 17 (March–April 1970): 102.

106. Howe, letter to Lew Coser, June 20, 1968, Coser Papers, Box 8, Boston College.

107. Howe et al., "How Shall We Vote?" *Dissent* 15 (November–December 1968): 469–472; Howe, "And Now, God Help Us, Nixon," *Dissent* 16 (January–February 1969): 19.

108. Paul Berman, "Democracy in the Streets," *New Republic*, August 10 and 17, 1987, 28–35; Todd Gitlin, *The Sixties: Years of Hope, Years of Rage* (New York: Bantam Books, 1993), 381–402.

109. Howe, "The Agony of the Campus," *Dissent* 16 (September–October 1969): 388.

110. Howe, interviewed by Enrique Krauze, in *Personas e ideas* (Mexico: Editorial Vuelte, 1989), 44–47, translated by Myra Sorin; Howe, interviewed by Todd Gitlin (audiotape, October 15, 1985).

111. Howe, "George Orwell: As the Bones Know," *Harper's* (January 1969): 98.

112. Howe, "Allard Lowenstein (1929–1980)," *Dissent* 27 (Spring 1980): 259; Martin Peretz, interviewed by author, August 28, 1997; Howe, letter to Lewis Coser, September 29, 1968, Coser Papers, Box 9, Boston College, indicates a $5,000 contribution from Peretz.

113. Howe, letter to Max Shachtman, May 3, 1969, Shachtman Collection, Reel 3379, Tamiment Institute, New York University.

114. Arien Mack, interviewed by author, October 12, 2000; Michael Weinstein, "A Long Lunch with Irving Howe," *New York Times*, May 10, 1993; Howe, *Margin*, 306. There are several variations of this story, but all are similar and contain the same dynamics. My version is a composite developed out of the three sources listed above.

115. Michael Walzer, interviewed by author, May 13, 1997; Howe, letters to Lewis Coser, September 15, 1968, September 29, 1968, September 18, 1969, and

November 1969, Coser Papers, Boxes 9 and 10, Boston College; Howe, letter to Max Shachtman, July 11, 1969, Max Shachtman Collection, Reel 3379, Tamiment Institute, New York University.

116. Howe, letter to Lewis Coser, March 21, 1969, Coser Papers, Box 9, Boston College.

117. Howe, letter to Tom Kahn, April 13, 1969, Max Shachtman Collection, Reel 3376, Tamiment Institute, New York University.

118. Howe, letters to Tom Kahn, June [n.d.] 1969, and June 10, 1969, Max Shachtman Collection, Reels 3379, 3380, Tamiment Institute, New York University.

NOTES TO CHAPTER 12

1. Howe, letter to Tom Kahn, June 10, 1969, Max Shachtman Collection, Reel 3380, Tamiment Institute, New York University Library.

2. Howe, *A Margin of Hope: An Intellectual Autobiography* (New York: Harcourt Brace Jovanovich, 1982), 328. For a perceptive and illuminating analysis of the seventies, see Bruce J. Schulman, *The Seventies: The Great Shift in American Culture, Society and Politics* (New York: Free Press, 2001).

3. Maurice Isserman, *The Other American: The Life of Michael Harrington* (New York: Perseus Press, 2000), 313.

4. Howe, *The Critical Point: On Literature and Culture* (New York: Horizon Press, 1973), 10.

5. Howe, *Margin*, 329–335; Howe, interviewed by Joseph Dorman (unpublished transcript, 1993), 32.

6. Todd Gitlin, interviewed by author, March 18, 1997; Howe, *Margin*, 331.

7. Howe, letter to Lewis Coser, November 1970, Coser Papers, Box 10, Boston College.

8. Howe, *The Critical Point*, 203–231.

9. Morris Dickstein, letter to author, November 12, 2001; Arien Mack, letter to author, November 12, 2001.

10. Howe, "On Sexual Politics: The Middle-Class Mind of Kate Millett, *Harper's* (December 1970): 120–129.

11. Some of my take on this is informed by discussions with the psychoanalyst and student of literature, Dr. Stanley Coen.

12. Howe, letter to Lionel Trilling, December 3, 1972, Trilling Papers, Columbia University.

13. Howe, *Margin*, 334.

14. Elizabeth Hardwick, quoted in David Laskin, *Partisans: Marriage, Politics, and Betrayal among the New York Intellectuals* (New York: Simon and Schuster, 2000), 192; Arien Mack, interviewed by author, October 12, 2000.

15. Interviews by author of Joanne Barkan, May 7, 1997; Paula Fox, March 31, 1997; Judith Walzer, May 13, 1997; Jane Wyman, February 26, 2001; Todd Gitlin, March 18, 1997; Michael Walzer, May 13, 1997. Howe, *Margin*, 333, 335.

16. Howe, *Celebrations and Attacks*, 36–38.

17. Howe, *Critical Point*, 146–147.

18. Howe, "Fiction: Bellow, O'Hara, Litwak," *Harper's* (February 1970): 106–114; Alfred Kazin, "The Jew as Modern Writer," in *The Commentary Reader*, ed. Norman Podhoretz (New York: Atheneum,1966), xvi. Donald Weber brought Kazin's article to my attention and generously shared with me his thoughts on Howe, Bellow, and "Jewish Opera."

19. Howe, *Critical Point*, 153–154.

20. Morris Dickstein, letter to author, October 18, 2001. It was Ilana Howe who told Dickstein that Irving was considering a new essay on Roth.

21. Philip Roth, *Reading Myself and Others* (New York: Penguin Books, 1985), 20.

22. Bernard Avishai, interviewed by author, April 7, 1997.

23. George Konrad, "Remembering Irving Howe," *Dissent* 40 (Fall 1993): 537.

24. James Atlas, "A Visit with Philip Roth," *New York Times Book Review*, September 2, 1979, 12–13. Like Roth, an extraordinary number of Howe's friends and colleagues thought Irving was a "real" reader, and writer, too. Most of them, especially the younger people contributing to *Dissent*, say they learned to write better under Howe's careful eye and critical but supportive tutelage. And they say still, years after his death, that when composing an article, they imagine Irving as their "designated reader." See "Remembering Irving Howe," *Dissent* 40 (Fall 1993): 514–551.

25. Roth, *Reading Myself*, 131.

26. For more on this, see Alan Cooper, *Philip Roth and the Jews* (Albany: SUNY Press, 1996), and Mark Shechner, *After the Revolution: Studies in the Contemporary Jewish-American Imagination* (Bloomington: University of Indiana Press, 1987), 196–238.

27. Ruth Prigozy, Celia Morris, LuAnn Walther, remarks at "Irving Howe and His World: A Memorial Conference" (audiotape, April 15, 1994); Morris Dickstein, interviewed by author, June 24, 1997.

28. Howe, letter to Harvey Swados, June 28, 1971, Swados Papers, University of Massachusetts at Amherst; Howe, letter to Lewis Coser, July 1971, Coser Papers, Box 11, Boston College.

29. Howe, letter to Lenore Marshall, September 18, 1971, Manuscript Collection, Columbia University. Marshall (1897–1971), was a poet, novelist, essayist, and political activist. In 1956 Marshall helped found SANE, the National Committee for a Sane Nuclear Policy.

30. Howe, letter to Lionel Trilling, December 3, 1972, Trilling Papers, Columbia University.

31. Howe had known Podhoretz since 1954. The relationship was always heated, never boring. But after 1973 they hardly ever spoke. "We had," Podhoretz said, "our ups and downs." *Intermountain Jewish News*, May 14, 1993. It is hard to resist including here a reference to Woody Allen's film "Annie Hall" (1977), in which he says, "I heard that *Commentary* and *Dissent* had merged and formed *Dysentery*."

32. Howe and Bernard Rosenberg, "Are American Jews Turning Right?" *Dissent* 21 (Winter 1974): 30–45.

33. Howe, letter to Lionel Trilling, December 3, 1972, Trilling Papers, Columbia University.

34. Howe, letter to Christopher Lasch, January 20, 1972, Lasch Papers, University of Rochester.

35. Michael Harrington, *Fragments of the Century: A Social Autobiography* (New York: Dutton, 1973), 245; Howe, letter to Michael Harrington, July 13, 1973, Harrington Papers, Tamiment Library, New York University.

36. Howe, letter to editors, September 17, 1974, Lewis Coser Papers, Box 13, Boston College; Howe, letter to Lewis Coser, October 10, 1974, Coser Papers, Box 14, Boston College; Howe, letter to Daniel Bell, n.d., Daniel Bell, personal collection.

37. Howe, "Socialists and Communists in European Politics," *Dissent* 22 (Fall 1975): 382–386; Howe, "Spain: Let Freedom Come!" *Dissent* 23 (Winter 1976): 5–6.

38. Howe, "Thinking the Unthinkable about Israel: A Personal Statement," *New York* 6 (December 24, 1973): 44–52.

39. Ibid.

40. Ibid.

41. Michael Walzer, interviewed by author, May 13, 1997.

42. Jeremy Larner, interviewed by author, June 19, 1997; Bernard Avishai, interviewed by author, April 7, 1997; Martin Peretz, interviewed by author, August 28, 1997; Menacham Brinker, "Remembering Irving Howe," *Dissent* 40 (Fall 1993): 522.

43. Howe, quoted in Leon Wieseltier, "Only in America," *New York Review of Books*, July 15, 1976, 27.

44. Jeremy Larner, interviewed by author, June 19, 1997.

45. Howe, letters to Lionel Trilling, September 18, 1971, and December 3, 1972, Trilling Papers, Columbia University.

46. Daniel Bell, interviewed by author, October 30, 1998.

47. Howe, letter to Lionel Trilling, July 5, 1975, Trilling Papers, Columbia University.

48. Arien Mack, interviewed by author, October 12, 2000.

49. Kenneth Libo, interviewed by author, January 30, 1997; Kenneth Libo, "Everyman's Intellectual: Remembering Irving Howe," *Judaism* 43 (Spring 1994): 191–195.

50. Howe, letter to Lewis Coser, November 1970, Coser Papers, Box 10, Boston College.

51. Howe, *World of Our Fathers: The Journey of the East Europeans to America and the Life They Found and Made* (New York: Harcourt Brace Jovanovich, 1976).

52. *World*, 171–177. Howe's animus toward Roth continued until at least 1979, and spilled over explicitly into *World* on pp. 596–597.

53. Irving Howe, "American Jews and Israel," *Tikkun* (December 1988): 73.

54. *World*, 225–249, 644, and throughout.

55. *World* (New York, 1990 ed.), xx. When Ken Libo told Howe to aim for more "detachment," Irving wrote back: "Detachment in behalf of what?" From "the terribly sophisticated notion that to express feeling directly, to invoke idealism, is somehow old hat, or something to be scorned, and that it's deprecation that should be appreciated? Well, Ken, I will just have to take the risk that people will respond to me that way." Ken Libo, "My Work on *World of Our Fathers*" (unpublished typescript, 2000), 14.

56. *Margin*, 339; Howe, interview with Susanne Klingenstein (audiotape, December 12, 1988).

57. Irving Howe, interview, *Jerusalem Post Weekly*, August 24, 1976.

58. *World*, 129.

59. Ibid., 96.

60. Ibid., passim and 645.

61. Howe, "Immigrant Chic," 76. Writing about the Lower East Side ten years before the publication of *World*, Howe did bemoan what he called the high price of progress for those who left the ghetto streets. But he also warned readers against even "for a moment sweeten[ing] the reality: those tenements were wretched, men did go hungry, life could be crippling." "The Lower East Side: Myth and Reality," *Midstream* (August–September 1966): 17, 62. When Howe, in the final words of *World*, tells us it is time to praise the "obscure men" of the Jewish immigrant community, it is clear from the bulk of the text that he means especially "the self-educated worker intellectual, still bearing the benchmarks of the Talmud Torah, forced to struggle into maturity for those elements of learning that his grandsons would accept as their birthright, yet fired by a vision of universal humanist culture and eager to absorb the world of Marx, Tolstoy, and the other masters of the nineteenth century." *World*, p. 22. And much earlier he had said "the greatest achievement of the Lower East Side . . . was that it nurtured a human type rare in this country, though for a time familiar in Europe: the intellectualized worker." "The Lower East Side," 17.

63. *World*, p. 247.

64. Howe, *Thomas Hardy*, 45.

65. Irving Howe, "The Limits of Ethnicity," *New Republic*, June 25, 1977, 18.

66. *Margin*, 341. In a letter to Marie Syrkin, September 18, 1976, Howe wrote: "Yes [*World*] has been a tremendous success. And what does it mean? Who knows? The last hurrah of what I write about?" Syrkin Papers, Jacob Rader Marcus Center of the American Jewish Archives, Cincinnati, Ohio.

67. Howe and Bernard Rosenberg, "Are American Jews Turning Right?" *Dissent* 21 (Winter 1974): 45.

68. The address was published in a somewhat shortened version as "The Limits of Ethnicity," 17–19; emphasis mine.

69. Irving Howe et al., "Liberalism and the Jews: A Symposium," *Commentary* (January 1980), 48.

70. Howe, "Liberalism and the Jews," 48.

71. Howe was witnessed at synagogue on various occasions by Morris Dickstein, Leon Wieseltier, and Seymour Martin Lipset. Morris Dickstein, interviewed by author, June 24, 1997; Leon Wieseltier, "Remembering Irving Howe (1920–1993)," *New York Times Book Review*, May 23, 1993; Joseph Dorman, *Arguing the World: The New York Intellectuals in Their Own Words* (New York: Free Press, 2000), 13.

72. Norman Podhoretz, *Breaking Ranks: A Political Memoir* (New York: Harper and Row, 1979), 65.

73. Howe, *Margin*, 346; Bernard Avishai, interviewed by author, April 7, 1997; Bernard Avishai, "Remembering Irving Howe," *Dissent* 40 (Fall 1993): 515; Mark Levinson and Brian Morton, "Irving Howe," *New Left Review* 202 (November 1993): 111–114; Brian Morton, interviewed by author, May 8, 1997.

74. *World*, 223–224, 646. See also Yehezkel Kaufmann, "Israel in Canaan," in *Great Ages and Ideas of the Jewish People*, ed. L. W. Schwarz (New York: Modern Library, 1956), 38–53; Gershom Scholem, *The Messianic Idea in Judaism* (New York: Schocken Books, 1971), 1.

75. *World*, 11, 16, 324.

76. Hasia Diner, "Embracing *World of Our Fathers*: The Context of Reception," *American Jewish History* 88 (December 2000): 449–450.

77. Edward Alexander, *Irving Howe: Socialist, Critic, Jew* (Bloomington: Indiana University Press, 1998), 187.

78. Howe, "Limits of Ethnicity," 18.

79. Howe, letter to Marie Syrkin, September 18, 1976, Syrkin Papers, Jacob Rader Marcus Center of the American Jewish Archives.

80. Howe, letter to Edward Alexander, April 21, 1998, cited in Alexander, *Irving Howe*, 265, n.29.

81. *Margin*, 339.

82. Howe, letter to Marie Syrkin, April 10, 1977, Jacob Rader Marcus Center of the American Jewish Archives.

83. Howe and Ilana Wiener Howe, eds., *Short Shorts* (New York: Bantam Books, 1983); Morris Dickstein, interviewed by author, June 24, 1997; Leon Wieseltier, "Remembering Irving Howe (1920–1993)," *New York Times Book Review*, May 23, 1993.

84. Arien Mack, interviewed by author, October 12, 2000.

85. Howe, letter to Marie Syrkin, September 18, 1976, Syrkin Papers, Jacob Rader Marcus Center of the American Jewish Archives; *Margin*, 339.

86. Nina Howe, "Remembering Irving Howe," *Dissent* 40 (Fall 1993): 533–534; Nicholas Howe, "Remembering Irving Howe," *Dissent* 40 (Fall 1993): 532–533; Howe, letter to Marie Syrkin, September 18, 1976, Syrkin Papers, Jacob Rader Marcus Center of the American Jewish Archives.

87. Howe, "The Cities' Secret," *New Republic*, January 22, 1977, 55–57; Howe, "On Pornography," *Dissent* 25 (Spring 1978): 204–205.

88. Howe, *Critical Point*, 57.

89. Howe, "The Cities' Secret," *New Republic*, January 22, 1977, 55–57; Howe, "The 'Animals' and the Moralists," *Dissent* 24 (Fall 1977): 345–346.

90. Howe, "The Right Menace: Why People Are Turning Conservative," *New Republic*, September 9, 1978, 12–22.

91. Howe, ed., *25 Years of Dissent* (New York: Methuen, 1979), xix.

92. Howe, *Leon Trotsky* (New York: Viking, 1978), 191–192.

93. Howe, "The Right Menace," 16. Howe had in mind Peter Viereck, Clinton Rossiter, Russell Kirk, and others whose main interest in conservatism was not to chip away at the welfare state, but a philosophical and programmatic search for general principles that might compete with liberalism in the American setting. *Margin*, 225. Howe's address to DSOC was published in the *New Republic*, March 26, 1977, 20–21.

94. Howe, letter to Victor Walter, April 11, 1955; Simone Plastrik, interviewed by author, May 8, 1997; Lewis Coser, interviewed by author, April 8, 1997; Howe, letter to Lionel Trilling, December 3, 1972, Trilling Papers, Columbia University.

95. Howe and Ruth Wisse, eds., *The Best of Sholom Aleichem* (Washington, D.C.: New Republic Books, 1979); Howe, letter to Marie Syrkin, April 10, 1977, Syrkin Papers, Jacob Rader Marcus Center of the American Jewish Archives; Howe, *25 Years of Dissent*, xix.

NOTES TO CHAPTER 13

1. Howe, letter to Bernard Avishai, March 26, 1981.

2. Howe, letter to Daniel Bell, July 30, 1981.

3. Ibid.

4. Howe, *A Margin of Hope: An Intellectual Autobiography* (New York: Harcourt Brace Jovanovich, 1982).

5. Robert Brustein, "Ciao, Manhattan!" *New York Review of Books*, February 3, 1983, 5–6; R. W. B. Lewis, "A Liberal Spirit," *New Republic*, November 1, 1982, 32–36; Vivian Gornick, "A Life of the Mind," *The Nation*, January 1–8, 1983, 20–22; Raymond Williams, "Generations Out of Joint," *Guardian Weekly*, March 20, 1983, 5; Robert Asahina, "The Autobiography of a 20th Century Socialist," *Wall Street Journal*, December 2, 1982, 28; Midge Decter, "Socialism and Its Irresponsibilities: The Case of Irving Howe," *Commentary* 74 (December 1982): 27–33.

6. Howe, letter to Marie Syrkin, February 24, 1983, Syrkin Papers, Jacob Rader Marcus Center of the American Jewish Archives; Howe, letter to Irving Panken, February 1, 1983, Glotzer Collection, Box 40, Hoover Institution, Stanford University.

7. Howe, *Margin*, 211–212.

8. Howe, letter to Hook, November 10, 1982, Hook Collection, Box 39, Hoover Institution, Stanford University.

9. Hook, letter to Howe, November 19, 1982, Hook Collection, Box 39, Hoover Institution.

10. Hook, *Out of Step: An Unquiet Life in the 20th Century* (New York: Harper and Row, 1987), 156–157; Hook, "Should Communists Be Permitted to Teach?" *New York Times Magazine*, February 27, 1949, 7–29. Daniel Bell recalled a phone conversation he had had with Hook about this time. Once a quite vigorous man, Hook had become frail, his voice shaky as he spoke from Stanford. But when Bell mentioned Howe, Hook's voice suddenly became powerful, his mood angry. Later, Bell mentioned this conversation to Howe, who replied, "Well, if I can keep Sidney Hook alive a little longer. . . ." Daniel Bell, interviewed by author, October 30, 1998; Joseph Dorman, *Arguing the World*, 6.

11. Joanne Barkan (NAM leader and later a contributing editor of *Dissent*), interviewed by author, May 7, 1997.

12. Maurice Isserman, *The Other American: The Life of Michael Harrington* (New York: Public Affairs, 2000), 348–349; Howe, interviewed by Isserman (unpublished transcript, April 26, 1991); Joanne Barkan, interviewed by author, May 7, 1997. "Common Dreams" is a term I borrow from Todd Gitlin's *The Twilight of Common Dreams: Why America Is Wracked by Culture Wars* (New York: Metropolitan Books, 1995).

13. Bernard Avishai, interviewed by author, April 7, 1997.

14. "Voices from the Left: A Conversation between Michael Harrington and Irving Howe," *New York Times Magazine*, June 17, 1984, 24–41; Howe, "From Roosevelt to Reagan," *Dissent* 30 (Winter 1983): 45–48; "Central America—Cry Halt!" *Dissent* 30 (Summer 1983), 279–281; "Grenada: 'Twas a Famous Victory!" *Dissent* 31 (Winter 1984): 7–8; "Reagan and the Left," *Dissent* 31 (Fall 1984): 389–391; "Four More Years," *Dissent* 32 (Winter 1985): 5–7; "The Spirit of the Times: Greed, Nostalgia, Ideology and War Whoops," *Dissent* 33 (Fall 1986):

413–425; "Reagangate: The Farce and the Shame," *Dissent* 34 (Spring 1987): 136–138.

15. Howe, "How It Feels to Be Hit By a Truck," *Dissent* 28 (Winter 1981): 7–14.

16. Howe, "Reagan and the Left," 391.

17. Howe, "Four More Years," 5; Joseph Dorman, *Arguing the World: The New York Intellectuals in Their Own Words* (New York: Free Press, 2000), 20.

18. Howe, letter to Marie Syrkin, July 6, 1978, Syrkin Papers, Jacob Rader Marcus Center of the American Jewish Archives; Bernard Avishai, interviewed by author, April 7, 1997.

19. *New York Times*, April 21, 1978.

20. Moshe Decter, "With 'Lifelong Friends' Who Needs Enemies?" *Midstream* (June–July 1978): 45–49; Howe, letter to Decter, July 1978, Marie Syrkin Papers, Jacob Rader Marcus Center of the American Jewish Archives.

21. Howe, letter to Marie Syrkin, July 6, 1978, Syrkin Papers, Jacob Rader Marcus Center of the American Jewish Archives; Bernard Avishai, interviewed by author, April 7, 1997; Michael Walzer, interviewed by author, May 13, 1997.

22. *New York Times*, June 30, 1982.

23. Carole Kessner, interviewed by author, July 26, 1997. Others who have received the award include Rabbis Ira Eisenstein and Irving Greenberg, and the noted Jewish historians Solomon Grayzel and Salo Baron. See the Web page of the Reconstructionist Rabbinical College.

24. Howe, letter to Marie Syrkin, January 7, 1983, Syrkin Papers, Jacob Rader Marcus Center of the American Jewish Archives.

25. An allegation by *Time* magazine that Sharon had encouraged the massacres was the subject of litigation in New York in 1984. In 1985 a jury in the New York Federal Court ruled that the allegation was false, and that *Time* had defamed Sharon, but the jury failed to find that the news magazine had acted with malice.

26. Howe, letters to Marie Syrkin, November 30, 1982, January 7, 1983, and February 24, 1983, Syrkin Papers, Jacob Rader Marcus Center of the American Jewish Archives.

27. Howe, "The West Bank Trap," *New Republic*, July 4, 1983, 18–21. It is interesting to note, and ironic given their history, that Howe's question is almost exactly the same question Philip Roth asks in *Counterlife* (1986), and later more radically in *Operation Shylock* (1993). Roth pictures Israel, especially the settlements, as "abnormal," as ghettoized; and he sees Jewish life in America as "normal" in the sense the Zionists really meant—having a place where Jews, like everyone else, are entitled to and are taking advantage of "self" determination, safety, and mobility. It is possible that Roth was influenced by Howe's writings on Israel. This is not something I could determine because Roth declined to be interviewed about Howe.

28. Howe, "Warm Friends of Israel and Open Critics of Begin-Sharon," *New York Times*, September 23, 1982, 27.

29. Howe, letter to Marie Syrkin, July 5, 1985, Syrkin Papers, Jacob Rader Marcus Center of the American Jewish Archives; Howe, "Thinking the Unthinkable about Israel: A Personal Statement," *New York* 6 (December 24, 1973): 52.

30. Morris Dickstein, interviewed by author, June 24, 1997; Dickstein, "A World Away, a Generation Later," *New York Times Book Review*, April 6, 1997.

31. Howe, *World*, 627; Howe, "How to Write about the Holocaust," *New York Review of Books*, March 28, 1985, 17.

32. Howe, "Writing and the Holocaust," *New Republic*, October 27, 1986, 27–39; Howe, "How to Write about the Holocaust," 14–17.

33. Howe, *Socialism and America* (New York: Harcourt Brace Jovanovich, 1985), ix, 86, 140.

34. Ibid., 31–32, 48, 141–142.

35. Ibid., 123.

36. Ibid., 86.

37. Howe, "Of Socialists, Liberals and Others," *Dissent* 35 (Winter 1988): 32; Howe, "Socialism and Liberalism: Articles of Conciliation," *Dissent* 24 (Winter 1977): 22–35; Howe, "On the Moral Basis of Socialism," *Dissent* 28 (Fall 1981): 491–494.

38. Mitchell Cohen, "Socialism as a Regulative Idea: Irving Howe's Politics," *Dissent* 42 (Spring 1995): 254–257; Mitchell Cohen, interviewed by author, October 30, 1997; Howe and Coser, "Images of Socialism," *Dissent* 1 (Spring 1954): 122–138.

39. Howe, *The American Newness: Culture and Politics in the Age of Emerson* (Cambridge, Mass.: Harvard University Press, 1986), 8–9, 21, and passim.

40. Howe, "Strangers," in *Celebrations and Attacks* (New York: Harcourt Brace Jovanovich, 1979), 14–16, originally in *Yale Review* 66 (June 1977): 486–487.

41. Howe, *The American Newness*, 42–48; Judith Walzer, interviewed by author, May 13, 1997.

42. Howe, *The American Newness*, 24–25.

43. Ibid., 15; Howe, interviewed by Susanne Klingenstein (audiotape, December 2, 1988).

44. Ibid.; Howe, *The American Newness*, 52–53.

45. Howe, *The American Newness*, 89.

46. Ibid., 76–77.

47. Paul Berman, "Remembering Irving Howe," *Dissent* 40 (Fall 1993): 521–522. The discussion between Singer and Howe was broadcast over Yale University Radio, and the transcript of their conversation was published in *Midstream* 18 (June–July 1973): 32–38.

48. Howe, interviewed by Charlotte Curtis, *New York Times*, February 14, 1984.

49. Howe, "Social Retreat and the Tummler," *Dissent* 34 (Fall 1987): 411.

50. Nina Howe, "Remembering Irving Howe," *Dissent* 40 (Fall 1993): 533–534.

51. Nicholas Howe, "Remembering Irving Howe," *Dissent* 40 (Fall 1993): 532–533.

52. Howe, "Notes from Jerusalem," *New York Review of Books*, September 29, 1988, 13.

53. Howe, "American Jews and Israel," *Tikkun* (December 1988): 74.

54. Howe, "A Mixed Response," *Dissent* 35 (Summer 1988): 266.

55. Howe, "Notes from Jerusalem," 13.

56. Howe, "American Jews and Israel," 74, 73.

57. Ibid.

58. Conference announcement in *Association for Jewish Studies Program* (Waltham, Mass., 1999). See also Jack Wertheimer, *A People Divided: Judaism in Contemporary America* (New York: Basic Books, 1993), and Gerald Sorin, *Tradition Transformed: The Jewish Experience in America* (Baltimore: Johns Hopkins University Press, 1997).

59. Howe, ed., *Jewish-American Stories* (New York: New American Library, 1977), 12, 16–17; Gerald Shapiro, ed., *American Jewish Fiction* (Lincoln: University of Nebraska Press, 1998); Andrew Furman, *Contemporary Jewish American Writers and the Multicultural Dilemma* (Syracuse: Syracuse University Press, 2000). It is difficult to determine from their work the particular degree of religious observance of each author. But almost all display impressive knowledge of Jewish rituals, mores, and historical developments in the U.S. and elsewhere. And most, even where criticism of Orthodoxy is implied, display sympathy and sensitivity in their work toward traditional religiosity. These writers may have lost a connection to the Old World and to immigrant life, but in their works they have begun to substitute their own different but rich social and personal experience, as well as their knowledge of Israel and the Holocaust, of ethnic and sexual diversity, and their own "spiritual itineraries ranging from neo-Orthodoxy and mysticism to Eastern religion." Morris Dickstein, "Never Goodbye, Columbus," *The Nation*, October 22, 2001, 25–34.

60. Howe, *The End of Jewish Secularism* (New York: Hunter College, City University of New York, 1993), 10, 15, 13; emphasis mine.

61. Howe, letter to Hook, December 13, 1988, Sidney Hook Collection, Box 39, Hoover Institution.

62. Ibid., January 30, 1989, Sidney Hook Collection, Box 39, Hoover Institution.

63. Howe, "The Value of the Canon," *New Republic*, February 18, 1991, 40–47; Howe, letter to Hook, December 13, 1988, Sidney Hook Collection, Box

39, Hoover Institution. By 1988 the battleground had extended to several universities in the Northeast, including Harvard and Columbia. The divisions were never completely clear or rigid, but at Columbia it often seemed that men were lined up against women, old guard against new, liberals against conservatives, close readers of text against new-theory advocates and multiculturalists.

64. Todd Gitlin, interviewed by author, March 18, 1997; Hook, letter to Howe, February 7, 1989; Howe, letter to Hook, January 30, 1989, Hook Collection, Box 39, Hoover Institution.

65. Howe, "Toward an Open Culture," *New Republic*, March 5, 1984, 25–29; Howe, "Again: Orwell and the Neoconservatives," *Dissent* 31 (Spring 1984): 236; Howe, "Interview" with William Cain, *American Literary History* 1 (Fall 1989): 556–564; Howe, "History and the Novel," *New Republic*, September 3, 1990, 29–34.

66. Howe, "The Value of the Canon," 45–46.

67. Howe, "The Treason of the Critics," *New Republic*, June 12, 1989, 30–31; John Ellis, *Literature Lost: Social Agendas and the Corruption of the Humanities* (New Haven, Conn.: Yale University Press, 1997).

68. Howe, "The Value of the Canon," 47.

69. Howe, *Margin*, 289; Gerald Graff, interviewed by author, April 14, 1997; Kay Seymour House, letter to author, May 30, 1997; Judith Walzer, interviewed by author, May 13, 1997; Willard Wyman, interviewed by author, October 18, 1997.

70. Howe, "The Value of the Canon," 47.

71. In a letter to Bernard Avishai, November 1982, Howe wrote: "Writing is a life-long struggle, if you take it seriously; and if you stop doing so, you can slip right back into the worst habits. . . . Achieve clarity and the rest may follow—may. But at least you'll have clarity."

72. Nicholas Howe, "Introduction," in Irving Howe, *A Critic's Notebook* (New York: Harcourt Brace Jovanovich, 1994), 14, 5.

73. Howe, "The Earth Still Turns," *Dissent* 35 (Fall 1988): 397–398.

74. Howe, "The First 35 Years Were Hardest," *Dissent* 36 (Spring 1989): 135; Howe, "China!" *Dissent* 36 (Summer 1989); 291–292; Howe, "Totalitarianism Reconsidered," *Dissent* 38 (Winter 1991): 63–71.

75. Howe, "The First 35 Years Were Hardest," 135; Howe, "Soviet Transformation," *Dissent* 37 (Spring 1990): 133.

76. Howe, "Notes from the Left," *Dissent* 37 (Summer 1990): 300–302.

77. George Packer, "Remembering Irving Howe," *Dissent* 40 (Fall 1993): 545.

78. Ibid.

79. Howe, "A New Political Situation: Revolutionary Changes in the World," *Dissent* 37 (Winter 1990): 5–6. For more on Howe's optimism, see also

Howe, "Soviet Transformation," *Dissent* 37 (Spring 1990): 133–135, and Howe, "From the Dustbin of History," *Dissent* 37 (Spring 1990): 184–186.

80. Howe, "Soviet Transformation," 133; Howe, "The World after Communism," *Dissent* 37 (Fall 1990): 435; Howe, "The Communist Collapse," *Dissent* 38 (Fall 1991): backcover, 604–605. Emphasis mine.

81. Howe, "By Way of a Beginning," *Dissent* 38 (Spring 1991): 165–169.

82. Nina Howe, "Remembering Irving Howe," *Dissent* 40 (Fall 1993): 534.

83. Howe, *Margin*, 347–348.

84. Leon Wieseltier, "Remembering Irving Howe," *New York Times Book Review*, May 23, 1993.

85. Ibid.

86. Joanne Barkan, interviewed by author, May 7, 1997; Paula Fox, interviewed by author, March 31, 1997.

87. Howe, interviewed by Joseph Dorman (unpublished transcript, 1993), 35. "I made a big mistake with Irving Kristol, and that was recruiting him to begin with." Kristol, Howe said, "wasn't . . . good material." Dorman, *Arguing the World*, 55.

88. Howe, *A Critic's Notebook*, 315.

89. Howe, letter to Glotzer, November 18, 1944, Glotzer Collection, Box 12, Hoover Institution; Howe, "The Road leads Far Away," *New Republic*, May 3, 1993, 36.

90. Howe, "Two Cheers for Utopia," *Dissent* 40 (Spring 1993): 131–133.

91. Howe, "On the Moral Basis of Socialism," *Dissent* 28 (Fall 1981): 491–494; Walzer quoted, 493. Howe never said it quite this way but his various writings on the subject strongly imply that a fully unfettered liberty would lead not only to gross inequality, but also, and ironically, to an overall *decrease* in liberty. Those without much material wherewithal forced to spend the greatest amount of their time "freely" scratching a living from an unyielding world would have neither the resources nor the leisure to exercise the liberty to which they were statutorily entitled. In the same way, a fully developed equality of condition (or even something approximating it) requiring the coercion and terror of authoritarians in control of the "political system" would also firmly institutionalize inequality—elites with political power and the masses with none.

92. Howe, "Questions We Ask Ourselves and Sometimes Answer," *Dissent* 39 (Spring 1992); 143–146; Howe, "Two Cheers for Utopia," 132–133. Days after Howe died, Alfred Kazin said in a handwritten addition to an unpublished typescript that Irving was "the last Jewish utopian" in a world grown "increasingly crass."

93. Howe, *Critics Notebook*, 196; Howe, *Politics and the Novel* (New York: Columbia University Press, 1992), 57–60; Mitchell Cohen, interviewed by author, October 30, 1997.

94. Leon Wieseltier, "Remembering Irving Howe"; Howe, *The End of Jewish Secularism*, 13.

95. Howe, *Critic's Notebook*, 315; Nicholas Howe, "Remembering Irving Howe," *Dissent* 40 (Fall 1993): 533; Mitchell Cohen, interviewed by author, October 30, 1997; Paula Fox, interviewed by author, March 31, 1997; Joanne Barkan, interviewed by author, May 7, 1997; David Bromwich, interviewed by author, May 7, 1997; Michael Walzer, interviewed by author, May 13, 1997; Brian Morton, interviewed by author, May 8, 1997; Nicholas Howe, "Remembering Irving Howe," 533.

96. Ibid.

97. The list is long and distinguished. In addition to dozens of *Dissent* people, it included, among many other writers, critics, and journalists: Jervis Anderson, Daniel Bell, Paul Berman, Morris Dickstein, Denis Donoghue, Paula Fox, Gerald Graff, Elizabeth Hardwick, James Houston, Johanna Kaplan, Alfred Kazin, Jay Neugeboren, Sanford Pinsker, Jonathan Rosen, Lee Siegel, Ilan Stavans, Leon Wieseltier, and Dennis Wrong.

98. This and much more was attested to in interviews with many on the *Dissent* board, especially Joanne Barkan, David Bromwich, Mitchell Cohen, Todd Gitlin, Brian Morton, Jim Sleeper, and Michael Walzer.

Glossary

heder	Literally "room," but in most usage, "elementary school" for Jewish study.
landmanshaft(n)	A fraternal and mutual aid organization of immigrants who originate from the same old-world locations.
mamaloshn	Yiddish, or mama's language, sometimes used pejoratively.
mazeltov	Good luck, congratulations.
mensh	A decent person.
menshlikhkayt	Decency, humaneness.
schmaltz	Sentimentality, sometimes maudlin.
schmutz	Dirt, pornography.
shtetl(ekh)	Small town(s).
shtikl(akh)	Small piece(s).
shul(n)	Synagogue(s).
shule(s)	School(s).
tikn olam	An injunction to repair or improve the world.
tsedakah	Charity, but more often social justice.
Yiddishkayt	The stuff of Jewish culture and personality.

References

Selected Works of Irving Howe

HOWE WAS EXTRAORDINARILY prolific. Not everything he wrote is listed below, but these titles represent a substantial portion of his most important work. Those of Howe's essays reprinted in the several volumes of his collected writings are not included here. The same holds for the several hundred pieces Howe did for *Dissent* over a forty-year period, and the dozens of articles he wrote for *Labor Action* and *New International*. For these individual items the reader should consult the footnotes throughout.

BOOKS

The American Communist Party, with Lewis Coser. Boston: Beacon Press, 1957.
The American Newness. Cambridge, Mass.: Harvard University Press, 1986.
Celebrations and Attacks: Thirty Years of Literary and Cultural Commentary. New York: Harcourt Brace Jovanovich, 1979.
The Critical Point. New York: Horizon Press, 1973.
A Critic's Notebook. New York: Harcourt Brace Jovanovich, 1994.
Decline of the New. New York: Harcourt Brace and World, 1970.
Leon Trotsky. New York: Viking, 1978.
A Margin of Hope: An Intellectual Autobiography. New York: Harcourt Brace Jovanovich, 1982.
Politics and the Novel. New York: Horizon, 1957.
Selected Writings 1950–1990. New York: Harcourt Brace Jovanovich, 1990.
Sherwood Anderson. New York: William Sloane, 1951.
Socialism and America. New York: Harcourt Brace Jovanovich, 1985.
Steady Work: Essays in the Politics of Democratic Radicalism. New York: Harcourt, Brace and World, 1966.
Thomas Hardy: A Critical Study. New York: Macmillan, 1967.
The UAW and Walter Reuther, with B. J. Widick. New York: Random House, 1949.
William Faulkner: A Critical Study. New York: Random House, 1952.
A World More Attractive. New York: Horizon Press, 1963.

World of Our Fathers, with the assistance of Kenneth Libo. New York: Harcourt Brace Jovanovich, 1976.

ARTICLES

"American Jews and Israel," *Tikkun* 4 (December 1988): 71–74.

"Ballet for the Man Who Enjoys Wallace Stevens," *Harper's* (May 1971): 102–109.

"The Burden of Civilization," *New Republic*, February 10, 1982, 27–34.

"The Cities' Secret," *New Republic*, January 22, 1977, 55–57.

"The Decline in Democratic Sentiment," *Harper's* (August 1970): 93–98.

"An Exercise in Memory," *New Republic*, March 11, 1991, 29–31.

"Falling Out of the Canon," *New Republic*, August 17–24, 35–37.

"Forming Dissent," in Walter Powell and Richard Robbins, eds., *Conflict and Consensus: A Festschrift in Honor of Lewis Coser*. New York: Free Press, 1983.

"Hemingway: The Conquest of a Panic," *New Republic*, July 24 1961, 20.

"History and the Novel," *New Republic*, September 3, 1990, 29–34.

"How to Write about the Holocaust," *New York Review of Books*, March 28, 1985, 14–17.

"Imagining Labor," *New Republic*, April 11, 1981, 28–33.

"Immigrant Chic," *New York Magazine*, May 12, 1986, 76–77.

"Journey of a Poet," *Commentary* 53 (January 1972): 75–77.

"The Limits of Ethnicity," *New Republic*, June 25, 1977, 17–18.

"Literary Criticism and Literary Radicals," *American Scholar* 41 (Winter 1971–72): 113–120.

"Lost Young Intellectual: Marginal Man Twice Alienated," *Commentary* 2 (October 1946): 361–367.

"Mid-Century Turning Point: An Intellectual Memoir," *Midstream* 20 (June–July 1975): 23–28.

"The New 'Confrontation Politics' Is a Dangerous Game," *New York Times Magazine*, October 20, 1968, 27–29, 133–135, 137–140.

"The New Yorker and Hannah Arendt," *Commentary* 36 (October 1963): 318–319.

"Notes on Mass Culture," *Politics* 5 (Spring 1948): 120–123.

"Of Fathers and Sons," *Commentary* 2 (August 1946): 190–192.

"On Ideas and Culture," *New Republic*, February 2, 1959, 17–19.

"Philip Rahv: A Memoir," *American Scholar* 48 (Autumn 1979): 487–498.

"Political Terrorism: Hysteria on the Left," *New York Times Magazine*, April 12, 1970, 25–27, 124–128.

"The Range of the New York Intellectuals," in Bernard Rosenberg, ed., *Creators and Disturbers: Reminiscences by Jewish Intellectuals of New York*. New York: Columbia University Press, 1982.

"The Right Menace: Why People Are Turning Conservative," *New Republic*, September 9, 1978, 12–22.

"The Road Leads Far Away," *New Republic*, May 3, 1993, 29–36.

"Sholom Aleichem and His People," *Partisan Review* 13 (November–December 1946): 592–594.

"The Stranger and the Victim: Two Stereotypes of American Fiction," *Commentary* 8 (August 1949): 147–156.

"Thinking the Unthinkable about Israel: A Personal Statement," *New York* 6 (December 24, 1973): 44–52.

"The Treason of the Critics," *New Republic*, June 12, 1989, 30–31.

"An Unknown Treasure of World Literature: Who Will Make Sholom Aleichem Available?" *Commentary* 14 (September 1952): 270–273.

"The Value of the Canon," *New Republic*, February 18, 1991, 40–47.

"The West Bank Trap," *New Republic*, July 4, 1983, 18–21.

"Writer Can't Keep to His Attic," *New York Times Magazine*, December 5, 1965, 43–45.

EDITED WORKS

Ashes Out of Hope: Fiction by Soviet Yiddish Writers, with Eliezer Greenberg. New York: Schocken Books, 1977.

Basic Writings of Trotsky. New York: Random House, 1963.

The Best of Sholom Aleichem, with Ruth Wisse. Washington, D.C.: New Republic Books, 1979.

Beyond the New Left: A Confrontation and Critique. New York: McCall Publishing, 1970.

Beyond the Welfare State. New York: Schocken Books, 1982.

Classics of Modern Fiction. New York: Harcourt Brace and World, 1968.

Edith Wharton, a Collection of Critical Essays. Englewood Cliffs, N.J.: Prentice-Hall, 1962.

Essential Works of Socialism. New Haven, Conn.: Yale University Press, 1976.

Fiction as Experience: An Anthology. New York: Harcourt Brace Jovanovich, 1978.

Israel, the Arabs and the Middle East, with Carl Gershman. New York: Bantam Books, 1972.

The Idea of the Modern. New York: Horizon, 1968.

Jewish American Short Stories. New York: New American Library, 1977.

The New Conservatives, with Lewis Coser. New York: Quadrangle, 1974.

Nineteen Eighty-Four Revisited: Totalitarianism in Our Century. New York: Harper and Row, 1983.

The Penguin Book of Modern Yiddish Verse, with Ruth Wisse and Khone Shmeruk. New York: Viking, 1987.

The Portable Kipling. New York: Viking, 1982.

The Radical Imagination: An Anthology from Dissent. New York: New American Library, 1967.

The Radical Papers. New York: Anchor Books, 1966.

Selected Stories: I. L. Peretz, with Eliezer Greenberg. New York: Schocken Books, 1974.

Selected Short Stories of Isaac Bashevis Singer. New York: Modern Library, 1966.

Selected Writings: Stories, Poems, and Essays, by Thomas Hardy. Greenwich, Conn.: Fawcett, 1966.

The Seventies: Problems and Proposals, with Michael Harrington. New York: Harper and Row, 1972.

Short Shorts, with Ilana Wiener Howe. New York: Bantam Books, 1983.

A Treasury of Jewish Stories, with Eliezer Greenberg. New York: Viking Press, 1954.

A Treasury of Yiddish Poetry, with Eliezer Greenberg. New York: Holt Rinehart and Winston, 1969.

25 Years of Dissent. New York: Methuen, 1979.

Voices from the Yiddish: Essays, Memoirs, Diaries, with Eliezer Greenberg. New York: Schocken Books, 1975.

The World of the Blue Collar Worker. New York: Quadrangle, 1972.

Yiddish Stories Old and New, with Eliezer Greenberg. New York: Holiday House, 1974.

ARCHIVAL SOURCES

Reginald L. Cook Papers, Middlebury College, Vermont

Lewis Coser Papers, Burns Library, Boston College

Malcolm Cowley Collection, Newberry Library, Chicago, Illinois

Democratic Socialists of America Papers, Tamiment Library, New York University

George Elliot Papers, University of Washington Library

James T. Farrell Papers, Charles Patterson Van Pelt Library, University of Pennsylvania

Waldo Frank Papers, Charles Patterson Van Pelt Library, University of Pennsylvania

Julius W. Friend Papers, Howard-Tilton Memorial Library, Tulane University

Albert Glotzer Collection, Hoover Institution, Stanford University

Elizabeth Hardwick Papers, Harry Ransom Research Center, University of Texas

Michael Harrington Papers, Tamiment Library, New York University

Granville Hicks Papers, Department of Special Collections, Syracuse University

Sidney Hook Collection, Hoover Institution, Stanford University
Christopher Lasch Papers, Special Collections, University of Rochester
League for Industrial Democracy Papers, Tamiment Library, New York University
Bernard Malamud, Harry Ransom Humanities Research Center, University of Texas
Lenore Marshall Papers, Manuscript Collections, Columbia University
Dwight Macdonald Papers, Manuscripts and Archives, Yale University
Benjamin Nelson Papers, Manuscript Collections, Columbia University
Random House Papers, Manuscript Collections, Columbia University
Theodore Roethke Papers, University of Washington Library
Anne Sexton Papers, Harry Ransom Humanities Research Center, University of Texas
Max Shachtman Collection (microfilm), Tamiment Library, New York University
Max Shachtman Transcript, Oral History Collection, Columbia University
Harvey Swados Papers, Special Collections and Archives, W. E. B. DuBois Library, University of Massachusetts, Amherst
Marie Syrkin Papers, The Jacob Rader Marcus Center of the American Jewish Archives
Lionel Trilling Papers, Manuscript Collections, Columbia University

AUTHOR INTERVIEWS

Anderson, Jervis, June 12, 1997
Avishai, Bernard, April 7, 1997
Barkan, Joanne, May 7, 1997
Bell, Daniel, October 30, 1998
Berlin, Susan, June 10, 1997
Berman, Paul, October 8, 1998
Bromwich, David, May 7, 1997
Cohen, Mitchell, October 30, 1997
Cohen, Sarah Blacher, March 2, 1997
Coser, Lewis, April 8, 1997
Dickstein, Morris, June 24, 1997
Fox, Paula, March 31, 1997
Gitlin, Todd, March 18, 1997
Graff, Gerald, April 14, 1997
Gropman, Donald, October 10, 1997
Gropman, Gabriella, September 30, 1997
Haskell, Gordon, December 12, 1996

Houston, James, March 19, 2001
Jacobson, Julius, March 17, 1997
Jacobson, Phyllis, March 17, 1997
Kazin, Alfred, May 15, 1997
Kessner, Carole, July 26, 1997
Kugler, Israel, April 3, 1997
Larner, Jeremy, June 19, 1997
Lelchuk, Alan, June 30, 1997
Levin, David, June 5, 1997
Libo, Kenneth, January 30, 1997
Mack, Arien, October 12, 2000
Morton, Brian, May 8, 1997
Murphy, Joseph S., December 4, 1997
Peretz, Martin, August 28, 1997
Plastrik, Simone, May 8, 1997
Price (Sugarman), Rachel, June 4, 1997
Sleeper, Jim, January 24, 1997
Stein, Maurice R., July 25, 1997
Walter, Vic, March 4, 1997; June 4, 1997; October 22, 1997
Walzer, Judith, May 13, 1997
Walzer, Michael, May 13, 1997
Wolitz, Seth L., December 17, 1996
Wrong, Dennis, October 15, 1997
Wyman, Jane, October 18, 1997; February 26, 2001
Wyman, Willard G., October 18, 1997

CORRESPONDENCE

Barkan, Joanne, October 11, 1997
Bell, Daniel, July 22, 1998; January 28, 2001
Bellush, Bernard, October 18, 2001
Coser, Lewis, March 7, 2001
Eisenstein, Ira, September 23, 1997
Glazer, Nathan, April 15, 1997
Glotzer, Albert, March 6, 9, 1997
House, Kay Seymour, May 13, May 30, July 14, 27, October 2, 1997
Klingenstein, Susanne, June 15, 1997
Kugler, Israel, April 7, 16, 1997; January 24, 2001
Libo, Kenneth, May 17, June 28, 1997
Mack, Arien, February 22, 28, 1997; November 14, 2001

Meier, Deborah, June 1, 1997

Moser, Thomas, October 26, 1997

Peretz, Martin, April 18, 1997

Sanes, Mick, March 20, 1997

Syracopoulos, Nicholas, April 19, May 14, 1997; July 18, 1998; November 20, 1999

Wald, Alan, March 2 and 3, 1997

Walter, Vic, January 26, May 16, 1997

Wrong, Dennis, November 28, 1997; December 19, 2000

Wyman, Willard, July 2, 1997

INTERVIEWS BY OTHERS

Coser, Lewis, by Maurice Isserman, May 3, 1985 (unpublished transcript)

Geltman, Emnauel, by Maurice Isserman March 19, 1985 (unpublished transcript)

Howe, Irving, by Joseph Dorman, 1993 (unpublished transcript)

Howe, Irving, by Todd Gitlin, April 15 1985 (audiotape)

Howe, Irving, by Maurice Isserman, January 24, 1982; October 21, 1982; March 26, 1991 (unpublished transcripts)

Howe, Irving, by Neil Jumonville, June 6, 1985 (unpublished transcript)

Howe, Irving, by Susanne Klingenstein, December 12, 1988 (audiotape)

SECONDARY SOURCES

Alexander, Edward. *Irving Howe and Secular Jewishness: An Elegy*. Cincinnati: University of Cincinnati, Judaic Studies Program, 1995.

———. *Irving Howe: Socialist, Critic, Jew*. Bloomington: University of Indiana, 1998.

Alter, Robert. "Yiddishkeit," *Commentary* 61 (April 1976): 83–86.

Atlas, James. "The Changing World of New York Intellectuals," *New York Times Magazine*, August 25, 1985, 22–25, 52–53, 70–73.

———. *Delmore Schwartz: The Life of an American Poet*. New York: Avon Books, 1978.

———. *Saul Bellow: A Biography*. New York: Random House, 2000.

Barrett, William. *The Truants: Adventures among the Intellectuals*. Garden City, N.Y.: Anchor Press/Doubleday, 1983.

Berger, Bennett. "The New York Intellectuals," *American Jewish History* 80 (Spring 1991): 382–389.

Berman, Paul. *A Tale of Two Utopias: The Political Journey of the Generation of 1968.* New York: W. W. Norton, 1996.

Bloom, Alexander. *Prodigal Sons: The New York Intellectuals and Their World.* New York: Oxford University Press, 1986.

Bromwich, David. "What Are Novels For?" *New York Times Book Review,* October 30, 1994.

Cohen, Robert. *When the Old Left Was Young.* New York: Oxford University Press, 1993.

Cooney, Terry. "New York Intellectuals and the Question of Jewish Identity." *American Jewish History* 80 (Spring 1991): 344–360.

———. *The Rise of the New York Intellectuals: Partisan Review and Its Circle.* Madison: University of Wisconsin Press, 1986.

Cooper, Alan. *Philip Roth and the Jews.* Albany: State University of New York Press, 1996.

Dickstein, Morris. *Gates of Eden: American Culture in the Sixties.* New York: Basic Books, 1977.

Diggins, John P. *Up from Communism: Conservative Odysseys in American Intellectual History.* New York: Harper and Row, 1975.

Dorman, Joseph. *Arguing the World: The New York Intellectuals in Their Own Words.* New York: Free Press, 2000.

Drucker, Peter. *Max Shachtman and His Left.* Atlantic Highlands, N.J.: Humanities Press, 1994.

Dvosin, Andrew James. "Literature in a Political World: The Career and Writings of Philip Rahv." Ph.D. dissertation, New York University, 1977.

Eliot, T. S. *After Strange Gods: A Primer of Modern Heresy.* New York: Harcourt Brace, 1934.

Ellison, Ralph W. *Shadow and Act.* New York: Random House, 1964.

Furman, Andrew. *Contemporary Jewish American Writers and the Multicultural Dilemma.* Syracuse: Syracuse University Press, 2000.

Gilbert, James B. *Writers and Partisans: A History of Literary Radicalism in America.* New York: John Wiley, 1968.

Gitlin, Todd. *The Sixties: Years of Hope, Days of Rage.* New York: Bantam Books, 1993.

Glaberson, Eric. "Historical Humanism in the Work of Two New York Intellectuals: Irving Howe and Alfred Kazin." Ph.D. dissertation, New York University, 1982.

Glick, Nathan. "The Socialist Who Loved Keats," *Atlantic Monthly,* January 1998, 99–105.

Goodheart, Eugene. "The Abandoned Legacy of the New York Intellectuals," *American Jewish History* 80 (Spring 1991): 361–376.

Graff, Gerald. *Literature against Itself.* Chicago: University of Chicago Press, 1979.

Harrington, Michael. *Fragments of the Century: A Social Autobiography*. New York: Dutton, 1973.

Hayden, Tom. *Reunion: A Memoir*. New York: Random House, 1988.

Hofstadter, Richard. "Two Cultures: Adversary and/or Responsible," *Public Interest* 6 (Winter 1967): 68–74.

———. *Anti-Intellectualism in American Life*. New York: Vintage, 1964.

Hollinger, David. *Science, Jews, and Secular Culture: Studies in Mid-Twentieth Century American Intellectual History*. Princeton, N.J.: Princeton University Press, 1996.

Hook, Sidney. *Out of Step: An Unquiet Life in the 20th Century*. New York: Harper and Row, 1987.

Hux, Samuel. "Uncle Irving," *Modern Age* 37 (Summer 1995): 330–336.

Isserman, Maurice. *If I Had a Hammer: The Death of the Old Left and the Birth of the New Left*. New York: Basic Books, 1987.

———. *The Other American: The Life of Michael Harrington*. New York: Public Affairs, 2000.

———. *Which Side Were You On? The American Communist Party during the Second World War*. Middletown, Conn.: Wesleyan University Press, 1982.

Jacoby, Russell. *The Last Intellectuals: American Culture in the Age of Academe*. New York: Basic Books, 1987.

Julius, Anthony. *T. S. Eliot, Anti-Semitism, and Literary Form*. Cambridge, U.K.: Cambridge University Press, 1995.

Jumonville, Neil. *Critical Crossings: The New York Intellectuals in Postwar America*. Berkeley: University of California Press, 1991.

Kazin, Alfred. *A Lifetime Burning in Every Moment*. New York: HarperPerennial, 1997.

———. *New York Jew*. New York: Random House, 1978.

Kessner, Carol. *The "Other" New York Jewish Intellectuals*. New York: New York University Press, 1994.

Klehr, Harvey. *The Heyday of American Communism: The Depression Decade*. New York: Basic Books, 1984.

Krauze, Enrique. *Personas e ideas*. Mexico: Editorial Vuelte, 1989.

Kristol, Irving. "Memoirs of a Trotskyist," *New York Times Magazine*, January 23, 1977, 42–43, 50–51, 54–57.

Krupnick, Mark. *Lionel Trilling and the Fate of Cultural Criticism*. Evanston, Ill.: Northwestern University Press, 1986.

Lasch, Christopher. *The New Radicalism in America (1889–1963): The Intellectual as a Social Type*. New York: Random House, 1967.

Laskin, David. *Partisans: Marriage, Politics, and Betrayal among the New York Intellectuals*. New York: Simon and Schuster, 2000.

Levin, David. *Exemplary Elders*. Athens: University of Georgia Press, 1990.

Longstaff, Stephen. "Ivy League Gentiles and Inner City Jews: Class and Ethnicity around Partisan Review in the Thirties and Forties," *American Jewish History* 80 (Spring 1991): 325–343.

Macdonald, Dwight. *Memoirs of a Revolutionist: Essays in Political Criticism.* New York: Farrar, Straus and Giroux, 1957.

Mishler, Paul. *Raising Reds: The Young Pioneers, Radical Summer Camps, and Communist Political Culture.* New York: Columbia University Press, 1999.

Morris, Willie. *New York Days.* Boston: Little Brown, 1993.

Nobile, Philip. *Intellectual Skywriting: Literary Politics and the "New York Review of Books."* New York: Charter House, 1974.

Oshinsky, David M. *A Conspiracy So Immense: The World of Joe McCarthy.* New York: Free Press, 1983.

Ozick, Cynthia. *Art and Ardor.* New York: Knopf, 1983.

Pells, Richard. *The Liberal Mind in a Consservative Age.* New York: Harper and Row, 1985.

Phillips, William. *A Partisan View.* New York: Stein and Day, 1983.

Pinsker, Sanford. "Lost Causes/Marginal Hopes: The Collected Elegies of Irving Howe," *Virginia Quarterly Review* 65 (Spring 1989): 585–599.

Podhoretz, Norman. *Breaking Ranks: A Political Memoir.* New York: Harper and Row, 1979.

———. *Ex-Friends.* New York: Free Press, 1999.

———. *Making It.* New York: Random House, 1967.

Raskin, Jonah. *For the Hell of It: The Life and Times of Abbie Hoffman.* Berkeley: University of California Press, 1997.

"Remembering Irving Howe," *Dissent* 40 (Fall 1993): 515–549.

Rizzo, Betty, and Barry Wallerstein, eds. *City at the Center.* New York: City College of New York, 1983.

Rodden, John, ed. *Lionel Trilling and the Critics: Opposing Selves.* Lincoln: University of Nebraska Press, 1999.

Rosenberg, Bernard, ed. *Creators and Disturbers: Reminiscences by Jewish Intellectuals of New York.* New York: Columbia University Press, 1982.

Rosenberg, Harold. "Does the Jew Exist? Sartre's Morality Play about Anti-Semitism," *Commentary* 7 (January 1949): 8–18.

Roth, Philip. *Reading Myself and Others.* New York: Farrar, Straus, Giroux, 1985.

Schalk, David L. *War and the Ivory Tower: Algeria and Vietnam.* New York: Oxford University Press, 1991.

Scholem, Gershom. *The Messianic Idea in Judaism.* New York: Schocken Books, 1971.

Shapiro, Edward S. "Jewishness and the New York Intellectuals," *Judaism* 38 (Summer 1989): 282–292.

Shechner, Mark. *After the Revolution: Studies in the Contemporary Jewish-American Imagination.* Bloomington: Indiana University Press, 1987.

Simon, John. "Irving Howe: A Triple Perspective," *New Leader*, May 21 1979, 19–21.

Teres, Harvey M. *Renewing the Left: Politics, Imagination, and the New York Intellectuals*. New York: Oxford University Press, 1996.

Trilling, Diana. *The Beginning of the Journey: The Marriage of Diana and Lionel Trilling*. New York: Harcourt Brace, 1993.

Trilling, Lionel. *The Liberal Imagination*. New York: Viking, 1950.

Trotsky, Leon. *The Defense of Terrorism*, trans. H. N. Brailsford. London: Allen and Unwin, 1921.

———. *Literature and Revolution*. New York: Russell and Russell, 1957.

Wald, Alan M. *The New York Intellectuals: The Rise and Decline of the Anti-Stalinist Left from the 1930s to the 1980s*. Chapel Hill: University of North Carolina Press, 1987.

Watts, Jerry G. *Heroism and the Black Intellectual: Ralph Ellison, Politics, and Afro-American Intellectual Life*. Chapel Hill: University of North Carolina Press, 1994.

Weinstein, Allen, and Alexander Vassiliev. *The Haunted Wood: Soviet Espionage in America—The Stalin Era*. New York: Random House, 1999.

Wenger, Beth. *New York Jews and the Great Depression*. New Haven, Conn.: Yale University Press, 1996.

Wisse, Ruth. "The New York (Jewish) Intellectuals, " *Commentary* 84 (November 1987): 28–38.

Wreszin, Michael. *A Rebel in Defense of Tradition: The Life and Politics of Dwight Macdonald*. New York: Basic Books, 1994.

Wrong, Dennis. "Thinning Ranks," *New Republic*, November 25, 1985, 30–34.

Zipperstein, Steven J. "The First Loves of Isaac Rosenfeld," *Jewish Social Studies* 5 (Fall 1998–Winter 1999): 12–13.

Acknowledgments

IT WOULD HAVE been much more difficult to write this book had it not been for the contributions of the historians and critics listed in the bibliography who have acquainted us so well with the New York intellectuals and their times. It would have been equally difficult without the help of many generous librarians and archivists, including John Atteberry, John J. Burns Library, Boston College; Ronald M. Bulatoff, the Hoover Institution; Carolyn Davis, Syracuse University; Jo Ellen Dickie, Newberry Library, Chicago; Peter Filardo, Tamiment Institute, New York University; Amy Filiatreau, Harry Ransom Humanities Research Center, University of Texas (Austin); Mary Huth, University of Rochester; Diane E. Kaplan, Yale University; Lisa C. Long, Brandeis University; William M. Roberts, University of California (Berkeley); Linda L. Seidman , University of Massachusetts (Amherst); Nancy M. Shawcross, University of Pennsylvania; Dorothy Smith, Jacob Rader Marcus Center of the American Jewish Archives; and Sydney Van Nort, City College of New York.

Indispensable help came, too, from the nearly four dozen men and women who graciously agreed to be interviewed by me, and from Todd Gitlin, Maurice Isserman, Neil Jumonville, and Susanne Klingenstein, who permitted me to listen to taped interviews or to read transcripts or notes of interviews they had done with Irving Howe. I have also had very useful correspondence with Joanne Barkan, Daniel Bell, Lewis Coser, Morris Dickstein, Ira Eisenstein, Todd Gitlin, Nathan Glazer, Albert Glotzer, Kay Seymour House, Nicholas Howe, Nina Howe, Maurice Isserman, Neil Jumonville, Israel Kugler, Kenneth Libo, Arien Mack, Deborah Meier, Thomas Moser, Martin Peretz, Mickey Sanes, Nicholas Syracopoulos, Alan Wald, Victor Walter, Dennis Wrong, and Willard Wyman.

Nicholas and Nina Howe graciously granted permission to quote from Irving Howe's published writings and from his letters. They also generously supplied family photographs and verified important factual information about their father for me. Awards from the Lucius Littauer Foundation and from SUNY, New Paltz, helped fund travel to conduct interviews and to search various archives.

The manuscript was read in whole or part by Lewis Brownstein, Morris Dickstein, Helen Fein, Richard Fein, David Krikun, Deborah Dash Moore, Derek Rubin, Myra Sorin, and Daniel Soyer, and benefited from their many valuable insights and suggestions. My debt to these people as well as those listed above is very large, but in no way are they responsible for the views expressed in this book or for any misstatements of fact. Myra Sorin deserves special thanks not only for her careful, sensitive, and acutely intelligent reading and rereading of every chapter, but, as important, for her inspiration, continued patience, and loving support during the more than six years that Irving Howe shared our lives.

Index